SCARBOROUGH
SNIPPETS

Some fascinating facts
about the town

Compiled by

DAVID FOWLER

This edition published in Great Britain in 2013
by
Farthings Publishing
8 Christine House
1 Avenue Victoria
SCARBOROUGH
YO11 2QB
UK

http://www.Farthings-Publishing.com

ISBN 978-1-291-46709-3

December 2013 (n)

DEDICATION

This book is dedicated to Jackie Link and the staff of Clock Café, Scarborough, in the Café's centenary year.

Scarborough Snippets has been produced and published by Farthings Publishing as a donation towards Clock Café charities. All profits from the sale of this book at the café will go to Clock Café's nominated charity, The Littlefoot Trust.

This Trust is a Registered Charity based in Scarborough. It runs year-round fund-raising activities which enable the trustees to take groups of local children from socially deprived areas in and around the town, on an annual educational and cultural trip. Head teachers from local schools help the trustees to select children who would otherwise not normally be able to make such a visit.

*

OTHER BOOKS BY DAVID FOWLER

God Bless the Prince of Wales – August 2008
National Service, Elvis & Me! – November 2009
Why Should England Tremble? – September 2012
The Clock Café Story – July 2013

(Copies of the above are available from the publisher – address on previous page)

ACKNOWLEDGEMENTS

Thanks are due to the following, from whose articles, text or photographs have been used in some cases by internet download. We have tried to acknowledge all extracts below but if any copyright holders have been missed please advise the publisher and a correction will be made in future editions.

Anne & Paul Bayliss; Bryan Berryman; Graham Bettis; Complete Internet Computing Ltd; Discover Yorkshire Coast.com; English Heritage; Farthings Publishing; Eileen Fowler; David G Futty; Friends of South Cliff Gardens; Robert Goddard; Michael Gorbert; Houlton Construction; Rob Janovski; Michael Lester; Jackie and Gary Link; The Ministry of Defence; David Mould; Freda and Joy Murdo; Peter Newham; Neil Pearson Illustrating & Design; RJ Percy; Maureen Robinson and Freddie Gilroy; St Martins-on-the Hill Church; Scarborough Archaeological and Historical Society; Scarborough Library & Customer Service Centre; Scarborough & Ryedale Astronomical Society; Scarborough Borough Council; Scarborough Civic Society; The BBC; The Clock Café staff; The late Roy Day; The late HW Marsden; The late Cyril Prescott; The Scarborough News; The Sons of Neptune; The late Sir Meredith Whittaker; The Stephen Joseph Theatre; The Theatre's Trust; Eric Truman, Pip Waller; Wikipedia; Ren Yaldren; Yorkshire Post Newspapers;

*

CONTENTS

CHAPTER	TITLE	PAGE
	Introduction	9
One	From 8000 BC – The Beginning	11
Two	From 1626 – Scarborough, the first British Seaside resort	22
Three	From 1660 – The Spa, Scarborough	29
Four	From 1804 – Artists who painted in the area	52
Five	From 1845 – Development of South Cliff	75
Six	From 1850 – St Martins-on-the-Hill Church	100
Seven	From 1902 – The Westwood School	105
Eight	From 1908 – Marine Drive	115
Nine	From 1912 – Clock Café	121
Ten	From 1914 – The Bombardment of Scarborough	153
Eleven	From 1932 – Merrie England to World War II	164
Twelve	From 1945 to the present time	178
	Postscript	198

INTRODUCTION

'Living in the past. It's always said pejoratively, as if the past is necessarily inferior to the future, or at any rate less important; nobody's ever condemned for looking forward, only back. But the truth is that we live in the past, whether we like it or not. That's where our life takes shape. Somewhere ahead, however near or far, is the end. But behind, shrouded in clouds of forgetting, lies the beginning'.

Robert Goddard

*

This book is unashamedly about looking back - from the first mention of the town in 8000 BC, to the present day

Whilst the details given in the book are believed to be true it is not intended as a formal history; rather a miscellany of fascinating facts culled from many sources and stretching back over the years.

Initially it was planned as a short booklet about and as a tribute to Clock Café in its 100th year. However, as research evolved, and expanded to the town and its people, the size of the manuscript grew rapidly.

I therefore ended up with two editions; the first and much shorter version being a booklet about the Clock Café, - *The Clock Café Story*. The second is this larger version *Scarborough Snippets,* which contains much additional information about both the town and its people over the years.

The Clock Café's opening in 1913 was just before the commencement of World War I and the café's terrace would have been a superb if somewhat dangerous viewpoint for the bombardment of Scarborough in 1914.

During World War II, Clock Café and the Spa, together with most large hotels in Scarborough and many public buildings, were closed to the public and were used for accommodation and training forces – predominantly RAF aircrew. The Clock Café was used for aircrew navigation instruction.

If the buildings themselves had been able to record all the experiences and sounds they had seen and heard over the last 100 years, what a story we would now have been able to tell.

I hope you enjoy this book as much as I have enjoyed putting it together. It consists of a compilation of material from far and wide and from many sources, although as a compilation there is a small degree of overlap of material.

And finally, as profits from sales of this book at Clock Café will go to its very worthwhile local children's' charity, 'The LittleFoot Trust', please give generously. In fact, why not buy copies as presents for family and friends?

Who knows, whether they are residents or visitors they might wish to know more about our historic town; the first seaside resort in Britain.

David Fowler

Farthings Publishing
August 2013

CHAPTER ONE

FROM 8000 BC –
THE BEGINNING

Whilst the town of Scarborough's acknowledged beginning was in 966 AD there was evidence of Stone - age settlers in the Scarborough area around the year 8000 BC.

Later, in 500 BC, relics of bronze-age man were found, and later still around 400 AD, the Roman signal Station was built on the headland on which now stands the castle, although the signal station was abandoned within a year.

So, while we acknowledge these earlier happenings, our story really starts around 966 AD when Thorgils nicknamed Skarthi (meaning Hare-Lip) and his Vikings decided to settle in the place they called Skarthi's Burgh, or Skarthi's Stronghold...

*

'A medieval Icelandic saga, Kormakssaga tells how two Icelandic Viking brothers called Kormak and Thorgils were the first men to 'establish the fort called Skardaborg'. The fort was named after one of its founder's nickname, for Thorgils was called Skardi, meaning hare-lipped, by his brother. It is now generally accepted that the name Skardaborg, which has come down to us as Scarborough, means 'the fort belonging to Skardi'.

Kormakssaga tells more about these brothers. Kormak was a talented poet, described as a wild man with black curly hair while Thorgils on the other hand was taciturn and easy-going. Both men had a taste for adventure and plundering around the coasts of Britain and Ireland. Around the year 966 they decided to make the sheltered waters of the south bay their base and built the fort. They may even have reused the ruins of the Roman Signal Station.

Kormak was later killed while raiding in Scotland.

However, the first occupants of Scarborough's dominant Castle headland formed a village settlement in the early Iron Age, although the earliest visible remains are those of a Roman Signal Station. It was late in the Roman occupation, soon after 370 AD, when the Signal Station on the Castle Hill was built. These signal stations were erected to cope with piratical raiders, but although manned by garrisons, their prime purpose was not defence; they were intended as look-out stations from which warning of enemy approach could be sent along the coast and to inland Roman garrisons.

William le Gros, Earl of Albemarle, who led the army of the Yorkshire Barons at the Battle of the Standard in 1138 near Northallerton, built the first Castle at Scarborough, on the headland. King John visited Scarborough Castle in 1201, 1210, 1213 and again in 1216. King Edward I held court at the Castle in 1275 and, when Richard III visited Scarborough in 1484, one of the towers on the curtain wall was occupied by his Queen.

The Castle has undergone five sieges, in 1312, 1536, 1557, 1644-45 and 1648. In the Civil War, Scarborough was ultimately the only royalist port on the East Coast, and it was not until 1645, with the garrison worn out and stores exhausted that the Castle surrendered to Parliament.

For more than a year (1665-66), George Fox, the founder of the Society of Friends, was imprisoned in the ruined Charles' Tower of the Castle. Here he suffered great hardships, before he was released by order of King Charles II.

Much more recently, in 1914, during World War 1, the German fleet bombarded the town and Castle. They damaged the keep and the 17th century barracks was almost entirely destroyed.

Scarborough's harbour is also steeped in history. In 1225, Henry III made a grant of 40 oaks from his woods to the men of Scarborough to use in the harbour. Later, in 1251, he granted Charter to 'His Bailiffs and Burgesses and other good men of Scardeburgh: it is for the benefit of the Town of Scardeburgh to make a certain new port with timber and stone towards the sea whereby all ships arriving thither may enter and sail out without danger as well at the beginning of Flood as at High water'.

In 1732, George II passed an Act to enlarge the harbour by building Vincents Pier and the present East Pier at a cost of £12,000. At this time there were upwards of 300 sailing ships berthed at Scarborough.

At the beginning of the 19th century, Scarborough was one of the principal ship building centres on the East Coast. From 1785 to 1810, 209 ships were built with a tonnage of 35,683 tons. As many as 15 ships were launched in one year. In 1849, a company was formed to provide means for repairing ships at Scarborough. A floating dock was built capable of taking ships up to 300 tons.

The first reference to a lighthouse at the end of Vincent's Pier occurs in 1804. A signal flag was displayed by day and a light by night when the depth of the water was not less than 12 feet. In 1914, the lighthouse was seriously damaged during the bombardment of Scarborough by German cruisers and the tower had to be dismantled. It was rebuilt in 1931.

Today, Scarborough is a popular holiday destination, with visitors able to enjoy both the natural beauty and rich historical significance of the area.'

*

CHRONOLOGICAL LIST OF DATES IN THE HISTORY OF SCARBOROUGH

8000 BC   Evidence of Stone Age settlers found in the Scarborough area.

500 BC   Relics of the Bronze Age man found from this period.

370/ 400 AD   The Roman Signal Station at Scarborough headland is built, but abandoned within the first year.

966   Thorgil nicknamed Skarthi (meaning Hare-Lip) and his Vikings decided to settle in the place they called Skarthi's Burgh, or Skarthi's Stronghold.

1000   A Christian chapel is built within Scarborough.

1066   Hardrada, King of Norway and Tostig burnt the town also destroying the chapel.

1100   Henry 1st gave the town its first Charter.

1125   St. Mary's Church was built circa 1125, based on a one room chapel.

1136   Scarborough Castle was built by William Le

Gros, Earl of Albermarle.

1157	The Castle was taken over and a new Keep was begun by Henry II.
1158	Henry II strengthened the Castle by adding a large tower and keep.
1225	The Borough was permitted to levy murage and quayage tolls.
1253	A Royal Charter gave permission for a Scarborough Fair to be held.
1256	A new quay was built for Scarborough Harbour.
1265	The town was taken into the King's hands, due to the local Burgesses attacking the Constable of the Castle.
1275	Edward I held court at Scarborough.
1295	Scarborough is represented in the first full Parliament session.
1300	The Old Three Mariners Public House was built in Quay Street and still stands in the same place today.
1314	Piers Gaveston was besieged in the Castle.
1318	The town was attacked by the Scots under Robert the Bruce.
1343	The Castle Barbican was built and the outer walls strengthened.
1381	Riots took place in Scarborough during the Peasants Revolt.
1485	A new constitution was granted by Richard III.
1536	The Castle was besieged during the Pilgrimage of Grace.
1564	Elizabeth I granted the sum of £500 for

	rebuilding the harbour, and 100 tons of timber and 6 tons of iron.
1626	Mrs Elizabeth Farrow discovered spring Spaw Water flowing into the sea.
1645	The Castle was besieged by Roundheads.
1648	The second siege of the Castle.
1660	Dr Wittie's book about the Spaw waters was published and led to many visitors arriving 'to take the water'.
1700	Dicky Dickinson built the first Spaw House.
1720	Dicky Dickinson became 'Governour of the Spaw'.
1732	The Harbour Pier was extended to 1200 feet. By an act passed by George II Vincents pier and the current East Pier were built at a cost of £12,000.
1735	The first bathing machines appeared in Scarborough's bays.
1735	The Spaw was destroyed by high seas.
1738	The Spaw was rebuilt larger and grander than before.
1738	The Spa was destroyed by earthquake.
1752	The York to Scarborough Turnpike Trust was set up.
1752	Vincents pier in the Harbour was completed.
1772	o There was much smuggling in the town. o John Wesley visited.
1787	There were 1500 seamen in Scarborough, 500 of who sailed for the East Indian Service.
1790	There was a Press gang for the Navy in Scarborough.

1800	Scarborough's first lifeboat was launched.
1801	A Lifeboat station was established.
1808	The Spaw suffered serious storm damage.
1820	The population of Scarborough was c. 8000 inhabitants.
1825	A coach to Scarborough overturned.
1827	The Spa Cliff Bridge was opened by The Cliff Bridge Co. Ltd on 19th July. Locally it was called the 'Penny Bridge' due to the Toll houses, at either end, charging a penny to pass over.
1845	The Scarborough - York Railway opened and many visitors travelled to the town by train.
1847	The Scarborough to Bridlington Railway line Opened. It joined the existing railway from Bridlington to Driffield, Beverley and Hull.
1853	The Market Hall was built.
1857	13th August, Scarborough was hit by a great flood which destroyed many buildings including St Mary's church yard.
1858	Joseph Paxton's new Spa Hall opened with a festival and a grand concert.
1865	Valley Bridge was built.
1866	The building of the North Bay pier was started, at a budgeted cost of £12,135. Woodhall and Hebden's bank (Now Barclays) financed the building.
1866	Scarborough Jail in Dean Road opened and inmates moved from the previous Castle Road Jail.

1867	The Grand Hotel was built.
1876	The Spa buildings were destroyed by fire on 8th September.
1877	Work was started on the new - and still the present - Spa buildings although there have been a number of renovations since. It was designed by Thomas Verity & Hunt of London.
1880	The New Spa Grand Hall was opened.
1886	The New Spa Grand Hall Restaurant opened.
1886	Valley Bridge was taken over by the Scarborough Corporation.
1897	The building of Marine Drive was started.
1898	Warwick Tower was opened to the public. Local opinion did not favour the tower and it was eventually demolished.
1902	The Municipal School at Westwood opened.
1908	Marine Drive opened.
1911	o Peasholm Park land was purchased and work started on the Japanese themed design. o South Bay Gardens were developed as part of the South Bay expansion.
1913	The South Cliff Gardens Café opened having been built on the site of a previous Reading room. It became known locally as 'The Café under the Clock' and was later renamed 'The Clock Café'

1914	The town was bombarded by German warships. 19 people were killed, the Lighthouse was destroyed and had to be demolished and rebuilt. There was damage to the Royal Hotel, Grand Hotel and the Town Hall, and, on Esplanade, The Prince of Wales Hotel, not to mention many other buildings. The furthest shell damage was three miles inland to a farm.
1915	The South bay swimming pool opened at a cost of £5000. This was part of the South Bay development.
1917	The population in Scarborough was c.40,000.
1924 – 1925	The Corner Cafe complex was built in the North Bay, originally for the entertainment of children.
1928	Valley bridge re-opened to the public after being widened.
1931	The Lighthouse was rebuilt replacing the one destroyed by the German Naval bombardment.
1931	Scarborough's North Bay Miniature Railway was opened, consisting of miniature trains, bridges, slopes and signals.
1932	North Bay Open-Air theatre opened with 'Merrie England'.
1940	A lone bomber dropped a mine on Potters Hill in the old town killing four people and damaging 500 houses. Most had to be demolished.
1941	On March 18th Scarborough had its worst air raid of WWII which became known as the 'March Blitz'. 1,378 buildings were destroyed or damaged, 28 people were killed and 100 injured.

1947	Scarborough Art Gallery opened.
1951	The Cliff Bridge was purchased by the Council from The Cliff Bridge Company for £22,500. The toll booths were dismantled and free access was provided.
1951	Wood End Natural History Museum opened.
1955	Stephen Joseph founded the UK's first ever professional Theatre in the Round, in the Concert Room at Scarborough Library.
1957	The Spa was bought by Scarborough Council from The Cliff Bridge Company for £110,000.
1962	The Scarborough to Whitby Railway line was closed. Stations included Scalby, Burniston, Cloughton, Hayburn Wyke, Ravenscar, Hawsker, and Robin Hoods Bay.
1966	Scarborough Millennium Festival. Many events were held to commemorate the town's 1000th anniversary.
1973	The Scarborough Indoor Swimming Pool opened following much private fund raising.
1981	£3 million restoration of the Spa was completed.
1993	Landslides at Holbeck Hill pulled the Holbeck Hall Hotel into the sea.
1996	The Stephen Joseph Theatre moved to its new home following conversion of the Odeon Cinema.
2001	'The Sands' North Bay development started.
2002	Marine Drive was partly closed to enable coastal defence work to take place.

A new protective wall also replaced the railings.

2006
- The disused South Bay bathing pool was converted into an illuminated Star Map.
- Wood End Museum was created from the Sitwell family's former home.

2009-2011
- The Spa was renovated at a cost of £8.7m.
- The Spa Bridge was closed for renovation costing £700,000.

2010
HM The Queen opened the new Open Air Theatre.

2011
A large steel sculpture of 'Freddie Gilroy and the Belsen Stragglers' was donated to the town and is situated on Royal Albert Drive.

2011-2014
Yorkshire Water are spending £50m to help the town meet European Bathing Water Directives. The Marine drive is temporarily restricted to one way traffic.

2013
- The Clock Café is 100 years old.
- Valley Bridge is to be part closed from August for restoration

2014
Centenary to be held of 1914 Bombardment of Scarborough.

***

CHAPTER TWO

FROM 1626 –
SCARBOROUGH – THE FIRST BRITISH
SEASIDE RESORT

Scarborough, the first ever British seaside resort, has been welcoming visitors for over 360 years and is still as popular as ever.

The town is a great a place to stay for a holiday or short break. The safe, sandy, North Bay and South Bay beaches are broken by a rocky headland on which stands a reminder of the past, the historic Scarborough Castle.

The resort offers first class attractions such as the Rotunda Museum, Scarborough Art Gallery, the award winning Sea Life Marine Sanctuary, the world famous Stephen Joseph Theatre and of course the newly refurbished Scarborough Open Air Theatre – claimed by The Theatre's Trust to be Europe's 'largest open air theatre'. To quote from the Trust:

'The largest open air theatre in Europe (since Antiquity) was built by Scarborough Corporation and opened by the Lord Mayor of London in 1932. It was a striking landscape feature with the action viewed across a lake. The first production was 'Merrie England'. There was fixed seating in five blocks for 5,876 with the balance made up of deck chairs. The house record, set in August 1952, was an audience of 8,983 - but an unofficial 11,000 was claimed for a free recording of 'It's a Knockout' in the 1960s. The theatre was built on the

site of Hodgson's Slack taking advantage of ground contours which created a natural amphitheatre. In its heyday it was an important theatrical venue of national repute mounting lavish musicals with casts (largely amateur) of up to 200. During the season of three months two performances were held each week. Musicals ceased in 1968 after 'West Side Story', apart from a YMCA production in 1982. For eleven years 'It's a Knockout' games were staged, and concerts with the likes of James Last filled the theatre in 1983 and 1986. In 1977 the dressing rooms and stage set building on the island were demolished. Several attempts to start a restoration were made, and the theatre was on The Theatres Trust's Theatre Buildings 'At Risk' register. Happily, in 2008 planning permission was approved for a major restoration as part of the North Bay Project. This [was proposed to] replace 5,510 folding seats on the theatre's hard surfaced terracing, a central canopy to protect audiences from the elements as well as restoring the original projection tower. Additional temporary seating can increase the venue's capacity to 7,000 when major events are staged.'

In the event the 'central canopy to protect audiences from the elements' was not included in the final design.

*

Situated very close to and possibly on part of the site of the Open Air Theatre is the Manor of Northstead. Readers might not know the background which leads to how retiring Members of Parliament may apply to become 'Steward of the Manor of Northstead'.

'The ancient boundary of the Borough of Scarborough, on the northern side, was Peasholm Beck. Immediately beyond that was the Manor of Northstead, although

modern boundary extensions have brought it entirely within the town boundary and the area has been built upon.

The site of what may have been the manor house is now covered by the lake in Peasholm Park, (the lake between the auditorium and the stage of the Open Air Theatre).

The Manor was purchased by King Richard III and, although Scarborough Corporation purchased the land (known as the Northstead Estate) from the Crown in 1921, the Lordship of the Manor was retained by the Crown. That is how the Stewardship of the Manor became, and still is, a Crown office.
In theory a Member of Parliament cannot resign. However, a person who holds an office of profit under the Crown is disqualified from being an MP. In practice, if an MP wishes to resign, he or she applies to be appointed as Steward of the Chiltern Hundreds, or of the Manor of Northstead. Although these offices are sinecures involving no actual duties, they are technically offices of profit under the Crown, so anyone appointed to either of those offices automatically ceases to be an MP and has, in effect, resigned. Appointments to these offices are normally made alternatively.'

The Chancellor of the Exchequer made the latest appointment recently when it was announced on 15th April 2013 that *'he had appointed David Miliband to be Steward and Bailiff of the Manor of Northstead - the process by which a Member of Parliament resigns their seat.*
A by-election will take place at a later date in the constituency of South Shields.'

As well as the Open Air Theatre, Scarborough can proudly boast another famous link - the Stephen Joseph Theatre – renowned throughout the world.

'The Stephen Joseph Theatre was founded in Scarborough by theatrical pioneer Stephen Joseph.

Stephen, the son of actress Hermione Gingold and publisher Michael Joseph, had seen theatre in the round in America and determined to bring it back to Britain. Frustrated by attempts to open a theatre-in-the-round in London, Stephen's plans came to fruition when his search for a suitable venue led him to the seaside town of Scarborough on the North-East coast. Here in 1955 he established the country's first theatre-in-the-round company on the first floor of the Public Library. His primary aim was to encourage new writing by new writers, which he was passionate about until his death in 1967, aged just 46.

Alan Ayckbourn, Stephen's protégé, was appointed Artistic Director of the company in 1972. Alan had begun working with the company as an actor in 1957 and had premiered his first play at the venue, The Square Cat, in 1959. Alan would remain Artistic Director until 2009 having encouraged Stephen's legacy of new writing with the world premiere of 239 plays by 87 writers during his tenure. Alan has also premiered the majority of his own plays at the theatre, more than half of which have gone on to the West End or the National Theatre. He was awarded a CBE in 1987 and in 1997 was knighted for services to the theatre.

The theatre continued to flourish and in 1976 moved to a supposedly temporary home on the ground floor of the former Scarborough Boys' High School at an initial conversion cost of £40,000.

However, a permanent home proved difficult to find and it wasn't until late 1988 and the closure of the local Odeon cinema by Rank Leisure that Alan Ayckbourn found a suitable venue.

By October 1990, the newly formed Scarborough Theatre Development Trust had gained the lease on the classic thirties building and fund-raising began in earnest.

This time, the conversion cost £5.2m of which £1.48m came from the National Lottery Arts Council of England; £500,000 from the Foundation for Sport and the Arts; £495,000 from the EC Objective 5(b) fund; £400,000 from Alan Ayckbourn personally; £240,000 from the Chairman of the Development Trust, Charles (Mac) McCarthy; and other amounts ranging from hundreds of thousands to pound coins dropped in a collection bucket after each performance and from a myriad of other fund-raising initiatives.

The entire conversion was chronicled extensively by the theatre and documentary photographer Adrian Gatie. The end result in excess of 5000 images offers a unique record of the entire conversion between 1993 and 1996.

The new theatre, known simply as the Stephen Joseph Theatre opened on 30th April 1996 and has two auditoria: The Round, a 404-seat in the round and The McCarthy, a 165-seat endstage/cinema. The building also contains a restaurant, shop, and full front-of-house and backstage facilities.

The Round boasts two important technical innovations: the stage lift, facilitating speedy set changes and the trampoline, a Canadian invention which allows technicians particularly easy access to the lighting grid.

Chris Monks succeeded Alan Ayckbourn as Artistic Director of the Stephen Joseph Theatre on 1 April 2009.

A theatre director and writer, he has a history of producing exciting, imaginative theatre in the round; the majority of his work has been for The New Vic, The Orange Tree Theatre, Bolton Octagon and the Royal Exchange Theatre in Manchester.'

*

'Scarborough is also proud to be the home of many festivals, including Seafest, the iconic Scarborough Jazz Festival, Bike Week, Cycling, Scarborough Fayre, the UK Pro Surf Championships and the Scarborough Cricket Festival, to name but a few. These provide visitors with year round events.

The Yorkshire Coast truly is The Festival Coast!'

But how did Scarborough become the first British seaside resort? The town's business and trading activities were in decline during the early 17th century and having experienced two sieges during the Civil War was showing little sign of recovery.

Scarborough's birth as a seaside spa resort, which brought renewed prosperity, developed from the almost accidental discovery of the mineral spring waters earlier that century.

In about 1626 Mrs 'Tomyzin' or 'Thomasin' Farrer, a woman of substance and wife of one of Scarborough's leading citizens, John Farrer, several times Bailiff of the town, discovered natural springs bubbling out beneath the cliff to the south of the town.

These waters, which stained the rocks a russet colour, tasted slightly bitter and cured minor ailments. She told her neighbours and friends about the beneficial effects and soon drinking the waters became the accepted medicine for Scarborough's townspeople. If further proof were needed, they were said to have cured scurvy suffered by the weakened garrison of the besieged Scarborough Castle in the civil War.

The medical profession analysed the mineral waters and found a high content of magnesium sulphate, its healing properties certainly as effective as Andrews Liver Salts.

'Taking the Water' quickly became Scarborough's accepted medicine and the town's fame spread worldwide.

***

CHAPTER THREE

FROM 1660 –
THE SPA, SCARBOROUGH

'It was Dr Robert Wittie who published 'Scarborough Spaw' in 1660 which advocated 'taking the waters' as a cure for all ills. He inadvertently initiated the summer season, recommending that the waters were best drunk mid-May to mid-September. Dr William Simpson, a contemporary rival from York, refuted the claims made for the mineral spring waters and the medical debate spread beyond local boundaries to the Royal Society in London. Despite the debate, or because of it, the gentry and well-to-do who were accustomed to making regular visits to health spas like Bath, Tunbridge Wells and Buxton were soon flocking to Scarborough.

About the same time doctors began promoting sea-bathing as a healthy pastime. The medics gave plenty of advice on the best way to bathe: briefly, healthy males for five minutes before breakfast daily; the 'weaker sex', invalids and children for three dips of two minutes duration, three hours after breakfast, three times a week!

To facilitate sea bathing a horse-drawn box on wheels could be hired to take the bather out into the sea, enabling the occupier to undress modestly inside before 'dipping' in the sea. In Scarborough Public Library there is a view of the town as it was in 1735 by John Setterington which shows people bathing and the first recorded evidence for the use of bathing machines.

It was quite acceptable for men to bathe naked until the later 19th century.'

A visitor writing a letter in 1733 describes the bathing at Scarborough:

'It is the custom for not only gentlemen, but the ladies also, to bathe in the seas; the gentlemen go out a little way to sea in boats (called here 'cobbles') and jump in naked directly: 'tis usual for gentlemen to hire one of these boats and put out a little way to sea a-fishing. The ladies have the conveniency of gowns and guides. There are two little houses on the shore, to retire for dressing in. What virtues our physicians ascribe to cold baths in general and are much more effectual by the additional weight of salt in sea-water: an advantage which no Spaw in England can boast of but Scarborough.'

Scarborough responded to the influx of visitors by providing every fashionable amenity. A Long Room in St Nicholas Street provided nightly dancing, music, gaming tables and billiards; in the afternoon plays were acted under the management of Mr Kerregan in 1733 and from 1767 evening performances were given in the Theatre. There were coffee shops and bookshops with circulating libraries and horse-racing on the sands.

A whole range of accommodation was offered to suit every pocket - board and lodgings, a room at inns and hostelries, renting a Georgian house or later, top-quality hotels.

The age of tourism began with Dicky Dickinson, a man reported to have little charm but far-sighted enterprise.

Self-styled governor of the Spa, Dicky rented the site from the Corporation and in around 1700 built the first Spaw house and two conveniences, *'one for the ladies and 'another house for the Gent'.*

DICKY DICKINSON,
Governour of Scarborough Spaw.

He was responsible for preserving order and collecting subscriptions from its patrons, *'some of which went to pay the poor widows who dispensed the waters from the newly built cistern'.*

These simple buildings and the mineral springs (above) were buried by a massive landslide in 1737 but fortunately the springs were quickly located and new, better buildings were constructed. Throughout the following century the reputation and popularity of the resort continued to grow.

Such was its appeal that in 1826 the Cliff Bridge Company was formed to erect an ornate iron bridge across the valley, giving easier access from the cliff and the town where elegant hotels and Georgian lodging houses were being more and more heavily patronised.

The Corporation granted the company a lease of the Spa grounds for the term of 200 years and although the taking of the waters tended to decline in popularity during the 19th century, the Spa's reputation grew as a fashionable place of entertainment and relaxation.

During the Spa's Victorian heyday, it was considered the most popular music hall venue outside London. The first orchestra appeared in the 1830s. Henry Wyatt's 'Gothic Saloon' of 1839 was enlarged to seat 500 in 1847 and Sir Joseph Paxton, designer of the Crystal Palace, added a Concert Hall in 1858 which was gutted by fire in 1876.

The 1880 Spa Building designed by Thomas Verity – the mecca of Victorian and Edwardian Scarborough

As part of the Paxton improvements a luxurious Spa Chalet was built which for many years was occupied by the Spa Manager. In 2009 this was sold by the Council on a long lease and 'The Scarborough News' reported on 2nd April 2009:

'The 150-year-old chalet has been restored to its former glory after Scarborough Council sold the 125-year lease for the building, which is now being used as a holiday home.

Before its transformation the chalet, which lies at the end of the Spa footbridge, consisted of three bedrooms, a sun lounge and reception room, one bathroom, and a kitchen with only a sink in it, all of which were on the first floor.

The ground floor rooms suffered from damp and were used only for storage.

However, following a nine-month renovation project, the chalet now boasts five bedrooms all with en-suite, a fully fitted kitchen, and a restored living room and sun lounge.

The ground floor now has three of the bedrooms, all with their own colour scheme and design, while the other two are on the first floor along with the other residential rooms.

The plans for the chalet, which is a Grade II listed building, were drawn up by Scarborough architects

Denton and Denton, and the work was carried out by Swalwell and Geraghty builders of West Ayton.

Belinda Denton, of Denton and Denton, said: "I have worked on a lot of buildings before but I have never come across a Swiss chalet, so it was an interesting challenge.

"The chalet was very dilapidated with only basic conveniences, however architecturally the building has always been lovely and its location is fantastic.

"It was a very exciting project to work on and it is absolutely lovely to see it finished. It is always nice to see a building renovated and back in use."

The Alpine-style chalet was designed by Sir Joseph Paxton in around 1858, at the same time as he designed the Spa pavilion, which incorporated what is now the site of the Grand Hall before much of the interior was lost to a fire in 1877.

It is believed the chalet was built at the same time as the Spa Pavilion and was occupied for many years by the manager of the Spa at that time.

It later became a private home and was lived in by Jessica Bearpark until her death in the summer of 2006. Miss Bearpark had been the secretary of Eric Horsfall Turner, the town clerk of Scarborough Corporation, and his successor Glynn Morgan. She then worked for Russell Bradley, who became the chief executive of the new Scarborough Council following the reorganisation of local government in 1974. Following the death of Miss Bearpark the council put up the lease for sale and it attracted the interest of more than 620 potential buyers from all over the country.

The sale was handled by Scarborough estate agent CPH which would not disclose the name of the buyer or the price paid for the lease; however it was asking for offers over £250,000.'

The existing Spa Grand Hall, Theatre and Buffet came into use in 1879. The Ballroom was built in 1925 and enlarged in the early 1960s. The pump room finally closed in 1939.

Escalating costs of repair and maintenance to the rambling buildings and the 11 acres of grounds forced the Spa Company into liquidation in 1957; the Corporation took back the lease and began the long task of rehabilitation and development.

After two seasons of Eugene Pini and his Orchestra, Max Jaffa (below) arrived in 1960 and stayed until 1986; steadily increasing his own and the Spa's reputation and decrying those who said that good music was dead.

Max Jaffa died on July 30th 1991

*

The delightful Victorian theatre, on whose stage many famous thespians have trod, was completely renovated in 1972. A massive programme of building renovation in the 1980s successfully combined the restoration of the buildings to their former glory with the development of the Conference and Entertainment Complex of today.

The most recent redevelopment of the Spa was in 2009 when a £7.8m scheme was undertaken by Houlton Construction of Hull. They describe it thus:

'When people talk of Scarborough Spa today they are referring to the buildings and to the activities and entertainment carried out there. But the origins of this noble Complex, and indeed the place in history of Scarborough as a resort town, are directly attributable to a natural resource - the Spa waters. Visitors to the Spa today can still see the great architecture of the 1880s and many are still surprised by the scale and style of the Grand Hall. The Complex today encompasses the Spa Theatre, the Grand Hall for concerts, the Ocean Room, the Promenade Lounge, Suncourt for open air concerts, and various other rooms, cafes and bar areas.

The development Houlton completed at the Scarborough Spa complex was in two phases, a 40 week £2.9m renovation in 2007 followed by a major £4.9m refurbishment in 2010-2011.

First phase works included removal and renewal of the roof coverings of the Grand Hall and Spa Complex, removal and reinstatement of ornate cast iron railings on the roof, renewal of light fittings, renewal of the glazed roof of the Roof Garden and numerous structural repairs and treatments to the existing buildings.

The second phase saw an extensive programme of re-modelling including a new main conference and meeting facility, the transformation of the 1900 seater grand hall, new roof and the installation of state of the art technical equipment in the theatre.

*Photos of the interior of the Spa since completion of
Houlton's restoration programme*

To allow construction of new changing rooms and storage areas below the hall floor and a large floor lift the existing structure was supported with a continuous reinforced piled wall tied back to the cliff face with rock anchors to allow a major excavation beneath the hall floor, treatment that will secure the venue's future for years to come.'

*

Shortly after completion of this work, and after a few landslips occurred behind the Spa buildings, Scarborough Council became concerned about the stability of the cliff and proposed that rock armour be placed to the frontage of the present Spa sea wall to protect the cliffs behind from further slippage.

The Yorkshire Post reported on April 27th 2013:

'Moves to install rock armour around the cliffs beneath Scarborough Spa are facing a wave of protest from hundreds of residents who have branded it a 'crime against tourism'..

Council bosses say the venue could become a casualty of a massive landslip without the boulders to protect it from battering by the sea.

But a growing army of objectors is criticising the £16.6m scheme as a massive waste of taxpayers' money which will scar the listed building.

Objectors are calling for a 'make do and mend' approach involving improved maintenance of the existing sea wall. Opposition to the scheme was underlined when a presentation at the Spa was packed by hundreds of protesters.

Acting chairman of Scarborough Civic Society Adrian Perry said: "I can't find anyone who thinks it is a good idea. People at the meeting were very angry and irate.

"The fundamental problem is the appearance of all this rock sat in front of a listed building.

"It is a very delicate situation for the council. They have a duty to maintain the sea defences. They have come to the conclusion this is the cheapest long-term solution. The fact everyone hates it, may or may not change their mind. The rock armour will obviously spoil the appearance of this beautiful building.

"On the other hand, if it is not protected and does get damaged by the sea everyone will be wringing their hands because there won't be the money to repair it.

"However, everybody in the Civic Society thinks there must be another way to protect the Spa."

A spokesman for Scarborough Council said the authority would take objectors' comments on board.

"While we fully understand people's concerns and emotions about the proposed scheme, we cannot avoid the fact that there are some very big issues that we must tackle in the area surrounding the Spa," he said.

"Significant erosion of the toe of the cliff after failure of the sea wall would trigger a large-scale landslide, putting homes and businesses on the Esplanade at risk."

He added: "Our aims with these proposals are to achieve long-term stability of the cliffs behind the Spa, reduce the wave over-topping to acceptable levels for pedestrians, to address current safety issues, to prevent a collapse of the sea wall, to provide a coastal defence asset with a design life of 100 years and to continue to defend South Bay in a cost effective way."'

The Sons of Neptune and their spokesman Freddie Drabble make the following contribution which is included in this chapter to provide continuity although it is also concerns the deterioration of view the rock armour will bring from Clock Café:

"You can go anywhere in the world and never see anything to compare with this." How many times do I overhear this appraisal on the terrace of the Clock Café on a clear day. The view changes with the tides and clouds but to be gazing over the sweeping sandy bay to the 12th Century Church and then to the ruins of the town's Norman Castle atop the majestic headland is the ultimate romantic journey beyond childhood into history. There can be few who do not feel privileged to live in this area of outstanding scenic beauty.

And if anything were to complement such scenery in gastronomic terms for me it has to be the Clock Café scones 'cooked on the hour and every hour' I am reliably informed. Very often in life on the sunniest of days, dark clouds threaten. So it is with the golden sands and rock pools of Childrens' Corner just below the Café and beyond the Spa itself. How many times have we raced to be the first to search the pools all over again, as the tide goes out for crabs and whatever else could be used to scare our sisters. After that, at the end of the day after the never forgotten rub down with the damp sandy towel, the treat of an ice cream up at the Café!

The dark clouds I refer to are a proposal by the local Council to lay down a massive barrage of black boulders running northwards from the slipway below the Café for 350 metres and extending 30 metres out to sea from the Spa sea wall. This heap of oversize rubble will be stacked up against the wall for as far as you can see from the Café's terrace.

The amount of access time to the sands, allowing for the tides, will be about half what we enjoy now. That magnificent example of Victorian marine engineering - the sea wall - which has proved itself fit for purpose for more than 140 years is to be cloaked forever in black rubble. It even withstood the great storm of 1953 and yet the Council's Consulting Engineers say it only has a few years' life left and it is best preserved by covering it up!

On behalf of the Sons of Neptune who are among the consultees, I can best give you my reaction in my statement to the Consulting Engineers on 4th October 2011 when I first heard of the proposal:

The existing stone wall is an integral part of the overall historic heritage of the Spa. It is a beautiful frame to a magnificent building of great architectural merit. The wall complements the building. Not only that, it is itself a fine example of Victorian marine engineering which has stood the test of time. I have been in the town since 1945 and have never heard of the wall being breached despite many high tides and, indeed, the exceptional one of 1953. This wall is at the forefront of old paintings and photographs. Its sweeping curves and massive stones are as impressive as the Spa buildings and perhaps more so as they not only boldly state their purpose but they have proved themselves fit for purpose. Your alternative solutions of either a heap of rubble euphemistically termed rock armour stacked against the wall or a massive concrete apron which engineers would prefer to confuse the unsuspecting with the French word "revetment" are an insult to Victorian engineers who had the talents to complement great scenery with inspirational use of local materials. Can I ask your managing director, as courteously as possible, to take a walk along the south sands on a fine day in the direction of the Spa and look at what your Company propose to destroy?

Destruction comes easy. Is it too much to ask if a company of international repute such as yours is capable of a sympathetic restoration scheme? This town's lifeblood is scenery. We need engineers with the skills of cosmetic surgeons - not butchers' apprentices - on this job! Your company gets paid but the town suffers a major loss.

Who can be happy unless both parties are winners when millions of taxpayers' money is being spent?"
I was asked if I wished to be consulted further. I said that I did. I have received no further approach from them. The reasons we are given for the requirement of the heap of rubble is that the wall is in danger of collapse; the cliffs behind the Spa are unstable and there is danger to the public from waves overtopping the sea wall. And yet - how can a conclusion over the state of repair of the wall be arrived at without a survey of it? We have yet to see a survey report. As to cliff instability - how can a heap of boulders on the sands stop the cliffs subsiding as the cliffs do not adjoin the sands? How can there be an alleged danger from overtopping waves when the council charge for car-parking right up to the sea wall on the promenade?

The Sons of Neptune have been heavily engaged for more than 25 years in the improvement of bathing water quality and are currently working in cooperation with Yorkshire Water to achieve the highest "Excellence" rating for both North and South Bay. It is ironic that as we have fought for years to make the sea clear of pollution and safe for bathers, the Council now propose to fill much it in with rubble which will endanger bathers and surfers alike! None of this is necessary. There are advanced engineering techniques to reinforce the present sea wall with minimal visual impact on its appearance.

An artist's impression of what the proposed Spa Sea Wall might look like with rock armour in place.

Neil Pearson Illustration & Design
Web: www.neilodesign.co.uk

In congratulating the Clock Café on its centenary and in appreciation of all the pleasure it gives and has given its customers over all those years can I just say - please, please carry on just as you are! Well done.

But and there is a big BUT, we need the cups of tea and coffee, the scones and, okay - the cakes and flapjacks - but we also need the glorious scenery and golden sands. We do not need rat infested rubble to endanger children and surfers.

*You can help. There is an online petition. Tell your family and friends to visit <u>http://www.scarboroughrocks.com</u> DO IT TODAY – **PLEASE!**'*

Freddie Drabble
http://www.sonsofneptune.co

Finally, as the book was nearing completion, the Whitby Gazette reported as follows on 30th July 2013:

BOY TRAPPED IN ROCK ARMOUR NEAR WHITBY

'Stay away from rock armour is the warning to people on the Yorkshire Coast from the Coastguard.

After a call from the Coastguard of a 15 year old youth with his leg trapped in rock armour near Whitby, firecrews from Lythe, Whitby and Scarborough were dispatched to the eastern side of Staithes last night.

The youth, believed to be on holiday from Oxfordshire, had slipped between two large rocks after fishing for mackerel, with his lower leg becoming stuck fast.

Firecrews deployed high pressure air bags and lighting, and managed to free the youth by slightly forcing the rocks apart. He was then given a precautionary check up in a nearby ambulance and shortly afterwards heading back to his residence on foot unharmed.

The Coastguard warns at a different time, with the tide coming in, the consequences could have been fatal.'

*

CHRONOLOGICAL LIST OF DATES IN THE HISTORY OF THE SPA

Circa

1626 Mrs Farrer claimed that the spring water had medicinal properties.

1698 First cisterns for holding water were built by the Corporation.

1700 First Spaw House was built by Dickie Dickinson, the first Governor of the Spaw.

1735 The staith (protective wharf) of the Spaw was washed away.

1736 The Spaw was rebuilt and enlarged.

1737 The staith was damaged by subsidence and the water springs were lost.

1738 2 February, the springs were rediscovered and the staith repaired.

1739 The Spaw House was rebuilt.

1808 o The Spaw House was damaged by storm.
   o The Spaw was rebuilt.

1825 The Spaw was severely damaged by a very high tide and nearly washed away.

1826 The Cliff Bridge Company was formed by a group of 26 who met at the 'George' Hotel in York. For the erection of the bridge Mr Outhett was appointed Engineer at a salary of £200. The waters had been retained and sold by the Corporation but from this year the Spa was taken over by the Cliff Bridge Company. The 'W' was omitted from 'Spaw' for the first time.

1827   The Cliff Bridge opened on 19th July.

1836   The House and Spa was again destroyed by a violent storm.

1837   Building commenced on the Gothic Saloon (plans prepared by Henry Wyatt). The original lease of the Spa was superseded by one dated 1st January 1837, for a 200 year term.

1839   The Gothic Saloon opened on 16th August.

1845   The Saloon was improved and enlarged.

1856   Sir Joseph Paxton was consulted, and he carried out a survey of the Spa.

1857   Work started on transformation and additions, according to his plans.

1858   The New Spa Hall opened on 20th July with a festival and a grand concert.

1857/58   Prospect Tower was added.

1861   Improvements were made to the Spa Gardens.

1871   The freehold of eight acres of land south of Spa was purchased.

1875
- South Cliff Tramway, the first cliff railway in England, was opened to link the Spa with the Esplanade.
- Wells were rehabilitated and sheltered by the erection of the Band Rotunda.

1876   The Grand Hall was gutted by fire on 8th September.

1877   The present Spa building commenced in October 1877, inside the original shell. The architect was Thomas Verity & Hunt, London.

1880 The Official opening of the new Grand Hall took place on 2nd August 1880 by Sir Francis Wyatt Truscott, Lord Mayor of London.

1881 The first experimental lighting of the Spa grounds with the 'Brush' system of electric light took place.

1886 The New Spa restaurant opened.

1887 Sunday Concerts began.

1894 Electric light was first used in the Spa theatre.

1904 Trams started running from the Spa carriage road to town and back by way of Vernon Road.

1911 Land was purchased in November for £7140 for extensions, planned south of the Spa.

1912-1914 Work was started to provide the South Cliff Gardens, South Cliff Gardens Café, (later the Clock Café) beach chalets and South Bay bathing pool.

1913 A new Band Stand with a marble forecourt, and colonnade and the Grand Hall Café were built.

1914 The Grand Hall Café opened.

1915 The South Bay swimming pool was completed at cost of £5000.

1920 Prospect Tower was removed from the Spa and a roof garden was added.

1924/25   The Ballroom was added.

1940/45   Following declaration of WWII the last concert was held on 6th July 1940. The Spa was used for RAF training during the war and reopened to the public on 21st May 1945.

1951   Spa Bridge was purchased by the Council for £22,500.

1953   The Toll pay boxes at the town end of Spa Bridge were removed in February.

1954   A glass screen was erected around the Band Stand (originally for an ice show).

1955   A new £2000 floor was laid in the ballroom and the ballroom was modernised and enlarged.

1957   The Spa was purchased by the Council from the Cliff Bridge Company for £110,000.

1957   A concert on the 26th October was the last event held under the old administration.

1958   The new Spa restaurant opened at a cost of £10,000.

1960
   o The Spa Ballroom reopened on 16th April after extensive alterations at cost of £26,000.
   o Max Jaffa concerts commenced.

1963
   o Two domes on the sea side of the Spa were demolished and removed in November.
   o The Grand Hall was modernised, the balcony was rebuilt and the rest of the hall reseated at cost of £27,550.

1965   In February the North West Dome and stone surround were demolished.

1967   The Spa Ballroom was improved to give it a new intimate atmosphere.

1968

o On the closing of the Olympia Ballroom on Foreshore after a disastrous fire, the Council decided to improve facilities at the Spa with the object of housing two separate conferences simultaneously.

o Work was undertaken including additional secretariat facilities for conferences at the Grand Hall, provision of new toilets, improvements to the Green Lounge Café area, provision of conference secretariat and improvements to stage and catering facilities in the Ocean Room.

1981

o The £3,000,000 scheme of improvement was completed, restoring the Spa Grand Hall to the full splendour of its Victorian heyday.

o The opening ceremony was performed on 23rd May by Mr Michael Montague, CBE, Chairman of the English Tourist Board, in the presence of Sir Denis Truscott, former Lord Mayor of London and grandson of Sir Francis Wyatt Truscott who had performed the same ceremony just a century before.

1984   The second phase of the total scheme of refurbishment for the Spa, comprising an entirely new east façade and Promenade Lounge with mezzanine bar and enclosed foyer approach was completed at a cost of approximately £2,000,000.

1986   A third and final phase costing £600,000 brought the Ocean Ballroom up to a much higher standard for multi-purpose use with additional catering facilities, passenger lift and new external staircase from the roadway to terrace.

2008   Clock Café, and the beach chalets were given Grade II listed building status.

2009-
2011   A new large Spa redevelopment contract costing £7.8m was undertaken by Houlton Construction of Hull.

2013   Scarborough Borough Council proposed installing rock armour against the Spa sea wall in a £16.6m scheme. This aimed to prevent further slippage of the cliff and protect the buildings on Esplanade.

The Spa was operated by Scarborough Corporation from 1698 to 1826, then by the Cliff Bridge Company between 1826 to 1957, then again by Scarborough Corporation from 1957 to date. (The Corporation later became Scarborough Borough Council following local authority reorganisation from 1st April 1974).

***

CHAPTER 4

FROM 1804 –
ARTISTS –WHO PAINTED LOCALLY

Out of over 120 artists painting from the Scarborough area in the 19th century we pick 7 as our artistic snippets.

FREDERICK WILLIAM BOOTY 1840-1924

Frederick William Booty was an artist, who initially lived in Brighton. He was also the author of the first postage stamp catalogue in English, and the first illustrated stamp catalogue anywhere.

In 1893, Frederick William Booty received a *Master of Arts* Degree from Cambridge University.

Booty's *Aids to Stamp Collectors, being a list of British and Foreign Postage Stamps in Circulation since 1840 - by a Stamp Collector*, was published in April 1862, just weeks before Mount Brown issued his more successful work, and when Booty was in his early twenties. The catalogue was partly based on earlier works produced in Belgium and France.

Later in 1862, Booty was also the first to issue an illustrated catalogue, titled *The Stamp Collector's Guide; being a list of English and Foreign Postage Stamps, with 200 facsimile drawings*. This edition listed 1100 stamps and Booty drew all of the illustrations himself.

"Whitby", a watercolour painting by Frederick Booty 1886

He reportedly used half a million stamps to compile the catalogue.

Booty also contributed to the *Monthly Advertiser*, published by Edward Moore & Co., in 1862. These catalogues appear to have been a business venture, capitalising on Booty's artistic skills, as there is no evidence that Booty was a philatelist.

Booty's watercolour landscape pictures are still regularly featured in art auctions in Britain. Although originally based in Brighton, his later work is mainly of scenes from Yorkshire and Humberside, including Hull and the ports of Scarborough and Whitby.

Harbour scenes were a popular subject with Booty. He also painted Yorkshire panoramas and the peacocks at Haddon Hall, Derbyshire.

*

HENRY BARLOW CARTER 1804-1868

Henry Barlow Carter by George Pycock Everett Green 1857

Henry Barlow Carter was born and brought up in Bermondsey, London. Like JMW Turner, he served in the Navy. He moved north after he met his cousin, Eliza, who lived in Durham.

They married at St Mary's Parish Church, Scarborough in July 1830.

Above: 'Whitby Abbey' HB Carter

As Carter's success grew over the next 30 years in Scarborough, so did his prosperity as can be seen from a progressive rise through ever more fashionable addresses in Scarborough, from Auborough Strret to Queen Street to York Place.

Nevertheless Carter still had to work for a living and whilst his artistic reputation is overwhelmingly connected with watercolour painting, his work for the Scarborough printer, SW Theakston provided an additional source of income. Theakston founded the Scarborough Gazette, opened the town's first art gallery and was one of Carter's most influential clients. The Victorian visitors to Scarborough and the surrounding area purchased Carter's paintings as souvenirs of the town and provided him with a regular income.

'Wreck off Scarborough' HB Carter

It is thought Carter offered tuition from his home in York Place – his pupils including his two sons, John Newington Carter and Henry Vandyke Carter.

Following the death of his wife in 1857, Carter left Scarborough in 1862 and moved to Torquay where he died in 1868 from bronchitis.

Carter is commemorated by a Blue plaque affixed to 16 York Place which was unveiled on 23rd March 2000. The house dates from about 1835, in white brick with stucco string courses and cornices.

In the 1973 edition of *The Streets of Scarborough* Fieldhouse & Barrett said, 'York Place must once have been one of the most dignified streets in the town, but many of the ground floors have been ruined by being put to commercial use....'

*

JOHN ATKINSON GRIMSHAW 1836-1893

John Atkinson Grimshaw is a remarkable painter who  is less widely appreciated than he should be, for many reasons: little is known of his life, he worked mainly in the north of England, most of his paintings are in private collections and he was unfashionably versatile yet he became one of the worlds' artists.

He first began painting while working as a clerk for the Great Northern Railway. He encountered bitter opposition from his parents, but after his marriage in 1858 to a cousin of TS Cooper, he was able to devote himself full time to painting. Self-taught, Grimshaw started exhibiting in Leeds in the 1860's with minutely observed still life's. By 1870, he was successful enough to rent a 17th century mansion in Scarborough, following the death of three of his children at his Leeds home. He called the Scarborough house Castle by the Sea, and it was (and still is) perched on a cliff top opposite St Mary's Parish Church and a short distance from Scarborough Castle. It has magnificent views of both the north and south bays. The name of his Scarborough house came from a poem by Longfellow. The move to the coast inspired much of the artist's most attractive work as throughout his career he was always attracted by ships, the sea and docks; in fact all things maritime.

In the 1870's he experimented with a looser technique and with classical subjects in the manner of Lawrence Alma-Tadema, historical subjects and contemporary ladies in the manner of Tissot. These last were particularly successful. But the real breakthrough at that time was the night-time scenes - the 'moonlights' with which he is usually associated today.

In the middle of the decade he took a second house in Scarborough, and there are many paintings of seascapes at night. He also travelled to Liverpool and London in search of material and diversified yet again into 'literary' subjects. Grimshaw painted mostly for private art patrons, and exhibited only 5 works at the Royal Academy between 1874 and 1886 and one at the Grosvenor Gallery. The towns and docks that he painted most frequently were Glasgow, Liverpool, Leeds, Scarborough, Whitby and London. Grimhaw's style and subject matter changed little during his career; he strove constantly to perfect his own very individual vision. He was interested in photography, and sometimes used a camera obscura to project outlines on to oil canvas, enabling him to repeat compositions several times. He also mixed sand and other ingredients with his paint to get the effects he wanted. Although he established no school, Grimshaw's oil paintings were forged and imitated in his lifetime.

Whilst his moonlit town views are his most popular works, he also painted landscapes, portraits, interiors, fairy pictures and neo-classical subjects. Around 1880 Grimshaw suffered some unknown financial crisis and retrenched, returning to Leeds and boosting his output to around fifty paintings a year.

Certain elements of social realism come into his paintings around that time, night being a good time to record less respectable forms of life. The output of moonlights continued during the 1880's, particularly of street and dockside scenes, but there were also continuing experiments.

He tried painting over photographs, shocking some modern art historians. He tried much less precise, almost naive, paintings, which reflected his friendship with that other nocturnal creature, Whistler, who, in a rare outbreak of generosity, had ceded to Grimshaw priority in the 'moonlight' oil painting genre. Grimshaw also tried fairy painting, especially the various versions of Iris which are popular posters today.

'Sic Transit Gloria Mundi – The Burning of the Spa Saloon' 1876
Atkinson Grimshaw

One of a number of Atkinson Grimshaw's paintings of 'Forge Valley - Scarborough'. Another was sold in July 2013 at auction by Bonham's of London for £68,450

During his early period he signed 'JA Grimshaw' but in 1867 dropped the 'J' and signed himself Atkinson

Grimshaw. He usually signed his pictures on the front and the back. Two of his sons, Arthur and Louis, were oil painters. It is difficult to know what this innovative and resourceful painter might have tried next, had he not died of cancer at the age of 57.

Scarborough Art Gallery holds 5 of his paintings — Lights in the Harbour' (1879), 'Sic Transit Gloria Mundi – The Burning of the Spa Saloon' (1876), [page 59] 'Scarborough Lights' (c1877), 'Yew Tree Court Scalby', and 'Burning Off' - a fishing boat at Scarborough (1877),

and for anyone interested in a moody, albeit perhaps romantic view of the town some 150 years ago, with views many of us can still recall, the Art Gallery to see these paintings is well worth a visit.

*

PAUL MARNY 1829-1914

Paul Marny was born in Paris 1829 and was a noted British- French artist. He died in Scarborough in 1914. Paul Marny first worked as a stage scene painter, and porcelain decorator for the Sèvres factory before joining a French architect in Belfast. He became a landscape and architectural painter and moved to Scarborough in 1860.

There he taught Albert Strange (who, in turn taught Frank Henry Algernon Mason – see next section) and many other Scarborough artists where he mostly remained until he died in 1914. After 1878 he sold almost all of his work to John Linn, a local dealer.

He exhibited at the RA.

In 1874 the British Journal of Photography reported that 'A Gallic brother, M. Paul Marny Godard, of Paris, has obtained a patent for the application of carbon printing to porcelain or other similar substance, which, after the picture is developed, receives a coating of transparent enamel ..."

He is famous for his painting of the *Loss of the Scarborough Lifeboat on 2 November 1861*. We have been unable to obtain a print of Marny's painting to include in this book but below is a copy of the painting of the same event by Ernest Roes which appears below.

'The loss of the Coupland' by Ernest Roes

The background to the tragedy is that before the lifeboat was called out the storm had already caused a lot of damage. The town itself had been hit by hurricane strength winds. Houses in New Queen Street had their roofs blown off and similar damage occurred in Falsgrave and to the Marionettes theatre. The huge seas nearly rose above the level of the West pier almost sweeping away the salesmen's offices. Many boats moored in Sandside were moved to the streets beyond to protect them.

Tragedy and loss of life had already occurred that night before the lifeboat Amelia was called out. A pilot named William Leadley had already escorted in "The Wave". [His local knowledge was vital as Scarborough is a tricky port to enter. There are cross currents on the entrance to the harbour and boats can easily miss the turn.] The master of the 'Wave' described two other vessels in trouble. William Leadley went back to sea to help. He was never seen again. Also, Mr Appleyard, the Harbour Master had already reported that a merchant ship or collier had foundered on rocks 3 miles to the south.

'At 12 noon "The Coupland", a schooner from South Shields attempted to gain entry to the harbour but failed. As it headed for the Spa promenade walls the Lifeboat was called out. The breaks were so huge that stones had already been dislodged on the parapet. The Lifeboat soon got into trouble as her coxswain was thrown overboard.

The Lifeboat floated on the water like a cork, but never capsized. In returning from the Spa sea wall after she had struck a second time, she lay partly on one side, a heavy sea washed several of the crew overboard, and some of the oars were also lost. Thomas Brewster was washed overboard and drowned. Nothing but the great excellence of the boat could have saved her from going to pieces, with the repeated dashings against the Spa.'

Notable deaths occurred in the crowd. Ropes were thrown from the spa promenade to the boat. The Lifeboat was pulled to some calmer water. But as the Lifeboat men jumped into the surf they were dragged out to sea in receding waves. Lord Charles Beauclerc died trying to help those in the sea.

Mr Sarony and Mr Rutter recovered the body of Lord

Beauclerc. They were nearly lost in the process. Mr Sarony was carried by the waves out of sight of the spectators. He was thrown a lifebelt Three hours passed before circulation to his body was fully restored.

Two of the Lifeboats crew were lost - Thomas Brewster and John Burton. The Coxswain Thomas Clayburn was swept away. He was saved but he was "much injured and has been confined to his room ever since." The remaining crew were James Banks, Thomas Ward, William Chambers, Isaac Morley, William Ruston, Robert Maltby, Richard Harrison and William Larkin. Several of these were also injured...

Mr Oliver Sarony, was a famous photographer who used some of his wealth to commission a painting called "The Shipwreck" by Paul Marny which was based upon the tragedy involving the "Coupland" and the "Amelia" that fateful day in 1861.'

*

On a personal note Paul Marny lived in South Cliff, Scarborough. Apparently his cashflow was often very stretched and one day he called into Smith's, Fishmongers and Game Dealers of South Street. Mr & Mrs Smith had been chasing him about an unpaid bill and when he visited the shop he was served by my aunt, then Phyllis Fowler. She had started work at Smiths very recently having just left the Municipal School.

Paul Marny explained to her that the Smiths had been in touch about an unpaid bill but that cash, he said, was tight so, 'Would this do instead?'

From his pocket he pulled a watercolour painting about a foot square, folded into four. My aunt didn't have authority to make such a decision so asked him to wait while she approached Mrs Smith who was upstairs.

Above: 'Scarborough by Night,'

'Abbeville Cathedral ' by Paul Marny

According to my aunt the Smiths felt sorry for him so said that 'on this occasion only' they would accept the painting in full payment of his overdue account,

Paul Marny went on his way happy to have resolved his financial difficulties and later that day Mrs Smith came into the shop around the time my aunt was due to leave. She was holding the painting. "You can have this as a gift." she said, "You never know. It might be worth a guinea or so in a few years' time."

My aunt thanked her, took the painting, smoothed out the folds and eventually framed it. She had it until a few years before her death and always said to me "that's for you David when I'm gone."

However, in her final years she became a little forgetful and this became known amongst various unsavoury characters who kept visiting her and offering ludicrously small sums of money for the few paintings and other antiques she had collected.

We were living away from Scarborough but one day we visited and I noticed the patch on the wall where 'my' Paul Marny had hung.

She saw me looking and said that a 'dealer' had called round and she'd told him the story of Paul Marny's bill. The dealer had promptly offered her twice the amount of Marny's original bill and had persuaded her that that was a very generous offer. She was taken in and sold it for around £10!

So, if any reader owns a Paul Marny watercolour about a foot square, which has obviously at one time been folded into four, I could be very interested in acquiring it!

*

FRANK HENRY ALGERNON MASON
1875 –1965

Frank Henry Mason, RBA, RI, RSMA was an artist best known for his maritime, shipping, coastal and harbour paintings and as a creator of art deco travel and railway posters. His style is described as a 'light impressionist' and he was a founder member of the *Staithes Art Club* whose members are known today as the *Staithes group* of artists, or the *Northern Impressionists*.

His fields were painting, drawing and etching and he was trained by Arthur Strange at Scarborough College of Art. Strange had, in turn been trained by Paul Marny.

Frank Henry Mason was born Frank Henry Algernon Mason in Seaton Carew, Hartlepool, County Durham, on 1st October 1875. He was the son of a railway clerk and was educated between 1880 and 1882 as a cadet at the HMS Conway Naval School at Birkenhead.

On leaving HMS Conway, Frank Mason spent time at sea then trained with Parsons as a marine engineer for steam powered ships working at Hartlepool, Leeds and Scarborough, eventually settling in Scarborough around about 1894.

Frank had been interested in drawing but had no formal training in art. There was however a strong artistic community in Scarborough at the time. Frank studied at the Scarborough School of Art with Albert Strange and made regular trips to Staithes to meet and socialise with the arts community there. By 1890 Frank's work had advanced to the point where he received commissions from art dealers, and around 1898 he decided to quit marine engineering and take up art full-time. In 1901 he became a founder member of the *Staithes Art Club*.

Frank married his wife Edith in 1899. He had lived at Blenheim Terrace in Scarborough but they relocated the short distance to lodgings in North Marine Road.

During 1914-1918, Frank Mason was appointed shipping war artist in the RNVR as lieutenant in command of a motor launch in the North Sea. The Imperial War Museum holds 56 of his paintings from this period.

On returning from the war Frank worked with the community at Ebberston Hall near Scarborough and he travelled abroad extensively undertaking an extended European tour. He painted many subjects - generally in water colour.

During the 1920s and 1930s he designed poster artwork for most of the countries railway companies, the Underground in London and ocean liner companies.

Frank Mason was elected to the Royal Society of British Artists in 1904 and elected to the Royal Institute of Painters in Water Colours in 1929.

Frank Henry Mason had exhibitions of his work at the Royal Academy from 1902 onwards. His work has been included in an exhibition in Liverpool and in 1973 there was an exhibition of his work at the National Maritime Museum. As well as the Imperial War Museum, Frank's work can be found in numerous galleries around the country - at Cartwright Hall Bradford, in Dundee, Hartlepool, and at Whitby.

Frank Mason wrote the book *Ashore and Afloat* (1929) about his water colour technique and with Fred Taylor, wrote the book *Water Colour Painting.*

'HMS Superb' by Frank Henry Algernon Mason

*

SARONY, OLIVER FRANCOIS XAVIER
1819-1879

Oliver Sarony trained as a daguerreotypist in New York before travelling to England. He set up his studio in

Alfred Street on South Cliff in 1857, in the fashionable resort of Scarborough, describing his business as a 'Photographic Institution'

He became one of the most commercially successful photographers of his day.

His gallery comprised no less than 98 rooms and up to 110 people were employed there at any one time. At the time of Sarony's death in 1879, the turnover of his studio was estimated at £20,000, and this in a season that only lasted three months.

Born Olivier François Xavier Sarony in Quebec in 1820, his name was Anglicized to Oliver sometime soon after his arrival in England in 1843. He operated first as an itinerant daguerreotypist and is known to have worked at different times in Bradford, Chesterfield, Mansfield, Huddersfield, Hull, Lincolnshire, and Doncaster. In 1854 he settled briefly in Wiesbach, before spending a year in Cambridge and then another in Norwich, finally settling in Scarborough in 1857.

The studio that he commissioned architects John and David Petch to build for him was *'one of the grandest in Europe'*; the Scarborough Gazette called it *'an establishment with every convenience for carrying out Photography to perfection.'*

Designed to impress his clients, it included a gallery long enough to place the camera 40 feet from the sitter with a direct north light. Built in the Louis XV style, Sarony called the premises Gainsborough House.

Sarony's buisness propsered. Not only from Scarborough's annual influx of royalty, nobility and gentry but also from the various technological innovations that the photographer invented and patented.

A major part of his business was the production of high quality photographs of paintings, for which he exploited the benefits of the new carbon process. Another important source of revenue was the production of large portraits, photographic enlargements finished in oils by skilful painters. By 1871, his studio was said to be the largest photographic establishment in Europe, but Sarony began to suffer from diabetes and grew increasing more debilitated. He collapsed in town one day and died at his home on 30 August 1879. He was buried in Scarborough cemetery.

Sarony is seen in this self-portrait (right) wearing the silver medal of the Royal National Lifeboat Institution for the Preservation of Life from Shipwreck, which he received for his bravery during a storm at Scarborough on 2nd November 1861 and described more fully in the Paul Marny section of this chapter, on pages 62 -64.

Above is Oliver Sarony's Grand Studio in Scarborough where he made portraits - painted onto an enlarged photographic base - into luxury products. At its height Sarony's studio was said to be the largest in Europe. The building on the left – built in a similar style - is now flats. Sarony's studio was later demolished, became tennis courts and is now a car park.

*

JOSEPH MALLORD WILLIAM TURNER

1775-1851

Whilst Turner must have been the most prolific painter of Scarborough seascapes, he never appeared to live in the town although he must have stayed for prolonged spells whilst undertaking his commissions.

'Regarded as the most important landscape painter of the 19th century, Joseph Mallord William Turner was born in 1775 in Covent Garden, London. His father ran a barber shop alongside a wig-making business. Possibly due to his mother's mental stability which later led to an early death, the young Turner was sent off to stay with his uncle in Brentford.

The young Romantic artist began expressing an interest in painting, and went on to attend the prestigious Royal Academy of Art at a mere age of 14. A watercolour piece Turner did a year later was accepted for the RA Summer Exhibition of 1790.

Frequent visits to the breath taking countryside of Yorkshire and West Sussex created such an impact on Turner that he began creating detailed, realistic drawings of the inspiring landscapes and seascapes. He stayed loyal to the traditional English landscapes for a couple of years but the subject matter of his later works – nature in its powerful destructive form – began to come into play in the 1812 painting of Hannibal Crossing the Alps.

Influential art critic John Ruskin described Turner, whose painting radiates a spectacular ephemeral quality, as the artist who could most "stirringly and truthfully measure the moods of Nature". And even though his palette was vibrant with rich tangerines, cerulean and violet, a layer of transparency and lightness exists amidst the violence of the shipwrecks and catastrophes.

Turner became more eccentric as he grew older, and his father's departure in 1829 had a profound effect on the pioneer British artist, causing bouts of depression. At 70, Turner eventually bought a house in Chelsea and retired due to deteriorating health. After his death in

1851, Turner was buried at St. Paul's Cathedral and bequeathed to the British government more than 20,000 drawings, oil paintings and watercolours

Two of JMW Turner's watercolours of Scarborough

***

CHAPTER 5

FROM 1845 -
THE DEVELOPMENT OF SOUTH CLIFF

With the expansion of Scarborough as a seaside resort, and the growing popularity of the Spa, it was logical that the South cliff area - up to then undeveloped - should expand. Hotels were needed for the increasing numbers of holidaymakers, some who would spend the whole 'season' in the town arriving with a retinue of staff.

The Crown Hotel (now the Crown Spa Hotel) was completed in May 1844 and opened for business on 10 June 1845. It overlooks the town's South Bay and is now privately owned by a local family.

The hotel was designed by the architect John Gibson, and when completed in 1844, was one of the first purpose-built hotels in the world, as well as the first purpose-built hotel in Scarborough. John Gibson chose a site overlooking the South Bay Beach and North Sea views and designed the hotel on a Greco-Roman theme.

The hotel's heyday was arguably during Victorian times, when wealthy society made up the establishment's clientele.

The hotel has been featured in television and film, chiefly being linked to the programmes and films, *Little Voice*, *Heartbeat*, *The Royal*, the *Acid Bath Murders* and many more.

In 2003, the hotel was renamed to the Crown Spa Hotel, to reflect the new facilities within the hotel. In

May 2008, after months of hard work and dedication to service, the hotel was awarded the four-star status by the AA.

The Prince of Wales Hotel (now luxury flats) was a little further south on Esplanade from the Crown but started life as a row of terrace houses, fronting Prince of Wales Terrace. This terrace extended right to the cliff edge with the garden of the end property adjoining the cliff edge with the garden of the end property going right to the cliff edge.

These houses were converted into a hotel, by demolishing the properties nearest to the cliff edge, then building a new frontage on Esplanade, to join to the existing properties built there. This also released land to enable Esplanade to be extended southwards – as part as a cantilevered extension over the cliff edge. Previously Esplanade had ended at the properties which now abutted the Prince of Wales, slightly to the north of Prince of Wales Terrace.

The hotel opened to the public in 1861. It gradually gained and nurtured the reputation of being at the luxury end of the market and its fastidious owners, starting with Richard Hunt, looked after its fabric, furniture and decorations and made sure they were always of the best quality and in impeccable condition.

But South Cliff was still somewhat remote from the rest of Scarborough and the area was then known as New Scarborough.

The Spa (or Cliff) Bridge had opened on 19th July 1827 and this gave much better access from the town to the Spa. But access to Esplanade, South Cliff and the growing number of new hotels in that area, was still difficult and meant a circuitous journey.

A carriage ride from York to Scarborough could take 7 hours of travel but things changed rapidly when the railway from York and further afield came to Scarborough in 1845, with the line to Bridlington – which then connected to Driffield, Beverley and Hull - following in 1847.

Scarborough Railway Station which reputedly has the longest station seat in the world

The railway brought a vast increase in passengers and the need for a more direct route from the central Railway station to South Cliff. Incidentally, it is not generally known that Scarborough Railway Station still has the longest station seat in the world. It is 152 yards (139 m) in length.

With the arrival of the railway, a bridge over Ramsdale valley was felt to be essential.

Building (top) and opening (bottom) of Valley Bridge.

One Robert Williamson who was interested in developing the largely unoccupied South Cliff, bought an iron bridge which had collapsed into the river Ouse at York. The Council decided to support his venture and the bridge was brought to Scarborough, re-erected and opened in 1865 with further road widening being completed by 1886.

Valley Bridge then became the main route to South Cliff and out of the town to the south and the distance from the railway station to Esplanade was cut by two thirds.

Michael Gorbert and Scarborough Civic Society give more clarity to the burgeoning expansion of South Cliff in the following extract:

'The Spa buildings and the gardens of the South Cliff are so much part of the Scarborough scene, taken for granted by residents and visitors alike, that it is hard to realize that at the time of Queen Victoria's accession, the cliff face south of Bland's Cliff was as undeveloped as White Nab remains today. [A point on the coastline just below Osgodby, south of Scarborough]

Early in the 19th century the town still enjoyed nationwide fame for its 'medicinal' waters, but in the face of competition from inland spas and south coast towns, Scarborough's popularity as a Spa town was declining. It was being abandoned by the very rich and a new social pattern was to emerge, bringing into sharp focus the changing needs of the visitors.

Although the Cliff Bridge had been opened in 1827 it led only to the rudimentary buildings and bare grounds of the Spa, overlooked by an undeveloped Belmont. Even the building of the elegant terraces, which included the Crown Hotel (1844), created an island remote from the town. More than 20 years were to pass before the opening of the first Valley Bridge provided a level traffic route to the expanding South Cliff area.

Concessions were being made however to the new generation of visitors - men and women who crossed the new Cliff bridge from St. Nicholas Cliff to the Spa as much to enjoy the music, the fireworks, and the promenading, as to take the waters and 'endure' the sea bathing. It was this demand for entertainment that led the Cliff Bridge Company (whose initials can still be found amongst the ironwork on the Spa buildings) to develop its grounds with walks, trees and gardens, and to replace their wooden structure with more distinguished Halls in 1839 and again in 1858. Sir Joseph Paxton added the Grand Staircase. Southwards however from these grounds the cliff face was bare, windswept and unvisited.

Gradually, as imposing buildings spread farther south along the Esplanade and inland towards Filey Road it became apparent that the neglected land offered opportunities for more gardens to complement those in the Spa grounds. Fortunately 13 acres of land were bought in 1883 by George Lord Beeforth, who was also responsible for many of the houses on the south Esplanade. On the storm-beaten cliffside he planted 14,000 rose bushes with trees to screen them and developed a cultivated vista from the seaward end of the subway which linked his own home 'The Belvedere' with his private garden and stone summer-house.

The Cliff Bridge Company had bought 8 acres of land to the south of the Spa, but sold 2 acres to the South Cliff Tramway Company for the erection of their steep track in 1875.

The subsequent history of the South Cliff is that of progression from private and individual enterprise to municipal control. Beeforth was to sell all 13 acres to the Corporation in 1912 and the Cliff Bridge Company sold all their land south of the Tramway. This allowed further development under the genius of Harry W. Smith, who devised so much of our parkland and floral heritage during his 37 years as Borough Engineer. Beeforth's Rose Garden was retained, other gardens developed, and in 1914 the new Italian Gardens, high above the almost completed bathing pool, were opened. Although the development of Holbeck Gardens with the putting green and pavilion had to wait until 1925, it is interesting to note how many postcard views of the earlier gardens in Holbeck Ravine survive, suggesting their great popularity. Much later, during the depression between the wars, unemployed men were found work in widening the paths of the Ravine.

Scarborough's first putting green soon found favour with visitors who passed under the Clock Tower which commemorates another benefactor, namely Alfred Shuttleworth. From his summer residence 'Red Court', Shuttleworth's view south-eastwards was impaired by another house. He eventually bought the house, demolished it to enjoy the unbroken view, and built Red Court Garden which he was to present to the town. (His earlier gifts had been the Clock Tower and the statue of Mercury in the Italian Gardens.) The Corporation renamed it the Shuttleworth Garden and eighteen months before the outbreak of the Second World War designed the attractive and ever-popular miniature garden.

The post-war period saw what was perhaps the logical 'democratisation' of the South Cliff. Public Service Vehicles appeared for the first time on parts of the Esplanade. Tolls of the Valley Bridge had long since

*been removed and now the Cliff Bridge was to be toll-free
so that all who would, might walk in the Spa grounds
without charge. With the acquisition by the Scarborough
Corporation in 1957 of the Spa and its grounds, all the
cliff face from Aquarium Top to Holbeck Ravine came
under municipal ownership, save for the tiny private
garden opposite 'The Belvedere' and the Tramway track
which slices the South Cliff in two, still offering (though
no longer for 1d!) an alternative to the 240 steps from the
South Sands to the Esplanade.*

*Perhaps now the evolution is complete and we are
fortunate to be the legatees of planners and gardeners
long ago departed. Sadly vandals daub Sir Joseph
Paxton's summer-houses, dogs foul pathways, shelters
and flower beds, the thoughtless cast their plastic trays
and tins amongst the primroses and flowers. But the
gardens remain, and season by season, year by year, in
their beauty and serenity the tired, the contemplative,
and the appreciative can still enjoy their glories and the
ever-changing seascape beyond.'*

Michael Gorbert's extract above mentions the South
Cliff Tramway Company and this was the final piece of
jigsaw needed to provide easy transport between the
beach, the Spa and the hotels and properties on
Esplanade. Until it was built the only access was via the
steep, winding paths up the cliff side and the many
steps.

The Spa Cliff Lift as it became known was Britain's first
cliff lift. It opened in 1875 having been built by the
Scarborough South Cliff Tramway Company Limited
to link the South Cliff and Esplanade to the beach and
especially the Spa – which at the time was the most
popular music venue outside London.

But what is not generally known is that the keenest proponent in providing the lift, who became a board member of South Cliff Tramway Company Ltd, was none other than Richard Hunt – proprietor of the Prince of Wales Hotel diagonally across Esplanade from the lift.

He had seen the need and the benefit to his hotel guests in providing transport to and from the Spa and beach and was instrumental in pushing through the project.

Church Parade on South Cliff- possibly viewed from the Prince of Wales Hotel, just over the road from the top Lift station.

'The system to link the South Cliff Esplanade to the Scarborough Spa, was designed and engineered by a Mr Lucas. Constructed by Crossley Brothers of Manchester for a cost of £ 8000, the track is 4 ft 8 ½ in (1,435 mm) wide and 284 feet (87 m) long, on 1 in 1.75 gradient.

The Spa Cliff Lift with the Prince of Wales Hotel at the top of the cliff.

Metropolitan Carriage of Birmingham constructed the two cars, each capable of carrying 14 seated passengers, to the bottom of which is attached a water tank. Each car is also attached to a twin-steel cable rope, which is operated by a brakeman at the top station.

'Using seawater pumped by two Crossley gas engines through a hydraulic system designed by Tangye Ltd in Smethwick, Birmingham,' the upper car's water tank was filled until the counterbalance point was reached. The cars then proceeded along their individual tracks, with speed and safety controlled by the brakeman. When the upper car reached the bottom of the incline, both cars were braked, and the seawater released. The procedure was then repeated.

The Cliff railway opened on 6 July 1875. The gas engines were replaced by steam pumps in 1879, and after refurbishment in 1947 the water system was replaced by a 90 hp electric engine. The cars were replaced by two built by Hudswell Clarke & Company in 1934-1935.

Scarborough Borough Council bought the funicular from South Cliff Tramway Company in 1993. In 1997, the lift was modified to be completely automatic.

*

The Friends of South Cliff Gardens add to Michael Gorbert's earlier extract:

'The layout of the paths appears in an artist's drawing of the plans by the architects Verity and Hunt in 1880. George Lord Beeforth created other large areas including extensive rose gardens in 1885; at a similar time William Skipsey began the landscaping of the Holbeck Gardens.

Yet it is the deep understanding of the area by Harry W Smith that gave rise to the gardens we see today.

'A brilliant design, bringing together old and new areas and seamlessly linking different skills and uses so effortlessly together.

Three rules were applied to these gardens for this final design. For the long-term preservation of the Esplanade it was essential to stabilize the cliffs, yet

equally every part must still give pleasure to the visitor, and finally to allow the undercliffs to contain attractive gardens, the plants must survive the salt laden winds...'
As Harry W Smith has had such a lasting impact on Scarborough it is worth looking further into his background and achievements.

'He was born on the 9th of October 1867 and was educated at various schools in Birmingham, Bristol and Bournemouth. In 1881 he was articled to Mr J Stevens FRIBA, an architect who was Surveyor and Sanitary Inspector in Bournemouth, where Smith completed his training. His final position in Bournemouth was Deputy Engineer. The value of Smith's work in Bournemouth amounted to £250,000. His projects included main drainage works, sea-outfalls, a sea-water scheme for road and sewage flushing, a refuse destructor, new depots, fire stations and the laying out of public parks and cemeteries.

The Chairman of the Scarborough Committee recommending his appointment to the Council said:

"We have found a young man who will suit you. You can bring him up just as you want him".

When Mr Smith appeared before the Selection Committee he was the owner of a black beard. It had been specially grown for the occasion to try and divert attention from his youthful appearance for he was only 30 years of age at the time of his appointment. After his appointment he quietly dispensed with the beard, it having served its purpose.

Harry W Smith took up his duties as Borough Engineer and Surveyor of Scarborough on 1st January 1897.

The driving force in his official life was to make the best possible use of natural beauty. Mr Smith was a great enthusiast for planting trees. He used to offer this advice to his assistants:

"If you do nothing else, whenever you can, plant a tree. It will be there when you are gone."

There was nothing pretentious or flamboyant about Harry Smith. He was a homely, friendly man, simple in his tastes, deeply interested in and dedicated to his job. His chief hobby was growing begonias in his greenhouse and tending his lawn. This was his particular pride and he would offer a shilling to any visitor who could find a weed in it.

Early in his career in Scarborough he designed the Borough Sanatorium which was a landscaped campus with three separate buildings for diphtheria, enteric fever, and scarlet fever and a further observation block. Some private patient rooms were also provided.

A porter's lodge at the entrance housed a discharge unit. He achieved a hospital site of attractive and functional buildings on a landscaped area which came in on budget and is still in use today as Cross Lane Hospital, Newby, albeit not now for infectious cases. A friendship between Harry Smith and a wealthy businessman Alfred Shuttleworth brought indirect benefits to Scarborough. Mr Shuttleworth lived at Red Court on the Esplanade and his view of the Castle Hill was spoiled by the Revolving Tower, an erection which since 1898 had stood out like a sore thumb on the skyline. In 1907, Mr Shuttleworth bought the Revolving Tower and paid for the cost of its removal.

To the south of Red Court was Holbeck Hurst, formerly the home of Cllr. RA Marillier, Mayor of Scarborough in 1896. Mr Shuttleworth also bought

Holbeck Hurst, had it demolished, and the site cleared, thus giving him an uninterrupted view of the cliffs to Filey Brigg. When Mr. Shuttleworth decided to leave Scarborough and sell Red Court, he called on the Borough Engineer and asked if he wanted a garden for the town. Mr Smith accepted this generous offer without demur and in due time the site of Holbeck Hurst became known as Shuttleworth Gardens.

He converted St. Nicholas House into the Town Hall. Of the latter, the Scarborough Mercury commented:

"The house, built by Mr John Woodall in 1845 as a private residence, is Elizabethan in character, and the additions both exterior and interior have been designed to harmonize as far as possible. Indeed, but for the newness of the colouring of the red bricks and stone facings of the new portion, it would be difficult to say exactly where it begins and the old portion ends".

He also laid out the gardens and opened them to the public. Residents as well as visitors were in Smith's thoughts when he designed new projects. He was responsible for Scarborough's earliest slum clearance and house building schemes, of which the authors of the 1938 Adshead Report wrote that *'Scarborough has done well'.*

At the time of his retirement Smith said that nothing had given him greater pleasure than to see the homes they had created for the working men of the town. Schemes such as the construction of Peasholm Park and the beach bungalows on the North Bay, and later Peasholm Glen, provided work for local men at times of high unemployment. Facilities such as the Manor Road

Bowling Green and the Mere provided leisure opportunities for residents.

Above: Shuttleworth Miniature Garden
Below: Scarborough Town Hall

Although the Alexandra field had been purchased by the Corporation in 1889 to prevent it falling into the hands of speculative builders, it was not until 1907 that any attempt was made to develop this four acre site. The scheme which Mr Smith prepared included the provision of two crown bowling greens, three tennis courts and an open space for entertainments. The estimated cost was a £4,000 including paths, floral beds and earthworks to provide shelter from the north and east winds. This improvement was opened on 27th June, 1908.

Three years later the Borough Engineer submitted a scheme for building a concert pavilion, providing covered accommodation for 1500 with additional space for a further 1500 in the open air.

The laying out of the Alexandra Gardens and the building of the Floral Hall was a major step forward in the development of the North side and the popularity of the Floral Hall in subsequent years proved how wrong the opponents were.

In the early days of the Floral Hall, Mr Smith made a feature of hanging baskets, flowering shrubs and sub-tropical plants in the hall, but in the course of time, as the Fol-de-Rols shows developed into full scale revue productions depending more and more on modern lighting effects, it was necessary to black-out the hall and the attractive floral features had to be sacrificed.

Whilst on a visit to Guernsey, Mr Smith had seen an open air tidal bathing pool. This idea appealed to him and he came back to Scarborough to explore the possibility of building a similar pool in the South Bay. Bathing at Scarborough was very popular but the facilities provided by the old bathing machines left much to be desired.

The proposal he submitted was to build an open air pool at the foot of the undercliff where the Italian Gardens were beginning to take shape. This pool which was being built at the outbreak of the 1914-18 war was the first of its kind in this country and with its diving boards, water-chute, varying depths of water, up-to-date dressing boxes, showers, and so on, provided facilities far in advance of anything which could be provided for beach bathers.

SCARBOROUGH
ITS QUICKER BY RAIL

Above: Rail poster showing the South Bay pool.
Below: Clock Café and chalets.

Early one morning in December 1914, the workmen engaged on the construction work at the pool had a rude shock when German cruisers steamed across the bay firing their broadsides. The workmen scurried for shelter as quickly as they could and found protection behind the new wall of the bathing pool as the shells passed overhead.

Mr Smith proceeded to lay out the land south of the Spa with paths of easy gradient, rose beds, beach bungalows, bathing shelters and the familiar 'Cafe under the Clock' (previous page).

The beach bungalows which are such a novel part of this development were first introduced on the North side in 1910. There is justification for claiming that Scarborough pioneered the beach bungalow idea.

The planning of the Italian Gardens (opposite) gave full scope to Mr Smith's genius for landscape gardening, and the result proved to be one of the Corporation's most popular features on the South side. The north shelter carries the date of 1914.

The centrepiece of the garden is a stone kerbed lily pond surrounding a pedestal surmounted by a figure of Mercury. On either side of the lily pond are rose beds laid out in formal design and at each end rise graceful terraces with stone retaining walls, surmounted by stone vases. Flights of steps lead to pergola shelters of classical design.

The gardens and shelters were furnished with comfortable teak seats enabling the visitor to enjoy the colourful and restful scene.

To ensure the position and size of Mercury were right, Mr Smith took one of his staff to pose on the pedestal so he could view it from all angles.

The stone required for the terraces and shelters was in the main reclaimed from the rocks excavated when the bathing pool was built.

Of the many spots in Scarborough that claim the amateur photographer's attention, the Italian Gardens is perhaps the most photographed of all.

Although the work Mr Smith had done in laying out the St. Nicholas Gardens and the Alexandra Gardens had met with general approval, it was the laying out of Peasholm Park that established his reputation as a landscape gardener of outstanding ability. Apart from the Clarence Gardens and the Alexandra Gardens the North side was still undeveloped and Mr Smith turned his attention to what was known locally as Tuckers Field. It was rather an unlovely, neglected area occupied in the main by allotments and piggeries. The stream running through Wilson's Wood crossed the site and emptied itself at Peasholm Gap.

Mr Smith could see beauty in the most unlikely places. He looked at Tucker's Field and dreamed a dream, and in due time translated this dream on to his drawing board. He would excavate the area around the island and use the stream to make a lake. Around the lake he would lay out pleasant paths with flower beds. A boathouse, cafe and bridge would be introduced in the Japanese style so that the whole effect would be like that of a Willow Pattern Plate.

The estimated cost of the scheme was £8,851 and despite opposition the scheme was approved and the work proceeded.

Peasholm Park was opened on 19th June 1912. Further additions to the Park were made from time to time including the Bandstand, the Waterfall and Pagoda, and the Miniature Golf Course together with a number of Japanese and Oriental statues and ornaments which were purchased by the Corporation from Kirby Misperton Hall.

Above: Miniature Railway in Northstead Manor Gardens
Below: Peasholm Park

With the purchase of the Northstead Estate in 1926, the area known locally as Hodgson's Slack was available for development. The central feature in the first stage of the development was to be a miniature railway which would connect the Peasholm area with Scalby Mills.

This railway would be seven-eighths of a mile long, with all the features of a normal railway i.e. tunnels, bridges, signal boxes and gradient boards all reproduced to scale.

The locomotives were to be scale models of the LNER's Gresley engine but instead of being driven by steam, a 26 BHP diesel engine was to be used.

Not everyone thought the miniature railway scheme a good one and the local press referred to it as *'The Toy Railway'* and *'The Borough Engineer's Toy'*.

Then Mr Smith considered the idea of building an open-air theatre.

The setting was ideal with the stage (bigger than Drury Lane) on an island in the middle of a lake, and with accommodation for 7,000 rising up the sloping banks facing the stage, and the hillside behind the island stage forming a natural backcloth.

The work went ahead and in the summer of 1932 Sir Edward German's popular light opera 'Merrie England' was produced by the Scarborough Operatic and Dramatic Society. The Lord Mayor of London, who attended the opening with the Lady Mayoress and his Sheriff said: *"The setting is ideal and constitutes a wonderful tribute to the imagination of whoever realised the possibilities to be derived from this particular part of the park, and also to the engineers who carried out the necessary embellishments and alterations which provide such a picturesque stage and background and also such splendid accommodation".* Perhaps the most apt description of the Open-air Theatre was penned by Mr John Bourne in 1936 when he called it *'The Drury Lane of the open air'*.

When Harry W Smith retired in October 1933, Mr FA White, presiding at a testimonial gathering in the Council Chamber, described the Borough Engineer as 'one who entered this town nearly 40 years ago and has done nothing in his life amongst us but to beautify everything he has touched'. Continuing, White said he could remember 'a town having from north to south many eyesores, which had been obliterated and in many places beauty spots had sprung up which it was never anticipated would be there'.

The Open Air theatre with the stage centre left, the lake, centre and audience seating centre right. The Miniature railway travelled from the station, front right, across the bottom of the photo, round the back of the stage area and on to Scalby Mills.

It is worth taking a few minutes to consider exactly what he did do to improve Scarborough. We tend to think first and foremost of the gardens and other landscape features that he laid out, for Smith was, in the words of the report of his death in the Scarborough Mercury of 4th August 1944, *'A landscape artist of rare genius with a passion for preserving and exploiting natural beauties ...'*.

The list includes the St. Nicholas, Alexandra and Italian Gardens, Peasholm Park and the later Peasholm Glen, and Northstead Manor Gardens. In some of these cases, notably the Alexandra Gardens and Peasholm Park, he saw potential in what were essentially neglected or waste areas and transformed them into beautiful attractions. He certainly lived by the injunction he gave to one of his juniors, *"If you do nothing else, whenever you can, plant a tree. It will be there when you have gone"*.

When laying out a new estate or making new roads the planting of trees was always of primary importance to him. On old photographs of Tucker's Field (Peasholm Park) and of Oliver's Mount and the Mere there is hardly a tree to be seen, while today through his foresight and skill, the trees he planted add greatly to the beauty and colour of these areas.

Not only did he plant many trees during his career as Borough Engineer, but also he left in his will £50 to the Corporation of Scarborough *'either for planting bulbs on the roadsides and open spaces or in commencing planting of azaleas and rhododendrons along the roadway through Raincliffe Woods"*.

Mr Smith's retirement did not go unnoticed and steps were taken privately by a number of well-wishers in the town, to mark this event.

They did so by presenting him with six Chippendale chairs and a cheque for £309. The meeting of subscribers at which the presentation was made was held in the Town Hall on 6th October 1933.

Acknowledging the gift Mr Smith replied and said:

"I have been surrounded throughout my stay here by a staff of young men, energetic, clever and loyal, who had stood by me through thick and thin and I gratefully acknowledge in public what I owe to them. In 1897 there were 55 acres of public pleasure grounds and today there are something, like 350 acres. I have always been a lover of the beautiful and it has been my endeavour to leave Scarborough a little better than I found it.

I have to confess that in my 36 years' service I have, God forgive me, spent on capital works alone, no less a sum than one million pounds of your hard earned money."

After his retirement Mr Smith served on the Board of the Scarborough Hospital for some years and supervised the laying out of the Hospital grounds. He also accepted invitations to advise local authorities in various parts of the country on their development schemes, and served on the Board of the Scarborough Building Society.

Harry W Smith died on 3rd August, 1944, at the age of 77.

Harry W Smith

CHAPTER SIX

FROM 1850 –
ST MARTIN-ON-THE-HILL CHURCH

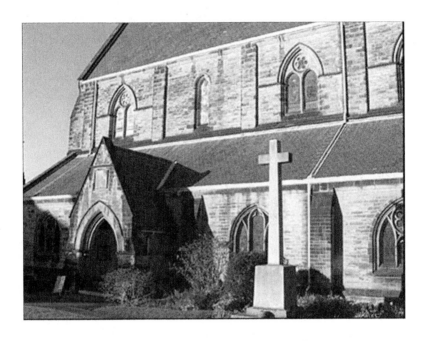

'St Martin's is the perfect High Victorian church. In its
history and within its walls can be found every sort of
Victorian concern and obsession. It was brought into
being by the rapid urban expansion of the 1850s and it
was made possible by the great generosity of a Victorian
spinster. Its outer form and furnishings are the product of
the medievalism of Victorian art: determined to recall an
earlier Age of Faith, its robust realism and its involved
symbolism. The church of St Martin, Scarborough,
remains to this day the physical and spiritual heir to the

love of ritual in worship which came out of Oxford in the 1840s. St Martin's represents an increasingly precious inheritance in art, history and worship.

Development came to the South Cliff of Scarborough late in the l840s with the building of the Crown Hotel and Crown Terrace at the northern end of what is now the Esplanade. It was linked to the medieval town of Scarborough by the Spa Bridge (built in 1827). By 1858 South Cliff was criss-crossed by a network of new roads and drains, and terraces and crescents were steadily rising as plots were acquired and developed. The medieval church of St Mary in the old town was hard-pressed to cope with the demand for seats in the summer. As a result, the worthies of the corporation of Scarborough and the directors of the South Cliff Company (who were more or less the same body of men) set up a committee to raise a new church in the expanding suburb.

Despite the company's gift of a building plot on Albion Road. the committee had not got very far with raising the necessary funds by 1859. When the scheme was on the point of foundering, a South Cliff resident, Miss Mary Craven, stepped in to rescue it. The committee had already secured her assistance to the total of £1,000; she now offered to guarantee the full £6000 estimated as the building cost, and another £1000 needed to endow the parish. Mary Craven (1814-1889) was one of the four daughters of Robert Martin Craven, a wealthy Hull surgeon who had retired to South Cliff (living at 5, Esplanade) and had recently died. She saw the new church as a memorial to her father. The dedication to St Martin of Tours was chosen by her as his name-saint; this was stated in the address she composed for the ceremony of laying the foundation stone in November 1861 (an event ill health obliged her to miss).

Mary Craven was responsible for more than the financing of the new church. Her family connection with Hull secured a vicar for the parish, the Rev'd Robert Henning Parr (1826-1888). Parr was an energetic and eloquent High Churchman, and had been connected with the church of Holy Trinity, Hull, since 1856, when he had been a curate there. He had moved from Hull to the archbishop of York's staff at Bishopthorpe, where he was examining chaplain to the archbishop. But a promising career on the ecclesiastical heights was cut short in 1860, at the death of his patron, Archbishop Musgrave. At a loose end once more in Hull, he accepted the invitation to take up the new living of St Martin's. Miss Craven may also have been responsible for the selection of an architect for the new church. George Frederick Bodley (1827-1907) was himself also the son of a Hull physician, William Hulme Bodley. Although the Bodleys moved to Brighton in the 1840s, they must have been well known to the Cravens, and there is the suspicion of a family connection. Both Parr and Bodley were in their mid-thirties at this time; energetic and forceful men at the beginning of distinguished careers. Through them, Mary Craven put a deep physical and spiritual imprint on the future of the church she had made possible.

The church designed by Bodley for Miss Craven was one of his earliest. Until 1851 he had been the pupil of one of the greatest of all Victorian church architects, George Gilbert Scott. Bodley's independent practice had only recently begun when he won the commission for St Martin's. However, a Cotswold church which he had already designed (France Lynch, 1855-7) had defined *his style. Reacting against Scott's preference for the English Decorated period, Bodley had embraced the simplicity of French Gothic of the thirteenth century. Another influence on Bodley at this time was the group of artists known as the Pre-Raphaelites. The leading members of this group: William Morris (1834-96), Dante Gabriel Rossetti (1828-82) and Edward Burne-Jones (1833-98) had recently become established figures in the world of art.*

In 1861, William Morris had masterminded the foundation of the firm of Morris, Marshall, Faulkner & Co. to promote his ideas of decor, particularly in church furniture. He worked closely in this enterprise with the architect and craftsman, Philip Speakman Webb (1831-1915). Bodley immediately engaged the services of the new company in his commission for St Martin's, working simultaneously with Morris and his associates on the churches of St Michael, Brighton and All Saints, Selsley, Gloucestershire. As early works of Morris & Co., these 'sister' churches are artistically most valuable, and of them all St Martin's is the most complete survivor; a remarkable treasury of Victorian art.

The original church of St Martin was designed, as Bodley's churches often were, as a simple structure of nave and chancel, with aisle and aisle chapels. Its distinctive tower was placed at the north west corner of the church; carefully sited to rise above the roof line of Albion Road, and on the very crest of the hill above the Ramsdale valley. It thus dominated southern views from the old town. Faithful to its French Gothic inspiration, the church is very high, and the tower (with the sort of saddleback roof commonly found in the parish churches of Normandy) is proportionally higher. As a result, the external and internal dimensions of the church are most striking. The impressive austerity of the architecture is emphasised by the simplicity of the ornament to the exterior: plain, plate tracery, simple pilaster buttresses and plain string courses. The ashlar stonework emphasises this simplicity. The Whitby stone used (from quarries at Aislaby, twenty-five miles away) has darkened over the years, and Sir Nikolaus Pevsner's word sketch of the church is very apt: 'Dark, sombre stone. Large, strong and never showy'.

The church was completed by April 1863, but at this point an ecclesiastical storm blew up, and delayed the consecration. It was still general at this time for an incumbent's income to be drawn from rented pews, rather than free collections. The Rev'd R.H. Parr decided as a matter of principle to forgo this sort of income. He was a supporter of the 'free and open' movement. This caused a considerable local row, and attempts were made through the archbishop to establish the traditional system at St Martin's. Part of the opposition can be accounted for by the suspicions of the dominant Low Church faction in Scarborough, which deeply suspected the 'poperies' of Parr and his patron. But with Miss Craven's support, the opposition was overcome, and the new church was consecrated by Archbishop Thomson on 11 July 1863.

The seating of the first St Martin's was inadequate for the demand for places in the summer season and Parr devised a grand scheme to extend the church on all fronts, including an extra south aisle, a bay and narthex at the west end, and a baptistry. In the event, there was not enough money for the aisle, but the rest was carried out to Bodley's design in 1879, increasing capacity to 1200.'

CHAPTER SEVEN

FROM 1902-
THE WESTWOOD SCHOOL

The Municipal School Scarborough around 1910 – 8 years after it opened. Note Oliver's Mount in the background completely treeless and without the war memorial or the much more recent television masts.

Few crossing the Valley Bridge or looking up from Valley Road these days at the sad and unloved superstructure of the former Westwood School, can appreciate its state of the art status at its opening in 1902, nor that it represented a first major work by the then rising Scarborough Architect, Edwin Cooper (later Sir Edwin Cooper.)

The sequence of events leading up to the construction of the School is ably recounted in ex-

Headmaster Henry Marsden's *"History of the Municipal School at Scarborough."*

At a time when the average school leaving age was 10, and when neither Whitby nor Filey had Secondary Schools, the financing and construction of such a major forward-looking educational establishment represented a bold and very far-sighted act of faith for the local Council of what was only a relatively small and isolated town.

Negotiations for the purchase of 18,000 square yards of land from the North Eastern Railway on which to build the School began in January 1896 and the land was subsequently purchased in 1896 at a then immense £5000, the School to be erected on the steeply sloping hillside; the principal classrooms and the Hall to be on the same floor and the approach road to be connected, as transpired, by mini-bridges. According to the Specification, in the basement there was to be a gymnasium, a swimming bath, a laundry, two dining rooms and a joiner's shop with 40 benches; on the principal floor 12 classrooms, the Hall was to be 3,600 feet square and a Headmaster's room was to be incorporated. On the upper floors were to be a library, chemistry and physics laboratories, a lecture room, art room and two teachers' rooms. The design was required to be "*serious, of good proportions, outline and detail and expressive of its purpose; being intended for public education and from its size and position ranking among the more important buildings of the town, it should in every way be worthy*"

Perhaps surprisingly in view of the size of the commission it was Edwin Cooper's local firm of Hall, Cooper and Davis whose plans for the building were accepted, and work commenced in 1897. With the exception of the swimming pool and a caretaker's house the plans were faithfully carried out, many of the facilities being radical for their day, including a dumb-waiter system for the transportation of coal, and ingenious systems for the circulation of warm air.

Building of the school commenced on September 26th 1897 at a contract price of £13,585: 4s: 3d.

The school originally opened on January 6th 1902, having taken just over 4 years in building - as Scarborough Municipal School – a co-educational Secondary school. It became Scarborough High School for Boys in 1922 when the girls moved to the new Girls High School at Westlands.

One of the classrooms at Westwood- around 1955

The home of Scarborough High School for Boys was situated at Westwood, overlooking Ramsdale Valley, for 57 years until 24th July 1959. On 14th September

1959, after the school's summer holidays, staff and pupils moved to a new, purpose-built school which had been built for them at Woodlands Farm, near Scarborough Hospital, for which land and buildings had cost £236,174. The school remained at that site until July 1973, at which time grammar schools were being phased out. The Woodlands building then became the home of Graham School, one of a new breed of comprehensive schools which were then the vogue.

At the same time the Girls' High School, by then having moved again and, from just before WWII being situated in Stepney road, closed and the building became the town's 6th Form college for both boys and girls.

After the Boys' High school had moved out, the Westwood building first became home to Westwood County Modern School before becoming an annexe for Raincliffe School, then, later an annexe for Scarborough Technical College, (now the Yorkshire Coast College).

Later, the ground floor of the building became home to the world famous Theatre-In-The-Round of which the artistic director was Alan (now Sir Alan) Ayckbourn when the theatre was required to move from the town's public library's concert room.

Eventually the Council wanted back the ground floor at Westwood to extend the Technical College so the theatre moved to a new site 100 yards away in the former Odeon cinema, where it is known simply as The Stephen Joseph Theatre.

Edwin Cooper (architect of the Westwood building) himself was born in humble surroundings in Nelson Street Scarborough in 1874. His talent for drawing was recognized at an early age, his initial education being at the old Scarborough Central School. He was then fortunate in being articled to the Scarborough practice of Hall and Tugwell, and after a brief period in London returned in 1893 with his friend Herbert Davis to found the practice known as Hall, Cooper and Davis. Local commissions, in particular the Westwood School, followed by Scarborough College, Filey Road (1898) provided an impressive start to his subsequent career, in which he continued, on his own account, to specialize in the design of large public buildings. The Edwardian bandstand and enclosed wings to the Spa in Scarborough further represent his local work.

The school in more recent years

The Guildhall at Hull, followed by a number of prominent London buildings, including Marylebone Town Hall and Lloyds headquarters in Leadenhall Street (now demolished) and subsequently the Port of

London Authority Building led to his knighthood in 1923, and he succeeded Sir Edwin Lutyens as the President of the Incorporated Association of Architects and Surveyors in 1937, dying in 1942 in London.

According to the architectural press, history has been less than kind to his output, but Westwood, which is described as *"an eclectic brick building showing signs of controlled romanticism,"* was almost ahead of its time in the architectural and educational concepts introduced, withstood solidly the test of time throughout our years of schooling until the 50's and 60's, and has been now recognized for its worth as a Grade II Listed Building, which hopefully may preserve it into the future.

*

The Municipal School, then its successor Scarborough High School for Boys, were much ahead of their time in many respects and provided, and still provide happy memories for many ex-pupils. But was the school haunted?

Long after the school had moved from Westwood to Woodlands, the Old Scarborians' Association, consisting of old boys and masters of the school, had arranged a visit when the building was part of what is now the Yorkshire Coast College. One member on that visit later mentioned that Graham Bettis, our guide for the afternoon who had worked at the former school for 14 years, had encountered two ghostly experiences in the building.

Graham told me an article had appeared in the Scarborough Evening News a few years ago relating to one of these happenings.

At that time I was editor of the Old Scarborians Magazine, and this comment rang a bell and I felt I had seen mention somewhere about both occurrences he mentioned. I searched through old copies of the magazine and found an article dating back to May 2003, written by Mick Jefferson who was then a journalist working for the Scarborough Evening News. Mick is a High School old boy himself and had written:

'A reader [this was Graham] who told me of some odd happenings at the Westwood school had the job, a few years ago, of opening up the lecture rooms on the upper floor at around 7 am each day. Twice he was walking along the corridor towards a particular room when, ten or twelve paces in front of him, he saw a figure reaching forward as though to open the door – and then disappear.

On both occasions this happened the corridor was well lit and the reader is very clear about what he saw – a figure in a gown and mortar board who was tall enough to have to reach down for the door handle. The room concerned was used as a chemistry lab.

In the author's [Mick Jefferson's] days at the school in the 1940's there were certainly no tales within the school of any such strange happenings – they would have gone around the 500 or so pupils like wildfire, but one thing does puzzle me about the description of the figure.

Although masters almost always wore academic gowns, mortar-boards were worn, if at all, on only one day in the school year, on speech day and that was not normally held on the school premises.

The question is, has anyone else had, or heard of such ghostly experiences, and, if so, perhaps they would like to share these in future pages.'

Graham said that after the article had appeared there was some speculation that the figure had been 'someone called Potts' – presumably because that was the name of the chemistry master - This seems unlikely as whilst 'Zenna' Potts ('Zenna' being his nickname – just think about it!) - invariably wore a gown, which I recall as a wonderful flapping version when he strode around, I never saw him in a mortar board.

Regarding the second occurrence which I don't think was mentioned in the press; Graham Bettis recalled having seen a schoolboy in uniform in the area of the old school basement toilets. In fact Graham was so sure it was a schoolboy up to no good that he challenged him, but the boy just melted away into the fabric of the building.

Whilst I have no information to link the schoolboy with the following incidents, it could just be possible, if ghosts exist, that the reports and the schoolboy are connected. And as far as ghosts existing I can personally vouch that they do as I took one from the Beansheaf Restaurant near Kirby Misperton to York Minster one cold wintry night! But that's another story.

In his memoirs late master Gerry Hovington recalls:

'World War II started on September 3rd, 1939, but my call-up was deferred to September the following year, because I was a schoolmaster. Then there was a further delay, because I had attended a school camp at Bromsgrove in the August, picking raspberries for the war effort. I was quarantined for a month, because one boy who had been on the camp died from polio and another was left a cripple. As a result, I was not called up until 17th October.'

Referring to the same incident, OSA members Ron Gledhill and Jack Layton, recalled in the following edition of the magazine:

'As part of the War effort, boys of 13 and above were invited to go on a fruit picking camp in Worcestershire.

Approximately 60 boys (including we two - both aged 14) volunteered to go. We left Scarborough by train and eventually arrived at Bromsgrove. We unloaded our bikes and cycled to Burcot, the luggage following on tractor drawn trailers. We were 'housed' in a double decker barn with a ramp leading up to the top half deck. We were allowed the use of Redditch swimming pool.

The majority of us slept on straw filled palliasses on the floor, with no pillows; and the washing and toilet facilities were open air and very primitive.

We were off each morning at 7.30 am to start our fruit picking, finishing at approximately 5.30pm with a half hour break for lunch at mid-day.

We picked raspberries for four and a half weeks and for each full 2lb chip, we received a metal token from the fruit farmers. These tokens were handed in to the pool at the end of each day.

Approximately two weeks into the camp tragedy struck. Fred Colley - who was an excellent swimmer - died, aged 14. We were not informed of the cause of his death.

Subsequently PF Watts, a visitor from Cambridge University and an old boy, contracted polio and spent the rest of his life in a wheel chair. This resulted in the rest of the boys being quarantined for a period.

...Strangely enough, the whole episode was played down, both at school and outside, after we returned to Scarborough.

It's a long shot, but could Fred Colley have 'found his way home' to the school, and he be the school boy Graham Bettis challenged all those years later?

If any reader can shed further light on these, or any other ghosts at Westwood, please let me know.

A wintry photograph of the school taken from Valley Bridge on 19th December 2010

***

CHAPTER EIGHT

FROM 1908 –
THE MARINE DRIVE

'Scarborough had been for centuries a popular fishing resort and its popularity increased further with the discovery of its health-giving Spa Water.

Following the completion of the York to Scarborough railway in 1855 its popularity increased further as a holiday resort. Famous also for its two bays, the commercial South Bay near to the town centre and the more serene North Bay beyond the Castle Headland, development had taken place separately and distinctly.

The influx of holidaymakers with the development of the railways resulted in huge development of the infrastructure of Scarborough and a new road was built along the Foreshore of the South Bay in 1879 and another (Royal Albert Drive) along the foreshore of the North Bay from Peasholm Beck to The Holms. This was completed in 1890 but, however, still left the two bays isolated from each other.

In 1896 the Scarborough Council decided to link the two bays by the construction of a 1,300 yard link road, around the castle headland, to be known as Marine Drive, from the East Pier to Royal Albert Drive.

Although there was much local opposition to the scheme there was also much support, not only for the commercial advantages but also due to the pressing need to prevent further coastal erosion. Land slips from the Scarborough Castle Headland were common and indeed over a period of 700 years the site of Scarborough Castle had dwindled from 60 acres to 16 acres due to erosion. 50% of the roman signal station has disappeared over the cliff edge into the sea because of erosion.

In October 1896 contractors were commissioned for construction of the sea wall and roadway at a cost of £69,270 with completion planned for August 1899 although many local councillors viewed both the anticipated cost and completion date with jocular hilarity.

A very experienced engineer, Mr J E Everett from Southampton was commissioned to oversee the works at the princely sum of £300.00 per annum.

The foundation stone was laid in June 1897, the whole town celebrating the ceremony, which was the chief feature of the local celebrations of Queen Victoria's diamond jubilee.

The scepticism of local councillors proved fully justified. A combination of legal wrangles and bad weather dogged the project from the start, although the 'lamentable lack of energy' of the workforce was the chief culprit for the horrendous delays and Mr Everett was largely blamed for this.

So bad was the situation that there was even a suggestion that the workforce be placed under military supervision. The Council invoked penalty clauses, withheld monthly payments and even set up a Committee For the Acceleration of Works. In 1899 the Scarborough Council obtained a three year extension for completion and later that year Mr Everett resigned under the wave of criticism.

Above and below: Work proceeds, with something looking like a railway bogey carrying steel girders, moving over a timber framework, and below, a crane lifting some heavy piece of machinery, or possibly a block of the wall, along the skeleton of the new Marine Drive.

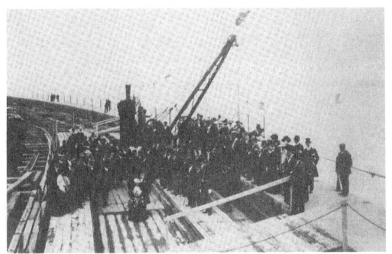

Above: the final stone is placed at the official opening, and, below, the Drive is complete and pedestrians are taking advantage of the ability to walk between the two bays.

Once eventually completed in 1908 – only 9 years after the anticipated date - the Marine Drive proved to be a resounding success both for the commercial aspects of the town and for its aesthetic value, the sea wall being originally topped by some 1,384 linear yards of cast-iron handrails.

Prevention of coastal erosion also proved to be very effective and for nearly 100 years the sea wall bore the brunt of the wild North Sea waves. Further coastal defence works were implemented in 2002 mainly by protecting the old sea wall with a rock barrier to protect the roadway and foundations.

By 2002 the old seawall was showing severe signs of decay, and higher tides with resultant overtopping, were causing damage to the Marine Drive road surface.

Above: A postcard showing the southern toll box at the Foreshore end of Marine Drive. The postal date was 4th August 1913

The aim was to protect the existing sea wall from further erosion by placing rock armour to the seaward side of it. To protect the roadway from higher wave overtopping the Victorian railings were to be replaced by a concrete wall.

The following appeared in the Scarborough Evening News:

'The first sections of Scarborough's controversial concrete sea wall have been unveiled. The one-metre-high structure, which replaces the existing Victorian railings, is part of a two-kilometre scheme designed to protect the resort. Councillors say the wall is vital to safeguard the 100-year-old Marine Drive, which is at risk from heavy sea. But many local people are unhappy their view of the town's North and South bays will be obstructed.

Peter Cooper, of the Scarborough Civic Society, said: "We felt there was a balance to be achieved between amenity and the need to preserve the headland - but we still don't feel the balance is right."

Other people in the town feel the sea front should be preserved as it is. Spokesman Freddy Drabble of the Sons of Neptune said: "If you put a wall there, people travelling around in cars can't see the sea."Now how can we have a seaside resort with no views? It's criminal." But Godfrey Allanson, of Scarborough Council, said the average tourist should have no trouble seeing over the wall to appreciate the view of the bay. "It [the wall] is essential. Because of rising sea levels and greater storm surges, we have to do this now," he added. "The government has given us this money and it has to last for the next 100 years."

Work on the coastal wall was completed early in 2005.

***

CHAPTER NINE

FROM 1912 – CLOCK CAFÉ

In the early 20th century, together with the Spa redevelopment; the redesign and planting of existing gardens and the development of new garden areas on South Cliff; the new South Cliff Tramway; the South Bay bathing pool and the building of beach chalets; there was one other item planned on Harry W Smith's South Bay improvement schedule – *'the provision of a café to the south of the Spa'.*

Folklore tells us that there was a reading room to *'the south of the Spa and built near to the cliffside.'* And *'...slightly above it* [the Spa] *on an open piece of ground, an old cottage stood which was subsequently demolished. It was the home of Jarvis the Quaker who sold flowers in the town – 'Who will buy my beauties?''*

Assuming folklore is correct and the reading room did exist it was likely to have been built when the first phase of the South Cliff gardens were constructed in 1861 – well before the time the café was built and opened for the 1913 season. It can only be supposition that the café was built on the reading room site but it does seem a possibility.

We had no early photographs of the café – until now!

Some months ago when we were planning a booklet about Clock Café, together with this book which would cover a wider field, a visitor to the café brought out his mobile phone and showed a member of the staff two photographs of the café being built. He said one of the workmen was his grandfather and he would pass on printed copies of the photograph to the café. Staff didn't know his name or how to contact him and weeks went by with no photographs. In the meantime the first two editions of The Clock Café Story had been published and sold, and it was only when we were preparing an update for the 3rd edition that a man walked into the café, left an envelope, and disappeared. In the envelope were two A4 sized photographs showing the birth of Clock Café. Both are undated and no names are available but if anyone can provide further information about the following two photographs it will be included in a later edition.

Workmen building Clock Café' (then The South Cliff Gardens Café) around 1911/12. The concrete foundations have been laid and the present supports around the perimeter of the café are in place. It also appears that the roof is in place as what appears to be a gutter is showing on the edge of the roof.

This photo is likely to have been taken before the previous one. It gives a better perspective of the building, much of which can still be recognised today. The young boy shown 3rd left on the previous photograph appears to be on the roof.

Better still, if the donor can get in touch we will be happy to mention him in acknowledgement of his donation of the first two known photos of the Café.

Right:
South Bay: Clock Café today, with the beach chalets below

This photo, left, is of Clock Café (then South Cliff Gardens Café) staff in what was its second season in 1914. The only person known is Minnie Pottage, kneeling right, who attended the Municipal School and took a job at the café during the school summer holidays.

From the start, the café – then known as South Cliff Gardens Café - was owned and operated by Scarborough Corporation, which became Scarborough Borough Council on local government reorganisation from 1st April 1974. At a later stage the Council decided to move a number of its catering outlets into the private sector and to rent out the premises to tenants who would then run them as individual businesses.

Information about the actual building and design of South Cliff Gardens Café is very sparse but we can assume that it has changed very little over the years.

During the World War II years the Spa, and *Clock Café,* together with most large hotels and other public buildings in Scarborough) were closed to the public and used for military training.

Clock Café was used for RAF navigation training. Navigation charts were said to still adorn the café walls when the café was handed back to the Corporation in 1945.

The Cliff Lift was closed for the duration of the war and airmen had to march down the cliff paths to and from the café. The South Bay bathing pool changing rooms were also used for RAF instruction.

*

Following publication of the first edition of *The Clock Café Story,* Eric Truman came forward and said his mother had worked at the café at one time

and he produced 3 photographs which are reproduced here.

His late mother, Freda Turner neé Haylett was born in 1918. He estimates she would be about 21 at the date of the photo on the previous page, which would place it at 1939, or just before World War II. She appears front bottom right in the photo in that photo and in the centre in the photo below.

In the photo on the following page the café can be seen, with the Prince of Wales Hotel, Esplanade, above, centre. There seems to be much more vegetation than appears today. To the bottom left of the top photo below is a woman's head. It is only supposition but this could well be Freda Turner at a later stage – possibly after World War II when the café reopened to the public.

*

The bottom photo above and the two on the next page were sent in by Pip Waller of Scarborough and are thought to be from the late 1940's early 1950s'.

The bottom photo on the last page and the top one above are of Pip's ex-girlfriend's mother, Freda Murdo. She had been manageress of, at first the Olympia Café, then the North Bay Pool café and finally Clock Café – all at that time operated by Scarborough Corporation. She appears in the first photo, front left looking away from the camera, and on the top photo on the previous page she is fourth from the left. It is also possibly her in the bottom photo on the previous page, back row second from left.

Her involvement would have been around the late 1940s to the early 1950s.

Mrs Murdo later had an accident and damaged her ankle badly, following which she retired and her eldest daughter Joy Murdo, was appointed manageress of Clock Café, being employed by the Council from early 1950 to around 1957.

*

Whilst I approached Scarborough Council in May 2013 seeking any information about Clock Café including managers or tenants of the café over the years, no information has so far been forthcoming. Should other facts become available these will be included in a later edition of this book.

Present tenants Jackie and Gary Link followed Maggie and Jim Hargreaves in 1993, Jackie having worked part time for Maggie during the previous year.

As Jim Hargreaves worked away from Scarborough and Maggie had got a little unhappy over frequent calls for her to attend the café in the early hours of the morning as there had been yet another break-in or yet more vandalism, they offered to sell the business to Jackie and her husband Gary.

After discussing matters with her family, Jackie and Gary agreed to take over from the weekend of 5th and 6th June 1993. They remember the day vividly two decades on as that was the same weekend that the

Holbeck Hall Hotel – just ¼ mile south from *Clock Café'*, collapsed down the cliff into the sea.

If you say you're from Scarborough people worldwide still say, 'Oh yes, that's the place where the hotel fell into the sea!'

*

Late in 2007 *Clock Café* leaseholders Jackie and Gary Link, learned that a well-meaning member of the public had applied for the café and beach chalets to become listed. This had been done in good faith as, because the café is in a somewhat isolated position it has, over the years, attracted much more than its fair share of vandalism and it was thought that listing could attract grants to help counteract this problem.

Unfortunately, after listing, and when Jackie Link sought help through landlords Scarborough Council she was told that grants were limited and were now only available for Grade I listed buildings. The café and chalets below it are Grade II.

As this book was being researched and written in 2013, the café needed reroofing and a quote of £50,000 has been received – a sum which would be hard to raise even if 2013 turned out to be the best season ever for the café. Luckily Gary Link is a builder and providing the work can be fitted into otherwise slack periods he hopes to do it for a lower sum.

Listing of the building has also brought some drawbacks. Some customers have commented on the somewhat old fashioned interior of the café and the fact that old coat hooks, door signs and so on, obviously from a long gone era, are still in existence. Why not just remove them and tidy the place up, goes the comment?

The answer is that as a listed building any changes have to be agreed by the listing authority, and listing does confer responsibilities on the tenant - such as retaining 'ancient coat hooks, door signs and so on!'

Listing consideration took place in 2007/8 following which the café and the nearby beach huts were formally listed. We are lucky to have a copy of the listing documentation which follows and which contains some useful history of the café:

'DESCRIPTION: BEACH HUTS AND CAFE

Grade: II
Date Listed: 28 April 2008
English Heritage Building ID: 504422
OS Grid Reference: TA0454287597
OS Grid Coordinates: 504542, 487597
Latitude/Longitude: 54.2733, -0.3961
Location: Esplanade, Scarborough,
North Yorkshire YO11 2AR
Locality: Scarborough
Local Authority: Scarborough Borough Council
County: North Yorkshire
Country: England
Postcode: YO11 2AR

SCARBOROUGH
782/0/10033 SOUTH CLIFF
28-APR-08 BEACH HUTS AND CAFE

Beach huts and café, early c20 with minor later c20 alterations. Constructed of timber boards, with timber verandas, orange roof tiles and glazed panels.

PLAN:

The beach huts and café are situated within South Cliff gardens, a public park to the south of Scarborough overlooking the sea. The café is situated upon a level upper terrace within a stone walled enclosure, and a stone stair with balustrades and interval piers with ball finials leads down the cliffside to the beach. The huts comprise two groups of 11 single cell beach huts, or changing rooms arranged on terraces set either side of the stone stairs immediately below the café. There are further rows of 6, 2 and 3 huts to the south.

EXTERIOR:

Beach Huts: the terraces of huts are constructed of overlapping timber boards, with original French doors, now with applied panels, painted in primary colours. All have white painted open latticework timber verandas. Roofs are hipped or pitched with orange tile and prominent sprockets; the most northerly two rows have modern replacement roof covering and projecting end bays with canted bay windows to their gable ends.

Café: projecting central section of 3 bays with a hipped roof; this is surmounted by a square clock tower with four faces and pyramidal roof bearing an ornate weather vane. Central projecting entrance bay has a dentilled segmental pediment carried on an entablature; below there are glazed French doors flanked by glazed windows. To either side of the 3 bay central section there are single storey ranges each of 3 bays formed by a wooden blind arcade of open latticework mirroring that of the beach huts; the first bay of each range contains glazed French doors with others having large glazed windows. The ends of each range are canted and formed of glazed windows. The building has prominent sprockets again mirroring those of the beach huts.

INTERIOR:

Beach Huts: very simple construction clad in tongue and groove timber, painted with dado rails. The floors are boarded and huts have double full height corner cupboards and small folding tables.

Cafe: the original plan form is retained and the central room has original wooden panelling with a delft rack and original coat hooks. Above the higher central section, access is gained to the clock tower, with original working clock, from a small loft.

SUBSIDIARY FEATURES: Stone steps flanked by balustrades with interval square piers, coping stones and ball finials.

HISTORY: Permanent bathing bungalows or beach huts first appeared in Britain in c.1910 in Bournemouth, but the idea of creating a series of cells in a permanent row was pioneered in Scarborough at its North Bay in 1911 followed on closely by these examples at South Cliff in 1911-12. Scarborough was the world's first seaside resort; it was essentially where the seaside was invented. By 1735 it had an early form of bathing machine, the wheeled precursor of beach huts, and continued to be a pioneer in all things seaside and many of the innovations begun there were copied elsewhere around the country. The building of such beach huts at seaside resorts was considered quite a desirable attraction, and formed an important element in the creation of the seaside resort in the early c20. Beach huts represent a fundamental change from the wheeled bathing machines previously used where people changed in private and modestly lowered themselves into the sea almost unseen. The concept of beach huts reflects changing ideas about social decorum: getting changed for bathing in a hut at the top of the beach and walking to the sea in full view was a rather liberated activity.

South Cliff, Scarborough, began to be developed as a select resort by the mid c19 with the construction of The Crown Hotel and the Esplanade in 1845. A new wave of development came in the years between 1864 and 1880 with South Cliff baths, a tramway, a new Spa Hall and grand terraces. The beach huts and cafe were clearly part of the overall scheme to improve visitor facilities in this part of the South Bay during the early years of the c20, close to the beach area known as 'Children's Corner'. South Cliff gardens were laid out from c. 1910 and included an Italian garden in 1912. In 1914 construction began on the South Bay Bathing Pool, which was also pioneering as one of the country's first tidally filled lidos and further additions took place in the 1930s.

SOURCES:

P Williams 'The English Seaside' 2005, English Heritage, p81
A Brodie and G Winter 'England's Seaside Resorts' 2007, English   Heritage
K Ferry 'Sheds on the Seashore: from bathing machines to beach huts' forthcoming.

REASONS FOR DESIGNATION DECISION

The beach huts and café at Scarborough are listed at Grade II for the following principal reasons:

- *The huts are examples of the first chalet style of terraced beach huts in England which contribute to the development of the building type*
- *The huts and cafe survive well and are relatively unaltered*
- *They have architectural interest both in their overall design and setting, and in the individual elaboration of the elements*
- *They are intact with original plans and interior features*
- *Although modest, they capture the spirit of the Edwardian seaside in the world's first seaside resort*
- *The beach huts compare well with the only other listed example in England.'*

*

In 1998 on the eve of the General Election that Tony Blair visited Scarborough and this caused problems for the *Clock Café* as reported in the Scarborough Evening News:

'APOLOGY BY BLAIR TO SHUT CAFÉ

A café owner who was forced to shut up shop when Tony Blair visited Scarborough on the eve of the general election has been invited to Downing Street by way of an apology.

Jackie Link, of the Clock Cafe on South Cliff, was so annoyed that she wrote to the Prime Minister. The closure happened for security reasons when he visited the town in 1998.

Mrs Link of Harcourt Avenue, said: "It was all a bit tongue in cheek really and I wasn't particularly expecting the reply I got. When he came on May 4 all the security precautions meant I wasn't able to get any deliveries. One van driver had to bring all my stock on a wheelbarrow."

In the letter she challenged the PM's attitude towards the working person and complained at having to close her cafe for a second time.

Mrs Link has now received a reply from 10 Downing Street, apologising for the inconvenience and inviting her to look around the Prime Minister's official residence — with friends Debbie Fields, Sue Bell and Jill Periera.

Mrs Link said: "It was fantastic when I got the letter. My friends couldn't believe it when I told them."

CHARITY EVENTS

The café and its staff have always supported various charities, and Jackie, herself, is a trustee of the LittleFoot Trust, a charity which benefits local needy childen.   The following report appeared in the Scarborough Evening News:

'A Scarborough charity worker, who will soon be taking a group of children to London, was delighted to receive a letter from Buckingham Palace.

Jackie Link, treasurer of the LittleFoot Trust children's charity, and proprietor of clock Café wrote to Prince Philip in the hope of organising a guided visit.

Just two weeks later she got a reply from his assistant equerry Captain Alexander Forster who has arranged for the group to be shown around the Royal Mews.

Mrs Link said: "I was so surprised to get this letter – I'm absolutely thrilled. All the children are really looking forward to it."

The LittleFoot Trust has been taking children who might not otherwise get a holiday to London for the past five years.

A group of 12 children aged 10 and 11 will be going on a five-day trip on February 14.

The youngsters will also visit Downing Street, the Houses of Parliament, Big Ben and the Tower of London, go to the Imax cinema, bowling and swimming.

She said: "We have had such fantastic feedback about these visits. It's the highlight of the year for everyone involved."'

In another item from the Scarborough Evening News:

'LITTLEFOOT TRUST PUPILS TREATED TO VIP TOUR OF NUMBER 10

A group of Scarborough school children enjoyed a tour of 10 Downing Street by the Prime Minister's wife Sarah Brown.

The children from Barrowcliff and Gladstone Road schools were given the VIP treatment as part of a five day trip to London organised by 'The LittleFoot Trust' charity.

The charity takes children from primary schools in Scarborough on educational visits to the capital.

The children had a packed programme of events during the five day trip which include theatre trips, visits to the Houses of Parliament, Buckingham Palace and other famous sites.

Mrs Link, owner of the Clock Café in between the Spa complex and the old South Bay swimming pool site, said: "The children had a fantastic time. It was definitely one of the highlights of this last trip, along with a visit to Chelsea Football Club.

"Mrs Brown was lovely. She made us feel very welcome and it was wonderful for the children to see all the different rooms. Her two boys were running around all over the place just like boys do.

"The people at Chelsea were also great, we got to see the FA Cup and everyone was so nice.

"The children were all very well behaved. In fact they were great ambassadors for our town and a credit to their families.'"

THE SCARBOROUGH NEWS REPORTED ON 7TH DECEMBER 2012 –

'Football fans are being offered the chance to get their hands on historic memorabilia belonging to a true legend of the sport.

Programmes, trophies and awards belonging to Scarborough-born ex-Tottenham Hotspur manager Bill Nicholson are being offered to football fans to help boost the coffers of a local charity.

The items were left to Jackie Link, who is the treasurer of the LittleFoot Trust children's' charity.

A neighbour of the footballing great's sister, she helped to care for her and her husband in their old age.

And Jackie, who admits she isn't a big footballing fan, is looking to sell the treasures to help youngsters with the charity.

"Someone would benefit from them far more than I would. I used to look after Bill's sister, and they gave me this memorabilia. Bill used to joke and say 'wait until I'm gone as it will be worth a lot more!"

She initially attempted to sell them to Tottenham Hotspur, where the late manager enjoyed considerable success in the 1950s and 1960s.

He guided the club to the first ever domestic league and cup double, and the street leading up to the ground is named after the late Scarborough great.

However, the Premiership giants offered a figure which fell way short of her valuation and she thought she could get a bit more for the charity than that."

Jackie considered holding a sportsman's dinner to help sell the lot, which includes the Scarborian's first ever trophy, along with bookends and match programmes.

However, she's now thinking of holding an auction to help sell the goods, although nothing is confirmed yet.

Tony Randerson and Jackie Link, left, trustee and treasurer of the Little Foot Trust charity, with memorabilia from Bill Nicholson, the Scarborough born, player and manager of Tottenham Hotspur FC in the 1950's and 60's.

Not only do Jackie and her staff work to support their charity but she is always keen to give support to other local charities.

'On 4ᵗʰ August 2008 the Scarborough branch of Epilepsy Action held an information day on Sunday from 10am to 4pm at the Clock Cafe near the South Bay chalets. There was also a tombola to raise funds for specialist Sapphire nurses who look after people with the condition. The Scarborough group has already sent out information packs to 50 GPs' surgeries and 150 schools in the area in a bid to raise awareness about epilepsy, which affects one in 220 children and one in 131 people overall.'

And, a year later:

'WALK OF AWARENESS FOR EPILEPSY CHARITY GROUP'

'Putting their best foot forward for Epilepsy Action proved a money winner for this group of volunteers. They raised over £400 for the charity by walking from the Spa to the Sea Life centre.
Tracey Vasey, chairman of the group's Scarborough branch, said: "It wasn't the nicest weather on the day – I thought we might get blown away! But despite that it was a fantastic day and we're very pleased with the amount raised.
"I'd like to thank the Clock Café who gave us a slap up tea at the end of the walk."'

*

As another example of the café's help The Friends of the Stephen Joseph Theatre held 5 successive September 'Griddle Gatherings' with profits going to the theatre. A barbecue was provided with raffles, roll a pound, quizzes and entertainment.

The café also helps other charities and individuals by selling period photos from the collection of the late Max Payne, books by David Fowler, and canvas printed photographs of Scarborough. The café accepts a small commission on sales towards the LittleFoot Trust.

VANDALISM

Vandalism of the café has always been a problem because of its somewhat isolated position especially on dark nights. Windows would be constantly smashed if steel covering panels had not been installed each evening when the café closes. Lighting installed in 2002 by the Council improved this problem and later, a surveillance camera was installed which again helped to pinpoint troublemakers.

However, on 23rd September 2002, only 2 nights after the security lighting was installed the following report appeared in the Scarborough Evening News:

VANDALS AGAIN TARGET CLOCK CAFÉ – 23RD SEPTEMBER 2002

Vandals left a trail of destruction outside a cafe less than 48 hours after two new security lights were installed.

The Clock Café, near the Spa, was left with a 2ft hole in its roof, dented shutters, graffiti and smashed tiles and windows after Friday's attack.

Security lights were put up 2 days before to illuminate the area and protect the chalets and café..

Scenes of crimes officers were at the location taking photographs of the damage on Saturday morning and comparing graffiti 'tags'.

Council workers repaired some of the damage.

Mother-of-four Jackie Link, 43, has run the Clock Cafe for 10 years, leasing the building from the council.

"It's so frustrating when this happens," she said.

"Thursday was the first night the new lights were switched on. They are meant to help people to see. It looks a nice place in the day, but in the dark it was very, very dark without lighting.

"I think everyone is trying to preserve the last bit of South Bay. It's a piece of heritage and customers who have been down are gutted."

Her friend Sue Bell, who was helping to clean up the cafe, said: "It was looking lovely before this happened."'

On a later occasion vandals climbed on to the roof of the café and bent out the hands of the clock by 90 degrees. New pointers had to be bought and to prevent similar vandalism a large circular clear plastic cover was installed over the clock face to protect the clock's hands.

LANDSLIP IN SOUTH BAY

On March 15th 2013 The Scarborough News reported that another landslip had occurred in Scarborough's South Bay near the Clock Café.

'A huge crack has appeared in the path above the cafe and to the right, near a group of four beach chalets.

The landslip is the latest in a series of similar problems in the area.

Just weeks ago, a path has to be cordoned off near the old South Bay pool after part of the cliff gave way. A Scarborough Borough Council spokesperson said: "We are making preparations to carry out some work to remove earth at the top of the slip, which will help to relieve some of the pressure on the slope and allow us to carry out further investigations.

"We advise members of the public to choose an alternative route when walking in the area."

*

MENUS – THE OLD

The menu below dates from the days when Scarborough Corporation both owned and ran Clock Café. The menus were printed by Boucher & Brown of North Street who were still in existence in the early 1960s - and probably later. The prices shown are pre-decimalisation which dates the menu before 15th February 1971. The menu mentions Scarborough Corporation which became Scarborough Borough Council on local Government reorganisation on 1st April 1974. It seems therefore that the menu is dated somewhere in the decade 1961 to 1971.

TARIFF

BEVERAGES.

Pot of Tea, per person	... 9d.
Pot of China Tea ...	... 9d.
Pot of Coffee, per person	1/-
Chocolate, per cup ...	... 9d.
Cadbury's Bournvita	... 8d.
Nestle's Milo	... 8d.
Horlicks made with milk	1/-
Bovril or Oxo with biscuits	8d.
Minerals	... 8d.
Fruit Squash	... 8d.
Britvic Fruit Cocktail	... 1/-

BREAD, TEACAKES, etc.

White or Brown Bread and Butter	... 4d.
Buttered Teacake or scone	5d.
Toasted Teacake ...	... 6d.
Toasted Muffin or Pikelet	5d.
Buttered Toast, per round	4d.
Roll and Butter	... 3d.

SANDWICHES, etc.

Ham or Beef, per half-round	9d.
Tongue "	... 9d.
Salmon & Cucumber "	... 9d.
Egg & Cress "	... 6d.
Various (Tomato, Cucumber, Salad, etc.)	... 6d.

CAKES, etc.

Meringues, Chocolate Eclairs, Cream Sandwich, Iced Fancies, Battenburg Squares, Fruit Cake, Almond Tarts, Macaroons, Buttercream	... 6d.
Cakes, Viennese Cakes, etc., Jam Sponge, Swiss Roll, Jam Tarts, Lemon Curd Tarts, Shortbreads, etc.	
Biscuits, assorted, per portion	... 4d.

ICES

Ices	... 9d.
Iced Drinks	... 9d.
Milk Shakes	... 1/-
Trifle and Ice Cream ...	... 1/-
Fruit Melbas and Sundaes, From	... 1/6

FRUIT, PRESERVES, etc.

Jam or Marmalade ...	... 3d.
Fruit Salad	... 1/3
Trifle or Fruit Jelly ...	... 8d.
Vita-Cream	... 3d.

SAVOURIES and SNACKS

Poached or Scrambled Egg on Toast	... 1/3
Sardines on Toast ...	... 1/3
Spaghetti and Tomato on Toast	... 1/3
Baked Beans on Toast ...	1/3
Welsh Rarebit	... 1/3
Cheese, Biscuit, & Butter	9d.
Green Salad	... 1/-
Cold Meat and Salad ...	3/6
Heinz Mayonnaise ...	... 2d.

... AND THE NEW

Below appears the 2013 menu although not shown is the wide variety of soft drinks, teas and coffees which the café also provides:

SCAMPI & CHIPS	£6.25
GAMMON EGG CHIPS	£6.25
CHILLI N RICE OR CHIP	£6.25
LASAGNE " "	£6.25
CURRY " " CHICKEN	£6.25
CHEESE N BROCCOLI PASTA BAKE N CHIPS	£6.25
FISH N CHIPS	£5.95
BREAKFAST	£5.50
CHICKEN FILLET BITES CHIPS	£6.00
BEEF BURGER N CHIPS	£4.50
CHICKEN BURGER N CHIPS	£4.50
SAUSAGE N CHIPS	£4.25
FISHFINGER N CHIPS	£3.75
CHILDRENS MEALS	£3.75
GIANT YORKSHIRE PUD	£3.10
EGG N CHIPS	£3.00
JACKET POTATOES VARIOUS FILLINGS FROM	£3.00
BEANS ON TOAST	£2.80
EGGS ON TOAST	£2.80
ASSORTED HOT AND COLD SANDWICHES FROM	£3.25
BURGERS	£2.70
VEGGIE BURGERS	£2.70
SOUP AND ROLL	£2.50
CHIPS	£2.00
HOT DOG	£1.50
JUMBO	£2.90

*

RECENT CUSTOMER REVIEWS

'An extremely popular place to visit is the well situated Clock Café just above the line of chalets on the South Bay. It makes a lovely focal point resting on the side of the cliff, and what a view! It is simply stunning and for the fortunate visitors offers plenty of outside seating from which to admire it. All the delicious cakes, scones and pastries are made on the premises and are really good value. Plenty of other choices are available with everything from a full English breakfast to fish and chips.
There is also a good selection of dishes for the children. All the sandwiches are made to order with a take away service also available. You get a good strong pot of tea, various coffees, milk shakes and ice-creams and lots more. Very busy in high season so be prepared to wait.'

*

'Halfway up the cliffs and behind the beach huts, overlooking Scarborough's South bay, the Clock Cafe serves basic foods (tea, coffee, sandwiches, homemade cake) at very affordable prices, and the view is spectacular.

*

'Lovely early 20th century café. Great location and the terrace is a perfect place to enjoy lunch or a coffee.'

*

'The Clock Cafe is beyond the Spa and is open when the flag is flying. Here you can sit outside and admire the view of the sea and harbour while eating decent home-made lunches and cakes.'

*

'I am almost reluctant to leave this review as you may take the last available seat on the terrace! The Clock Café is not fine dining, it's an egg and chips, cup of tea and a slice of cake, type of place, and I love it. The view is just stunning across the South Bay, great to sit out and while away a happy hour, your dogs and children are all welcome...

*

'The Clock Café - A hidden gem.'

*

'If you're after good honest food and a view money can't buy, well this is the place for you. It's slightly off the beaten track, but you won't be disappointed.
The staff are great and very helpful.'

*

'Lovely cafe, home bakes, beautiful view.'

*

'The Clock Cafe located on a very steep bit somewhere beyond the Spa - sit outside with a strawberry milkshake and a sticky bun for the best view.'

*

'Wander down the cliff paths to the south of Scarborough's Spa to the Clock Café which was used for RAF navigation training during World War II.
It has some of the best views in Scarborough, arguably the best scones and toasted teacakes in the area, and lemon meringue pie to die for!'

*

As a somewhat humorous addition to this chapter, there was recent concern that Jackie and Gary Link might have been thinking of selling their business at

Clock Café, and that Scarborough Borough Council also intended selling 'the family jewels' - the nearby historic Spa buildings.   On 21st February 2013 an online auction site advertised:

'CLOCK CAFÉ AND SPA, SCARBOROUGH, FOR SALE

Rumours flying round the town were increased by press comment that the Council had announced some time earlier that it had been looking to find a company to take over the management and promotion of the Spa. Surely this was a joke? Surely it wasn't 1st April?

Further investigation revealed that the web site had only set a reserve price of 60p for the 'buildings' and that the auction would end in 10 days' time.

It emerged it was actually a picture postcard of the Spa and Clock Café from the 1920's which was for sale – shown below!

*

With Saturday 29th June 2013 being part of the café's centenary celebrations as well as Scarborough Armed Forces Day; and with a packed programme of events, what better viewpoint could there have been than the terrace of *Clock Café* overlooking South Bay? According to ITV news Forces Day brought over 20,000 additional people to Scarborough.

The café was crowded from opening at 10.00 am until the early evening and, in fact broke its own record by serving more meals than ever before during Jackie Link's 20 year ownership.

The first display was of a Eurofighter Typhoon, a twin-engine, canard-delta wing, multirole fighter. This display had the audience gasping at the sheer power and agility of the aircraft which flew low over the bay before climbing vertically at great speed, then diving at even greater speeds.

The Typhoon is capable of flying at twice the speed of sound.

The Typhoon was followed by a display of breath-

taking split-second timing by the Red Arrows (left) who weaved patterns across the afternoon sky in red, white and blue.

Scarborough had managed the not insignificant coup in obtaining the only Red Arrows display that day and congratulations are due to whoever managed to make the booking.

Following on came the historic Battle of Britain Memorial Flight (right), consisting of Lancaster, Spitfire and Hurricane aircraft. Majestic and beloved though these planes are, they obviously belong to a different era in comparison with the Typhoon and Red Arrows.

The Battle of Britain Memorial Flight was followed by the Ravens parachute display team –where 4 members parachuted into a marked area on the beach and this was followed by a flypast of a RAF Sea King helicopter.

It was a wonderful day's entertainment, in decent weather, viewed from a prime vantage point by those lucky enough to find a table on the terrace at Clock Café. And the fly-pasts by Typhoon, Red Arrows and Battle of Britain Memorial Flight were surely a most fitting way to celebrate Clock Café's centenary year.

ALAN COLES

If you ever come across a very active, distinguished looking man at *Clock Café,* delivering orders, clearing and cleaning tables, making sure customers are comfortable and being generally very affable, it will be Alan Coles.

Often described by customers as the café's 'Meeter and Greeter', and by some who think he is the café's proprietor, Alan is officially none of these.

In view of his previous employment he could even be described as the café's fraud officer but even this would be wrong.

Alan is a volunteer worker at the café who gives his time free, firstly in memory of his late wife Jennifer who loved the café and the area, and secondly through his own love of the town and the café. He describes his role as a "fetcher and carrier".

Before retiring Alan worked for the Police for 30 years specialising in the fraud squad. Twice a year he and Jennifer travelled from their home in Stamford, Lincolnshire where they lived for 18 years, to Scarborough on holiday. There they got to know the café and the staff and became friendly with proprietor Jackie Link and her 2 i/c Sue Bell.

9 years ago Alan retired from the police aged 60 and they sold their Stamford house and moved to a spacious flat in Westbourne Grove, Scarborough. Tragically Jennifer died from breast cancer 5 years ago aged only 61 and a bench inscribed to her memory stands on the café's terrace.

Alan says she was 'a wonderful woman who had a good knowledge of antiques and of interior decorating which she used to good effect on the Scarborough flat. She was also a good 'people person' having the knack of being able to get on with most people.'

*

And finally, to celebrate their centenary, Clock Café staff members were presented by Jackie Link with new uniforms in the style of the original 1913 photograph which appears on page 18.

The 2013 uniform is shown below with Jackie Link seated front right:

***

CHAPTER TEN

FROM 1914 –
THE BOMBARDMENT OF SCARBOROUGH
16th December 1914

Just months after the South Bay Gardens Café opened, the town was bombarded by the Imperial German Navy from the sea. What a sight that would have provided - albeit dangerous - for anyone brave enough to sit on the café's terrace!

On 4th August 1914 Great Britain declared war upon Germany. Initially, one could have been forgiven for thinking that the country was still at peace. There was no panic-stricken departure by the visitors; the only sign of war being the queues of young men at Army recruitment centres. Why should anyone panic? Visitors and locals alike felt completely safe knowing that the Royal Navy, the mightiest in the world, was not only guardian of the Empire but of the shores of Britain herself.

However, an event on Wednesday, 16th December 1914 sent shock waves through the British Isles.

At 8am on that fateful day a grey fog clung to the coast obscuring visibility. Slowly and silently the menacing silhouettes of two German battle cruisers, the Derrflinger and the Von Der Tann, accompanied by the light cruiser, Kolberg, steamed into full view and closed to within one mile of the resort. The smaller ship made off in a southerly direction laying mines as she went. The two remaining battle cruisers trained their 11- and

12-inch guns on the ancient battlements of the castle where the gunners knew the Admiralty Signal Station was situated. An accurate salvo reduced the building to rubble. The Germans were reluctant to move in closer to the shore as they were under the impression that Scarborough was a fortified town. In actual fact the only armaments were four rusty 18th-century cannon that stood in the castle yard.

Above: SMS Derrflinger; Below: SMS Von der Tann

Seeing that there was no answering fire the ships closed in and with a mighty roar opened up a steady fire upon the peaceful town.

The bombardment lasted about half an hour and within that time over 520 shells had exploded resulting in the deaths of 18 people including eight women and four children.

Merryweather's shop on the corner of Prospect road. A shell hit the shop killing the proprietor's wife Mrs Merryweather

Over 210 buildings suffered varying degrees of damage. Churches were struck and the Grand Hotel and Royal Hotel suffered severely. On Esplanade the Prince of Wales Hotel was badly hit, the Spa was hit and the lighthouse was hit and put out of operation.

The Town Hall, Workhouse, Gladstone Road School and the Hospital all shuddered under the impact of direct hits.

Many years later the shelling of the Prince of Wales Hotel led to an amusing story. In the late 1990's I lived in the property and noticed 3 men closely studying a piece of the Esplanade frontage of the hotel – by then flats. I asked if I could help.

Above: Damage to the Spa
Below: More damage, this time to a property on Esplanade

On Esplanade the Prince of Wales Hotel was hit with damage being visible to the first two windows on the first floor. The ground floor railings were also damaged

The men introduced themselves as 'World War 1 experts' and said they knew the hotel had been shelled and they were certain a piece of shell was buried in the wall. They had apparently found some surface rust near to the ground floor door.

I tried to keep a straight face but then told the men that they were wrong. They started to argue that 'they had found the evidence' until I cut them short and explained that the Esplanade frontage of the hotel had been completely demolished a few years earlier because of foundation problems and the frontage they were examining was completely new, so, in no way could it contain a shell fragment from 1914! 3 very downcast 'experts' gathered up their tools and cameras and went on their way...

The Prince of Wales Hotel after the Esplanade frontage had been demolished but before it had been rebuilt.

Another hotel badly hit – this time The Royal in St Nicholas Street. As well as the damage that can be seen, over 150 windows were smashed.

During and after the bombardment panic set in and people ran out into the street shouting that the enemy was coming. Whole families made their way into the outlying villages; some just wandered about in a daze. There were constant streams of people trying to get out of the town – Scalby road, Filey road, and the York road became crowded with people.

Above, the national press gave headlines to the bombardment of the town.

A message was telegraphed to York where the 8th West Yorkshire Regiment was billeted. They quickly mobilised and arrived in Scarborough at 2.30pm by train. (This was only 6 hours after the shelling had ceased!) They positioned themselves at strategic points throughout the town but this military show of strength was all in vain. By that time the enemy ships were safely back in home waters after successfully evading Beatty's squadron which had steamed to intercept them.

We now know that the Admiralty knew of this attack well in advance but dared not send warships as they feared the Germans would realise that their codes had been broken.

Slowly the residents of Scarborough returned home but there was always the dread of another attack. A poster, 'Remember Scarborough', became famous and the bombardment was used by the government to encourage men to join the army and recruitment soared.

As the months and years passed by, the public's fears lessened.

There was still the Zeppelin to contend with but, even though their steady drone overhead made peoples' hearts pound that bit quicker, no bombs fell on Scarborough itself; the nearest landing at Seamer some three miles away. Then, on 6th September 1917 their deep-rooted fears materialised. At 6.45pm on a beautiful sunny evening when the Foreshore was crowded with locals and a few visitors who had braved wartime travel, an enemy U-boat surfaced four miles off the resort. It lay there for 15 minutes before opening fire. Thirty rounds were fired at the town. Half of the shells fell among fishing and pleasure boats in the bay causing no noticeable damage. The other half smashed into buildings and caused the deaths of three people and injured another five.

Ironically, minesweepers laying at anchor in the bay had chosen to ignore the submarine until it was too late. Although they raised steam and set off in pursuit, the enemy vessel had submerged and made its escape.

On 11th November 1918, the Prime Minister announced to cheering crowds that the Armistice had been signed and that all hostilities would cease at 11 am. In Scarborough the news was greeted with jubilation but also with great sadness for the families of the 636 local men who, up to the end of the war were known to have been killed.

It was the following year, 19th July 1919, when the town celebrated in style. Fireworks and rockets soared into the night sky and burst over the Castle Hill. There was dancing on the Spa to Alick Maclean and his Orchestra and at 11 pm. the celebrations came to a grand finale when the ancient beacon on the castle wall was set alight.

Everyone said it was the war to end wars. The boys were arriving home and the future looked secure. But it would only be 20 years before the next major world conflict arose.

Alick Maclean and his Orchestra played at The Spa

***

CHAPTER ELEVEN

FROM 1932 –
'MERRIE ENGLAND', TO ENGLAND AT WAR

In 1908 the massive engineering undertaking, the Marine Drive, linking Scarborough's North and South Bays was opened. This was followed in 1928 by the opening of a widened Valley Bridge spanning Ramsdale Valley and this provided far better access between the town and its South Cliff.

In the late 1920's and 1930's these developments gave the impetus to energetically develop the town, with the aim of making Scarborough an attractive, welcoming and top-class seaside resort with few equals. We have already seen that Borough Surveyor Harry W. Smith was the catalyst who made a lot of this possible.

In the Old Town many streets of fishermen's cottages, churches and public buildings were demolished to make room for redevelopment – and to provide car and coach parks for the burgeoning increase in motoring which brought holiday makers to the seaside.

The North Side, and Tucker's Field, where now lies Peasholm Park, was previously a rural backwater but was transformed by excavation and inspired design to provide an attractive lake with an island in the centre. There were boating facilities for the visitors, ducks and swans to feed, an aviary, new gardens, seating and terraced areas, cafés and many grassed areas. A Japanese theme was adopted which lasts to this day, and there was even a floating bandstand in the centre of the lake on which many military and brass bands played over following years. The highlight of the scheme was an attractive illuminated waterfall starting at the top of the Island and cascading over rocks down to the lake.

Merrie England at the Open Air Theatre in 1936.

Across the road from Peasholm Park another great project was being completed - the Northstead Manor Gardens.

This was a large, attractively laid out area which included more gardens, seating, shelters and café areas, a small gauge railway running to and from

Scalby Mills – still known as The Miniature Railway to this day, and the biggest innovation of all, the Open Air Theatre.

This opened in 1932 with a season of 'Merrie England'.

The theatre boasted 5876 fixed seats and a total capacity of 11,000.

To say the Open Air Theatre shows were spectacular is an understatement. There were casts of hundreds, and an illuminated glass raft on which a ballet was performed as the raft was pulled from one side of the lake to the other in front of the stage area.

The final phase of the North Bay development took place in 1938 when the North Bay Swimming Pool was opened.

In 1937, at the Spa in the South Bay Alex Maclean's Orchestra was still playing to packed audiences, but the war clouds were gathering and during the Munich crisis of 1938 when Prime Minister Chamberlain returned from Germany to declare, 'We have peace in our time', gas masks were already being issued to the residents of Scarborough.

Two days before war was declared on 3rd September 1939, the first batches of evacuees arrived from Hull, Middlesbrough and West Hartlepool. Over the following weeks 14,000 refugee families were to be billeted in Scarborough.

Everyone had to carry their gasmasks, and was allocated an identity card which had to be carried at all times.

Ration Books were first distributed in Scarborough in November, 1939. Queues for rationed, and even non-rationed goods were the norm.

People were urged to take fewer baths, do fewer washes and to change their clothes and sheets less frequently to save water, soap and fuel.

With the shortage of cloth, skirts became shorter. Buttons vanished from men's sleeves when the new Utility suits came on to the market. Double breasted suits and turn ups on trousers were also abandoned and there were also fewer shades of colour and fewer styles available.

After the town was declared a prohibited area the threat of invasion was on everyone's minds. Troops started pouring into Scarborough and the RAF took over many hotels for aircrew training. The Grand and The Prince of Wales hotels and Scarborough College became respectively 10 Initial Training Wing (ITW), 11 ITW and 17 ITW.

Londesborough Road Excursion Railway Station was taken over by the military when war broke out and it was not until May, 1946 that the station was returned to LNER.

Barbed wire was installed on slipways leading to the sands. Some of the South Cliff gardens were barricaded, as were the North Side Gardens and promenade.

Concrete anti-tank blocks were erected along the Royal Albert Drive and on the piers. The Castle Holmes was mined, as was the entrance to the harbour.

Barriers and 'pillboxes' were erected at all entrances to the town – and all these areas were manned by soldiers.

Concrete Pill Boxes were erected. The cliffs above Scalby Mills were used for bomb and rifle training by the Home Guard and the pits can still be seen today. Water tanks, or static tanks as they were called, were constructed at various places in the town for use in case of fires from incendiaries.

A static tank full of water, situated in wartime near to where the St Thomas Street Casino now stands.

Initially, cinemas and entertainment centres were closed but they soon re-opened to the public with restricted hours although no one was allowed in without their gas mask.

To help pedestrians in the blackout all kerb edges, trees and other obstacles were marked with white lines. Trees had a white band painted round them.

The beaches, cliffs and promenades resembled a filmset for a battlefield as barbed wire and mines were laid in case of an invasion. On the outer harbour wall and at the South Bay Pool were located machine gun posts. A heavy naval gun was installed at the bottom of Wheatcroft Avenue.

The harbour was mined and the plunger to detonate the mines was located in a Pill Box disguised as an ice cream kiosk at the bottom of Bland's Cliff. This was manned 24 hours a day by the Army.

At a talk I gave recently an old man approached me afterwards and said he worked for the Corporation after the war and remembered being involved in clearing the cables for the plunger which led to the mines. Whilst this was cleared from the ice cream kiosk and from under Foreshore road it was cut just beyond the railings at the edge of the beach and as far as he knew the cable still remains there under the sand.

Summer 1939 had seen the resort packed with holidaymakers. The same could not be said of 1940. The sands were bare of holidaymakers and were prohibited areas except for a small area reserved for families. Anyone venturing outside this area stood the risk of being shot and one young lady did lose her life one night when a sentry shot her after she ignored his challenge.

The hotels and boarding houses had been full of visitors on the first Christmas of the war but this was all to change as one by one they were taken over by the military for the billeting and training of armed forces.

North Bay is prepared for invasion

Many shop and house owners taped up their windows to stop glass damage in case of air raids.

Scarborough's first air raid warning sounded at 9.25am on 29th January 1940 following German planes being spotted flying over Cayton Bay. On this occasion nothing occurred but the following months saw the town subjected to tip-and-run raids which caused considerable damage to property. However, much worse was to come as Scarborough had too many important targets, including the Admiralty's Wireless Station, Army Barracks and Harbour, and since the start of the war the RAF Initial Training Wings and the other military presence in the town.

On 10th October 1940 a German plane swooped over Castle Hill and dropped a landmine on the densely populated old town. The crater in Potter Lane measured 60ft across and 30ft deep. Four people died in this raid and 500 houses were either damaged or destroyed. In the photo below, the Grand Hotel, home to 10 ITW RAF, can just be seen at the top right edge.

On 18th March 1941 the sirens sounded the
alert at 8.10pm as 98 enemy aircraft flew in over
the Wolds and showered the villages of Flixton and
Folkton with incendiaries. At 9.00pm they closed in
on Scarborough and subjected the town to two
delayed action bombs, parachute mines and
thousands of incendiaries. There then followed
sporadic attacks when further parachute mines
were dropped.

What became known locally as the 'March
Blitz' proved a trying time for the town's war-time
services. During the war, the biggest fire in the town

was at ETW Dennis' printing works in Melrose Street on 18th March 1941.

During the raid the first incendiaries fell on this building at about 9.15pm. The staff had only left at 9.00pm and the building soon became a blazing inferno with the lead type melting in the composing room and running as a river of metal on the floor. The firemen fought valiantly to put out the fire often having to put up with unexploded bombs and bombs and incendiaries which were still falling around them.

ETW Dennis's printing works fire

Luckily only one fireman was injured. ETW Dennis moved to temporary premises at 10 York Place and it took only 4 months to rebuild the factory despite it being wartime and numerous other buildings being damaged. That raid on Scarborough continued until 4.30 am. The result of the raid was that 1,378 buildings had either been destroyed or damaged. There had been 27 fatalities - a high number when one considers the then size of Scarborough - with a further 45 being injured. The All-Clear sounded at 4.30 am the following day.

In September 1941, it was the turn of Prospect Mount Road, near Manor Road (above) when a single plane released two bombs. Four houses were demolished and flames from a fractured gas main shot 40 feet into the air. Luckily there were no serious casualties.

On a lighter note, ladies' stockings were very scarce and in May, 1942 it was reported that 3 million pairs of silk and silk mixture stockings had reached the shops in Great Britain. One lady queued for a pair of silk stockings but then complained afterwards that she had had to wait an hour before being served. She probably needed them for a special event but her complaint during wartime, and in the circumstances of that period seemed very incongruous.

VE Day, (Victory in Europe) on 8th May 1945 brought the threat of air attack to an end. The town had suffered 21 air raids and five machine gun and cannon attacks.

There had been 47 deaths from bombs and mines with a further 137 wounded. Over 3,000 of the town's buildings were destroyed or damaged.

After VE Day the town very slowly started to get back to normality. Most of the hotels were de-requisitioned and returned to their owners but with the shortage of linen and soap they had a difficult job re-opening to the public.

On 21st September 1944, The Prince of Wales Hotel, 11 ITW RAF during wartime, was bought by Mr WH Cockerline, a shipping and horse racing magnate for a sum of around £100,000 possibly before the hotel was derequisitioned.

The North Cliff Golf Course turf had to be completely re-laid in 1946 because during the war years the 18½ acres had been used for growing cereals.

Troop trains which had arrived hourly at Londesborough Road Railway Station laden with tanks, Bren gun carriers and all types of military vehicles, which vehicles could be seen in almost constant convoy through the streets of the town, suddenly ceased.

On 8th December, 1945 the last troop train left Scarborough at 10.00am bound for Richmond. This last troop train marked the end of a vast number of especially laid-on trains which carried troops and supplies during the war years.

Although many troops were still in the town, they left on future dates by regular passenger trains.

It was not until 1947 that the Grand Hotel opened again to visitors, and similarly The Zylpha Hotel on Albion Road did not re-open until April, 1947.

After the war the hotels and businesses slowly began to repair damage that had been sustained through either neglect or enemy action.

The Spa was de-requisitioned in March, 1945 and was open to the public for that season. The Balmoral Hotel re-opened the same month but many hotels had to wait another year or so before the Forces moved out.

After the war, encouragement of the tourist trade was top priority but had to take second place until a solution to the homeless problem could be found. A large estate was built at Sandybed in 1945 where 'pre-fabs' - pre-built properties which were easy and fast to erect – were built using prisoner-of-war labour, and another estate was laid out at Barrowcliff which eased the situation.

Building permanent houses at Highfield estate Newby – off Throxenby Lane, was started a little later.

The military was still in many of the hotels and it was well into 1947 before all of them were de-requisitioned and they could be refurbished and returned to their original holiday use. There was still a shortage of soap and linen but by the late 1940s most of the problems had been overcome and by the start of the new decade in 1951 Scarborough was once again being hailed as a premier holiday resort and 'The Queen of Watering Places'.

*

Roy Day had been training to be a dentist when he was called up by the RAF. He was posted to 11 ITW – The Prince of Wales Hotel - to train as aircrew and eventually became the pilot of a Lancaster bomber.

'...*After passing out from ITW 11 at the Prince of Wales Hotel I was posted to 50 Squadron just outside Lincoln.*

But that was not the end of my association with Scarborough. By VE Day I had completed only 23 Operational Sorties out of the required 30 of an Operations 'Tour', so I was posted to another Squadron to train for 'Tiger Force' to finish my 'Tour'. Tiger Force involved bombing operations against Japan.

The training was boring and uninteresting so on the evening of July 6th after a session of practice bombing on the Wainfleet range I decided to divert on the way back, to Scarborough to take a look at my old Initial Trainnig Wing, The Prince of Wales.

I made about four low passes over the hotel and the South Bay and town, then returned to our base at Spilsby in Lincolnshire.

What I did not know was that in passing low over Scarborough and my nostalgic visit to see the Prince of Wales Hotel, the roar and reverberation of the four Merlin engines on the Lancaster had drowned out the RAF orchestra which was playing at an open air concert being held at the Spa.

Attending, among others, was the Mayor and an RAF Air-Vice Marshal!

On my return to Spilsby I was arrested and I was found guilty at the subsequent Courts-Martial. By the time sentence came through the war had ended and, to discourage an expected spree of low flying, they made an example of me and I was 'Dismissed the Service'!

What I did not realise at the time of my premature release from the RAF was that it was a golden opportunity to get into Civil Aviation. I wasted a year first, trying to get back into Dental College and, when I did eventually start studying at Swansea University I found myself out of my depth after a four year break in my education.

I saw from the advertisement columns of 'Flight' and 'Aeroplane' that they were crying out for Pilots so I quit Dental College and went to the Merchant Venturers Technical College at Bristol and studied for my 'B' Pilots Licence and 2nd Class Navigators Licence.

Armed with these I had my pick of jobs and chose Silver City Airways – a newly formed well-funded charter company.

I flew until my retirement, was never out of work, and never looked back.'

***

CHAPTER TWELVE

FROM 1945-
TO THE PRESENT TIME

SCHOOLBOY MEMORIES FROM THE '40s, '50s, and '60s

Trawling the memories of life in the 40's, 50's, and 60's may strike a few chords among readers:

- **Saturday Morning Cinema** at the Odeon, — 6d to pay and a succession of cartoons, then Flash Gordon, the Rough Riders, Roy Rodgers, Laurel and Hardy, and Abbot and Costello, and a number of short 'B' pictures so unmemorable that they completely defeat recollection some 50 years on. A greater extravagance was a visit to the then several other cinemas in the town as a treat. The Futurist, the Londesborough, and the Aberdeen were reminders of the heyday of British cinema entertainment before the insidious advent of Television as the universal panacea for boredom!

- **Television** — for those of us then still at school, less of a distraction from homework than now, with the newsreaders, McDonald Hobley and Mary Malcolm, unbelievably in evening dress. And then a gap after the news before the more adult and serious programmes for the night commenced. Some readers may even recall watching the Coronation all day, possibly with pre-made sandwiches for lunch, and with curtains drawn to assist the viewing of a flickering small screen, accompanied by the reverential tones of Richard Dimbleby.

- **The Open Air Theatre** — Memory brings to mind a number of magical visits on warm summer evenings to packed houses with colourful, musical entertainment of operettas and musical shows. Shows such as Robin Hood, Faust, The Bohemian Girl, Vagabond King, Song of Norway and many, many more.

Memories of the excitement and the buzz of conversation before the show started; the orchestra, attired in evening dress, moored in a barge-like 'pit' at the edge of the lake; of the powerful spot lighting operated from a tall purpose built brick tower at the very back of the auditorium. And of the sheer expanse of the stage and scenery and costumed cast – often well above 200 - which took up the entire frontage of the island (unlike today's tiny weather–proofed stage area which protects the comparatively tiny casts and which obscures a full view for the majority of ticket buyers). Only arenas such as Verona now continue to provide the sort of spectacle Scarborough enjoyed in those halcyon days.

Of the world famous illuminated glass raft which moved from one side of the lake to the other and on which a full ballet performed.

Of cushions, to ease the hard bench-like seating, which could be hired for 6d, and the coffee and sandwiches and blankets which most people took with them – certainly the former two not being confiscated at the gate as seems to be the practice at the present 'modern' open-air theatre.

Then, a few years on into our late teenage years, actually taking part in the shows; rehearsing at Gladstone road school during the winter evenings and needing to promise 4 evenings a week for the entire summer (2 for actual performances and two the following nights in case the performance night was rained off).

Open Air Theatre- Song of Norway 1951

Extremely popular in its time, bringing thousands of people to the town each week during the summer weeks, and the actual capacity audiences in those days never having so far been surpassed by the modern theatre, it was however overtaken eventually by the increasing sophistication of public demands for entertainment in front of the television set; the onset of central heating in most homes which made people more averse to sitting out in the cold or the rain and the vagaries of Scarborough summer weather!

- **Shopping** in the town, and being parentally dragged round those havens of middle-class department store refinement, Rowntrees, or Marshall and Snelgrove in St. Nicholas Street, the disappearance of which, and the advent of the faceless multiples having taken much of the character out of the occasion. Woolworths was a very different store in those days, and many of us will recall wandering round the multiplicity of individual cheap buys at lunchtime. Whatever you wanted, they probably had it — it was more like a penny bazaar. Stamp collectors could buy for 6d mixed packets of gaudy foreign postage stamps which would satisfy even the most ardent junior philatelist.

Still on the subject of Woolworths, and lowering the tone several notches, I have it on good authority from someone slightly older than me, that among the trinkets for sale, ladies 'gold' wedding rings could be purchased for as little as 3/6d. He explained to me that these were suitable for illicit boarding house weekends with one's current enamoured, though the same good authority alleged that after several days' wear they turned green, as did the finger in question! Of similar prurient interest to those of us who were more shy, repressed or perhaps just downright envious were the somewhat embroidered tales of several of our more liberated school mates of their nocturnal exploits at their parents' homes of what can tactfully be described as *rapprochements* with the girls from Scarborough Girls High School, although the wilder excesses of this did require envious digestion with several pinches of salt!

- **The Cricket Festival** – This was another feature and still is, each summer; a notable event even for those who were not very enthusiastic about the game, and the likes of Hutton, latterly Truman, Close, Peter May, and the Bedser Brothers, Alec and Eric, bring back memories which will be largely lost on modern fans. In those days the Festival was very much a prestigious event. The Festival, and its stars, and seeking and getting autographs; meeting BBC commentator Peter West (and others); seeing the BBC radio 'transmitter room' – I think it was a disused coalhouse - under the grandstand with great glowing glass valves; and collecting rubbish after the match, payment being a free ticket for the next day. Magic!

*

BOYS' HIGH SCHOOL MEMORIES –

The following are a few personal memories specific to the High School.

- A fine autumnal morning, September 1949. Me, a very nervous new boy, in new uniform, short trousers, school socks, black shoes, grey shirt, tie, sweater, blazer and cap – and a new very, very, stiff leather satchel.

- The service bus from Newby to and from school – and the monthly bus tickets printed on blue card with which we were issued, which gained punch holes round the edges as the month progressed.

- The Westwood School building; the smell of it - especially at the start of a term when floors had been varnished and black boards blackened.

- The bike sheds – always overcrowded – and, looking up, the beams and floor boards of the classroom above.

- The smell in the Chemistry labs – a mixture of experiment leftovers from the last 50 years.

- German Master Bon Clarke, and his weekly tests, always with 4 questions. And everyone sitting in alphabetic order.

- The magazine we produced under English master Gerald Hinchliffe's guidance, and particularly the smell of printing ink for the duplicator.

- Chalk dust and blackboards.

- French master Les Brown, sweeping into the room to start a lesson, gown flapping – then realising it was the wrong room and sweeping out again.

- Cycling to and from the school playing fields at Oliver's Mount. We were exhausted before we even started games.

- Showers after PT with sports master Jock Roxburgh – particularly the last shower which was cold and which he made sure we did not miss – and the strict time limit he gave us to get dressed.

- The strict stair code at school – up one set and down another.

- The School library – where pupils at least made a semblance of being quiet and industrious.

- Teacher Eddie Colenutt's Lambretta scooter – one of the first, if not the first in Scarborough. It had ivory, (presumably imitation), brake handles.

- The school choir attending and winning their class at the Eskdale Tournament of Song.

- The school visit to the Festival of Britain; staying in the wartime dormitories deep beneath Clapham Common – and restored for the Festival from the war days. And the Skylon at the Festival.

Memories, memories. It is ironic how, after all these years, small but vivid vignettes of memory, often of really trivial events, come back, when more recent recollections prove totally elusive.

*

FYLINGDALES – THE SECRET BASE WHICH HAS WATCHED SPACE FOR 50 YEARS - 1963

The Scarborough News recorded the 50th Anniversary of the base on September 17th 2013 -

Cloaked in secrecy, RAF Fylingdales has stood sentry over the North York Moors for half a century.

It was built during the Cold War, a time when tensions were high between the world's great superpowers, and the threat of nuclear war was very real.

On Tuesday 17th September the base celebrated its

anniversary, 50 years after Air Marshal Sir Douglas Morris commissioned the base, saying: 'This is not the first time that a station of this kind has been established here on the Yorkshire moors - about 1,000 years ago a warning post was set up near Whitby, some 10 miles from here, to provide warning of attack by sea invaders from Scandinavia on their approach to these shores. The threat and equipment has changed in the intervening years, but the purpose remains the same.'

This historic outpost inspired the station's crest, showing the White Rose of Yorkshire surmounted by a Viking Fire Warning Basket.

Appropriately, the Fylingdales motto, Vigilamus, means 'We are watching'.

First using the famous 'golf balls', then later the 'pyramid', a team of British and American personnel have indeed watched, originally able to spot missile launches 2,000 miles away.

In 1960, soon after the base was announced, Pentagon sources were quoted as saying the base would give the USA up to 15 minutes extra warning, should an attack be launched, but the UK would be

unlikely to benefit. 'Russians would use intermediate range missiles and you would get no warning worth mentioning', was the brutally honest reply.

The £43m project announced by the North Atlantic Treaty Organisation was the first in which the UK had made a contribution, and at a meeting of Whitby Luncheon Club at Botham's Cafe in 1961, a representative explained how its proximity to the coast and lack of population in the vicinity made the moor the only candidate. He also pledged that when the station was no longer required, the moor would be restored to its original condition.

Work began on the first of the three 140 ft golf balls in 1962 and at the station's opening in September of the following year, both the American Stars and Stripes and the British Union Flag flew side by side in a statement of defiance against Soviet aggression.

In 1973 it was claimed by Conservative MP Geoffrey Stewart-Smith that the Russians had used spy-ships disguised as trawlers to bug the station.

The three original domes were dismantled between 1982-84 and replaced. However, the new golf balls were to be operational for less than a decade, before being replaced by the pyramid which became operational in 1992 and still stands today.

The replacement system was set to be a massive upgrade, and was able to track a football-sized object at 3,000 miles.

It could also scan in 360 degrees and was not restricted to just the north and east like the old system.

Eighty RAF personnel join around 300 other contractors, military police and various other staff in calling the base home.

In 50 years, there have only been 14 hours where the radar has not been operational.

Around 12 times a year the unmistakable alarm sounds which signifies a missile launch somewhere in the world. The five-man shift then has just 60 seconds to discover if the alert is genuine. Crew commander Jim Garlick said: "It can be horribly unpleasant but at the same time it's what we are here to do and so it's exciting.

"We have a minute to make a decision as to whether the radar is working properly or if World War Three has started."

If a threat was confirmed the crew would call an American Air Force base in Colorado to inform them an attack was imminent. The line must be tested daily.

But these events are rare and for the remaining 99 per cent of the year, the crew spends the majority of their 12-hour shift working through a list of targets, sent through from the United States, that they must track in space.

In the early years of its life the new system had attracted a large amount of controversy. Peace protesters feared the new £160m radar system could be used to fire weapons from space as part of America's 'Star Wars' project.

Several people have also been taken into custody over the years following demonstrations close to the base.

Concerns over Fylingdales' inclusion in the 'Star Wars' project continued for over a decade.

In 2003, Defence Secretary Geoff Hoon angered locals by announcing America would be allowed to use Fylingdales in the defence programme, despite large-scale protests. Campaigners feared the base could become a target for terrorist attacks.

Now, the base continues its fourfold mission relating to missile defence and satellite tracking. And Fylingdales has become an accepted part of the community.

It remains a large-scale employer, maintains 3,000 acres of moorland, and the rumours of radiation death rays that accompanied the base's launch in 1963 have, thankfully, proved untrue.

HOLBECK HALL HOTEL – 1993

Holbeck Hall Hotel was a cliff top hotel to the south of Scarborough, owned by the English Rose Hotel group. The hotel had scenic views of the sea and surrounding area. It was built in 1879 by George Alderson Smith as a private residence, and was later converted to a hotel.

The drama attracted world-wide news and television coverage of the site with pictures and commentaries being beamed all over the world.

'The first signs of any trouble at Holbeck Hall were when hikers noticed cracks and bulges had appeared in the land surrounding the hotel on the previous Thursday, 3rd June 1993. By the Friday morning the earth movement had gouged a massive cleft in the cliffside in front of the hotel.

By the following morning staff and residents awoke to find a earth movement had created a new cliff edge just 20 yards from the hotel and the rose garden had disappeared and was now well below the new cliff edge. During the day further slippage occurred and 80 guests and staff were evacuated as the cliff edge continued to crumble, taking the hotel another 10 yards towards the sea.

The hotel began to crumble on the Friday afternoon and on Saturday 5th June the main entrance to the hotel and the front wall collapsed down the cliff. Later the same day the central part of the seaward wing crashed down together with the Rose Lounge.

Luckily, there were no casualties or even fatalities and all staff and residents were able to get out safely.

There were no more landslips at that site but the remaining part of the hotel was eventually demolished by July 29th.

In 1997, the loss of the Holbeck Hall became the subject of a significant court case in English civil law (Holbeck Hall Hotel Limited and another v. Scarborough Borough Council) when the owners of the hotel attempted to sue Scarborough Borough Council for damages, alleging that as owners of the shoreline they had not taken any practical measures at all to prevent the landslip.

The claim was rejected on the grounds that the Council was not liable for the causes of the landslide itself.'

*

SCARBOROUGH STAR DISK – 28th JANUARY 2006

Scarborough's Star Disk is the largest such illuminated Disk in the UK, and possibly in Europe at 26m in diameter. It was officially switched on by the Deputy Mayor of Scarborough Cllr. Jim Preston on January 28th 2006, at 7pm.

The disk, constructed on the site of the South Bay Pool, which closed because of structural problems, contains, as fibre optic terminals, the 42 brightest circumpolar stars (stars which never set) as seen from Scarborough. It also marks the positions of the sunrise points over the North Sea for various dates in the year.

'The idea for this stage in the development of the South Bay Pool was instigated by 'Create', an arts and cultural agency, specialising in the setting up of temporary works of art and events. Also involved in the ongoing project is the Scarborough Urban Renaissance

*of Public Space Group working in conjunction with
Scarborough Borough Council. Funding was provided
by Yorkshire Forward and the Borough Council.*

*Because of the extensive involvement in the
preparatory work for this project done by John Harper,
as President of Scarborough and Ryedale Astronomical
Society, it is rather fitting that the educational
'illumination' became operational within a month of the
30th birthday of the Society!*

*The North-South line points to St. Mary's Church
Tower.*

*A large Public Star Party was held at the South Bay
Pool site, attended by members of Scarborough and
Ryedale Astronomical Society and nearby Whitby and
District Astronomical Society. The major attraction for
members of the public was the chance to observe
through the telescopes Saturn with its beautiful ring
system and major satellites. The planet was at
Opposition and its nearest to Earth on January 27th, the
day before the event!'*

*

NORTH BAY DEVELOPMENT - 2001

In 2001, development work started to bring up to
date the somewhat run-down North Bay area. The
Corner café was demolished and replaced by two blocks
of luxury flats overlooking the sea. The old North Bay
bathing pool was closed and has not yet been
redeveloped.

Forest chalets are proposed to be built in the old
Kinderland site on Burniston road; the old Mr Marvel's
Fun Park is to be developed, and there is hope that the

North Bay indoor pool will be replaced by a larger, modern up to date pool in a different part of the town.

Work is expected to start shortly on a water themed park off Burniston road, planning permission having been granted.

The Open Air theatre, re-opened by HM The Queen on May 20th 2010

The one-time derelict Open Air Theatre, originally built in 1932, was rebuilt in Northstead Manor Gardens at a cost of £3.5m and was opened by HM The Queen on 20th May 2010. Seating capacity is approximately 6,500.

*

THE SPA RENOVATED 2009-2011

Between 2009 and 2011 Scarborough Spa was renovated by Houlton Construction at a cost of £8.7m.

The Spa Bridge was also closed for improvements to the footway at an additional cost of £700,000.

*

FREDDIE GILROY 2011

'Freddie Gilroy and the Belsen Stragglers'

In 2011 a sculpture called Freddie Gilroy and the Belsen Stragglers was donated to the town by Maureen Robinson and erected on Royal Albert Drive.

The Scarborough Evening News reported:

'A pensioner from Scarborough has donated £50,000 to keep a sculpture as a permanent fixture for the town.

The steel work on the North Bay, which depicts an old soldier sitting on a bench, was initially loaned for one month by artist Ray Lonsdale.

Resident Maureen Robinson has now donated the money to keep the artwork in the town.

She said she bought it as a 'thank you to the people'. The piece, called Freddie Gilroy and the Belsen Stragglers, is based on the former miner who was one of the first Allied soldiers to enter the Belsen concentration camp on its liberation in World War II.

"I've been saving up for years to buy something for Scarborough and the opportunity has never arisen," said Mrs Robinson.

"When we saw Freddie, I said, 'This is my dream come true. It seemed the perfect thing, as a thank you to Scarborough... and for the happy years we have spent here."

Mrs Robinson said the artist Mr Lonsdale was a 'genius with tremendous talent'.

Mr Lonsdale, who is based in County Durham, said: "From the minute this sculpture hit the ground it got a lot of interest."

He said he was flattered with the interest in his work.

A second sculpture loaned to the council, A High Tide in Short Wellies, is sited on Whitby's West Pier.'
[Since that report appeared a further sculpture has been provided to Filey, and a 2nd to Scarborough]

*

'YORKSHIRE WATER TO CARRY OUT £50M SCHEME TO IMPROVE WATER QUALITY - 2012-14

Yorkshire Water submitted plans to install a huge new storage chamber under Marine Drive in a bid to improve *bathing water quality and fall into line with new European rules.'*

As this book is nearing completion, the work is progressing well and whilst through traffic is only allowed from the south to the north bays and this caused severe congestion throughout the rest of the town during summer months, the work appears to be on schedule.

The work is expected to be completed by mid-2014.

VALLEY BRIDGE TO BE REFURBISHED AT A COST OF £250,000

'One of Scarborough's most historic landmarks is set to receive £250,000 of refurbishment work funded by North Yorkshire County Council.

Valley Bridge will be renovated and repaired as part of the council's planned maintenance programme, which will span a number of years.

Concerns had been raised locally about the current state of the bridge, as parts of it are in poor repair with rust and broken sections clearly visible.

However, a spokeswoman from the county council explained that in September, the council arranged specialist access contractors to remove any deteriorating, non-structural components on the bridge that were in danger of falling off.

She explained that although the bridge looks visually worse as a result of this work, it is safe.

The county council is now in the middle of a £250,000 procurement exercise to buy new components such as handrails, fascia panels and different cappings to replace cracked and rusting parts of the parapet.

David Bowe, the county council's corporate director for business and environmental services, said: "Last September we employed civil engineers, specialised in rope access, who abseiled along the Valley Bridge structure on both sides to inspect the decorative balustrade and to remove any components that had the potential to come loose. We are now in the process of awarding a contract for replacement components for the balustrade which have to be specially cast.

"We wish to reassure members of the public that the bridge is structurally sound and that no loose components have fallen from the bridge – all have been safely removed.

"The structural stability of the bridge has not been compromised and the bridge is fit for purpose.

"We now intend to push ahead with awarding the contract for casting the new parts so they can be fitted later this year. In the meantime we will continue to monitor the bridge.

"The renovation work will be undertaken over a 22-week period, but will not require closure of the bridge to traffic or pedestrians."

The plan was welcomed by Scarborough's MP Robert Goodwill - although he believes that the work is somewhat overdue.

Mr Goodwill added: "However, I'm pleased that county are looking at it."

Adrian Perry, chairman of Scarborough Civic Society, said that he was pleased to hear about the work, as the bridge is an important historical landmark.

He said: "It's good that they're making the investment. It's a very important arterial road and a very important structure.

"It's got a very interesting history and was bought originally as a bridge that had collapsed over the River Ouse in York."

The renovation work follows renovation work at Spa Bridge in 2009/10, just a couple of hundred yards along Valley Road.'

***

POSTSCRIPT

So, very briefly, we have covered from 8000 BC to 2014 AD – 10,014 years in 193 pages – just under 52 years a page!

Obviously I do not claim this to be a complete or formal history of Scarborough. It is merely intended to scatch the surface and whet the appetite of readers; to show just a miniscule part of what has gone on, in, to and by the town and its inhabitants, during those 10,014 years. Hence the book's title *'Scarborough Snippets'*.

Some will claim that arguably important facts have been omitted; others will claim many items mentioned have been given more space and prominence than is warranted. Both might be correct but my intention when I started this project was to entertain and to provide background to some of the major events which have taken place in Scarborough.

If I have succeeded in this and you have bought a copy and enjoyed it I shall be happy. And if you have bought your copy from Clock Café I shall be delighted as all profits from Clock Café sales of this book will go to their very worthwhile, local charity – The LittleFoot Trust.

Hence the length of the Clock Café chapter!

David Fowler

Scarborough
October 2013

Printed in Great Britain
by Amazon

57095208R00119

PERSPECTI
ENVIRONMEN
SCHOLAR

This collection invites environmental law scholars to reflect on what it means to be an environmental law scholar and to consider how and why environmental law scholars engage in environmental law scholarship. Leading environmental law scholars from different backgrounds and jurisdictions offer their personal reflections on the nature, form, quality and challenges of environmental law scholarship. The collection offers the first honest introspection on what environmental law scholarship is and is not. It considers the unique contributions of environmental law scholarship to legal scholarship more generally, reflecting on what sets environmental law scholarship apart from other disciplines of legal scholarship and the challenges arising from these differences.

OLE W. PEDERSEN is Reader in Environmental Law and joint Director of Research at Newcastle Law School. Dr Pedersen actively researches the areas of environmental law, enforcement, justice and rights, and hydraulic fracturing and his scholarship engages with conceptual and foundational issues of environmental law and scholarship as well as the role of the courts in shaping modern environmental law. He is joint author of an established textbook on environmental law and Deputy Director of the Global Network of Human Rights and the Environment.

PERSPECTIVES ON ENVIRONMENTAL LAW SCHOLARSHIP

Essays on Purpose, Shape and Direction

Edited by

OLE W. PEDERSEN

Newcastle University

CAMBRIDGE
UNIVERSITY PRESS

CAMBRIDGE
UNIVERSITY PRESS

University Printing House, Cambridge CB2 8BS, United Kingdom

One Liberty Plaza, 20th Floor, New York, NY 10006, USA

477 Williamstown Road, Port Melbourne, VIC 3207, Australia

314-321, 3rd Floor, Plot 3, Splendor Forum, Jasola District Centre, New Delhi - 110025, India

79 Anson Road, #06-04/06, Singapore 079906

Cambridge University Press is part of the University of Cambridge.

It furthers the University's mission by disseminating knowledge in the pursuit of education, learning and research at the highest international levels of excellence.

www.cambridge.org
Information on this title: www.cambridge.org/9781108465984
DOI: 10.1017/9781108635929

First published 2018
First paperback edition 2020

A catalogue record for this publication is available from the British Library

Library of Congress Cataloging in Publication data
Names: Pedersen, Ole W., editor.
Title: Perspectives on environmental law scholarship : essays on purpose, shape and
direction / edited by Ole W. Pedersen, Newcastle University.
Description: Cambridge, United Kingdom ; New York, NY, USA : Cambridge University
Press, 2018. | Includes bibliographical references and index.
Identifiers: LCCN 2018035532 | ISBN 9781108475242 (hardback)
Subjects: LCSH: Environmental law – Study and teaching. | BISAC: LAW / Environmental.
Classification: LCC K103.E58 P47 2018 | DDC 344.04/6–dc23
LC record available at https://lccn.loc.gov/2018035532

ISBN 978-1-108-47524-2 Hardback
ISBN 978-1-108-46598-4 Paperback

CONTENTS

List of Contributors   *page* vii

1 Introduction   1
   OLE W. PEDERSEN

2 What Legal Scholarship Can Contribute
   to Environmental Law   10
   TODD S. AAGAARD

3 Back to Basics: Thinking About the Craft of
   Environmental Law Scholarship   26
   ELIZABETH FISHER

4 Environmental Law Scholarship: Systematization,
   Reform, Explanation, and Understanding   41
   DANIEL BONILLA MALDONADO

5 (Un)Making the Boundaries of Environmental Law
   Scholarship: Interdisciplinarity Beyond the Social
   Sciences?   60
   MARGHERITA PIERACCINI

6 Crossing Disciplines in Planning: A Renewable Energy
   Case Study   79
   MARIA LEE, SIMON LOCK, LUCY NATARAJAN AND
   YVONNE RYDIN

7 Economics and Environmental Law Scholarship   96
   CAROLINE CECOT AND MICHAEL A. LIVERMORE

8 What Is the Point of International Environmental Law
   Scholarship in the Anthropocene?   121
   TIM STEPHENS

9 Reflections on the Future of Environmental Law
   Scholarship and Methodology in the Anthropocene   140
   LOUIS J. KOTZÉ

10 The Unifying Force of Climate Change Scholarship   162
   DANIEL A. FARBER

11 Environmental Law Scholarship in a Developing
   Country – An Alternative Discourse   178
   CAMENA GUNERATNE

12 President Trump, the New Chicago School
   and the Future of Environmental Law and Scholarship   195
   JASON J. CZARNEZKI AND SARAH SCHINDLER

13 EU Environmental Law and European Environmental
   Law Scholarship   212
   LUDWIG KRÄMER

14 The Culture of Environmental Law and the Practices of
   Environmental Law Scholarship   227
   OLE W. PEDERSEN

   Index   239

CONTRIBUTORS

TODD AAGAARD is Vice Dean and Professor of Law at the Charles Widger School of Law, University of Villanova

CAROLINE CECOT is Assistant Professor at the Antonin Scalia Law School at George Mason University

JASON J. CZARNEZKI is the Gilbert and Sarah Kerlin Distinguished Professor of Environmental Law and Associate Dean and Executive Director of the Environmental Law Programme at the Elizabeth Haub School of Law, Pace University

DANIEL A. FARBER is Sho Sato Professor of Law at University of California, Berkeley

ELIZABETH FISHER is Professor of Environmental Law at Corpus Christi College and Faculty of Law, University of Oxford

CAMENA GUNERATNE is Professor of Law and Dean of the Faculty of Humanities and Social Sciences at the Open University of Sri Lanka

LOUIS J. KOTZÉ is Research Professor at North-West University, South Africa

LUDWIG KRÄMER teaches environmental law across several European universities and worked for the European Commission for more than three decades, including as head of the legal unit of the Directorate-General for the Environment

MARIA LEE is Vice Dean (Programme Planning and Development) and Professor of Law, University College London

MICHAEL A. LIVERMORE is Associate Professor of Law at the University of Virginia School of Law

SIMON LOCK is Lecturer at the Department of Science and Technology Studies, University College London

DANIEL BONILLA MALDONADO is Associate Professor and Director of the Public Interest Law Group at the University Los Andes

OLE W. PEDERSEN is Reader in Environmental Law at Newcastle Law School

MARGHERITA PIERACCINI is Reader in Law at the University of Bristol Law School

LUCY NATARAJAN is Research Associate at the Bartlett School for Planning, University College London

YVONNE RYDIN is Chair of Planning, Environment and Public Policy at the Bartlett School for Planning, University College London

SARAH SCHINDLER is the Edward S. Godfrey Professor of Law and Associate Dean for Research at University of Maine Law School

TIM STEPHENS is Professor of International Law and Australian Research Council Future Fellow at the University of Sydney

1

Introduction

Today seems a good point in time at which to be an environmental law scholar. In fact, it might even be the best. There are more of us than ever. There are more journals and periodicals than any time before in which to publish the fruits of one's labour and most academic publishing houses now dedicate specific catalogue space to environmental law. And environmental law scholars seemingly take advantage of this by publishing more and more work. As a result, there is an abundancy of environmental law scholarship out there. With abundance, however, also comes the risk of oversupply. With oversupply comes the risk of spam jurisprudence in which 'there is more, vastly more, of nothing happening',[1] resulting in scholarship being met with, in James Boyd White's words, 'a feeling of guilty dread and with an expectation of frustration'.[2]

With abundancy therefore also comes responsibility. Responsibility to pause and reflect on the joint enterprise that is environmental law scholarship. It is in part in an attempt to dislodge this responsibility that this collection of essays has been brought about. The presence of an obligation to reflect on the practice of the scholarly endeavour might be particularly acute in environmental law scholarship if indeed the discipline is seen as suffering from immaturity as argued by some commentators.[3] But there is more to it than a sense of responsibility. For in addition to providing a subset of scholars with an opportunity for

I am grateful for the invaluable support provided by Sarah Mackie in preparing this collection.

[1] Pierre Schlag, 'Spam Jurisprudence, Air Law and the Rank Anxiety of Nothing Happening (A Report on the State of the Art)' (2009) 97 Geo. L.J. 803.
[2] James Boyd White, 'Intellectual Integration' (1988) 82 *Nw. U. L. Rev.* 1, 5.
[3] Elizabeth Fisher and others 'Maturity and Methodology: Starting a Debate about Environmental Law Scholarship' (2009) 21 *JEL* 213.

disciplinary introspection and reflection, an additional driver behind the collection is an interest and curiosity about environmental law scholarship and an interest in pondering what it is we do as environmental law scholars.

Lurking in the desire to reflect on the practice of scholarship is of course a series of underlying concerns – perhaps even a disciplinary anxiety. Concerns about what actually constitutes scholarship, considerations about the quality of scholarship as well as considerations about why environmental law scholars do what they do and for what reasons. Initially, the curiosity behind this collection of essays found expression in a series of questions: What is the purpose of environmental law scholarship – what is the point of the enterprise? Why is environmental law scholarship often said to require appreciation of interdisciplinarity? What relationship does environmental law scholarship enjoy with other legal and non-legal disciplines? Does environmental law scholarship require the possession of specific methodological skills? For whom does the environmental law scholar write? Does environmental law scholarship have any impact beyond the academy? And if not, does it really matter? What are the main differences in scholarship between jurisdictions? Is environmental law scholarship necessarily more instrumental than other disciplines (in the sense that environmental law scholars are wedded to particular purposes and outcomes)? Does environmental law scholarship suffer from a lack of rigour?

While some of these points are likely to be perceived as controversial, the premise of the project was always to facilitate an honest self-assessment from within the discipline from some of the discipline's leading contributors. In a sense, an implicit purpose of the project was to engage head-on with any latent scholarly anxieties arising from contemplating the specific concerns just listed. Embracing and engaging any scholarly anxiety would ideally serve the overall good of the discipline of environmental law scholarship insofar as 'a scholarly work's ability to engender [anxiety] should be treated as a mark of excellence.'[4] With this in mind, the contributors to the collection were invited to offer their personal reflections in response to some of these concerns. The results yielded from this invitation follow in the subsequent pages.

From this emerges a rich and multifaceted picture of environmental law scholarship. One of the more obvious points is of course that

[4] Edward L. Rubin, 'The Evaluation of Prescriptive Scholarship' (1990) 10 *Tel Aviv U. Stud. L.* 101, 112.

environmental law and environmental law scholarship do not operate in a legal vacuum isolated from external influences be they political, economic, social, scientific or moral considerations. Notwithstanding this, in producing environmental scholarship, environmental law scholars, as highlighted by Aagaard, have a real comparative advantage compared to those who seek to influence the law from the perspective of a policymaker, compared to a non-academic lawyer/legal practitioner and compared to non-legal scholars. Obvious as this may seem, the environmental law scholar's real advantage lays in her ability to understand the subject as a distinctive legal discipline rich in legal 'ambiguities, contingencies, interdependencies [and] implications' that might not be readily apparent to non-legal scholars and commentators.[5] The ability of the environmental law scholar to challenge what Aagaard sees as methodological and ideological orthodoxies is consequently a skill unique to the legal scholar. This alone ought to dispel disciplinary anxieties.

Like Aagaard, Fisher reminds us that in undertaking environmental law scholarship, the endeavour is, at heart, about expertise. To Fisher, expertise takes the form of a craft which focuses on 'the desire to do a job well for its own sake.'[6] The commitment to do something for its own sake does not, however, suggest that the craft of scholarship takes place in a void sealed off from external drivers and considerations. On the contrary, Fisher highlights how the practice of crafting environmental law scholarship is an inherently social practice which is shaped by the institutional environment in which it is conducted and moulded by the materials that each scholar engages with (be it international law or specific decisions from a subset of jurisdictions). An important point made by Fisher is, however, that the environmental law scholar ensures that the vigour which the scholar puts into the scholarly endeavour (what Fisher sees as 'obsessive energy') is put to appropriate use to avoid bad scholarship. Bad scholarship is making scholarly arguments not substantiated by the materials being analysed. To Fisher, obsessive energy is thus important but it must be used with caution and in moderation to avoid the scholars channelling themselves into the rabbit warren of their own narrow research agendas isolated from the rest of the scholarly practice.

The importance of scholars keeping an eye on the social practice in which they take part when conducting research is further highlighted by Maldonado who identifies and dissects four main types of scholarship

---

[5] Aagaard, Chapter 2, this volume.
[6] Fisher, Chapter 3, this volume.

prevalent in environmental law. Maldonado thus identifies the paradigmatic models of environmental law scholarship as being the systematisation effort, the reform model, the explanation paradigm and the understanding effort. Each of these models will be familiar to most environmental law scholars and most of us will use each of the models interchangeably. Importantly, however, echoing Fisher's point that no particular approach to scholarship is necessarily superior to another as long as it is done well, Maldonado points out that each model serves a purpose which stands apart from any of the other models but that each of the four models has its own shortcomings and problems. It is the job of the diligent scholar to bear these shortcomings in mind and to be honest and open about them when engaging in scholarship.

Being social and engaging with other scholars does, as we all know, have its own problems and challenges. Some of these challenges are, as Pieraccini drives home, institutional, whereas others are epistemological. Pieraccini thus highlights how institutional pressures have the potential to impede the environmental law scholar (in particular the sociolegal environmental scholar) from producing optimal scholarship which truly engages with interdisciplinary considerations. Though some of the challenges highlighted by Pieraccini – such as audit culture – are more prevalent in certain jurisdictions, some of the drivers behind this culture (that of marketization of higher education) are increasingly found in most countries.[7] Consequently, Pieraccini's argument serves as a warning call to the architects of higher education policy (wherever they might be) – a warning call which cautions against micromanagement of research agendas and scholarship.[8]

For those brave enough to engage in interdisciplinary research notwithstanding the challenges highlighted by Pieraccini, like Lee, Lock, Natarajan and Rydin, it is evident that interdisciplinary scholarship holds real rewards. Rewards for those involved in the work as well as rewards for those of us who have the pleasure of reading the work. Relaying their experience from taking part in a funded and interdisciplinary research project, examining the decision-making process for so-called nationally significant infrastructure projects, Lee, Lock, Natarajan and Rydin are admirably honest about the challenges and problems faced in undertaking this work. One problem encountered by the

[7] On this, see Stefan Collini, *Speaking of Universities* (London: Verso, 2017).
[8] For a fruitful discussion of the values of higher education and academic research, see e.g. Stanley Fish, *Versions of Academic Freedom* (Chicago: University of Chicago Press, 2014).

interdisciplinary team of researchers centres on disciplinary identification. That is, is the project really an environmental law project or is it something else? Another problem relates to the risk of disciplinary misunderstandings and the realisation that methodologies vary significantly from discipline to discipline. In being so forthright and by sharing their story of the challenges they have encountered, Lee, Lock, Natarajan and Rydin demonstrate the ultimate collegial commitment to the practice of environmental law scholarship (and arguably beyond to other disciplines) insofar as their experience serves as an inspiration, albeit a personal one, for other scholars.

In related fashion, and echoing Aagaard's argument about the relevance of legal know-how, Cecot and Livermore draw attention to how environmental law scholars potentially can play an important role in interdisciplinary research by bringing to the fore their specific legal expertise as this relates to familiarity with administrative and legal decision-making processes and institutional contexts. The environmental lawyer, Cecot and Livermore argue, has the potential to act as a facilitator between disparate disciplines. Unfortunately, there remains one area in which environmental law scholars are perhaps lacking behind other legal scholars when it comes to facilitating fruitful exchanges with other disciplines. Cecot and Livermore thus call attention to the relative dearth of engagement with quantitative empirical work by environmental law scholars. Though one gets the impression that the hesitancy in engaging with quantitative work is not as widespread as it once was, Cecot and Livermore point out that the lack of such work is particularly surprising in environmental law scholarship given the wealth of empirical questions ripe for examination (including those pertaining to valuation of costs and benefits, the real-life impacts of policies and the effectiveness and efficacy of environmental policies). One hypothesis potentially explaining the relative lack of engagement with quantitative empirical work, Cecot and Livermore theorise, is that environmental law scholars have traditionally been unsympathetic towards 'economic worldviews', viewing environmental goods and benefits as deontological entities not susceptible to cost-benefit valuation. In pondering the reasons behind the lack of quantitative empirical work, Cecot and Livermore draw attention to the dangers emerging when a scholarly practice is primarily inward looking and isolated. Where this is the case, Cecot and Livermore's analysis convincingly argues that environmental law

scholars are doing a disservice to their discipline and practice, ultimately running the risk of the practice becoming overly arcane.

With environmental law scholarship being shaped by factors ordinarily perceived as being external to the discipline, Stephens, Kotzé and
Farber all consider the impacts that emerging paradigms have on environmental law scholarship. In considering the impacts of the emerging
concept of the Anthropocene on international environmental law scholarship, Stephens argue that the disruptive nature of this new epoch
represents a critical turning point for the study of international environmental law. This argument is in part driven by an assumption that to
date, international environmental law has not been entirely effective in
halting environmental degradation (though that may well of course be
because too much is expected of the discipline) and international environmental law scholars have perhaps been slower in engaging with the
emergence of the Anthropocene than domestic environmental law scholars. Stephens cautions against being overly defeatist when responding to
the immense challenges associated with the Anthropocene, and his
argument for a pragmatic result-orientated reconfiguration of international environmental law and international environmental law scholarship is admirable. Stephens thus argues that one challenge for
international environmental law and international environmental law
scholarship is to identify the conditions for a legal order which is both
equitable and effective. In one sense, the adoption of the Paris Agreement
arguably represents a tentative move towards answering Stephens's call.
Finally, when it comes to the question of how best to respond to the
challenges of the Anthropocene, international environmental law scholars arguably have one advantage over scholars engaging with domestic
questions insofar as international law recognises the writings of learned
scholars as a subsidiary source of law.[9] In light of this, there is seemingly
plenty of scope for international environmental law scholars to influence
debates on the shape and content of international environmental law in
the Anthropocene.

Whilst the onset of the Anthropocene poses challenges for international environmental law and international environmental law scholarship, Kotzé drives home the point that the Anthropocene similarly poses
methodological challenges for environmental law scholars. On the premise of never wanting to waste a good crisis, Kotzé argues in favour of
a more radical reconfiguration of our approaches to environmental law

[9] E.g. Statute of the ICJ Article 38(1)(d).

scholarship. Though critics might argue that the prefix of 'critical' ought to be superfluous insofar as any scholar ought to be 'critical' towards the material with which she engages, there is a refreshing radicalness to Kotzé's thesis. Kotzé thus argues that the present state of environmental law scholarship is insufficiently aligned with ideas of earth system complexities and too accommodating of what he terms 'neoliberal anthropocentrism'. To Kotzé the Anthropocene offers a unifying background paradigm against which environmental law scholars ought to study the role of law – a new intellectual paradigm for environmental law scholars. However, to fully grasp the opportunity, environmental law scholars will, echoing the argument of Cecot and Livermore, have to get out of their comfort zones and engage with transdisciplinary and transnational agendas (though many environmental law scholars already do so to a great degree).

When it comes to the potential for emerging scholarly paradigms to act as unifying backgrounds for scholarship, Farber argues that the problem of climate change has the potential to provide one such background. In making this argument, Farber highlights how in the absence of such a unifying paradigm, environmental law resembles Easterbrook's idea of 'law of the horse' which suggests that many emerging areas of law (like environmental law) do not make for a coherent body of law but instead are made up of disparate areas of law tangentially relevant to the environment.[10] The argument that environmental law as a body of law is incoherent seems by now to be beyond dispute.[11] But Farber's argument that the law relating to climate change (which to some might in itself represent 'a law of the horse') has the potential to unify the discipline of environmental law is all the more relevant when considering, as Farber does, how legal initiatives aiming at dealing with climate change often take the form of transplants which are based on experiences and methods from other jurisdictions. As Farber points out, 'someone who understands California's climate change regime would find it easier to understand the EU's climate change regime.'[12] Implicitly picking up the points made by Stephens and Kotzé, Farber similarly drives home how in the context of climate change law, the international v. domestic dichotomy is breaking down. Necessarily, the scholarly engagement with

---

[10] Frank H. Easterbrook, 'Cyberspace and the Law of the Horse' (1996) *U. Chi. Legal F.* 207.
[11] E.g. Todd Aagaard, 'Environmental Law as a Legal Field: An Inquiry in Legal Taxonomy' (2010) 95(2) *Cornell Law Review* 221; and Ole W. Pedersen, 'Modest Pragmatic Lessons for a Diverse and Incoherent Environmental Law' (2013) 33 *OJLS* 103–131.
[12] Farber, Chapter 10, this volume, 170.

different regimes of climate change law – be it international, domestic or comparatively – ought to bear in mind the differences between legal cultures and jurisdictions which likely reveal finer details and differences between the legal regimes.

Some of these differences as they pertain to environmental law scholarship are brought into perspective by Guneratne when she details the development of environmental law and environmental law scholarship from the perspective of a developing country scholar. Guneratne argues that environmental law scholarship necessarily varies from jurisdiction to jurisdiction, reflecting unique legal cultures and practical circumstances. One such example highlighted by Guneratne is the argument that environmental law scholarship in some developing countries has a stronger element of activism to it than seen in developed countries. In the context of Sri Lanka, Guneratne thus argues that scholarship is necessarily predicated on a foundation of sustainable development and social change. In making this argument, it is evident that the definition of environmental law scholarship developed by Guneratne (and possibly legal scholarship more generally) is anchored in the idea that scholarship has potential to facilitate profound changes in society. The desire to reach out to a wider audience than the immediate community of scholars is not one which is unique to developing countries though it evidently takes on an added urgency in the context of those countries.

Echoing the point made by Guneratne about the necessary contingency of scholarship, Czarnezki and Schindler bring to the fore the potential impacts which the Trump presidency in the USA might have on the practice of environmental law scholarship. Czarnezki and Schindler point out that the boundaries of what constitutes environmental law continue to expand, resulting in a discipline which constantly reinvents itself through the use of alternative methods of regulation. This move away from traditional means of regulation means that environmental law scholars will have to reorientate themselves to ensure that the scholarly practice keeps up with the dynamic understanding and definitions of the law. Against this, the election of President Trump has real potential to impact the nature of environmental regulation and thereby implicitly also the practice of scholarship. One argument put forward by Czarnezki and Schindler is that the Trump administration's willingness to (at least on the rhetorical level) question the role of the administrative state has the potential to shape significantly the form and content of environmental law. One need look no further than to the recent resignation of the administrator of the USA Environmental Protection Agency (EPA), Scott Pruitt, to appreciate that political cultures have real potential to alter the legal landscape and thereby also the dynamics of scholarship.

Against the politically volatile background of the Trump administration, the chapter by Krämer considers environmental law scholarship in the context of the European Union (EU). Unlike that the present situation in the USA, the EU has gained a reputation as a body polity which is willing to put in place comprehensive systems of environmental regulation. In light of this, Krämer's account of how relatively small a role environmental law scholars have played in shaping this extensive system of law might surprise some. Krämer's argument is of course not that there is no or little EU environmental law scholarship but that those scholars who have dedicated their attention to EU environmental law have often done so from the perspective of their own member states. Though there is evidence to suggest that the tendency for scholars to remain anchored in their own domestic context is waning,[13] Krämer highlights how it has nevertheless resulted in environmental law scholars yielding little influence over the form and content of EU environmental law. As Krämer argues, that is a shame considering the many environmental challenges facing the EU (notwithstanding its rich environmental law history).

Finally, against these different reflections on environmental law scholarship which, as noted, in a sense reflect the personal, jurisdictional and political circumstances of each scholar, it bears noting that the stocktaking exercise of this volume is not intended as a self-indulgent, self-aggrandising exercise of navel gazing, allowing scholars to reflect on the strength of their own work. Instead, the main purpose of this collection of essays is altogether more modestly to invite environmental law scholars and colleagues to pause and consider the scholarly practice and enterprise of environmental law scholarship. The main point is that such disciplinary self-subversion is 'while often experienced at first as traumatic, [it is also] eventually rewarding and enriching.'[14] With that in mind, it is the hope that this collection will aid such self-subversion.

---

[13] Most recently Suzanne Kingston, Veerle Heyvaert and Aleksandra Čavoški, *European Environmental Law* (Cambridge: Cambridge University Press, 2017) and Maria Lee, *EU Environmental Law* (Oxford: Bloomsbury, 2014).

[14] Albert O. Hirschman, *A Propensity to Self-Subversion* (Cambridge, MA: Harvard University Press, 1995) 91.

What Legal Scholarship Can Contribute to Environmental Law

TODD S. AAGAARD

Debates over environmental law and policy benefit from a variety of participants with differing perspectives. Active contributors to such debates include academics from other fields, government agencies, industry professionals, trade groups, advocacy organizations, and think tanks. Among this crowd, it may not be immediately clear what distinctive contributions legal scholars can make to advance conversations about environmental law. Legal academics generally lack the technical education and training of a scientist, economist, or engineer or the ongoing work experience of a practicing lawyer.

This chapter argues that legal academics have at least three key areas of comparative advantage with respect to environmental policy debates, and that the legal academy should foster scholarship that leverages these advantages. First, legal scholars make law the focal point of their analysis and so bring a more sophisticated understanding of individual laws as they operate in the context of broader legal systems. Second, whereas environmental law practice and policy debates often tend toward siloed analysis of discrete policy problems, environmental law scholarship is more conducive to integrative and crosscutting work. Third, environmental law scholarship is well poised to challenge methodological and ideological orthodoxies that stagnate policy innovation. The best environmental law scholarship exhibits these attributes, and environmental law scholars need to do more in their work to leverage these potential advantages.

I Comparative Advantages of Legal Academics

Scholars produce scholarship because we are driven to think and write – to contemplate the subjects of our research to almost obsessive extents and then to peddle our ruminations in the marketplace of ideas. That drive is why we become scholars in the first place and why most of us cannot imagine being anything but academics. But ultimately the value and worth of our scholarly endeavors depend on what we contribute to the collective understanding of the subjects we examine in our work.

When thinking about what legal scholarship can contribute to environmental law, environmental law scholars must consider that they are not the only ones thinking and writing about environmental law. Environmental law as a subject of research and analysis is clearly not the exclusive province of legal academics. This is true in at least two respects: work by nonlegal scholars and work by nonacademic lawyers. Legal scholarship focusing on environmental law contributes most when it focuses on work in which environmental law scholars have a comparative advantage versus academics from other disciplines and nonacademic lawyers.

A   Contributions of Nonlegal Scholars

Scholars and academics from disciplines other than law frequently write about environmental statutes and regulations.[1] The work of these nonlegal scholars contributes greatly to our collective understanding of environmental statutes and regulations. Such work may analyze, for example, the health impacts of regulation or the costs associated with regulatory compliance. The distinctive contribution of legal academics to environmental law is not, then, merely a focus on environmental law as a topic of scholarly research.

Indeed, looking at the work of scholars from other fields that examines environmental law, it may not be clear what legal scholars have to contribute. Generally a legal scholar is unlikely to have better insights into the economics of environmental policy than an economist, better insights into the public health aspects of environmental policy than a public health specialist, or better insights into the politics of environmental policy than a political scientist. To the extent that legal scholarship attempts to replicate the work of other disciplines, it is likely to be second rate to the contributions of specialists working within those

---

[1]   See, e.g., Jonathan M. Samet, "The Clean Air Act and Health – A Clearer View from 2011" (2011) 365 *New England Journal of Medicine* 198; David Lewis Clark, *Characterization of the Potential Hazards Associated with Potential RCRA Treatment Noncompliances* (OSTI Technical Report, 2015); Dallas Burtraw et al., "The Costs and Consequences of Clean Air Act Regulation of CO_2 from Power Plants" (2014) 104 *American Economic Review* 557.

fields. Legal scholarship, to be useful, must emphasize the distinctive contributions that lawyers can make to understanding law.

This is probably true of legal scholarship generally, but it is especially true of environmental law. Environmental law is highly technical. Some of its technical complexity is legal complexity, which lawyers and legal academics are well equipped and placed to address. But much of environmental law's technical complexity derives from its scientific, engineering, or economic underpinnings. For example, for many Environmental Protection Agency (EPA) regulations, the length of the codified regulatory standards themselves is far exceeded by the length of the technical appendices and guidance to the standards. The Clean Air Act's National Ambient Air Quality Standards comprise fewer than fifteen pages of the Code of Federal Regulations. The appendices to those standards, which explain how to measure ambient air quality for purposes of the standards, comprise 138 pages of the Code.[2] A different set of regulations filling 110 pages provides additional detailed instructions regarding the standards.[3] Even most lawyers who specialize in the Clean Air Act have little understanding of these technical specifications. Thus, the answer as to what environmental lawyers can contribute cannot be that we understand environmental law categorically better than other disciplines, because much of environmental law can only be understood through the expertise of other fields.

Our comparative advantage as lawyers is understanding law as law, not merely as policy. Most nonlegal commentators and academics engage with law only as policy – that is, as a course of action or set of outcomes decided upon by a government that then through its operation induces certain effects, some intended and some not. Reading a statute, regulation, or permit, they see a series of decisions made by regulators – for example, how much of a pollutant a factory can discharge into a river – with effects that are primarily contingent on the context in which they operate. Each field views that context somewhat differently, through the focus of its discipline – for example, an economist looks at how laws operate through the medium of economic systems, and an ecologist looks at how laws operate through the medium of ecological systems. Scientists thus see law as science policy, economists see law as economic policy, and so forth.

[2] 40 C.F.R. Part 50.
[3] 40 C.F.R. Part 53.

Lawyers, by contrast, understand that law operates first and foremost within a legal system. That legal system has certain intrinsic and extrinsic features that shape law's content, meaning, and subsequently its consequences. Lawyers understand that law acts and takes form in complicated ways, resulting in applications and effects in the real world that are unpredictable and hard to decipher for non-lawyers who are not trained and experienced in legal methods. Individual laws cannot be analyzed merely as isolated policies because they operate as components of a complex legal system.

Take, for example, the law's meaning. Attorneys constantly grapple with questions regarding the meaning of laws. To offer a specific example from environmental law, the Clean Water Act requires permits for discharges of pollutants to "navigable waters."[4] Accordingly, much rides on the meaning of the term "navigable waters" in this context.[5] Construing the term narrowly – and therefore the scope of the Clean Water Act narrowly as well – saves industries from the time and expense of obtaining permits but results in more water pollution. Construing the term more broadly has the opposite effect, increasing costs but reducing pollution. But clearly the task of interpreting the term "navigable waters" is something different from just making a policy decision regarding the appropriate balance of regulatory costs and benefits. Law is not just policy.

How, then, to construe the term "navigable waters" in the Clean Water Act? Does its meaning depend primarily on the dictionary definitions of "navigable" and "waters," on the historic legal interpretations of "navigable waters," on the legislative and regulatory history of the term "navigable waters" in the Clean Water Act, or on how different options for interpreting the term "navigable waters" influence the effectiveness of the Clean Water Act in achieving its objectives?

Moreover, the meaning of a term such as "navigable waters" must be discerned under conditions in which the relevant statutory provision was enacted by Congress against the backdrop of the common law and existing statutes, implemented and interpreted by multiple administrative agencies over time and in different forms, and interpreted by courts in numerous decisions according to interpretive canons and

---

[4] 33 USC § 1362 (12) (2012).

[5] See *Rapanos* v. *United States*, 547 US 715 (2006); *Solid Waste Agency of Northern Cook County (SWANCC)* v. *U.S. Army Corps of Engineers*, 531 US 159 (2001); *United States* v. *Riverside Bayview*, 474 US 121 (1985).

constitutional principles. In the meantime, Congress may have considered amending the statute several times.

How should interpretation of the term take all of this information into account? Which institutions should play what role in determining the meaning of the provision? Nonlegal disciplines tend neither to focus on such questions nor even to have appropriate methods of inquiry to engage in such analysis. Politics, science, and economics provide context for the policy debate over what the Clean Water Act should regulate, but the debate over the meaning of the statute's terms is fundamentally a legal question, for which training and experience in the law are crucially important. And the meaning of the law plays a formative role in determining its consequences.

Lawyers may not have definitive answers to the questions regarding the meaning of laws – the law is rife with indeterminacy – but they are well versed and familiar with methodological tools standard in legal analysis that can identify and address questions about meaning in the law. Lawyers can look at a legal principle or piece of statutory or regulatory text and see things – ambiguities, contingencies, interdependencies, implications – that others will not see.

At the same time that law offers distinctive methodological perspectives and insights on the questions it seeks to answer, it still relies heavily on contributions from other disciplines. Law is inherently interdisciplinary. Both lawyers and non-lawyers ultimately care about the law because of its consequences, and those consequences cannot be fully understood except through the contexts in which the law applies, which are formed as networks of interwoven political, economic, social, and scientific systems.

Law generally is interdisciplinary, and environmental law is even more so. Environmental law's interdisciplinarity is one of its more interesting, but also challenging, features. A mind-boggling variety of disciplines contribute to the base of knowledge and experience relevant to environmental law: medicine, public health, ecology, chemistry, physics, earth science, engineering, psychology, sociology, economics, political science, and public administration, among others. Law sits at the intersection of these other disciplines. To understand environmental law, we must understand how these other disciplines interact to form the context in which environmental law applies. Whether a national ambient air quality standard for nitrogen dioxide at the level of 100 parts per billion protects the public health with an adequate margin of safety as required by

Section 109 of the Clean Air Act is both a legal question and a public health question.[6]

Lawyers often play the role of translators – explaining the law to their clients in terms that their clients can understand, and explaining the situation of their clients to judges, legislatures, agencies, and other parties so that laws reflect an understanding and sensitivity to the context in which they operate. Legal academics can play similar roles in scholarly research as interdisciplinary translators, bringing to bear the insights of other disciplines on law in all of its complexity and as it actually applies in the real world, and explaining to scholars in other disciplines how the law works in practice.

B   Contributions of Nonacademic Lawyers

Legal academics are not unique in applying legal analysis to environmental law. Nonacademic lawyers also think and write insightfully about environmental law and policy. Government agencies, industry professionals, trade groups, citizen advocacy organizations, and think tanks all actively contribute to analyses of environmental law. Indeed, academics frequently rely on the work of these experts – briefs, government reports, and white papers – in their scholarly research.

Nonacademics have several advantages over legal academics. Nonacademics tend to have a particularly practice-based focus on the consequences of regulation. They analyze issues with an immediacy borne of proximity to their ongoing professional experience. They see from the inside what academics must try to observe from the outside – for example, how a business is likely to react to a more stringent regulatory standard. Nonacademics also have access to different information and perspectives than academics. They attend meetings with interest groups, they lobby government officials, and they respond to questions and comments from the public.

Nonacademics write to have an immediate impact on ongoing policy debates in which they actively participate. They distinguish, perhaps with some disdain, their work from work that addresses questions that are merely "academic." Thus, when an EPA lawyer crafts a preamble to a new final rule, the lawyer is not just writing to understand or to explain the new rule; rather, she is writing to decide what the rule means and to offer a reasoned justification that will be the basis for a court's judicial review

[6]   42 USC § 7409(b)(1) (2012).

of the rule. Similarly, an attorney authoring a General Accountability Office or Congressional Research Service report is writing to answer a question that has been posed to the agency by the legislators who draft the law. A practicing attorney's policy work is thus part of the lawmaking process itself, not just an outside observation.

But academics have their own advantages over nonacademics. An insider's position is not always the best perspective to gain the deepest insights. Whereas practicing lawyers are able to write from direct ongoing experience, academics have the important advantages of time and distance. Practicing lawyers work from tight deadline to tight deadline churning out work product tailored to their clients' specific problems and interests – a permit application, a brief, an opinion letter, an agreement. Everything in legal practice is about practical consequences. The close frame of analysis tends to generate a narrow and siloed analysis. The need to prevail on behalf of a client tends to constrain the range and originality of the practicing attorney's thinking.

Academics, by contrast, have the luxury of time to step back and think deeply and broadly about what they observe. An academic may ruminate on an idea for months or years before publishing any work on the topic. Academics choose their research topics, their methodological approaches, and their conclusions. Academics can look retrospectively at past developments to glean insights that apply to future developments. Academics can look toward the future.

Legal academics work in a markedly different ethical context than practicing lawyers do, in ways that give academics much broader discretion. This is not to say that one is more or less ethical than the other, but rather that their ethics point them in potentially different directions with their research. Ethical codes obligate attorneys to pursue the interests of their clients.[7] Even when free from a client's ethical imperative, a lawyer looking to keep her clients and attract new clients is unlikely to take public positions that undermine clients' and potential clients' interests. Legal academics, at least in their scholarly work and teaching, lack clients and therefore the ethical obligations that attach to clients. Legal academics owe their professional duties to pursuing truth and increasing knowledge.[8] Academics can also afford to be wrong, which allows them to take risks and argue positions that practicing attorneys cannot take

---

[7] *Evans v. Jeff D.*, 475 US 717, 728 (1986).

[8] This is not to claim that there is necessarily an objective and verifiable truth to be discovered. Rather, the idea of the pursuit of truth represents the law's ultimate objective to find the right or just answer to the question at hand, however one defines right or just.

without endangering their clients' interests. This difference – between an ethical obligation to the client and an ethical obligation to pursue truth – creates a strong distinction between the work of lawyers and the work of legal academics. That difference creates opportunities for legal academics to make contributions with their scholarship that would be unlikely from nonacademic lawyers.

In reality, the difference in ethical orientation between academics and attorneys may be somewhat less chasmic than it appears in principle. Practicing lawyers can and do engage in inquiry, debate, and commentary outside of the context of representing a client; in those roles, they are free to pursue inquiries and articulate views that do not necessarily reflect a client's interests.[9] And academics, although free from ethical constraints to clients, tend to have their own biases. They may have fixed underlying worldviews, viewpoints, and political orientations that guide their research. Some scholars may write to advance a political agenda and so either intentionally or subconsciously conform their research to positions and reasoning that advance a particular political cause. Incentives for academic research also may carry certain biases. Some viewpoints may be more popular than others. Journals and peers may prefer work that follows settled assumptions – or that upends such assumptions with novel positions. No one seeks the truth with completely unfettered inquiry, nor is the truth necessarily definitively discernible. That said, legal scholars undeniably stand in a different position ethically with respect to their analysis of law – with much more freedom and independence – than do practicing lawyers with clients to represent.

At its best, academic scholarship is deeply open minded and rewards searching analysis. The essence of academic research is a willingness to subject everything to critical inquiry. This places academics in a position to challenge orthodoxies and settled assumptions. Even as among academics generally, legal academics are in a particularly strong position to challenge orthodox thinking, in both law and other disciplines, because the training and experience of lawyers encourage them to question and to look for flaws in lines of reasoning.

Legal academics should demand more exacting methodological standards than nonacademics for their scholarly work. Outside of ethical constraints, a practicing lawyer's commitment to a method of analysis is

---

[9] See Restatement (Third) of the Law Governing Lawyers § 125 cmt. e (2000) ("In general, a lawyer may publicly take personal positions on controversial issues without regard to whether the positions are consistent with those of some or all of the lawyer's clients.").

largely instrumental to the lawyer's goal in the particular matter. It is perfectly appropriate for an attorney to adopt a position or method of analysis in one case that is at odds with the same attorney's position or analysis in another case. Although trained and experienced in the adversary system, attorneys can sometimes find strategic advantage in concealing their underlying assumptions and premises or their logical leaps. Academics should be committed to the integrity of their methods, an objective best effectuated by maintaining scrupulous transparency in their assumptions, their methods of inquiry, and the steps in their logical reasoning. Scholarship should confess its potential weaknesses in service of the overall advancement of knowledge. It will undoubtedly fall short of that demanding objective, but it can distinguish itself from nonacademic work merely by achieving moderate success in this regard.

C   Distinctive Role of Legal Academics

Environmental law scholars contribute most to environmental law when they leverage their comparative advantages over academics from other fields and nonacademic attorneys. Lawyers enjoy advantages over scholars from other fields: an ability to understand law as it operates within legal systems, and an ability to integrate insights and methods from multiple perspectives and disciplines. There also are advantages that legal academics enjoy over practicing attorneys – most notably, an ability to challenge orthodox thinking and generate new ideas. Environmental law scholarship should focus on work that exhibits these features.

Examining some select pieces of environmental law scholarship, we can see some of the attributes that distinguish it from contributions of nonacademics and academics from other disciplines. Each of these works has added significantly to our collective understanding of environmental law, in ways that are difficult to imagine coming from somewhere other than legal scholarship. The following examples are merely illustrative. Although they are written by well-respected scholars and widely read, they are not intended as a list of the best environmental law scholarship, and there are many other examples that could have been included.

Christopher Stone's classic 1972 article "Should Trees Have Standing?" written early in the history of modern American environmental law provocatively argues that legal rights, including standing to bring suit, should be extended to the natural environment itself.[10] Traditionally the law protects the environment only by protecting the rights of people who hold public or private interests in the environment. Stone builds a case that the natural environment is not so different from other "in-animate rights-holders" previously recognized by law, such as trusts, corporations, partnerships, governments, and ships.[11] Because natural objects cannot represent themselves, Stone advocates using guardianship-type relationships to allow humans to advocate on behalf of nature. Stone acknowledges that extending legal rights to nature runs contrary to centuries of legal precedent but compares his argument to prior innovations that have extended legal rights to previous unrecognized interests such as the right of citizenship to African Americans, the right of Chinese persons to testify against white men in criminal matters, and the rights of Jews in thirteenth-century Europe.

Stone's article exemplifies scholarly work that leverages the comparative advantages of a legal scholar. By his account, his idea originated spontaneously while teaching a first-year Property course.[12] He developed the idea into a law review article that analyzes legal precedent in detail but also draws on diverse sources such as Charles Darwin, W. E. B. DuBois, David Hume, J. L. Austin, and Arthur Schopenhauer. But Stone's work also has a strong practical orientation. His article, in addition to explaining his general theory as to why the natural environment should have legal rights, propounds specific prescriptions for how to grant legal rights to nature – for example, by allowing the recovery of damages that would be placed in trust funds. Stone also specifically chose to highlight his theory's application to a pending Supreme Court case, and he targeted publication of his article so that it would be read by Justice William O. Douglas – the Court's foremost environmentalist – while the case was still pending in the Court. Justice Douglas went on to adopt Stone's theory in his dissent in the case, citing Stone's article.[13]

In his 1999 article, "Taking Slippage Seriously," Dan Farber examines the gap between the facial requirements of regulatory standards and how

---

[10] Christopher D. Stone, "Should Trees Have Standing? – Toward Legal Rights for Natural Objects" (1972) 45 *Southern California Law Review* 450. Stone subsequently expanded the article into a book. Christopher D. Stone, *Should Trees Have Standing?: Law, Morality, and the Environment* 3rd edn (Oxford: Oxford University Press, 2010).

[11] Stone, "Should Trees Have Standing?" p. 452.

[12] Ibid. xi–xii.

[13] See *Sierra Club* v. *Morton*, 405 US 727, 742 (1972).

regulated parties actually behave, which he calls slippage.[14] Farber notes
that most environmental scholarship focuses exclusively on regulatory
standards, neglecting the more important matter of how regulated parties
act, which determines the actual consequences of environmental laws.
Noncompliance is pervasive, Farber contends, but most analyses of
regulatory programs are premised on assumptions of full compliance.
For example, he notes that in light of slippage, the actual costs and
benefits of a regulatory program may differ substantially from the costs
and benefits of the program under conditions of full compliance, which is
generally assumed for such analyses.

Richard Lazarus's 2004 book, *The Making of Environmental Law*, provides a conceptual account of environmental law as the law's response to
the vexing policy problem of ecological injury. Ecological systems are
complex and dynamic. Ecological injuries can be irreversible, nonlinear,
catastrophic, exponential, persistent, or latent. These characteristics make
it often difficult to determine definitive cause-and-effect relationships.
Environmental law must address complexity, uncertainty, dynamism,
precaution, and controversy. The institutional structure of our governments and the nature of our political systems are in important respects ill
suited to meeting such challenges. Despite these obstacles, environmental
regulation has become entrenched in the American legal system and
persistent despite repeated political attacks, because the public has supported it. Over time, the loosely associated collection of statutes that
comprise environmental law have come to exhibit a core commonality
built around certain key components, including broad delegations of
authority to administrative agencies, permit programs, and regulatory
standards derived from a balance of health- and technology-based factors.

Although historical in its analysis, Lazarus does not offer a detailed
factual recitation of historical events. Instead, he provides an explanation
of environmental law's history based on a conceptual analysis of the
context in which environmental law operates and how that context
poses challenges for effective lawmaking to address environmental problems. Lazarus does not analyze from the perspective of ecology, medicine, economics, or political science, although he draws on insights from
each of those fields. Lazarus methodically builds a theoretical framework
for understanding environmental law as a legal system formed in

[14] Daniel A. Farber, "Taking Slippage Seriously: Noncompliance and Creative Compliance
in Environmental Law" (1999) 23 *Harvard Environmental Law Review* 297.

response to its nonlegal context but not wholly determined by that context.

Ann Carlson's 2009 article, "Iterative Federalism and Climate Change," offers a novel and insightful explanation for why and how states have taken affirmative steps to regulate climate change despite the strong economic disincentives to do so.[15] Carlson notes that states seeking to address climate change face a classic collective action problem: any particular state that attempts to regulate climate change bears the full costs of regulation; however, because climate change is a global problem, the benefits of reduced greenhouse gas emissions are globally dispersed. To explain why states nevertheless embark on climate change regulatory initiatives, Carlson explains that state climate change initiatives are not solely the product of state law. Rather, such initiatives arise within a federal regulatory framework under the Clean Air Act that authorizes a state or group of states to regulate subject to certain conditions. Thus, either the federal government or states take regulatory action, triggering a response by the other. Carlson calls this process iterative federalism, which she argues has encouraged and allowed useful regulatory experimentation that to some extent offers the benefits of both devolution and centralization, thereby transcending some of the federalism debates in environmental law.

A 2014 article by Professors Eric Biber and J. B. Ruhl proposed a conceptual framework for understanding administrative permit programs.[16] Administrative permits are ubiquitous in modern regulatory programs such as the Clean Water Act and the Clean Air Act, yet little if any scholarship analyzes the power of permitting generally. Biber and Ruhl offer an analysis that explains how permitting fits conceptually with other common regulatory tools such as exemptions and prohibitions. Permits fit within a continuum that spans from regulatory exemptions to general permits to specific permits to regulatory prohibitions. Biber and Ruhl examine the choice in designing a permit program between general permits and specific permits, a choice that requires lawmakers to balance the risk of harm from the regulated activity against the burden of transaction costs the permitting program imposes.

In his 2015 article, "Going the Way of the Dodo: De-extinction, Dualisms, and Reframing Conservation," Alejandro Camacho uses the

[15] Ann E. Carlson, "Iterative Federalism and Climate Change" (2009) 103 *Northwestern Law Review* 109.
[16] Eric Biber & J. B. Ruhl, "The Permit Power Revisited: The Theory and Practice of Regulatory Permits in the Administrative State" (2014) 64 *Duke Law Journal* 133.

emerging concept of "de-extinction" to illustrate problems that can arise when environmental law relies on simplified categorization.[17] De-extinction involves reviving extinct species – or approximations of extinct species – through selective breeding or biotechnological processes. As the technology of de-extinction becomes more viable, scholars have begun thinking about how existing conservation laws might govern de-extinction efforts. Camacho shows how the potentially applicable conservation laws rely on dualistic categorization that does not reflect the complex realities of a deeply human-impacted biosphere in the Anthropocene period. Conservation laws adopt a goal of protecting the natural from the unnatural, a dichotomy that assumes the existence of distinctions between humans and nature and between native and invasive species. But the reality is that humans have affected ecological processes to an extent that the boundaries between these categories are more porous than the conservation laws assume. As a result, conservation laws might well prohibit many de-extinction projects on the basis that they require a level of human involvement that renders them unnatural and nonnative. Camacho argues that wildlife management laws should reject simplistic dualities in favor of more nuanced approaches that base management decisions on how an action is likely to impact ecological health.

Jody Freeman's 2017 article, "The Uncomfortable Convergence of Energy and Environmental Law," examines the relationship between federal energy law and environmental law.[18] Traditionally energy law and environmental law have been quite different and separate fields. The Federal Energy Regulatory Commission (FERC) and the EPA have different policy goals, different statutes, different stakeholder groups, different Senate oversight committees, and different agency cultures. Noting that other legal scholars have advocated a convergence of energy and environmental law and have identified positive signs that such a convergence may be starting, Freeman strikes a more cautionary and skeptical tone. To the extent energy law and environmental law have become somewhat more complementary, Freeman argues, this has come as a coincidental development rather than a purposeful move by Congress, the president, or the agencies toward a consolidated approach. These changes are unlikely to continue unimpeded in light of the deeply

---

[17] Alejandro E. Camacho, "Going the Way of the Dodo: De-extinction, Dualisms, and Reframing Conservation" (2015) 92 *Washington University Law Review* 849.

[18] Jody Freeman, "The Uncomfortable Convergence of Energy and Environmental Law" (2017) 41 *Harvard Environmental Law Review* 339.

entrenched differences between FERC and EPA. Freeman's analysis adds deeper institutional context to the understanding of the FERC-EPA relationship and why it is likely to "remain stubbornly separate, at least for now."[19]

Each of these works substantially contributes to our understanding of environmental law by making important observations about topics that are central to the field. In doing so, they find innovative insights in a variety of areas. Some of these areas, such as environmental federalism, are well worn. Others, such as slippage and permitting power, are long neglected. Still others, such as de-extinction, are new altogether.

It is difficult to imagine anyone other than a lawyer writing any of these articles. Each of them has law as its focal point of analysis. Even the most theoretical of the works – such as Stone's argument for giving legal rights to the natural environment, Lazarus's conceptualization of environmental law, or Biber and Ruhl's permitting power framework – burrows deeply into the law. It is only by engaging directly with law that these scholars can see the nuances of law in all of its complexity and interdependencies, such as Carlson's analysis of state climate change regulation, Freeman's examination of differences between energy statutes and environmental statutes, or Camacho's analysis of how conservation statutes might govern de-extinction.

It is equally difficult to imagine anyone other than an academic writing any of these works. Each of these scholars clearly thought deeply and creatively about the topic, unmoored to a particular case or problem of a client. The questions these scholars are answering cut deeper and wider than the issue presented in a case or even the topic of a policy white paper. This breadth and depth enable the scholars to see patterns that transcend specific legal issues, such as Carlson's theory of iterative federalism, Freeman's skepticism toward an energy-environment convergence, and Camacho's critique of dualisms. All of the works generate policy implications, but those implications are derived from broader normative insights that form the author's core theses. The authors are not writing simply to argue a position on a policy issue.

Collectively, these articles and books illustrate key characteristics of scholarship that leverages the comparative advantages of legal academics. First, as already noted, each work makes law the focus of its analysis and analyzes law in the context of the complex legal system that determines

---

[19] Freeman, "The Uncomfortable Convergence of Energy and Environmental Law," 346.

its meaning and therefore its effects. These scholars see law as law, not merely as policies.

Second, the works are integrative and crosscutting. They think broadly, as broadly as the entire field of environmental law in the case of Lazarus, or environmental law and energy law in the case of Freeman. Even when they appear narrow, such as Camacho's examination of how conservation laws would govern de-extinction or Carlson's study of state climate change regulation, they end up being about much more – the downsides of dualisms for Camacho and the process of iterative federalism for Carlson.

Third, these works use their analyses to challenge entrenched assumptions in legal practice – for example, that only people can have standing, that federalism is an either/or allocation of power, or that regulated parties comply with environmental standards as written. It is precisely because academics frame issues differently and approach them differently that they are able to generate new insights not noticed by nonacademics. The open-mindedness of the academic perspective allows creativity, risk taking, and originality in thinking. Stone's argument for conferring legal rights on the natural environment exemplifies such thinking, but all of the works exhibit innovative insights that would be difficult to replicate in nonacademic work.

II   Reason for Caution

As academics, we enjoy a special position and ability to contribute to policy discussions by virtue of the unique place academics occupy in society. Academics have the time, perspective, and freedom to pursue inquiries that nonacademics will not. These inquiries generate insights that other, nonacademic work will not generate. We thus have every right, and indeed an obligation for the greater good, to add our views to policy debates. But one of the paradoxes of the position of academics is that when we participate as advocates, we tend to develop vested interests. In developing these vested interests, we to some extent endanger our special position as academics. The credibility of our advocacy depends on that special position – for example, whether it appears that we followed facts to their conclusion, rather than reverse engineered and found facts to support the conclusion we chose first. There is no easy answer to this dilemma between scholarship and policy advocacy, and so it requires constant diligence.

Many of the best environmental law academics are actively engaged in nonacademic work that gives them some of the perspective and immediacy to the issues that practicing lawyers have. Academics brief and argue cases in the courts, serve on the boards of corporations and nonprofit organizations, work temporarily in government positions, write comments on proposed regulations, and advise clients. Such work is valuable and should be encouraged in the profession. But it also poses a risk to academics, because it can erode some of the comparative advantages that come with an academic position. The academic, although not neutral, comes to her scholarly work without a predefined role. This freedom and independence allow us to bring a unique perspective to our research. The more we engage in nonacademic work, the more we endanger that perspective and associate ourselves with a role or viewpoint. It is in everyone's interest for us academics to retain the comparative advantages we enjoy – not just for our own good, although the position is an enviable one for those so inclined, but also to be able to retain the unique and invaluable perspective that an academic can contribute through her scholarly research.

Bibliography

Biber, Eric & Ruhl, J. B., "The Permit Power Revisited: The Theory and Practice of Regulatory Permits in the Administrative State" (2014) 64 *Duke Law Journal* 133.

Camacho, Alejandro E., "Going the Way of the Dodo: De-extinction, Dualisms, and Reframing Conservation" (2015) 92 *Washington University Law Review* 849.

Carlson, Ann E., "Iterative Federalism and Climate Change" (2009) 103 *Northwestern Law Review* 109.

Farber, Daniel A., "Taking Slippage Seriously: Noncompliance and Creative Compliance in Environmental Law" (1999) 23 *Harvard Environmental Law Review* 297.

Freeman, Jody, "The Uncomfortable Convergence of Energy and Environmental Law" (2017) 41 *Harvard Environmental Law Review* 339.

Stone, Christopher D., *Should Trees Have Standing?: Law, Morality, and the Environment*, 3rd edn (Oxford: Oxford University Press, 2010).

Back to Basics: Thinking About the Craft
of Environmental Law Scholarship

ELIZABETH FISHER

Being an environmental law scholar is a frenetic business. The changing state of environmental laws in different jurisdictions keeps us busy,[1] as do the multiple methodological and theoretical approaches to the subject.[2] There are also different and changing institutional expectations – we are encouraged to have 'impact beyond academia',[3] to be published in certain places, and/or to have a significant Altmetric number.[4] It can also be unclear who the specific audience is for any particular publication. Given all this it is easy for environmental law scholars to be confused about what it is we should be doing. Or more specifically, to figure out when we are doing our job well.

In this piece, I go back to basics. My starting point is that environmental law scholarship is a form of expertise.[5] Specifically, the expertise of environmental law scholars, like the expertise of all scholars, should be understood as a craft expertise. By that I mean it is a body of expertise focused on producing scholarship that is driven forth by 'the desire to do

I would like to thank Randall Stephenson for the outstanding research assistance he provided to this project and to Sanja Bogojevic, Ole Pedersen, Eloise Scotford, and Steven Vaughan for comments on a previous draft. Any errors or omissions are my own.

[1] Elizabeth Fisher et al., 'Maturity and Methodology: Starting a Debate about Environmental Law Scholarship' (2009) 21 *Journal of Environmental Law* 213 at 228–231.

[2] Andreas Philippopoulos-Mihalopoulos and Victoria Brooks (eds.), *Research Methods in Environmental Law: A Handbook* (Cheltenham: Edward Elgar, 2017).

[3] This, for example, is one of the features of the current Research Excellence Framework in the UK. See www.ref.ac.uk/about/whatref/.

[4] Altmetric, www.altmetric.com.

[5] I began to do this in Elizabeth Fisher, 'The Rise of Transnational Environmental Law and the Expertise of Environmental Lawyers' (2012) 1 *Transnational Environmental Law* 43; Elizabeth Fisher, 'Climate Change Litigation, Obsession and Expertise: Reflecting on the Scholarly Response to Massachusetts v EPA' (2013) 39 *Law and Policy* 236; and Elizabeth Fisher, 'Making Sense of the WTO Sanitary and Phyto Sanitary Agreement: An Essay About Scholarly Expertise' in Bettina Lange, Fiona Haines and Dania Thomas (eds.), *Regulatory Transformations: Rethinking Economy-Society Interactions* (Oxford: Hart Publishing, 2015).

a job well for its own sake'.[6] Understanding this highlights a number of important features of what environmental law scholars do, which I explore in Sections 2–4: scholarship takes place within an institutional context, it is focused on the materials that scholars work with, and a major challenge is learning to use 'obsessive energy well'.[7]

Three points should be made before starting. First, like all articulations of good scholarship or good method, my argument has a normative dimension. In my description of what is, there is a promotion of what ought to be. Second, I make no pretence to have mastered environmental law scholarship. I developed the idea of craft to help me in my own struggles with developing my own expertise. The point about the discussion here is not that it provides a neat checklist of how to 'write a scholarly article in ten days or less' (or something equally preposterous), but rather it provides a framework for how to think through the tasks and challenges involved in environmental law scholarship. Third, I refer to examples of what I see as paradigms of good environmental law scholarship throughout this piece. These references are not exhaustive. My general point is that there is much to admire in the general state of environmental law scholarship. Or to put the matter another way, there are many examples of environmental law scholars doing their job well.

1 Environmental Law Scholarship as Craft Expertise

This chapter is about scholarly expertise, but ideas of scholarly expertise are relatively alien to environmental law scholars. They are rarely used to discuss what we do. Rather, the vocabulary of method and methodology dominates discussion. These are 'skills' that we as scholars are told we must master. Not surprisingly some scholars rankle against this characterisation.[8] It is also the case that environmental law is not a subject that yields easily to the traditional lines of scholarly analysis. Much of that is to do with the polycentric, scientifically uncertain, dynamic, and controversial nature of many environmental problems that results in much environmental law being novel, legislative based, and cutting across existing legal orders in a variety of different ways.[9]

---

[6] Richard Sennett, *The Craftsman* (London: Allen Lane, 2008), 9.

[7] Ibid. 243.

[8] Paul Kahn, 'Freedom and Method' in Rob van Gestel, Hans-W Micklitz, and Edward Rubin (eds.), *Rethinking Legal Scholarship: A Transatlantic Dialogue* (Cambridge: Cambridge University Press, 2016).

[9] Elizabeth Fisher, 'Environmental Law as "Hot" Law' (2013) 25 *Journal of Environmental Law* 347.

Individual environmental law scholars have had to develop their own methodological toolkit, tailored specifically to particular environmental problems. The multi-scalar nature of climate change[10] requires a different set of research and scholarly methods from a study of environmental adjudication.[11]

This state of affairs is one of the reasons why there is a lot of soul searching on the part of environmental law scholars. A decade ago, I contributed to an article, 'Maturity and Methodology: Starting a Debate about Environmental Law Scholarship'.[12] The catalyst for the article was the perception of environmental law scholars that the subject had 'never grown up'. After charting many of the intricacies of the subject, one of our conclusions was the need for environmental law scholars to think more about their method.[13] Our hope was this conclusion would liberate and empower environmental law scholars – liberate them from unrealistic expectations about the subject's maturity and empower them to embrace the sheer complexity of the subject.

In particular, one conclusion was that scholars should find solace in the need to develop their methodological repertoire.[14] The danger with this conclusion is that it can give the impression that environmental law scholars are perceived as just stockpiling an inventory of different research techniques – a bit of empirical research here, a scattering of theoretical analysis there, and some decent old-fashioned doctrinal inquiry for good measure. While that has its merits, it also carries with it the risk that it undermines the broader point we were making – the need to develop a critical and self-reflective discourse about environmental law scholarship. In particular, it can emasculate what we saw as an important feature of any discourse – the need to have a discussion about quality.[15] Poor scholarship is often the product of the formulaic application of a method,[16] and no method is 'immune to poor applications'.[17]

[10] Hari Osofsky, 'The Geography of Climate Change Litigation Part II: Narratives of Massachusetts v. EPA' (2008) 8 *Chicago Journal of International Law* 573.

[11] Ceri Warnock, 'Reconceptualising Specialist Environment Courts and Tribunals' (2017) *Legal Studies* 391.

[12] Fisher and others, 'Maturity and Methodology'.

[13] Ibid. 226, 244, 246.

[14] Ibid. 244–245.

[15] Ibid. 248–249.

[16] Amy Poteete, Marco Janssen, and Elinor Ostrom, *Working Together: Collective Action, the Commons, and Multiple Methods in Practice* (Princeton, NJ: Princeton University Press, 2010), 3–4.

[17] Ibid. 4.

The inherent methodological pluralism of legal scholarship[18] – there are many research techniques in the study of law – reinforces this perception of environmental law scholarly method having a pick-and-mix quality. As does the way in which methodology is taught as a set of 'skills' to be 'trained in' as part of doctoral programmes. As Steven Vaughan has recently argued, there is a need for a deeper and more reflective approach to scholarly method in the environmental law sphere.[19] Vaughan is right, and he is not alone in arguing this.[20]

Any deeper approach requires the contextualising of our research method. Methods are being deployed as part of the wider scholarly practice of environmental law scholarship. That practice, while it can take different forms, is a form of expertise. It requires the development of skills, experience, and knowledge that others do not have. Some of this is explicit (explainable) and some of it is tacit (difficult to explain, intuitive).[21] Expertise is something that is gained by learning over time through frames for learning and assessing expertise.[22] Milestones mark the acquiring of expertise. Some may be formal – the gaining of the PhD or the awarding of the title of professor. Other may be more semi-formal – the acceptance of work for publication for example.

As Collins and Evans state, the acquisition of expertise is a 'social process – a process of socialization into the practices of an expert group', and, as a result, individuals gain expertise by 'social immersion' in groups that possess an expertise.[23] Expertise is not a free-floating 'thing', but a concept that only gains substantive meaning embedded in social practices that delineate what knowledge, skills, and experience count as

---

[18] Christopher McCrudden, 'Legal Research and the Social Sciences' (2006) 122 *Law Quarterly Review* 632.

[19] Steven Vaughan, '"The Law Is My Data": The Socio-Legal in Environmental Law' OUP Blog, 4 September 2017, https://blog.oup.com/2017/09/socio-legal-in-environmental-law/.

[20] Eloise Scotford, *Environmental Principles and the Evolution of Environmental Law* (Oxford: Bloomsbury, 2017).

[21] Harry Collins, *Tacit and Explicit Knowledge* (Chicago: University of Chicago Press, 2010).

[22] Elizabeth Fisher, 'Expert Executive Power, Administrative Constitutionalism and Co-Production: Why They Matter' in Maria Weimer and Anniek de Ruijter (eds.), *Regulating Risks in the European Union: The Co-production of Expert and Executive Power* (Oxford: Bloomsbury, 2017).

[23] Harry Collins and Robert Evans, *Rethinking Expertise* (Chicago: University of Chicago Press, 2007), 3.

expertise.[24] Scholarship is not pure thought, but also about day-to-day practice within particular contexts.[25]

The expertise of environmental law scholars like all social practices can be understood in different ways.[26] Any particular form of environmental law scholarly expertise is not a given. Choices can be made. If we (and there is a question of who the 'we' is) want environmental law scholarly expertise to be skills, knowledge, and experience focused on collating environmental laws and nothing more, environmental law scholarly expertise can take that form. Furthermore, behind every discussion of expertise is a theory of expertise. To be blunt, behind our plea for scholarly reflection in 'Maturity and Methodology' was a normative theory of the expertise of environmental law scholars. The nature of that theory can best be seen by scrutinising our definition of legal scholarship which we took from David Feldman.[27] Feldman was writing explicitly against a 'scientific' understanding of scholarly expertise.[28] He was dismissing the notion that legal scholarship was objective, although he did recognise that legal scholarship did adhere to certain 'formal values'.[29] Feldman stated:

> I define scholarship as action informed by a distinctive attitude of mind . . . Legal scholarship is a conception which results from the application of the concept of scholarship to the special kinds of problems that are discovered in the study of laws and legal systems.[30]

He defined that 'attitude of mind' in the following way:

> Scholarship is . . . guided by certain ideals, which distinguishes scholarship both from the single-minded pursuit of an end and from dilettantism . . . The ideals include: (1) a commitment to employing methods of investigation and analysis best suited to satisfying that curiosity; (2) self-conscious and reflective open-mindedness, so that one does not assume the desired result and adopt procedures to verify it, or even pervert one's material to support a chosen conclusion; and (3) the desire

[24] Expert Group on Science and Governance, *Taking European Knowledge Society Seriously* (Brussels: European Commission, 2007), 79.
[25] Steven Shapin, *Never Pure* (Baltimore, MD: Johns Hopkins University Press, 2010), 5.
[26] On ideas of expertise as a social practice, see Sheila Jasanoff, 'Serviceable Truths: Science for Action in Law and Policy' (2015) 93 *Texas Law Review* 1723.
[27] Fisher and others, 'Maturity and Methodology', 216.
[28] David Feldman, 'The Nature of Legal Scholarship' (1989) 52 *Modern Law Review* 498, 499–502.
[29] Ibid. 498.
[30] Ibid. 502.

to publish the work for the illumination of students, fellow scholars or the general public and enable others to evaluate and criticise it.[31]

Feldman also noted:

> What is important is how one behaves. A degree of rigour; an open minded, self-critical attitude to one's work; careful research; careful thought; careful clear writing up; these are the essence of scholarship, in law as in other disciplines.[32]

There are three things to note about this discussion. The first is that there is a particular job that Feldman is identifying that legal scholars do – 'the desire to publish the work for the illumination of students, fellow scholars or the general public and enable others to evaluate and criticise it'. While the audience may vary, the end result is legal scholarship. Second, Feldman's other two ideals are all about the process of production – scholarship is not just information but something shaped by intellectual activity – the application of method, self-reflection, and a desire to write something that 'illuminates'. Third, integral to that process of production is behaviour.

My view is that Feldman's characterisation of legal scholarly expertise is as a form of craft expertise. Feldman is arguing that the process of production is, and should be, driven forth by a sense of craftsmanship. As Sennett notes: 'craftsmanship names an enduring, basic human impulse, the desire to do a job well for its own sake.'[33] Thus the craft of legal scholarship is about the desire to carry out the process of doing scholarship well. Environmental law scholarship, to use Sennett's phraseology, is 'quality driven work'.[34] The idea of legal scholarship as a craft is not new to legal scholarship; in particular, it is inherent in Llewellyn's ideas of legal reasoning as a form of craft.[35] He saw craft as 'an organised, persisting body of skills and men to get some line of work done'.[36]

---

[31] Ibid. 503.

[32] Ibid. 508.

[33] Sennett, *The Craftsman*, 9.

[34] Ibid. 24.

[35] Karl Llewellyn, 'My Philosophy of Law' in Julius Rosenthal Foundation for General Law (ed.), *My Philosophy of Law: Credos of Sixteen American Scholars* (FB Rothman, 1941); Karl Llewellyn, 'The Crafts of Law Re-Valued' (1942) 28 *American Bar Association Journal* 801. See also Llewellyn, 'Law in Our Society' included as an Appendix in William Twining, *Karl Llewellyn and the Realist Movement* (London: Weidenfeld and Nicolson, 1973), 505–512.

[36] From his manuscript *Law in Our Society* which was published as an Appendix in Twining, *Karl Llewellyn and the Realist Movement* [2.1.1].

All well and good you may be thinking, but what does this actually mean for environmental law scholarship? Is this just a hipster way of describing what we do? It is a fair point. But here it is important to remember that the idea of craft is not just a descriptor; it denotes a set of practices that delineate a field of expertise. Thinking of environmental law scholarship as a form of craft expertise highlights a number of important features of environmental law scholarship which bear directly on method. I consider the most fundamental three here: institutional context, the importance of the material scholars work with, and 'learning to use obsessive energy well'. By scrutinising each of these, a clearer picture of the expertise of environmental law scholars emerges and thus an understanding of what it is we are doing and what we should be doing. As will also become clear, there is a relationship between these different aspects of craft expertise.

2   Institutions

Any expertise, no matter how it is understood, operates within institutional contexts. This is one consequence of its being a social practice. Those contexts will shape processes of gaining expertise. They will create yardsticks for prioritising and assessing scholarship.[37] They determine who our audiences are and why we are seeking to illuminate them through our scholarship. Given that scholarship is the fostering of expertise over time and the production of work can be over many years, the influence of institutional contexts has longevity.[38] Likewise, the longevity of expertise depends on its relationship with its institutional context. The more 'sociable' expertise is, the more skills are shared and fostered, the more likely it can be sustained over time.[39] In this regard, 'anyone pursuing knowledge will have to balance two different models of social life: individualism and communitarianism.'[40] Training and practice do not operate in isolation but within cultures and contexts.[41] Institutional context is easy to forget. As I noted earlier, scholarly method is often treated as 'technical' and as such 'kettled' off from the rest of

[37] Feldman, 'The Nature of Legal Scholarship', 508.
[38] Aaron Wildasky, *Craftways: On the Organisation of Scholarly Work*, 2nd enlarged edn (New Brunswick: Transaction Publishers, 1993), 5–6.
[39] Sennett, *The Craftsman*, 246.
[40] Feldman, 'The Nature of Legal Scholarship', 507.
[41] Michele Lamont, *How Professors Think: Inside the Curious World of Academic Judgment* (Cambridge, MA: Harvard University Press, 2009).

society.[42] While it is tempting to see any academic discipline in a thin sense as a vocabulary or as a positivistic body of knowledge,[43] disciplines are far more culturally 'thick'.[44] A discipline is a community and a social practice.[45]

Arguing this is not to argue that disciplines do not produce authoritative knowledge, but rather to understand that disciplines are sustained and operate through institutions. Institutions also delineate the yardsticks by which the quality of work will be assessed. In regards to environmental law as a scholarly discipline, the gaining, assessing, and operating of that expertise is done primarily through higher education institutions. What that practically means will vary between jurisdictions, but generally speaking we understand environmental law scholarship as part of the study of *law* in universities.[46]

One important implication of this is that the expertise that environmental lawyers are developing primarily contributes to law and legal discourses. It can do so in many different ways. Scholarship can illuminate understanding in relation to teaching, theory, practice, and research for example. But the bottom line is how the expertise of environmental lawyers directly relates to law. That is not to say that other types of expertise are not needed. Environmental law is inherently interdisciplinary.[47] The law cannot be understood without understanding the problems it applies to.[48] But the expertise needed to interact with other disciplines is distinct. In particular, there is no expectation that environmental law scholarship will directly relate or contribute to those other disciplines.[49]

---

[42] Theodore Porter, 'How Science Became Technical' (2009) 100 *Isis* 292; Elizabeth Fisher, 'Sciences, Environmental Laws, and Legal Cultures: Fostering Collective Epistemic Responsibility' in Jorges Viñuales and Emma Lees (eds.), *The Oxford Handbook of Comparative Environmental Law* (Oxford: Oxford University Press, forthcoming).

[43] Jerome Kagan, *The Three Cultures: Natural Sciences, Social Sciences, and the Humanities in the 21st Century* (Cambridge: Cambridge University Press, 2009).

[44] Fiona Cownie, *Legal Academics: Culture and Identity* (Oxford: Hart Publishing, 2004); Andrew Abbott, *The System of Professions: An Essay in the Division of Expert Labor* (Chicago: University of Chicago Press, 1988); and Lamont, *How Professors Think*.

[45] Sennett, *The Craftsman*, 58–65.

[46] It of course may have a vexed relationship with mainstream legal study. See Fisher and others, 'Maturity and Methodology', 221–223.

[47] Gavin Little, 'Developing Legal Scholarship: Going Beyond the Legal Space' (2016) 36 *Legal Studies* 48; Ole Pedersen, 'The Limits of Interdisciplinarity and the Practice of Environmental Law Scholarship' (2014) 26 *Journal of Environmental Law* 423.

[48] Fisher, 'Environmental Law as "Hot" Law'.

[49] I say 'directly' because the practice of law will indirectly have an influence. See Jasanoff, 'Serviceable Truths'. This also informs her critique of Collins and Evans. See

Understanding the importance of institutions for environmental law scholarly expertise highlights three important aspects of that expertise that need to be fostered. First, environmental law scholars need to have an understanding of the institutional contexts they are operating in and the specific institutional contexts other environmental law scholars are working in. Those contexts will delineate what is expected of their scholarship and thus what is understood as possible forms and lines of scholarship. This understanding needs to be of a questioning sort. Not all yardsticks that academics are assessed by further the values articulated by Feldman.[50] A higher Altmetric number does not necessarily ensure that anyone was illuminated. True, institutional self-reflection can get self-indulgent and it is not the primary focus of scholarship; but without having a critical awareness of institutional context, it is easy to lose focus on what we should be doing. It also becomes impossible to engage in constructive discourses that focus on improving scholarship.[51]

Second, emphasising institutional and community context also emphasises communicating with an audience. As Feldman notes; 'the communication of ideas is one of the innate goods, or part of the inner morality, of scholarship.'[52] If scholars are not effectively communicating with their audience, then they are not illuminating their audience. Given the diversity, complexity, and novelty of much environmental law and the many theoretical and conceptual issues it raises for legal thinking, the question of communication is a fraught one. Trying to find the words and the ideas to explain things is challenging. Writing about environmental law is an expertise in its own right. It involves developing skills and experience in how to express things *and* how to structure analysis and argument. As Pinker notes about the latter:

> A coherent text is a designed object: an ordered tree of sections within sections, crisscrossed by arcs that track topics, points, actors and themes, and held together by connectors that tie one proposition to the next. Like other designed objects, it comes about not by accident but by drafting

Sheila Jasanoff, 'Breaking the Waves in Science Studies: Comment on H.M. Collins and Robert Evans, "The Third Wave of Science Studies"' (2003) 33 *Social Studies of Science* 389.

[50] Ulrike Felt, 'Under the Shadow of Time: Where Indicators and Academic Values Meet' (2017) 3 *Engaging Science, Technology and Society* 53.

[51] In a different context, see Elizabeth Fisher, Pasky Pascual, and Wendy Wagner, 'Rethinking Judicial Review of Expert Agencies' (2015) 93 *Texas Law Review* 1681, which shows how a focus on yardsticks can improve decision-making.

[52] Feldman, 'The Nature of Legal Scholarship', 505.

a blueprint, attending to details, and maintaining a sense of harmony and balance.[53]

Third, thinking about the institutional context is a reminder about what it is we are really fostering. For example, interdisciplinary engagement must ultimately be tied to the developing of legal expertise. By understanding more about the problems that law governs, we gain a deeper understanding of law and its operation. Those problems may be about an object that law applies to – take for example Jasanoff's work on genetically modified organisms.[54] But they may also be about the conceptual ideas that drive forth social institutions. Bogojevic's study of the co-production of markets and states is a paradigm of this type of work.[55] The important point is that these forms of analysis provide deeper insight into both the internal and external dynamics in regards to law. Interdisciplinary study, as a form of interactional expertise, plays a role in facilitating contributory expertise.

3   Material

Craft is about working with something. Environmental law scholars are never working from a blank slate. As Adamson notes, 'craft always entails an encounter with the properties of a specific material.'[56] As my co-authors and I pointed out in 'Maturity and Methodology', environmental law scholars work with a wide range of material – cases, legislation, policy, empirical data, and other scholarly works. They also 'work' with the problems that environmental law applies to. Thus, Rajamani is directly engaging with the legal nature of the United National Framework Convention on Climate Change Conference of Parties Agreements.[57] Scotford is immersed in the case law of particular

---

[53] Steven Pinker, *The Sense of Style: The Thinking Person's Guide to Writing in the 21st Century* (London: Allen Lane, 2014), 186.

[54] Sheila Jasanoff, *Designs on Nature: Science and Democracy in Europe and the United States* (Princeton, NJ: Princeton University Press, 2005). See also Elizabeth Fisher, 'Chemicals as Regulatory Objects' (2014) 23 *Review of European, Comparative and International Environmental Law* 163.

[55] Sanja Bogojevic, *Emissions Trading Schemes: Markets, States and Law* (Oxford: Hart Publishing, 2013).

[56] Glenn Adamson, *Thinking Through Craft* (Oxford: Berg, 2007), 39.

[57] Lavanya Rajamani, 'The 2015 Paris Agreement: Interplay Between Hard, Soft and Non-Obligations' (2016) 28 *Journal of Environmental Law* 337; Rajamani, 'The Devilish Details: Key Legal Issues in the 2015 Climate Negotiations' (2015) 78 *Modern Law Review* 826.

jurisdictions that pertains to environmental principles.[58] Vaughan is interrogating the soft law realm of the REACH regime.[59]

What they have in common is they are tactile when it comes to working with their legal material. This is important. As Grayson Perry has noted:

> Craftsmanship is often equated with precision but I think there is more to it. I feel it is more important to have a long and sympathetic hands-on relationship with materials. A relaxed, humble, ever-curious love of stuff is central to my idea of being an artist.[60]

Thus, the expertise of an environmental law scholar and the integrity of legal scholarship are closely related to how well scholars understand the material they work with.[61] It is important to have 'fidelity to subject matter'.[62] What this means is the fostering of scholarly expertise requires the fostering of an understanding, both tacit and explicit, of the materials we are studying. This is a hands-on process that requires learning-by-doing.

It is also the case that the sheer diversity of material that environmental law scholars need to work with means that they need knowledge and understanding of a range of different things. It is thus not surprising, and as noted in 'Maturity and Methodology', that environmental law scholars tend to cluster around certain types of legal material.[63] But even given that, a single scholar often has to develop expertise in regards to a range of different types of material in relation to the same topic. Thus Lee, in illuminating our understanding of EU regulatory regimes for genetically modified organisms (GMOs), needs to engage with EU law, World Trade Organisation (WTO) law, the science of GMOs, and the complexity of GMO disputes.[64] France-Hudson, in writing about the property and environmental law interface, has to have a serious working knowledge of property law, property law theory, environmental problems, and legislative regimes.[65]

---

[58] Scotford, *Environmental Principles*.
[59] Steven Vaughan, *EU Chemicals Regulation* (Cheltenham: Edward Elgar, 2015).
[60] Grayson Perry, *The Tomb of the Unknown Craftsman* (London: British Museum Press, 2011), 169.
[61] Sue Rowley, 'Introduction' in Sue Rowley (ed.), *Craft and Contemporary Theory* (St Leonards: Allen & Unwin 1997), xv.
[62] Wildasky, *Craftways*, xiv.
[63] Fisher and others, 'Maturity and Methodology', 230–231.
[64] Maria Lee, *EU Regulation of GMOs: Law and Decision Making for a New Technology* (Cheltenham: Edward Elgar Publishing,2008).
[65] Ben France-Hudson, 'Surprisingly Social: Private Property and Environmental Management' (2017) 29 *Journal of Environmental Law* 101. See also Eloise Scotford and

It is also useful to consider why environmental law materials are being worked with. Much of the time it is simply to illuminate understanding – casting light on legal complexity and much else besides.[66] Sometimes it is about attempting to improve what already exists. This may be about repairing the law,[67] improving it,[68] or even transforming it.[69] These all require different skills and different ways of working with legal material.[70] What scholarly task is being undertaken will relate to the wider context. For example, Christopher Stone's famous work 'Should Trees Have Standing' emerged out of a legal brief before the US Supreme Court.[71]

Closely related to understanding materials is the choice of methodologies that scholars use to investigate those materials and make sense of them. These methods are akin to the craftsperson's tools and what are classically understood as legal methodology.[72] This is what doctoral students are 'trained in'. Methodology in this regard can refer to many things: doctrinal method, comparative law method, empirical methods, and theoretical approaches to law are just a few examples. Part of the expertise of legal scholars is choosing the most appropriate methods for their scholarly purpose and for the material they are working with.

Take for example, Keith Hawkins's famous sociolegal work *Environment and Enforcement*.[73] The book is grounded in more than two years' empirical research of the work of officers in two water authorities that enforce pollution law in the United Kingdom. It's easy to pigeonhole this book as a study of the 'extralegal' process of enforcement. But it is much more than that. It is also a study of the uncertainty of

---

Rachael Walsh, 'The Symbiosis of Property and English Environmental Law – Property Rights in a Public Law Context' (2013) 76 *Modern Law Review* 1010.

[66] Emily Barritt, 'Conceptualising Stewardship in Environmental Law' (2014) 26 *Journal of Environmental Law* 1; Lovleen Bhullar, 'Ensuring Safe Municipal Water Disposal in Urban India: Is There a Legal Basis?' (2013) 25 *Journal of Environmental Law* 235.

[67] Perhaps Christopher Stone, 'Should Trees Have Standing?: Towards Legal Rights for Natural Objects' (1972) 45 *Southern California Law Review* 450 is an example of this.

[68] Peter Kunzlik, 'Green Public Procurement – European Law, Environmental Standards and "What to Buy" Decisions' (2013) 25 *Journal of Environmental Law* 173.

[69] William Howarth, 'The Progression Towards Ecological Quality Standards' (2006) 18 *Journal of Environmental Law* 3.

[70] Richard Sennett, *Together: The Rituals, Pleasures and Politics of Co-operation* (London: Allen Lane, 2012), 212–220.

[71] Stone, 'Should Trees Have Standing?' The case in question was *Sierra Club* v. *Morton* 405 US 727 (1972).

[72] McCrudden, 'Legal Research and the Social Sciences'.

[73] Keith Hawkins, *Environment and Enforcement: Regulation and the Social Definition of Pollution* (Oxford: Oxford University Press, 1984).

regulatory law and thus law itself. Prosecution may be a last resort as Hawkins shows, but law is ever present. While the transcripts of interviews with pollution officers describing their work and the interactions with those they regulate may not directly be about law, they tell the reader a lot about what law can be. The stories about bluffing, bargaining, and officers appearing on 'plush carpets' in 'dirty wellies' because they have been investigating oil pollution are not just random stories, but a careful piece of 'interpretative sociology' that helps us understand something about law's place in the world.

The overall point is that the application of method is not a mechanical enterprise – it requires practice and the development of understanding over time. Knowing the limits of particular techniques or methods is also part of the expertise in relation to methods.[74] Given the diversity of environmental law, it is no surprise that scholars most develop their methodological range. Thus Scott has taken a range of methodological approaches in her work which encompasses EU law, WTO law, multi-level governance, and forms of private governance.[75] Or take for example Lange and Shepheard's work[76] on developing an eco-social-legal approach to thinking about water regulation. Their method, which encompasses different types of material, pursues fidelity to that material. Overall, at the heart of good environmental law scholarship is developing an understanding of the relationship between method, material, and the questions being asked.

4   Using Obsessive Energy Well

Sennett describes craftsmanship as 'quality driven work' where the challenge for individuals and organisations is 'learning how to use obsessional energy well'.[77] He also notes: 'obsession risks deforming the character; in action obsession risks fixation and rigidity.'[78] That in turn creates the risk of the production of poor scholarship.

[74] Feldman, 'The Nature of Legal Scholarship', 501.
[75] Joanne Scott, *The WTO Agreement on Sanitary and Phytosanitary Measures* (Oxford: Oxford University Press, 2007); Joanne Scott and David Trubek, 'Mind the Gap: Law and New Approaches to Governance in the European Union' (2002) 8 *European Law Journal* 1; Joanne Scott and others, 'The Promise and Limits of Private Standards in Reducing Greenhouse Gas Emissions from Shipping' (2017) 29 *Journal of Environmental Law* 231.
[76] Bettina Lange and Mark Shepheard, 'Changing Conceptions of a Right to Water – An Eco-Socio-Legal Perspective' (2014) 26 *Journal of Environmental Law* 215.
[77] Sennett, *The Craftsman*, 243.
[78] Ibid.

An important part of using obsessive energy well is managing perfectionism. As Sennett himself has highlighted, there is a need to see 'contingency and constraint' in a positive light, to avoid 'self-conscious demonstration', and to avoid 'pursuing a problem relentlessly to the point it becomes perfectly self-contained'.[79] This advice sounds obvious, but as every scholar knows it is challenging to achieve in practice.

Highlighting obsessive energy makes clear that scholarship is about production and the focus must always be on that. Seeing it is about a craft also makes clear that there are tensions in its practice. Craft is about production, but it takes time to produce. Most publications require several iterations. This is particularly true in the environmental law sphere, where the lines of analysis are not always clear. Likewise, craft is creative but must remain true to the material. The descriptive parts of legal scholarship are fundamental to its success and are often the hardest to write. Craft may also be driven forth by aspiration, but the aspirations should not overtake what is possible.

The flipside of this argument is that highlighting obsessive energy also provides a guide for bad scholarship. Evidence of not wanting to do a good job – being shoddy with the use of the material, being unreflective about method, being uninterested in how scholarship is structured– is evidence of poor scholarly work. A fundamental point about this definition of 'bad scholarship' is that it does not coral people into certain techniques and certain ways of doing things. Foucauldian approaches to environmental law questions are not more or less superior to doctrinal approaches. Empirical studies do not inherently have the edge on jurisprudential approaches. The key issue is whether there has been an attempt to do the job well.

But there is also another dimension to managing obsessive energy – ensuring the operation of expertise is sociable; that is, a community of good practices is fostered.[80] That requires the building of relations among experts, with an emphasis on mentoring and sharing experiences about producing scholarship. To put the mater another way, it is important to ensure scholars are interacting with one another and discussing what it is they do. Edited collections such as these are not just navelgazing but part of fostering expertise.

What this also means is that craftsmanship is not about being crafty. As the artist Grayson Perry notes:

[79] Ibid. 262.
[80] Ibid. 246–252.

> There is also a mystical resonance to the word craftsman. He is crafty. A trickster, a sorcerer, an androgynous shaman communing with the spirit world, a member of a secretive guild holding his alchemical secrets close to his chest.[81]

While there are not many shamans stalking the halls of environmental law scholarship, there are definitely those who wish to see themselves as alchemists and who in doing so 'mythologise' themselves.[82] Opening up what we do to discussion is important.

5   Conclusion

Describing legal scholarship as a craft is not a cure for all the anxieties that anyone writing environmental law scholarship may feel, but it does contextualise them and make clear that the production of great legal scholarship requires an awareness of context, material, and the desire to do a job well. Method is not just methodology, but something more deeply embedded in expertise. It is not gained through the click of the fingers but over time through the fostering of expertise. While any act of describing expertise is normative, describing environmental law scholarship as a craft is not an act of romantic utopianism. Rather, it provides a hands-on vision about what we do as environmental law scholars. In this regard, the 'back to basics' in the title emphasises what is 'fundamental' and 'essential' in environmental law scholarship.[83]

Short Bibliography

David Feldman, 'The Nature of Legal Scholarship' (1989) 52 *Modern Law Review* 498.

Elizabeth Fisher and others, 'Maturity and Methodology: Starting a Debate about Environmental Law Scholarship' (2009) 21 *Journal of Environmental Law* 213.

Richard Sennett, *The Craftsman* (London: Allen Lane, 2008).

---

[81] Perry, *The Tomb of the Unknown Craftsman*, 23.
[82] Ibid.
[83] Taking this definition of 'basic' from the *Oxford English Dictionary*.

4

Environmental Law Scholarship: Systematization, Reform, Explanation, and Understanding

DANIEL BONILLA MALDONADO

Environmental law scholarship is not monolithic. It does not offer a unique way of approaching its object of study; it is internally diverse. Environmental law scholars, on many occasions, start from dissimilar premises, pursue different ends, and put into action different research methods.[1] Environmental law scholars begin with different political assumptions. They are, for example, conservatives, liberals, or progressives. These political positions determine, among other things, the specific objects of study that they consider relevant and the criteria for evaluating the legitimacy of environmental legal norms. Scholars also differ about what the aims of environmental law scholarship should be. There is no agreement on whether this type of legal scholarship should, for example, assess the efficacy of environmental legislation, the economic costs of environmental case law, or the justice of the allocation of scarce resources generated by environmental legal rules and principles.[2] Finally, environmental law scholars differ on the means for exploring their object of study; for example, they differ on whether they should examine environmental law using social sciences empirical research methods, the various types of conceptual analyses used by analytical philosophy, or the interpretative methods proposed by the cultural studies of law.

I would like to thank Natalia Serrano and Julián Díaz for the extraordinary work that they did as research assistants. I would also like to thank Colin Crawford for his comments.

[1] E. Fisher et al., 'Maturity and Methodology: Starting a Debate about Environmental Law Scholarship' (2009) 21 *Journal of Environmental Law* 213–250 at 216–217; T. Jewell & C. Reil, 'Environmental Law', in D. Hayton (ed.), *Laws Future(s): British Legal Developments in the 21st Century* (Oxford: Hart Publishing, 2000), 209.

[2] Fisher et al., 'Maturity and Methodology', 225; B. Richardson & S. Wood, 'Environmental Law for Sustainability', in B. Richardson and S. Wood (eds), *Environmental Law for Sustainability* (Oxford: Hart Publishing, 2006).

This chapter aims to examine four paradigmatic models of environmental law scholarship: systematization, reform, explanation, and understanding. In this chapter, I describe and examine these models as ideal Weberian types. Consequently, I present the basic structure of each of these forms of scholarship only. This way of articulating the work of environmental law scholars has a cost and a benefit. The cost of these abstractions is that they obscure the richness, variety, and lack of precise limits that comprise environmental law scholarship. Environmental law scholars continuously cross the borders that separate these four ideal types and do many more things than the models are able to give an account of. A research project in environmental law, for example, may have as a goal to systematize as well as to reform its object of study. Similarly, the models do not describe all the dimensions that constitute the systematization process of environmental legal rules and principles. The benefit of these abstractions is that they allow us to see clearly the constitutive elements, not the marginal or accidental ones, of the diverse forms of environmental law scholarship. Similarly, they allow us to compare these constitutive elements accurately and make explicit their strengths and weaknesses.

The chapter is divided into four parts to meet this objective. In the first part, I critically examine the model of systematization; in the second, the model of reform; in the third, the model of explanation; and in the fourth, the model of understanding. This chapter, therefore, aims to contribute to comprehending environmental law scholarship. Legal scholars rarely analyse the assumptions, objectives, and means of the type of research we put into operation; we are so immersed in its practice that we lose sight of its perspectival character and its limits. Now, the ideal types discussed in this chapter, it is important to note, are not exclusive of environmental law. Rather, they are forms of scholarship that cut across the legal academy. Environmental law scholarship's models are not idiosyncratic. These models reproduce forms of scholarship that are common in other areas of law.

1   Systematization, Teaching, and Environmental Law

The first model of environmental law scholarship is systematization. This model starts form three premises: (i) environmental law is (and should be) a hierarchically organized subsystem; (ii) the subsystem has (and should have) legal rules and principles as its basic units; and (iii) environmental law rules and principles, as well as their relations, are (or should be) clear and precise. As a consequence, the model imagines the ideal environmental law as a set of well-defined legal norms that is pyramidally organized.[3] In this structure, each legal norm plays a specific role and has a particular relationship with other legal norms.[4] Nevertheless, the model recognizes that, in practice, environmental law can be incoherent, vague, ambiguous, its norms dispersed, and the links between them imprecise. From this perspective, then, the task of environmental law scholars is to elucidate the content of environmental law rules and principles and to specify the relationships between them, for example, relationships of subordination or superiority, generality or specialty.[5] Environmental law scholarship should make the environmental law that 'is' closer to the environmental law that 'should be'. Environmental law norms should contribute to create a closed, complete, coherent, and univocal legal system. The systematizing legal scholar therefore uses reason to reconstruct environmental law. She uses reason to make environmental law the best expression of itself.[6]

The academic product par excellence for the systematizing model is therefore the environmental law treatise – a book that presents this particular area of the law organized systematically and hierarchically. Environmental law treatises are generally organized deductively, and

---

[3] E. L. Rubin, 'Legal Scholarship', in D. Patterson (ed.), *A Companion to Philosophy of Law and Legal Theory* (Cambridge, MA: Blackwell, 1996), 565.

[4] C. Von Savigny, *Of the vocation of our Age for Legislation and Jurisprudence*, A. Hayward (trans.) (London: Littlewood, 1831), 38–39.

[5] J. M. Smits, *The Making of European Private Law* (Antwerp, Oxford, New York: Intersentia, 2002).

[6] The systematizing model in legal academia has its roots in German historicism and the French school of exegesis. Historicism, represented paradigmatically by Carl Von Savigny, identifies the law with mathematics. The law starts from axioms, principles, from which the lower norms, legal rules, should be derived rationally. Historicism considers that the primary source of the creation of law must be custom. This is the direct creation of the people and expression of the nation's ethos. The legal academic must therefore induce the principles that are implicit in the custom. He or she must subsequently derive these rules that must control the behaviour of citizens more precisely. At the same time, he or she must organize and specify the content of the legal norms created by those institutions that concentrate the creative capacity of law in the political community. If, for historicism, the principles are always contextual, for the school of exegesis these are the product of human reason. The Napoleonic Civil Code of 1804, the legal product par excellence for the school of exegesis, is thus a product that is exportable to any nation; it is a product that can be transferred without major obstacles across the borders that separate France from other States. Manuel Atienza, *El Sentido del Derecho* (Barcelona: Ariel, 2003) 277.

they replicate the structure of the environmental law code or environmental statutes of a country. In each of their sections, treatises present the basic contents of the environmental code or statutes that are their object of study. In addition, these treatises usually include glosses that seek to clarify the contents of environmental legal norms.[7] These glosses, among other things, resolve incoherencies, reproduce judicial interpretations on certain rules or principles, and show the connections that should be made between environmental legal norms so that they can be duly applied in practice. Environmental law treatises then usually start with a definition of environmental law and its principles. They then sequentially go down the pyramid structure of environmental law and describe subjects like the State institutions in charge of protecting the environment; the procedures for obtaining an environmental licence; and how different natural resources, such as water, forests, and minerals, are regulated.

Treatises usually focus on national environmental law. However, sometimes they focus their systematizing efforts on international or regional environmental law, such as the Convention on Biological Diversity, the United Nations Framework Convention on Climate Change, or the Treaty of Amsterdam. Treatises are also used in national and international environmental law courses, and they usually become central points of reference for practitioners, judges, and students of environmental law. In continental Europe and Latin America, for instance, these are the materials that law students have typically been educated with. In these parts of the world, treatises are updated and edited every now and then, constituting intergenerational teaching books. Professors and students of environmental law thus are educated with the same legal materials, although the students' books are updates (ten or fifteen editions later) of these successful 'law books'. Environmental law treatises, we cannot forget, are a secondary source of law in the civil legal family. Environmental legal doctrine is formally understood as a part of the national legal system.

The systematizing model, when properly implemented, generates some positive consequences for environmental law: it collects and organizes the scattered set of legal norms that usually constitutes the environmental law of a State, simplifies and makes accessible a subfield of law

---

[7] These comments are connected and echo the long tradition of European glossators, particular the Italians in the eighteenth century, who systematized Roman law. These glossators made comments in the margins of the Roman legal texts that they compiled and reproduced. See A. Watson, 'The Importance of Nutshells' (1994) 42(1) *American Journal of Comparative Law* 1–24.

characterized by its technical complexity, and introduces the topic to the new generations of environmental law students.[8] However, the model also generates some negative consequences for environmental law. Two are, perhaps, the most important. On one hand, the model runs the risk of radically separating environmental law and social reality.[9] The legal subfield that emerges from the model's efforts may pass reason tests, may be accepted in the 'heaven of legal concepts', but it will probably not be very useful for the legal and political community. A national environmental law treatise, for example, can offer a precise description of the concept of 'environmental licence' and can organize logically the legal steps needed to obtain it. Nevertheless, these descriptions are typically presented in a decontextualized manner and do not say anything about the effects that the rules regulating environmental licences have had on the protection of the environment or in strengthening citizen participation. They do not examine either the differences between the procedures for obtaining an environmental licence on paper and the procedures in action. In the model's effort to transform environmental law into a true subsystem – in its aspiration to specify the contents of its concepts and the relationships they have with the subsystem's rules and principles – the model ends up creating a perfect abstract world that is gladly distant from the untidy environmental world we actually live in.

On the other hand, when the systematizing aims of the model are not realized in an ideal way, the products of environmental law scholarship end up being excessively similar to the materials created by the legislature or the judiciary. The materials generated by the model recreate the content and structure of environmental law. These are materials that are not intellectually challenging or useful for understanding the complexity of environmental law. Thus, for example, the typical treatise on international environmental law reproduces in analogous wording the content of the Rio Declaration, the Kyoto Protocol, or the Basel Convention, to list three of the best-known international environmental instruments. The description offered by the treatise focuses on the most relevant mandates of international environmental law. The central rules and principles of these international instruments are presented in the abstract. Occasionally, the treatise also includes the contents of the official interpretative documents of these instruments. The glosses of

---

[8] Watson, 'The Importance of Nutshells', 17–18; O. Pedersen, 'The Limits of Interdisciplinarity and the Practice of Environmental Law Scholarship' (2014) 26 *Journal of Environmental Law* 423–441.

[9] Fisher et al., 'Maturity and Methodology', 240–241.

the environmental law scholar make reference, for instance, to the official meaning of climate change, the definition of 'hazardous wastes', or the interpretation of a regional court on the duties imposed by the Convention of Biological Diversity.

2 Reform, Justice, and Environmental Law

The second model of environmental law scholarship is reform. Reformist environmental law scholarship usually moves in a cycle of critique and transformation: it questions the existing law and proposes to modify it.[10] The law that 'is' has to be transformed into the law that 'should be'. The environmental law scholar uses reason to show the reason of environmental law. The reforms proposed by the scholar to this legal subsystem do not come from an alternative normative system such as morality or politics. It is environmental law that shows how it should be.[11] Environmental law scholars do not present their proposals as based on their particular forms of understanding environmental justice; they present them as the best possible interpretation of existing environmental law. The critical and normative character that environmental law scholarship usually has is not only motivated by the political commitments of law professors. This type of legal scholarship is a form of legal practice.[12] It is not different, for example, from judicial practice.[13] Both environmental law scholars and judges are always seeking the law that should be. Environmental law itself is understood as always approaching what it ought to be.

Environmental law scholarship is therefore usually committed to its object of study;[14] it is a form of realizing the internal logic that cuts across environmental law. There is no distance between environmental law scholars and the legal reality that they examine. By their scholarship and teaching, environmental law scholars reproduce the dynamics that shape the subsystem that is their object of study.[15] They reproduce the practices of justification and questioning that are part of a liberal State

---

[10] P. Kahn, *The Cultural Study of Law: Reconstructing Legal Scholarship* (Chicago: University of Chicago Press, 1999), 7–30.

[11] Ibid., 18–30.

[12] E. J. Weinrib, *The Idea of Private Law* (Cambridge, MA: Harvard University Press, 1995); Rubin, 'Legal Scholarship', 565.

[13] J. M. Smits, *The Mind and Method of the Legal Academic* (Cheltenham: Edward Elgar, 2012), 44.

[14] Kahn, *The Cultural Study of Law*, 7.

[15] Pedersen, 'Limits of Interdisciplinarity', 12.

formed by free and equal citizens – a State in which all of its members are subordinated to legal rules and principles.[16] The model of reform in environmental law scholarship is not identified with a particular political position. It is not identified with a specific research method either. Conservative, liberal, or progressive environmental law scholars can put the model into operation. Environmental law scholars that use socio-legal, philosophical, or doctrinal methods can also do it. They all use the same argumentative movement: description of a part of environmental law, negative evaluation of some of its sections, and articulation of a proposal for how these segments should be reinterpreted or modified.[17]

Thus, for example, a conservative environmental law scholar can present the legal rules that create a CO_2 market in the Kyoto Protocol; assess them negatively because they excessively regulate the supply, demand, or price of the goods exchanged; and offer an interpretation of these legal rules that marginalizes the role of States and international institutions in the trading process. Likewise, continuing with the examples, a progressive environmental law scholar can begin her work by recounting how in the negotiations of international environmental law treaties, there has not been a horizontal relationship – one of equals – between the countries of the Global North and South; then, evaluate the imperial character of these negotiations negatively; and finish with a normative proposal on how non-vertical negotiations on environmental issues among States could be created.

The contribution that this model makes to the environmental law community is notable. First, it starts with the premise that law and justice intersect.[18] From this perspective, environmental law is not understood as a technique that is value-neutral. It is not understood as a technique for which the context in which it is applied is irrelevant either. Environmental law scholars committed to this model, therefore, ask valuable questions about the legitimacy or efficacy of their object of study. They ask, for example, about the political morality arguments that ground Ecuador's proposal on how the Global North should compensate the Ecuadorian State for not exploiting the Amazon economically. Second, environmental law scholars consider legal knowledge to be an instrument of social transformation. Their legal products should contribute to the creation of a more just society. These scholars,

---

[16] Kahn, *The Cultural Study of Law*, 7–18.
[17] O. Pedersen, 'Modest Pragmatic Lessons for a Diverse and Incoherent Environmental Law' (2013) 33 *Oxford Journal of Legal Studies* 103–131.
[18] Pedersen, 'Limits of Interdisciplinarity', 14.

for example, might describe, negatively evaluate, and present a proposal for modifying indigenous people's right to prior consultation. This right can assist in protecting indigenous people's ancestral territories, which, in many cases, overlap with natural reserves or are territories at risk from an environmental point of view.

Finally, this model of environmental law scholarship supposes a commitment to its object of study.[19] It is a way of realizing the internal logic that cuts across environmental law; it is a means of contributing to its consolidation and reproduction – which is no small task given that all democratic systems are threatened by authoritarian or anomic tendencies. Thus, the model's cycles of description, critique, and reform allow for strengthening what we could call the environmental rule of law. The model emphasizes that all actors in the environmental field must act in accordance with pre-existing legal norms.[20] This, which is theoretically obvious in a liberal democracy, is continually questioned in practice given the immense economic and political interests involved in most environmental matters.

Nevertheless, this last strength also makes clear the model's limits. There is no distance between environmental law scholars and the legal reality that they examine. Scholars reproduce the dynamics that shape environmental law by means of their writings and teaching.[21] Environmental law scholarship is interpreted as a form of legal practice that is not different from judges' and litigators' practice.[22] Being immersed in the reproduction of the environmental rule of law, however, scholars cannot pay attention to, among others, the conditions of possibility that allow for the emergence of environmental law, its genealogy, or its conceptual structure. The model does not allow scholars to take distance from environmental law in order to understand it.[23]

3   Explanation, Social Sciences, and Environmental Law

The third environmental law scholarship model aims to make explicit the causal links that explain the contents, efficacy, or legitimacy of its object

[19] Smits, *The Mind and Method of the Legal Academic*, 120.
[20] Ibid.
[21] P. Schlag, *Laying Down the Law* (New York: New York University Press, 1996), 141.
[22] E. L. Rubin, 'The Practice and Discourse of Legal Scholarship' (1988) 86 *Michigan Law Review* 1835–1905 at 1859; R. A. Posner, 'Legal Scholarship Today' (2002) 115 *Harvard Law Review* 1314–1326 at 1315.
[23] Kahn, *The Cultural Study of Law*, 7.

of study.[24] This model is closely linked to the social and natural sciences. It aims to explain social phenomena (environmental law) by means of other social phenomena (culture and economy, for example) or by means of some natural phenomena (the chemical composition of the earth or the biological structure of animals, among others). As a consequence, this model gives prevalence to empirical research methods, from structured and semi-structured interviews to statistics and economic regression models to ethnography and participative research.[25] Environmental law scholars committed to the model of explanation are social scientists who have the environmental law subsystem as their object of study. They are also scholars who use the natural sciences literature to explain some aspects of environmental law or use the scientific method to achieve their explanatory objectives.[26]

This model takes on different forms in environmental law scholarship.[27] On one hand, a scholar focusing on the sociology of environmental law might seek, for instance, to make explicit the reasons that determine the enactment of a specific environmental law statute by means of analysing the interests, interactions, and power of the relevant legal and political actors – including national and multinational mining companies, non-governmental organizations, legislators, and members of the executive branch. This environmental law scholar seeks to articulate a narrative that describes the balance of power that conditioned the enactment and contents of the environmental law statute that she is studying. This scholar describes the processes of negotiation or imposition of the legal actors' points of view after interviewing relevant representatives of each interest group.

On the other hand, a scholar focusing on the anthropology of environmental law might use ethnography to describe, for example, how low- and mid-level bureaucrats process environmental licences. These ethnographies allow the scholar to describe the difference between environmental law on paper and environmental law in action. The micro-decisions made by these bureaucrats are what determine the

---

[24] Smits, *The Mind and Method of the Legal Academic*, 28–32.

[25] D. Owen and C. Noblet, 'Interdisciplinary Research and Environmental Law' (2015) 41(4) *Ecology Law Quarterly* 887–938 at 905.

[26] J. McEldowney & S. McEldowney, 'Science and Environmental Law: Collaboration across the Double Helix' (2011) 13 *Environmental Law Review* 169–198; M. J. Angelo, 'Harnessing the Power of Science in Environmental Law: Why We Should, Why We Don't, and How We Can' (2008) 86 *Texas Law Review* 1527–1573.

[27] Owen and Noblet, 'Interdisciplinary Research', 904.

speed of the process and the decision to grant or deny an environmental licence. In this example, the environmental law scholar's starting point is that the bureaucrats' interpretations of environmental law are what determine the true rights and obligations of individuals or companies requesting an environmental licence. This type of environmental law scholarship would also allow the scholar to describe and analyse the structures and internal dynamics of the environmental bureaucracies that constitute a liberal State.

Finally, an environmental law scholar focusing on the economic analysis of environmental law might have the objective of explaining, for instance, why the economic incentives articulated by environmental law such as lowering taxes or promoting subsidies for companies were not effective in decreasing environmental contamination in a specific country.[28] This environmental law scholar would focus on gathering quantitative information that would allow her to explain why these mechanisms did not make companies lower contamination levels in their production processes or treat waste residues before pouring them into the environment.

Two positive consequences of this type of research are noteworthy. First, the model of explanation is able to offer precise descriptions and analyses of the material sources and efficacy of environmental law.[29] Environmental law is therefore thought of not as a closed subsystem that does not interact (or interacts only marginally) with other normative systems.[30]The model assumes that environmental law has particular characteristics and functions in a specific manner, due in part to its exchanges with other social fields, among others, morality, culture, and the economy. Second, the interdisciplinary character of the model enriches environmental law scholarship.[31] The causal ties between social and natural phenomena and environmental law that the model makes explicit are a consequence of environmental law scholars' use of the social and natural sciences methods.[32] The use of substantive concepts

[28] See, for example, J. E. Velentzas, K. K. Savvidou, and G. K. Broni, 'Economic Analysis of Environmental Law: Pollution Control and Nuisance Law' (2009) 8(3) *Journal of International Trade Law and Policy* 252–271; R. A. Westin, 'Understanding Environmental Taxes' (1993) 46(2) *The Tax Lawyer* 327–361; C. R. Sunstein, 'The Arithmetic of Arsenic' (2001) 90 *Georgetown Law Journal* 2255–2309.

[29] Fisher et al., 'Maturity and Methodology'.

[30] Owen and Noblet, 'Interdisciplinary Research', 904.

[31] Ibid., 892–895.

[32] D. A. Farber, 'Probabilities Behaving Badly: Complexity Theory and Environmental Uncertainty' (2003) 37 *University of California Davis Law Review* 145–173; D. Owen,

originating in other disciplines – including the concept of anomia, the one- or two-directional relationship between culture and law, and the notion of efficiency – also add complexity to the study of environmental law.[33] The methodological interdisciplinarity and cross-fertilization between the content of environmental law and the content of the social and natural sciences enhance the analysis of environmental law rules and principles.[34] Both increase the theoretical and methodological tools that environmental law scholars can use to approach their object of study.[35]

Nevertheless, the cost that environmental law scholars committed to the explanatory model have to pay is not negligible:[36] the model obscures the content and practices of environmental law; it obscures environmental law's conceptual structures and internal dynamics.[37] The model of explanation moves away from what is within environmental law to focus on what is beyond it. The extralegal elements, sociological, anthropological, and economic, among others, are what allow scholars to give an account of environmental law.[38] They are what allow the realization of environmental law's aims as well. To grasp environmental law, we have to go beyond it. Thus, if the systematizing model does not pay any attention to what is outside of environmental law, the model of explanation pays little attention to what is within environmental law.

Finally, the model of explanation also runs the risk of creating an environmental law scholarship that is so specialized that it excludes people without advance training in the intersecting social or natural

'Mapping, Modeling, and the Fragmentation of Environmental Law' (2013) *Utah Law Review* 219–281; J. B. Ruhl, 'Complexity Theory as a Paradigm for the Dynamical Law-and-Society System: A Wake-Up Call for Legal Reductionism and the Modern Administrative State' (1996) 45(5) *Duke Law Journal* 849–928.

[33] Smits, *The Mind and Method of the Legal Academic*, 22–28.

[34] D. Owen, 'Critical Habitat and the Challenge of Regulating Small Harms' (2012) 64(1) *Florida Law Review* 141–199 at 151–152, 170–172.

[35] Smits, *The Mind and Method of the Legal Academic*, p. 22–28.

[36] About the disadvantages of interdisciplinary legal research, see Brian Leiter, 'Intellectual Voyeurism in Legal Scholarship' (1992) 4 *Yale Journal of Law & the Humanities* 79–104; Martha Nussbaum, 'The Use and Abuse of Philosophy in Legal Education' (1993) 45 *Stanford Law Review* 1627–1645, 1641–1643; Charles Collier, 'The Use and Abuse of Humanistic Theory in Law: Reexamining the Assumptions of Interdisciplinary Legal Scholarship' (1991) 41 *Duke Law Journal* 191–273; D. W. Vick, 'Interdisciplinarity and the Discipline of Law' (2004) 31 *Journal of Law and Society* 163–193, 166–168. For a similar description about the limits of interdisciplinary research in environmental law, see Pedersen, 'Limits of Interdisciplinarity'.

[37] D. A. Kysar, *Regulating From Nowhere: Environmental Law and the Search for Objectivity* (New Haven: Yale University Press, 2010).

[38] Smits, *The Mind and Method of the Legal Academic*, 28.

sciences from the discussion.[39] This, however, is not a necessary consequence of the model. The economic analysis of environmental law can
create a centripetal force that marginalizes from the discussion, and from
the decision-making processes, those practicing attorneys, citizens, and
legal academics who do not have in-depth knowledge of, among other
things, econometric models, the mathematical structures that ground
economics, and the substantial premises that macro- and microeco-
nomics start from.[40] Therefore, explaining the relationship between
environmental law and nature or social reality passes through
a tremendously specialized knowledge that further concentrates the
power in some parts of an already elitist legal academia.[41]

4   Culture, Law, and Critique

The aim of the understanding model is to describe and analyse environmental law in order to comprehend it,[42] not to systematize, modify, or
explain it. The model can take various forms, among others, interpretive
anthropology of environmental law, analytical philosophy of environmental law, and the cultural studies of environmental law. The model,
therefore, usually generates academic products with a high degree of
generality and theoretical content.[43] In this chapter, for reasons
of space, I focus only on one of these perspectives: the cultural studies
of environmental law. This perspective starts from the premise that
environmental law is a part of culture, not its consequence.[44] For this
model, environmental law is not an epiphenomenon of culture.
Environmental law is part of the horizon of understanding that we are
immersed in. This horizon is a world of meaning that we simultaneously
inherit and construct:[45] it already exists when we arrive in the world; it
does not stop existing when we disappear. In fact, when we are born this
web of meanings already constitutes us: we describe ourselves and

---

[39] Owen and Noblet, 'Interdisciplinary Research', 905–907.
[40] Eric D. Roy et al., 'The Elusive Pursuit of Interdisciplinarity at the Human-Environment
      Interface' (2013) 63 *BioScience* 745–753.
[41] M. Tushnet, 'Legal Scholarship (1): In the Law Reviews' (6 August 2013) at https://balkin
      .blogspot.com/2013/08/legal-scholarship-1-in-law-reviews.html.
[42] Smits, *The Mind and Method of the Legal Academic*, 32–34.
[43] Ibid.
[44] P. Kahn, 'Comparative Constitutionalism in a New Key' (2003) 101 *Michigan Law Review*
      2677–2704.
[45] P. Kahn, *The Reign of Law: Marbury v. Madison and the Constitution of America* (New
      Haven: Yale University Press, 1997).

interact with the world by means of its categories. Our identities, the meaning we give to the world, and the ways we relate to the external reality do not exist outside of this web of meanings. Of course, the world exists as materiality, independent of these categories. However, it exists as an entity without meaning. Culture, and environmental law as part of it, articulates the narratives by which we respond to key existential questions such as the following: Who are we? What do we do? What should we do? And what have we experienced?

The model of understanding aims to clarify the conditions of possibility of the world we live in. In particular, it aims to describe and examine how environmental law constructs our imagination and therefore how environmental law constructs the world we occupy.[46] The model of understanding is thus a critical enterprise in a Kantian sense: it aims to describe the structure and borders of this form of experiencing the world.[47] Nevertheless, the model is also a critical enterprise in another sense: it aims to clarify the ideological horizons that make the existence of those webs of meaning possible.

As a consequence, the model of understanding can help us make explicit and analyse, for example, the conditions of possibility of the anthropocentric and biocentric views that have historically sustained or questioned Western environmental law. This genealogy of the grounds of environmental law can lead us, for instance, to exploring the relationship between nature and human beings in contractualism – one of the paradigmatic ways of justifying the modern State. Contractualism understands that, in the state of nature, the relationship between human beings and nature has particular characteristics. Nature is a divine creation, the resources it contains are limited but abundant, and all human beings have the same right to appropriate natural resources for their survival. The religious echoes in contractualism are therefore powerful. Categories like creator/creature, Eden and manna, equality of God's creations, and nature as an instrument to satisfy human needs are all present in its narrative. The form par excellence of founding the modern State secularly intersects with Christianity. The marks of Christian theology appear in this central stage of modern law in general and environmental law in particular. In contractualism, moreover, the move to the civil state should be made because there is no impartial third party

---

[46] P. Kahn, 'Freedom, Autonomy, and the Cultural Study of Law' (2001) 13 *Yale Journal of Law & the Humanities* 141–171.

[47] Kahn, *The Cultural Study of Law*, 34–35.

capable of resolving the conflicts that emerge around natural resources. Nature is a source of conflict in modern contractualism, though not the only one.

Now, for the model of understanding, the categories that constitute environmental law are always part of conceptual networks.[48] These categories do not exist as monads in a world of abstract and universal ideas. They do not exist as isolated units: they construct and give meaning to the reality that human beings inhabit by their intersection – by the construction of narratives that aim to persuade the 'other', and ourselves, of the value of the legal world of meanings we are immersed in. These conceptual networks shape the narratives we use to construct our individual and collective identities. Who we are as individuals and collectivities is always a consequence of these narratives.

The model of understanding can help us comprehend, for instance, in what sense the new Latin America constitutional environmental law, which is articulated paradigmatically in the constitutions of Bolivia and Ecuador, is nurtured by and distanced from modern constitutionalism.[49] The model can also help us understand what types of subjects this new constitutional environmental law creates, as well as the history and geography that these subjects inhabit. Thus, the model can help us analyse how the principles of plurinationality and interculturality reinterpret the collective subject that is the political community.[50] This is a reinterpretation that simultaneously uses and distances itself from the concepts of nation, people, and culture that constitute the grammar of modern

---

[48] Ibid., 102–106.

[49] M. Aparicio, 'Nuevo Constitucionalismo, Derechos y Medio Ambiente en las Constituciones del Ecuador y Bolivia' (2011) 9 *Revista General de Derecho Público Comparado* 1.

[50] C. Gregor, 'Nuevas Narrativas Constitucionales en Bolivia y Ecuador: el Buen Vivir y los Derechos de la Naturaleza' (2014) 59 *Latinoamérica* 9–40; R. Lalander, 'Entre el Ecocentrismo y el Pragmatismo Ambiental: Consideraciones Inductivas Sobre Desarrollo, Extractivismo y los Derechos de la Naturaleza en Bolivia y Ecuador' (2015) 6 *Revista Chilena de Derecho y Ciencia Política* 109–152, 146–148; K. Zimmerer, 'The Indigenous Andean Concept of "Kawsay", the Politics of Knowledge and Development, and the Borderlands of Environmental Sustainability in Latin America' (2012) 127(3) *Publications of the Modern Language Association of America* 600–606; Eduardo Gudynas, 'La Ecología Política del Giro Biocéntrico en la Nueva Constitución de Ecuador' (2009) 32 *Revista de Estudios Sociales* 34–47; R. Ávila, *El Neoconstitucionalismo Transformador: el Estado y el Derecho en la Constitución de 2008* (Quito: Ediciones Abya-Yala, 2011).

constitutionalism.[51] This reinterpretation also serves as the foundation for the construction of nature as a subject of rights and the
inclusion of the principle of 'good living' in the constitutions of
Ecuador and Bolivia. The principle of good living imagines nature
in a holistic and biocentric way; it imagines nature as constructed by
the principles of rationality, complementarity, balance, and
reciprocity.[52] Nature then emerges as a subject analogous to the
subject of individual rights. Human beings, more than rights, have
obligations with regard to nature, and they have a relationship not of
dominance but of equality with the rest of the organic and inorganic
world.[53]

The purpose of this research project would not be to systematize the
Ecuadorian or Bolivian environmental law doctrine or to criticize or
reform it. The model does not intend to contribute to making environmental law a coherent or more just subsystem, and it does not intend to
contribute to the solution of difficult environmental cases. All of these are
valid objectives. Nevertheless, they are aims that start from
a commitment to the object of study – that believe that it has value and
that it needs to be reproduced. The model of understanding values the
distance between scholars and object of study, not because it allows them
to capture absolute truth or to annul their perspectival character, but
because distance gives them freedom with regard to the practices and
beliefs that they are examining.

The purpose of the research project also would not be to clarify why
the constituent assemblies of Bolivia and Ecuador created this new
constitutional environmental law. The model of understanding does
not pursue the aims of the social sciences that have culture as their object
of study, sociology and anthropology, for example. The model does not
aim to offer a set of explanations that allows for understanding how the
environmental law culture came to be what it is. It does not aim to clarify
relationships of cause and effect. These kinds of explanations are useful
for shedding light on the external phenomena that determine the

---

[51] For an analysis of the traditional liberal interpretation of these concepts, see W. McNeill,
Polyethnicity and National Unity in World History (Toronto: University of Toronto Press,
1986).
[52] Raúl Llasag Fernández, 'El Sumak Kawsay y Sus Restricciones Constitucionales' (2009) 12
Revista de Derecho Universidad Andina Simón Bolívar 113–125.
[53] Rickard Lalander, 'Rights of Nature and the Indigenous Peoples in Bolivia and Ecuador:
A Straitjacket for Progressive Development Politics?' (2014) 3 *Iberoamerican Journal of
Development Studies* 148–173.

construction of an environmental law culture. Nevertheless, they do not allow for understanding its substantive content. Rather, the objective of the environmental law scholarship implementing the model of understanding is to comprehend the world of meaning created by the constitutional environmental law of Ecuador and Bolivia – the type of subjects, geographies, and history created by this culture of environmental law.

The model of understanding, therefore, does not use empirical research methods to specify the reasons why a culture has some characteristics and not others.[54] It does not make use of statistics, surveys, or structured interviews to make explicit the external variables that give an account of the internal elements or dynamics that constitute an environmental law culture. The model does not revolve around the collection and interpretation of quantitative information. It is a humanist interpretative practice that examines how an environmental law culture constructs a world of meaning.[55] The model of understanding does not believe that a culture can be described, the environmental law culture in particular, pointing towards something that is beyond it.[56] The content of an environmental law culture is understood by going inside of its conceptual networks. The model of understanding aims to understand this set of beliefs and practices on its own terms; it aims to create a dense description of the networks of meaning that these beliefs and practices construct.[57] The aspiration of the model of understanding, after the process of free self-examination that requires the temporary suspension of our commitments to environmental law, is that we will better understand who we are:[58] what type of individuals and collectivities we have constructed, what type of subjects we have made of ourselves.

In addition, the model of understanding believes that the micro and the macro intersect.[59] In this sense, when it analyses a particular environmental law product, the model considers that it can find some of the central elements of the environmental law culture. The model of understanding therefore tends to focus on a few environmental law products. The macrocosm of the legal subsystem appears in the particular

---

[54] P. Kahn, 'Prólogo a la Edición en Español', in P. Kahn, *El Análisis Cultural del Derecho* (Bogotá: Siglo del Hombre Editores, 2014), 11.
[55] D. Bonilla, 'El Análisis Cultural del Derecho. Entrevista a Paul Kahn' (2017) 46 *Isonomía* 131–154.
[56] Ibid.
[57] C. Geertz, *The Interpretation of Cultures* (New York: Basic Books, Inc., 1973).
[58] Kahn, *The Cultural Study of Law*, 6.
[59] Ibid.

environmental law product. The description and analysis of modern environmental law as anthropocentric and as secularized Christianity does not emerge from examining all environmental law products. There are too many environmental law institutions, rules, and principles; they are too disperse and diverse; and they emerge from heterogenous sources. Rather, this description and analysis arise from the interpretation of legal materials that represent environmental law paradigmatically or from the central theoretical constructions environmental law is founded on.

The strength of this model, the distance it creates vis-à-vis its object of study, is at the same time its weakness: the model does not aim to transform environmental reality.[60] In an environmental world as deeply unjust and deteriorated as ours, this characteristic of the model of understanding can be presented as one of its limits. A second weakness of the model is that by focusing on the web of meanings that constitutes environmental law, it loses sight of the material conditions that construct this legal subsystem. The model, therefore, is not capable of accounting for the relationships and balances of power that create environmental law. It cannot help to understand who wins and who loses with the distribution of scarce resources created by environmental law. Finally, the model does not generate knowledge products that can directly help those who are immersed in the practice of environmental law. Understanding the conceptual geographies that environmental law creates is irrelevant to those who want to use it in litigation, business, or politics.

Conclusion

Environmental law scholarship is structured around four ideals: systematizing, reform, explaining, and understanding. The four models focus on different aspects of environmental law. They clarify and examine different dimensions of environmental legal discourse and practice. The systematizing and reformist models want to bring the environmental law that is closer to the environmental law that should be; they want to make environmental law the best version of itself. The former aims to organize its conceptual structure, to make it clear and precise; the latter

---

[60] About the normative and prescriptive nature of environmental law and legal scholarship, see Pedersen, 'Limits of Interdisciplinarity', 12; Pedersen, 'Modest Pragmatic Lessons'; Rubin, 'The Practice and Discourse of Legal Scholarship', 1847–1853.

aims to interpret or transform environmental law so that it will be coherent with the highest ideals of justice promoted by the subsystem itself. The model of understanding, in contrast, aims to describe and analyse the internal point of view of a member of the practice or the basic structure of the subsystem. It aims to understand the web of meanings that constitutes the environmental world that the legal subject inhabits or the units that constitute environmental law. Finally, the model of explanation emphasizes what is beyond environmental law, what makes environmental law what it is – its causes. Environmental law scholarship, therefore, is multiple. Each of these four models contributes differently to the understanding of their common object of study. Each model, however, has deficiencies that must be made explicit and discussed among environmental law scholars. Each model aims to solve some of the problems posed by its rivals, but it creates others by doing it.

Bibliography

Fisher E. et al., 'Maturity and Methodology: Starting a Debate about Environmental Law Scholarship' (2009) 21 *Journal of Environmental Law* 213–250.

Jewell T. & Reil C., 'Environmental Law', in D. Hayton (ed.), *Laws Future(s): British Legal Developments in the 21st Century* (Oxford: Hart Publishing, 2000).

Kahn P., *The Cultural Study of Law: Reconstructing Legal Scholarship* (Chicago: University of Chicago Press, 1999).

Kysar D. A., *Regulating From Nowhere: Environmental Law and the Search for Objectivity* (New Haven: Yale University Press, 2010).

McEldowney J. & McEldowney S., 'Science and Environmental Law: Collaboration across the Double Helix' (2011) 13 *Environmental Law Review* 169–198.

Owen D. & Noblet C., 'Interdisciplinary Research and Environmental Law' (2015) 41 *Ecology Law Quarterly* 887–938.

Pedersen O., 'Modest Pragmatic Lessons for a Diverse and Incoherent Environmental Law' (2013) 33 *Oxford Journal of Legal Studies* 103–131.

Pedersen O., 'The Limits of Interdisciplinarity and the Practice of Environmental Law Scholarship' (2014) 26 *Journal of Environmental Law*, 423–441.

Posner R. A., 'Legal Scholarship Today' (2002) 115 *Harvard Law Review*, 1314–1326.

Richardson B. & Wood S., 'Environmental Law for Sustainability', in B. Richardson & S. Wood (eds), *Environmental Law for Sustainability* (Oxford: Hart Publishing, 2006).

Rubin E. L, 'The Practice and Discourse of Legal Scholarship' (1988) 86 *Michigan Law Review*, 1835–1905.

Rubin E. L., 'Legal Scholarship', in D. Patterson (ed.), *A Companion to Philosophy of Law and Legal Theory* (Cambridge, MA: Blackwell, 1996).

Schlag P., *Laying Down the Law* (New York: New York University Press, 1996).

Smits J. M., *The Mind and Method of the Legal Academic*, (Cheltenham: Edward Elgar, 2012).

Watson, A., 'The Importance of Nutshells' (1994) 42 *American Journal of Comparative Law* 1–24.

(Un)Making the Boundaries of Environmental Law Scholarship: Interdisciplinarity Beyond the Social Sciences?

MARGHERITA PIERACCINI

1 Introduction: Interdisciplinarity and Environmental Law Scholarship

Despite its recent origins, public international law has developed at great speed to solve and react to current environmental crises. Academics interested in the subject have had little time to reflect on the identity and boundaries of the subject. As Fisher et al. argue,[1] it is time for environmental law academics to pause and begin an internal reflection on their academic subject. This call has been taken up by some scholars, who have discussed the (lack of) coherence of environmental law scholarship[2] and the challenges arising from its perceived interdisciplinarity.[3]

This chapter contributes to these existing critical reflections by focusing on the problematic relationship between natural sciences and environmental law scholarship. To explore this relationship, it focuses on two key challenges: institutional and epistemological, which confront the growth of an interdisciplinary agenda aimed at bringing natural sciences and environmental law scholarship together.

---

[1] Elizabeth Fisher et al., 'Maturity and Methodology: Starting a Debate about Environmental Law Scholarship' (2009) 21 *Journal of Environmental Law* 213.

[2] Ole Pedersen, 'Modest Pragmatic Lessons for a Diverse and Incoherent Environmental Law' (2013) 33 *Oxford Journal of Legal Studies* 103; Andreas Philippopoulos-Mihalopoulos & Victoria Brooks (eds.), *Research Methods in Environmental Law: A Handbook* (Cheltenham: Edward Elgar, 2017).

[3] See, for example, Ole Pedersen, 'The Limits of Interdisciplinarity and the Practice of Environmental Law Scholarship' (2014) 26 *Journal of Environmental Law* 423; Dave Owen & Caroline Noblet, 'Interdisciplinary Research and Environmental Law' (2015) 41 *Ecology Law Quarterly* 887.

As a starting point, it should be stated that there is not a unified version of what environmental law is and this of course has repercussions on the way a critique of the discipline and its relationship to natural sciences disciplines can be approached. The meanings of both the 'environment' and 'law' are complex and varied and subject to contestations of a jurisprudential nature. The divide between doctrinal and sociolegal research, which permeates the whole discipline of law, shapes the way in which environmental law scholarship is constructed and the possibilities for interdisciplinary research. This chapter adopts a sociolegal approach to environmental law. There is no agreed definition of sociolegal research,[4] and its strength possibly lies in its 'anarchic heterogeneity".[5] For example, sociolegal studies range from empirical studies of law in action under the legal consciousness umbrella,[6] to studies of legal pluralism,[7] the latter being an attractive and complex concept to study multilayered normative orders and discourses.

Law in action is what legal consciousness scholars have always been concerned with, focusing on the engagements with law by ordinary people, often working-class individuals or people at the margin. Many legal consciousness studies explore experiences and attitudes to power/ domination and resistance in ordinary people's experiences of law. Subjective experiences of law recorded by the legal consciousness literature not only bring law in dialogue with society but also help rethinking the boundaries of law itself beyond legal texts. Similarly, at the core of legal pluralism lies an understanding of law as a complex and varied occurrence. Legal pluralists have opened law to embrace different types of legal orders, not necessarily tied to the state machinery. A well-known definition of legal pluralism is the presence in a social field of more than

---

[4] D. R. Harris, 'The Development of Socio-Legal Studies in the United Kingdom' (1983) 3 *Legal Studies* 315; William Twining, *General Jurisprudence: Understanding Law from a Global Perspective* (Cambridge: Cambridge University Press, 2009)

[5] Roger Cotterrell, 'Subverting Orthodoxy, Making Law Central: A View of Sociolegal Studies' (2002) 29 *Journal of Law and Society* 632, 632.

[6] Patricia Ewick & Susan S. Silbey, *The Common Place of Law. Stories from Everyday Life.* (Chicago: University of Chicago Press, 1998). On environmental law scholarship, see Simon Halliday & Bronwen Morgan, 'I Fought the Law and the Law Won? Legal Consciousness and the Critical Imagination' 66 *Current Legal Problems* 1.

[7] See, for example, Sally Engle Merry, 'Legal Pluralism' (1988) 22 *Law and Society Review* 869; Simon A. Roberts, 'After Government? On Representing Law without the State' (2005) 68 *Modern Law Review* 1; Emmanuel Melissaris, *Ubiquitous Law: Legal Theory and the Space for Legal Pluralism* (Farnham: Ashgate, 2009).

one legal order.[8] According to Griffith, the 'myth' of legal centralism has
been an obstacle to developing analyses of tribal law or religious law, as
they did not deserve to be called law. Against this Western ethnocentr-
ism, legal pluralism flourished to recover those normative orders left
silenced and described their interactions with more formal orders. More
recent legal pluralist scholarship, such as the work of the De Sousa
Santos, has described more complex power relationships between legal
orders showing the hybridisation between legal spheres. For De Sousa
Santos, 'legal pluralism is the key concept in a postmodern view of law . . .
we live in a time of porous legality or of legal porosity, of multiple
networks of legal orders forcing us to constant transitions and trespas-
sing. Our legal life is constituted by an intersection of different legal
orders, that is, by interlegality.'[9] Such legal porosity and complexity are
not confined to postcolonial societies as they also shape Western contexts
and operate at different jurisdictional scales. Adopting a legal pluralist
perspective enables environmental law scholarship to explore through
empirical studies the multiple meaning of law in social-ecological systems and requires scholars to engage with a variety of legal and other
cultures participating in the shaping of environmental regulation.

Despite the many variants of legal consciousness and legal pluralism
and the existence of other sociolegal approaches, at its minimum
common denominator, it can be argued that sociolegal research, following Wheeler and Thomas,[10] is an academic phenomenon requiring
scholars to study the context in which law operates and to engage with
sociological, historical, political, cultural, economic or other forces,
which force us to rethink legal boundaries. Sociolegal research is
therefore inherently interdisciplinary. It is not by chance that sociolegal research in environmental law scholarship is carried out by
academic alliances between lawyers, sociologists, political scientists,
human geographers and anthropologists, among others.[11] However,

[8] John Griffith, 'What Is Legal Pluralism?' (1986) 24 *Journal of Legal Pluralism and Unofficial Law* 129.
[9] Bonaventura de Sousa Santos, *Toward a New Common Sense: Law, Science and Politics in the Paradigmatic Transition* (London: Butterworths LexisNexis, 2002), p. 437.
[10] Sally Wheeler & P. A. Thomas, *Socio-Legal Studies* (Oxford: Hart Publishing, 2000).
[11] Anne Griffiths, Franz von Benda-Beckmann & Keebet von Benda-Beckmann, *Spatializing Law: An Anthropological Geography of Law in Society* (Farnham: Ashgate, 2009); Margherita Pieraccini & Emma Cardwell, 'Divergent Perceptions of New Marine Protected Areas: Comparing Legal Consciousness in Scilly and Barra, UK' (2015) 119 *Ocean and Coastal Management* 21; L. C. Natarajan et al., 'Navigating the Participatory

the interdisciplinarity of sociolegal studies is very much confined within the social sciences.[12]

What happens when such sociolegal environmental research attempts to move beyond the boundaries of the social sciences and encounters the natural sciences? To what extent can environmental sociolegal scholars research and write with natural scientists? These are the key questions this chapter focuses on. Environmental sociolegal scholarship cannot ignore the natural sciences as the majority of environmental law as a field depends on it or more precisely on scientific constructions of what the environment and its sustainable thresholds are. Environmental law's engagement with natural science is unique compared to other law disciplines and has contributed to the shaping of this area of law as extensively discussed in the environmental legal literature,[13] less, I argue, to the shaping of legal scholarship to date. This is because of various constraints that can be subsumed under two main pillars: the institutional and the epistemological.

Institutionally, I will focus specifically on what has been termed the 'audit culture'[14] in which universities are immersed. A consideration of the United Kingdom Research Excellence Framework (REF) will be provided. There are plenty of academic critiques regarding the rise of the neo-liberal university and providing a critical account of the REF.[15] It is not the intention here to reproduce such critiques. The REF will be explored to the extent to which it facilitates or hinders the possibility for interdisciplinary research between environmental sociolegal scholars and natural scientists. Before moving to the epistemological constraints, I intend to discuss also another type of institutional challenge that

Processes of Renewable Energy Infrastructure Regulation: A "Local Participant Perspective" on the NSIPs Regime in England and Wales' *Energy Policy* (forthcoming).

[12] Notable exceptions exist. For a recent example, see Bettina Lange et al., 'A Framework for a Joint Hydro-Meteorological-Social Analysis of Drought' (2017) 578 *Science of the Total Environment* 297.

[13] See, for example, Dan Tarlock, 'Environmental Law: Ethics or Science?' (1996) 7 *Duke Environmental Law & Policy Forum* 193; Dan Tarlock, 'Who Owns Science?' (2002) 10 *Pennsylvania State Environmental Law Review* 135; John McEldowney & Sharron McEldowney, 'Science and Environmental Law: Collaboration across the Double Helix' (2011) 13 *Environmental Law Review* 169.

[14] Marilyn Strathern (ed.), *Audit Cultures: Anthropological Studies in Accountability, Ethics and the Academy* (Abingdon: Routledge, 2000).

[15] See, for example, Sheila Slaughter & Gary Rhoades, 'The Neo-Liberal University' (2000) 6 *New Labor Forum* 73; Susan Wright & Cris Shore (eds.), *Death of the Public University? Uncertain Futures for Higher Education in the Knowledge Economy* (Berghahn Books, 2017); Stefan Collini, *Speaking of Universities* (Verso, 2017).

concerns early-career researchers. This is the rise of doctoral training centres, which are recent cross-institutional centres to fund doctoral researchers and offer interdisciplinary pathways and cross-council scholarships.

Even in an ideal world in which all institutional constraints are overcome, the collaboration between natural scientists and sociolegal environmental scholars may still be a difficult one due to epistemological differences between science and law. To explore the epistemological boundaries will require a brief excursus into the philosophy of science and the demystification of the positivist paradigm by sociologists of scientific knowledge. Many of the critiques that will be presented here draw on the literature of Science and Technology Studies (STS). Such literature proves useful in both tackling the institutional and epistemological challenges and showing the connections between them. Indeed, STS have critically investigated the rise of entrepreneurialism as the organising principle of academia[16] and the introduction and effects of audit and assessment procedures on researchers' subjectivities, careers and publication practices.[17] At the same time, STS scholars have problematised the notion that scientific knowledge is distinct from other types of knowledge. Although my institutional analysis is based on examples from UK universities, the epistemological challenges that will be discussed are of a wider relevance as they focus on the relationship between environmental law scholarship and other forms of knowledge.

2   Institutional Constraints

2.1   Audit Cultures

'[E]very established order tends to produce ... the naturalization of its own arbitrariness.'[18]

UK academics are immersed in a pervasive 'audit culture'. *Audit Cultures* is the title of a book edited by the anthropologist Marilyn Strathern in 2000.[19] The book has many contributions from scholars critically

---

[16] Sheila Slaughter & Larry L. Leslie, *Academic Capitalism: Politics, Policies, and the Entrepreneurial University* (Baltimore, MD: Johns Hopkins University Press, 1998).

[17] For example, Strathern, *Audit Cultures*; Angela Brew & Lisa Lucas, *Academic Research and Researchers* (Society for Research into Higher Education and the Open University Press, 2009).

[18] Paul Bourdieu, *Outline of a Theory of Practice* (Cambridge: Cambridge: University Press, 1977), p. 164.

[19] Strathern, *Audit Cultures*.

reflecting on the auditing practices primarily in their academic environments. As Strathern argues, audits permeating public institutions such as universities are more than practices concerning 'style and presentation' as they become part of 'the general fabric of human interchange';[20] they are a cultural movement becoming a central organising principle of society in particular contexts and creating new auditable individuals participating in rituals of verification.

Building on Power's *The Audit Explosion*,[21] audits are more than just a quantitative neutral technique for improving the accountability and efficiency of an organisation. Audits spread a culture of administrative control and contribute to the making of knowledge and auditees by articulating values and frameworks under which the subjects of audits can move. Audits therefore are active. In the words of Power, 'audit actively constructs the context in which it operates … audits do not passively monitor auditee performance but shape the standards of this performance in crucial ways.'[22] They construct definitions of quality and performance as much as monitoring them. Self-reflexivity is encouraged by the audits but within fixed parameters and frameworks. Hence audits significantly shape the production of knowledge and scholarship and, I will argue later, in how far environmental sociolegal scholars can push the boundaries of their research. I will make this argument by reference to the quintessential example of auditing in UK universities, the REF.

The REF plays a major role in the allocation of resources and in giving visibility and credibility to the institutions and their individual departments. The REF was first carried out in 2014, replacing the previous Research Assessment Exercise (RAE). The first of such auditing exercises dates back to 1986, the time of Margaret Thatcher's government. It was conceived as a means to decide the allocation of funding at a time of austerity. Several refinements and amendments to the exercise over time relate to what to grade, how to grade and who could participate.[23]

---

[20] Ibid. p. 4.

[21] Michael Power, *The Audit Explosion* (New York: Demos, 1994).

[22] Ibid. 7.

[23] For a review of the history, please see Kate Williams & Jonathan Grant, 'A Comparative Review of How the Policy and Procedures to Assess Research Impact Evolved in Australia and the UK' (2018) *Research Evaluation* (forthcoming); John Brennan & Sofia Branco Sousa, 'UK Research Excellence Framework and the Transformation of Research Production' in Christine Musselin and Pedro Teixeira (eds.), *Reforming Higher Education. Higher Education Dynamics* (New York: Springer, 2013); Ben Martin, 'The Research Excellence Framework and the "Impact Agenda": Are We Creating a Frankenstein Monster?' (2013) 20 *Research Evaluation* 247.

The key criteria for assessing outputs in the REF 2014 were originality, significance and rigour, and it is expected that they will be used in the REF 2021. Originality referred to the innovative character of the output such as engagement with new/complex problems and developing innovative research methods and methodologies. Significance referred to the development of the intellectual agenda, which may be theoretical, methodological, substantive. Finally, rigour referred to the intellectual precision, robustness and appropriateness of the output.

It is useful to note that in the REF 2014, the scope of research that could be submitted to the law sub-panel was widely constructed comprising 'all doctrinal, theoretical, empirical, comparative, critical, theoretical, historical or other studies of law and legal phenomena including criminology and sociolegal studies'.[24] Saliently, it was stated that research in law might intersect and draw upon a variety of disciplines and methodologies. This encompassing understanding of legal research clearly opened spaces for interdisciplinary research, at least within the social sciences.

Nevertheless, as discussed in the Stern Review in 2016,[25] despite the growing importance of interdisciplinary research, often required by grant calls to address global challenges, the disciplinary 'silos' in the Unit of Assessment panel structure were perceived as discouraging such work. Thus, many departments adopted a risk-adverse strategy by not submitting as many interdisciplinary outputs as available. The Stern Review recommended the placing of more emphasis on and providing more guidance to the panels to recognise interdisciplinary work through the appointment of interdisciplinary 'champions' on the sub-panels with interdisciplinary expertise and to introduce interdisciplinarity also in the environment element of the REF 2021.

To address such calls for further developing interdisciplinary research, an Interdisciplinary Research Advisory Panel (IDAP) has been established to advise the REF team, REF panel chairs and the UK funding bodies on the approach for submitting and assessing interdisciplinary outputs in the new REF 2021. Following the IDAP's advice, the REF 2021 will have in each sub-panel at least one appointed interdisciplinary research adviser to oversee the equitable assessment of interdisciplinary

---

[24] Part 2C Main Panel C Criteria, REF 2014, 60, www.ref.ac.uk/2014/media/ref/content/pub/panelcriteriaandworkingmethods/01_12_2C.pdf.

[25] Building on Success and Learning from Experience: An Independent Review of the Research Excellence Framework, Department for Business, Energy and Industrial Strategy, July 2016, www.gov.uk/government/uploads/system/uploads/attachment_data/file/541338/ind-16-9-ref-stern-review.pdf.

research. Interdisciplinarity will also figure in the environment template to describe how the submitting unit's structures support interdisciplinary research. Finally, the so-called interdisciplinary identifier will be retained in the submission system as an optional field to better identify interdisciplinary research for which the appointed members will have oversigh.[26]

The inclusion of interdisciplinary research advisers on each sub-panel and of a new interdisciplinarity section in the environment template is a welcome development, which shows the institutional willingness to support interdisciplinary work. The extent to which these will make a difference on the assessment of interdisciplinarity is however unknown. Decisions regarding who will be appointed in the REF sub-panel to oversee interdisciplinarity have not been made at the time of writing and the way in which institutions and departments will complete the interdisciplinary section of the environment template is also unknown.

Whether these developments will minimise the risk-adverse strategy permeating REF 2014 leaves a question mark, especially in relation to outputs bridging natural and social sciences. Indeed, as in the past REF 2014, in the REF 2021 each sup-panel sits within a main panel. Law sits within Panel C (Social Sciences), whilst, for example, life sciences sit under Panel A (Medicine, Health and Life Sciences). In REF 2014, the biological sciences sub-panel admitted outputs that crossed other disciplines within the main panel but did not refer to research crossing other main panels.[27]

Thus, even if REF sup-panels have shown openness towards publications in non-disciplinary journals in the last REF and the definition of legal research as reported earlier is very inclusive and the renewed emphasis on interdisciplinarity for REF 2021 constitutes a positive sign, departments may still be adopting a risk-adverse strategy for outputs crossing natural sciences and social sciences due to lack of explicit connections in the REF definitions of research between the 'macro' subjects. This may also be due to issues such as journal formatting and expectations regarding authorship and length of articles that differ greatly between, in our case, legal research and natural sciences. If co-authorship is contemplated in law and in the REF sub-panel, the majority of outputs of legal scholars are often single authored or have at most a handful of writers. In the natural sciences, long lists of authors appear,

---

[26] See REF 2021, Interdisciplinary Research at www.ref.ac.uk/about/ir/.
[27] Part 2D Main Panel Criteria, REF 2014, 21, www.ref.ac.uk/2014/media/ref/content/pub/panelcriteriaandworkingmethods/01_12_2A.pdf.

with the first and last occupying the key places and the length of publications tends to be much shorter than in law. Also, formatting of papers
is more rigid in the natural sciences, which often require a standardised
format with headings such as 'material and methods' and 'results'. Such
formatting and length may not work for environmental legal scholarship.
All of this implies that even if co-authorship is possible and interdisciplinary research is well regarded in the REF, legal scholars may avoid
submitting for the REF outputs that are the product of intellectual
exchanges with natural scientists for fear of not being equitably assessed.
It may be safer for environmental lawyers to push the disciplinary
boundaries nearer home, engaging with other social scientists given
that sociolegal research is firmly written into the definition of legal
research, as discussed earlier.

2.2   Training Interdisciplinary Scholars

The previous section argued that, cumulatively, a particular auditing
culture embodied by the REF, next to different publication styles and
perceptions of scholars and schools, constitutes an apparatus that challenges the possibility of interdisciplinary research between the natural
and social sciences. This is however at odds with a grant culture that
pushes for creative interdisciplinary research across the sciences.
The Global Research Council has addressed the growing recognition of
funding interdisciplinary research worldwide.[28] At the UK level,
Research Councils encourage cross-council collaborations advertising
joint calls to address global sustainability challenges.[29] Such collaborations are encouraged at the very early stages of the academic career;
indeed, there are instances in which cross-council funding (for example,
Natural Environment Research Council/Economic and Social Research
Council) is available for PhD students. With the rise of doctoral training
partnerships in the country, interdisciplinary pathways are flourishing.
Most are internal to either the social or natural sciences, for example,

---

[28] 'Statement of Principles of Interdisciplinarity', Global Research Council, available at www
.rcuk.ac.uk/documents/documents/GRC2016Interdisciplinarity-pdf/.

[29] See, for example, 'The UK Strategy for the Global Challenges Research Fund',
Department for Business, Energy and Industrial Strategy, 2017 at www.rcuk.ac.uk/docu
ments/documents/global-challenges-research-fund-gcrf-strategy-pdf/. The Global
Challenges Research Fund brings together the UK Research Councils with other funding
bodies including UK Higher Education Funding bodies, the Academy of Medical
Sciences, Royal Society, British Academy, the Royal Academy of Engineering and UK
Space Agency.

requiring students to have proposals bridging law and geography and a supervisory team representing the different disciplines. This is of course positive for environmental sociolegal researchers.

To provide an example within my own institution (University of Bristol), the Economic and Social Research Council South-West Doctoral Training Partnership,[30] which is a collaboration between the universities of Bristol, University of the West of England, Bath, Exeter and Plymouth, hosts among its interdisciplinary pathways one called Sustainable Futures,[31] which attracts, inter alia, law students who are interested in exploring the interface between law and other social sciences disciplines in the field of sustainability. Such cross-institutional and cross-disciplinary perspectives have their institutional challenges: from the funding which is assigned to the school of the first supervisor, to different PhD handbooks in different schools with different reference styles and methodologies and different requirements for tracking students' performance during the course of the PhD programme. These are all elements of the audit culture, challenging the development of inter-disciplinary research.

Those challenges are exacerbated when attempts at cross-council studentships are made. Once again, speaking from my own experience, in recent years the Economic and Social Research Council (ESRC), South-West Doctoral Training Partnership has provided matching funding for scholarships with the Natural Environment Research Council Great Western Four+ Doctoral Training Partnership, a partnership designed to train earth and natural scientists in Bath, Bristol, Exeter and Cardiff.[32] The challenges of such cross-council scholarships are more substantial than the challenges mentioned earlier within interdisciplinary pathways such as Sustainable Futures. These begin with different approaches to the development of research proposals: in the natural sciences, students are asked to apply to proposals designed by supervisors in advance and they are assessed on the basis of their fit within that proposal; in the social sciences, students are asked to develop their own proposals and the choice of whom to fund heavily relies on the academic quality and feasibility of the proposal. This implies that when cross-council student-ships are advertised, a choice between the social or the natural science

[30] See South West Doctoral Training Partnership, www.swdtp.ac.uk/.
[31] See 'Sustainable Futures', South West Doctoral Training Partnership, www.swdtp.ac.uk /home-page-2/prospectivestudents/pathway-information/sustainable-futures/.
[32] See NERC Great Western Four+ Doctoral Training Partnership, https://nercgw4plus.ac .uk/.

approach needs to be made by the governance bodies of the doctoral training partnerships. Applicants trained in natural sciences may find it difficult to develop their own proposals from scratch, and applicants from the social sciences may find applying to an already existing proposal intellectually constraining. Second, it is difficult to find students who have been trained in both natural and social sciences and therefore capable of excellent performance in both elements of the PhD research: undergraduate and masters degree programmes generally sit within either social or natural sciences.

The example of doctoral training centres shows how the institutional constrains of bridging natural and social sciences explored earlier in the context of the REF examples are also present from the early stages of an academic career. However, if we, as environmental sociolegal scholars, are serious about engaging with the environment, rather than only with rules regarding the environment, it is essential that a radical shift in the organisational structure of universities, beginning from teaching up to research auditing exercises, occurs to facilitate interdisciplinary research encounters. For example, more interdisciplinary teaching programmes at the undergraduate and postgraduate levels could be developed. If this already occurs in certain subjects crossing the human and physical dimensions of knowledge, such as geography, it is much more challenging for law, which is more inward looking, probably also due to its vocational nature, which requires the syllabus to cover subjects for a qualifying law degree. Nevertheless, law school could offer options of joint honours degrees with natural sciences. As for research audits, a more explicit consideration of interdisciplinary research among the macro subjects could be made, as well as the development of clear guidelines regarding its assessment to incentivise such types of outputs.

Provided that the institutional challenges described earlier are overcome with time, there remains another set of key challenges of an epistemological nature, which may render improbable solid interdisciplinary research between sociolegal scholars and natural scientists. The next section explores such epistemological differences and in doing so it asks to what extent these are inherent in the nature of the disciplines or, at least partially, institutionally constructed and reproduced.

3   Epistemological Challenges

Wilhelm Windelband, a neo-Kantian philosopher, made the well-known distinction between different approaches to knowledge and knowing: the idiographic and the nomothetic. Such division is between those studying values and subjectivities and those concerned with the search for generalisable laws (*nomos*) based on systematic empirical observation of facts. The extent to which this distinction corresponds to that between positivist natural sciences (the nomothetic) and interpretivist social sciences (the idiographic) determines the possibility of interdisciplinary scholarship.

Positivists, arguing that social sciences are also nomothetic, have questioned such a distinction. Notable in this respect is the early positivist position articulated by Comte, followed by the sociology of Durkheim based on the argument that social facts should be treated in the same ways as the objects of scientific inquiry and also the refinements of the neo-positivism of the Vienna School in the 1920s, which attempted to apply the atomistic philosophy of natural sciences to the social sciences and argued more fundamentally that science is the description of experience.

Positivists, as is well known, are proponents of the verifiability of knowledge, its neutral (value-free) character and the experimental method based on observational units. Valid knowledge is produced independently of ethical or subjective elements. From a positivist standpoint, the union between natural and social sciences exists on the basis that all science should be based on the nomothetic approach. Comte's thesis on the unity of science indeed implies that there cannot be a distinction between the natural and social sciences.

However, the core elements of positivism have been criticised since the 1950s, most famously with Popper's argument that science proceeds deductively through the principle of falsification (rather than verification) or with the Kuhnian concept of paradigm and the importance assigned to the historical and social contexts that allow revolutions and new paradigms to emerge.

Positivism has also been strongly rejected by one the one hand, the critical theorists of the Frankfurt School and, on the other, by Science and Technologies Studies (STS). I am focussing here on some of the insights offered by STS because, in critiquing positivism, they, differently from the traditional position of the Frankfurt scholars,[33] question its validity also in the context of the natural sciences. Their critiques are highly

---

[33] See Barry Barnes, *Interests and the Growth of Knowledge* (Abingdon: Routledge, 1977).

relevant for social-legal environmental law scholarship.[34] In doing so, the STS scholars highlight the societal, historically contextual character of scientific knowledge and offer the opportunity to recover epistemological bridges between the natural and social sciences.

3.1 Beyond Nature and Culture, Beyond Natural Scientists and Environmental Law Scholars?

Following Jasanoff,[35] the STS literature can be divided into two strands: the 'constitutive' and the 'interactional'. The first strand, associated most predominantly with the work of Latour and fellow Actor-Network-Theory scholars,[36] is more concerned with metaphysical questions regarding the boundaries between the natural and the social. The second strand, rooted in the Edinburgh school of sociology of scientific knowledge, focuses on epistemology, more specifically 'knowledge conflicts within worlds that have already been demarcated, for practical purposes, into the natural and the social'.[37]

Of course, the two strands inform each other and produce overlapping critiques. Indeed, in studying science as a social practice, the 'constitutive' STS literature has shown how science establishes itself with a demarcated identity and authority. In *Science and Action*,[38] for example, Latour's argument is that what distinguishes science from other regimes is not its rationality but the way in which science-objects are constructed within particular networks of discourses, materials and practices. These networks in a sense enact the scientific, bringing into being what they discover. The STS literature has demonstrated how the social elements of scientific knowledge and how the boundaries between scientific objects and social values are blurred in real life. The detachment of the research object from the observer (the scientist) is put into question in these studies. To bring another example, Latour and Woolgar's (1986)

---

[34] It could be argued that they are less useful for doctrinal legal studies, given their legal positivist underpinning.
[35] Sheila Jasanoff, *States of Knowledge: The Co-Production of Science and Social Order* (Abingdon: Routledge 2004).
[36] Bruno Latour, *We Have Never Been Modern* (Cambridge, MA: Harvard University Press, 1993); Andrew Pickering, *The Mangle of Practice: Time, Agency, and Science* (Chicago: University of Chicago Press 1995).
[37] Jasanoff, *States of Knowledge*, p. 19.
[38] Bruno Latour, *Science in Action: How to Follow Scientists and Engineers through Society* (Cambridge, MA: Harvard University Press, 1987).

classical study of the daily practices of scientists working at
a neuroendocrinology laboratory at the Salk Institute of Biological
Sciences showed that positivist analyses of rationality, of evidence, of
truth were not overly relevant to understanding the production of
scientific knowledge.[39]

The 'interactional' approach focuses even more explicitly on
knowledge conflicts, and its insights are very relevant for thinking
about possible bridges between sociolegal environmental scholarship
and the natural sciences. Shapin and Schaffer make the argument
that claims to reliability and truth are sustained through techniques
of validation, and social practices render scientific knowledges more
credible than others, defining science and scientists.[40] The validation
of science as a distinguished subject is not independent from the
political and the subjective. Similarly, the 'boundary work' of Gieryn
shows how particular social, institutional practices and discursive
representations help in demarcating the boundaries of science.
Carving a special place for scientific disciplines is therefore
a 'boundary-work': 'their [scientists] attribution of selected characteristics to the institution of science (i.e., to its practitioners, methods, stock of knowledge, value and work organization) for purposes
of constructing a social boundary that distinguishes some intellectual
activities as "non-science"'.[41] Its boundaries are always in the making so that scientific epistemologies are flexible, varying historically,
geographically and politically.

The STS literature has made a strong case against the bounded-
ness of disciplines, showing that they are not closed and homoge-
nous systems but have porous borders.[42] Relatedly, they have made
the argument that epistemological clashes are also present within
a particular discipline and therefore disciplines are not necessarily
uniform. As Lowe et al. argue, 'what holds most disciplines together
is a collective claim to authoritative understanding of certain

---

[39] Bruno Latour & Steve Woolgar, *Laboratory Life: The Construction of Scientific Facts*
(Princeton, NJ: Princeton University Press, 1986).

[40] Steven Shapin & Simon Shaffer, *Leviathan and the Air-Pump* (Princeton, NJ: Princeton
University Press, 1985).

[41] Thomas F. Gieryn, 'Boundary-Work and the Demarcation of Science from Non-Science:
Strains and Interests in Professional Ideologies of Scientists' (1983) 48 *American
Sociological Review* 781, 782.

[42] Andrew Abbott, *Chaos of Disciplines* (Chicago: University of Chicago Press, 2001).

problems or objects and an evolving nexus of institutional connections'.[43]

These observations are relevant in at least two respects. First, they support the dismantling of dichotomies such as the nomothetic vs the idiographic, the facts vs values, the natural sciences vs the social sciences showing how natural science itself has a strong subjective element and is not a-political or a-contextual. Rather than following a positivistic pathway of the unity of science, STS studies rekindle the social and natural sciences by showing their 'co-production', to use Jasenoff terminology.[44] This opens windows of opportunity for collaborative and interdisciplinary research. Second and even more telling, these observations help us reconnect with the institutional challenges discussed earlier in showing that institutions themselves, including academia, are a space for boundary demarcation between the disciplines and the fortification of their epistemological differences. Institutionalised ways of characterising knowledge have an effect on the possibility for interdisciplinary research between environmental law and natural scientists and in doing so they foster the perceptions of unsurmountable epistemological differences. A brief sociological excursus into the history of science shows us that the way we understand valid and rigorous knowledge has been subject to change. Academic institutions play a major role in defining knowledge and its boundaries and in doing so produce the naturalisation of epistemological openings or closures. The epistemological issues cannot therefore be disentangled from the institutional ones.

Conclusion

Environmental law scholarship is caught in a dilemma. On the one hand, as a relatively young discipline, it needs to establish firm borders, 'discipline' itself so as to gain authority by having an agreed set of problems, theories and methods that are perceived to be rigorous. On the other hand, because of the nature of its object (the environment) and because of the spaces in which environmental law is produced (often at the interface between the legal and the political), environmental law scholarship cannot isolate itself, for its very existence depends on science, politics and also culture(s) of legal subjects.

---

[43] Philip Lowe & Jeremy Phillipson, 'Barriers to Research Collaboration Across Disciplines: Scientific Paradigms and Institutional Practices' (2009) 41 *Environment and Planning A* 1171, 1173.

[44] Jasanoff, *States of Knowledge*.

The question of interdisciplinarity is indeed not an add-on to environmental law scholarship but inherent in the essence of its subject matter. If sociolegal scholarship in environmental law is sufficiently developed, with scholars sitting in law schools borrowing insights from sociological theories, political science, anthropology and human geography, the connections between environmental law scholarship and natural science scholarship is more embryonic. This is not to say that environmental law scholars are not engaging with science and technology: from the very beginning environmental law scholars have studied and questioned the role of science in the production and reproduction of environmental law. However, it is science, rather than scientific disciplines, and environmental law, rather than law scholarship, that are at the core of existing academic analyses. This chapter has put the question of interdisciplinarity between natural sciences and environmental law scholarship at the centre, signposting some of the challenges of pushing the boundaries of environmental law scholarship beyond the social sciences. The discourse of interdisciplinarity is well established in academic circles and research councils, and other funding bodies are making efforts to establish cross-council funding opportunities to tackle complex environmental problems.[45] Following Gibbons et al.[46] and Nowotny et al.,[47] this can be characterised as part of a shift from 'Mode 1' to 'Mode 2' knowledge production, the latter characterised by research aimed at transcending disciplinary boundaries and also academic and non-academic interests.[48]

However, this chapter has argued that there are some key institutional and epistemological challenges that are interrelated and that should be taken seriously, prior to concluding that Mode 2 knowledge production guarantees the possibility for interdisciplinary work between natural scientists and environmental law scholars.

Perhaps what is more realistic at present is to make a case for multidisciplinary rather than interdisciplinary research, so that cooperation happens without attempts at synthesis or integration given the challenges identified. This however accords to what Pedersen has called, a 'service' version of interdisciplinarity, which consists in environmental lawyers

[45] Lowe & Phillipson, 'Barriers to Research Collaboration Across Disciplines'.
[46] Michael Gibbons et al., *The New Production of Knowledge: The Dynamics of Science and Research in Contemporary Societies* (Sage, 1994).
[47] Helga Nowotny et al., *Re-Thinking Science. Knowledge and the Public in an Age of Uncertainty* (Polity Press, 2001).
[48] Notable in this respect is the Impact culture in REF, which is assigned even more weight in REF 2021.

contributing 'to a self-contained piece of scholarship or a research project as part of a larger endeavour, counting scholars from different backgrounds amongst its contributors'.[49] A multidisciplinary option is epistemologically less challenging because it does not require scholars to rethink the production of knowledge within their field. A 'service' version however reinforces the production of disciplinary differences. Even if we accept this very soft version of interdisciplinarity, we still run against some of the institutional challenges identified earlier, such as current auditing mechanisms not so ready to assess research that crosses the main REF panels. Indeed, the key message of this chapter is that unless the institutional frameworks are revised to give serious weight to interdisciplinary scholarship, either service versions of interdisciplinarity or more 'interactional' versions are risky endeavours.

Bibliography (Cited Academic References)

Abbott A., *Chaos of Disciplines* (Chicago: University of Chicago Press, 2001).

Barnes B., *Interests and the Growth of Knowledge* (Abingdon: Routledge, 1977).

Bourdieu P., *Outline of a Theory of Practice* (Cambridge: Cambridge University Press, 1977).

Brennan J. and Branco Sousa S., 'UK Research Excellence Framework and the Transformation of Research Production', in C. Musselin & P. Teixeira (eds), *Reforming Higher Education. Higher Education Dynamics* (New York: Springer, 2013).

Brew A. & Lucas L., *Academic Research and Researchers* (Society for Research into Higher Education and the Open University Press, 2009).

Collini S., *Speaking of Universities* (London: Verso, 2017).

Cotterrell R., 'Subverting Orthodoxy, Making Law Central: A View of Sociolegal Studies' (2002) 29 *Journal of Legal Studies* 632.

de Sousa Santos B., *Toward a New Common Sense: Law, Science and Politics in the Paradigmatic Transition* (London: Butterworths LexisNexis, 2002).

Engle Merry S., 'Legal Pluralism' (1988) 22 *Law and Society Review* 869.

Ewick P. & Silbey S. S., *The Common Place of Law. Stories from Everyday Life* (Chicago: University of Chicago Press, 1998).

Fisher E. et al., 'Maturity and Methodology: Starting a Debate about Environmental Law Scholarship' (2009) 21 *Journal of Environmental Law* 213.

Gibbons M. et al., *The New Production of Knowledge: The Dynamics of Science and Research in Contemporary Societies* (London: Sage, 1994).

---

[49] Pedersen, 'The Limits of Interdisciplinarity', 427.

Gieryn T. F., 'Boundary-Work and the Demarcation of Science from Non-Science: Strains and Interests in Professional Ideologies of Scientists' (1983) 48 *American Sociological Review* 781, 782.

Griffith J., 'What Is Legal Pluralism?' (1986) 24 *Journal of Legal Pluralism and Unofficial Law* 129.

Griffiths A., von Benda-Beckmann F. & von Benda-Beckmann K., *Spatializing Law: An Anthropological Geography of Law in Society* (Farnham: Ashgate, 2009).

Halliday S. & Morgan B., 'I Fought the Law and the Law Won? Legal Consciousness and the Critical Imagination' 66 *Current Legal Problems* 1.

Harris D. H., 'The Development of Socio-Legal Studies in the United Kingdom' (1983) 3 *Legal Studies* 315.

Jasanoff S., *States of Knowledge: The Co-Production of Science and Social Order* (Abingdon: Routledge, 2004).

Lange B. et al., 'A Framework for a Joint Hydro-Meteorological-Social Analysis of Drought' 2017 578 *Science of the Total Environment* 297.

Latour B., *Science in Action: How to Follow Scientists and Engineers through Society* (Cambridge, MA: Harvard University Press, 1987).

Latour B., *We Have Never Been Modern* (Cambridge, MA: Harvard University Press, 1993).

Latour B. & Woolgar S., *Laboratory Life: The Construction of Scientific Facts* (Princeton, NJ: Princeton University Press, 1986).

Lowe P and Phillipson J, 'Barriers to Research Collaboration Across Disciplines: Scientific Paradigms and Institutional Practices' (2009) 41 *Environment and Planning A* 1171.

Martin B., 'The Research Excellence Framework and the "Impact Agenda": Are We Creating a Frankenstein Monster?' (2013) 20 *Research Evaluation* 247.

McEldowney J. & McEldowney S., 'Science and Environmental Law: Collaboration across the Double Helix' (2011) 13 *Environmental Law Review* 169.

Melissaris E., *Ubiquitous Law: Legal Theory and the Space for Legal Pluralism* (Farnham: Ashgate, 2009).

Natarajan L.C. et al., 'Navigating the Participatory Processes of Renewable Energy Infrastructure Regulation: A "Local Participant Perspective" on the NSIPs Regime in England and Wales' (2918) 114 *Energy Policy* 201.

Nowotny H. et al., *Re-Thinking Science. Knowledge and the Public in an Age of Uncertainty* (Cambridge: Polity Press, 2001).

Owen D. & Noblet C., 'Interdisciplinary Research and Environmental Law' (2015) 41 *Ecology Law Quarterly* 887.

Pedersen O. 'Modest Pragmatic Lessons for a Diverse and Incoherent Environmental Law' (2013) 33 *Oxford Journal of Legal Studies* 103.

Pedersen O. 'The Limits of Interdisciplinarity and the Practice of Environmental Law Scholarship' (2014) 26 *Journal of Environmental Law* 423.

Philippopoulos-Mihalopoulos A. & Brooks V. (eds.), *Research Methods in Environmental Law: A Handbook* (Cheltenham: Edward Elgar, 2017).

Pickering A., *The Mangle of Practice: Time, Agency, and Science* (Chicago: University of Chicago Press, 1995).

Pieraccini M. & Cardwell E., 'Divergent Perceptions of New Marine Protected Areas: Comparing Legal Consciousness in Scilly and Barra, UK' (2015) 119 *Ocean and Coastal Management* 21.

Power M., *The Audit Explosion* (New York: Demos, 1994).

Roberts S. A., 'After Government? On Representing Law without the State' (2005) 68 *Modern Law Review* 1.

Shapin S. & Shaffer S., *Leviathan and the Air-Pump* (Princeton, NJ: Princeton University Press, 1985).

Slaughter S. & Leslie L., *Academic Capitalism: Politics, Policies, and the Entrepreneurial University* (Baltimore, MD: Johns Hopkins University Press, 1998).

Slaughter S. & Rhoades G., 'The Neo-Liberal University' (2000) 6 *New Labor Forum* 73.

Strathern M. (ed.), *Audit Cultures: Anthropological Studies in Accountability, Ethics and the Academy* (Abingdon: Routledge, 2000).

Tarlock D., 'Environmental Law: Ethics or Science?' (1996) 7 *Duke Environmental Law & Policy Forum* 193.

Tarlock D., 'Who Owns Science?' (2002) 10 *Pennsylvania State Environmental Law Review* 135.

Twining W., *General Jurisprudence: Understanding Law from a Global Perspective* (Cambridge: Cambridge University Press, 2009).

Wheeler S. & Thomas P. A., *Socio-Legal Studies* (Oxford: Hart Publishing, 2000).

Williams K. & Grant J., 'A Comparative Review of How the Policy and Procedures to Assess Research Impact Evolved in Australia and the UK' (2018) 27 *Research Evaluation* 93.

Wright S. & Shore C. (eds.), *Death of the Public University? Uncertain Futures for Higher Education in the Knowledge Economy* (New York: Berghahn Books, 2017).

6

Crossing Disciplines in Planning: A Renewable Energy Case Study

MARIA LEE, SIMON LOCK, LUCY NATARAJAN AND
YVONNE RYDIN

Introduction

One of the most heartening things about the community of environmental law scholars is the openness of the sub-discipline, which rarely
succumbs to a theatrical policing of internal legal boundaries and is
underpinned by a recognition of other disciplinary (including other
legal) perspectives. Some incoherence, and even (dare we say) some
poor quality scholarship,[1] is a small price to pay for this openness, for
avoiding a world in which 'sensible' people know and police what constitutes 'good' environmental law scholarship. The absence of a 'single
guiding logic' for environmental law scholarship is neither unique to this
element of legal academia nor a bad thing.[2]

But reflection and self-criticism can also be bracing. One of the striking
themes of environmental law scholarship is an assumption about the
necessity and ease of interdisciplinarity (a tricky term, to which we
return), including in the lone scholar model of law. This chapter provides
personal reflections on collaboration between academics from different
disciplines in a project on public participation and knowledge construction during decision-making on major renewable energy projects.
The four individuals involved (the authors of this chapter) work at
University College London (UCL), based in the Faculty of Laws, the
Department of Science and Technology Studies and the Bartlett School
of Planning. We work in cognate areas, and we share a fundamental belief

This work was supported by ESRC Award No. 164522. We are grateful to Chiara Armeni and
Steven Vaughan for comments on this chapter.

[1] Ole Pedersen, 'The Limits of Interdisciplinarity and the Practice of Environmental Law
  Scholarship' (2014) 26 *Journal of Environmental Law* 423.
[2] Elizabeth Fisher et al., 'Maturity and Methodology: Starting a Debate about Environmental
  Law Scholarship' (2009) 21 *Journal of Environmental Law* 213 at 219.

that words matter and institutions matter. We take, broadly, a social constructionist approach to our work, and a co-productionist approach: 'the facts' cannot be taken for granted, but neither can 'the social'; the facts and society are mutually constitutive.[3] Perhaps self-evidently, we also share an interest in the governance processes around a transition to renewable energy, and we have all studied in different ways on knowledge and expertise, and on public participation. We understand planning as an element of broader democratic processes and seek to explore that.

Our shared perspectives and languages have made this collaboration less difficult than others can be. But even here, reflecting on our methods prompts interesting and occasionally challenging questions about our own and one another's disciplines. We have all worked in cross-disciplinary teams before, on big projects and small, within UCL and beyond, with more or less joy and success, but we focus here on our joint project. Following a brief introduction to that project, we discuss inter-disciplinarity and the nature of our collaboration. We then turn to reflect on lessons learned in this project. The social side of our collaboration has been crucial. Working with people you like, and whose work you respect, is perhaps not a bad starting point for scholarship across disciplines. But a cohesive team does not just happen, and we would like to reflect a little on the factors beyond the personal that have contributed to that.

The Project

Our project, *Evidence, Publics and Decision-Making for Major Wind Infrastructure*, funded by the Economic and Social Research Council (ESRC), examines the decision-making process for Nationally Significant Infrastructure Projects (NSIPs) under the Planning Act 2008, with a focus on renewable energy development. Applications for a Development Consent Order are made to an Examining Authority, appointed by the Planning Inspectorate, which makes recommendations and reports its findings and conclusions to the Secretary of State. The Secretary of State makes the final decision. The Planning Act (and associated regulation such as environmental impact assessment) pro-vides a number of opportunities for interested parties to be consulted on applications for development consent. The strong policy commitment to certain low carbon energy infrastructure raises questions about the

---

[3] Sheila Jasanoff (ed.), *States of Knowledge: The Co-Production of Science and Social Order* (Abingdon: Routledge, 2004).

ways in which decision-makers might take local impacts and the views of affected communities into account. This 'public participation' strand interacts with an exploration of the construction and use of 'knowledge' in the process, and the ways in which diverse professional, government and lay actors introduce knowledge claims into the process, and how they are heard and used as evidence in the reasoning and justifications for recommendations.

A total of fourteen renewable energy projects had gone through the process at the start of our empirical research. Three of these were taken out of the assessment as being so far out to sea that they raised relatively few issues for 'local' publics, although we did return to them for some of the work on evidence. We initially selected eleven cases to study,[4] adding the Navitus Bay wind farm a few months later, when it became the first (and still only) offshore 'nationally significant' wind farm to be refused consent.[5]

We discuss 'our differences' later and hope that the necessarily messy nature of even the apparently neatest methodology comes out there. In this project, we combined the insights from our multiple methods, triangulating and enriching insights from one with the results from another. Almost all of the documentation submitted to the Examining Authority (ExA) in respect of NSIP development consents is kept on the Planning Inspectorate website, providing an extraordinarily rich source of material.[6] We focused on reading and analysing all of the ExA Reports and Secretary of State decision letters, as well as a certain amount of other material submitted during the examination. Alongside this close reading, the documents were coded to enable comparison and identification of themes under the five headings of actors, impacts, evidence, deliberative processes and mitigation (and dozens of subheadings). The coding was conducted in NVivo and tested through blind re-coding of randomly sampled text extracts by two coders. Code runs were iteratively

---

[4] Kentish Offshore Wind Farm Extension, Galloper Offshore Wind Farm, Burbo Bank Offshore Wind Farm Extension, Rampion Offshore Wind Farm, Walney Offshore Wind Farm Extension, Triton Knoll Offshore Wind Farm, Brechfa Forest West Wind Farm, Clocaenog Forest Wind Farm, Swansea Bay Tidal Lagoon, North Blyth Biomass Plant, Rookery South Energy from Waste Plant. All of the documents can be found at https://infrastructure.planninginspectorate.gov.uk/.

[5] On Navitus, see Maria Lee, 'Landscape and Knowledge in Nationally Significant Wind Energy Projects' (2017) 37 *Legal Studies* 3. The Mynydd y Gwynt *onshore* Wind Farm application was rejected on 20 November 2015.

[6] https://infrastructure.planninginspectorate.gov.uk/.

undertaken to build up the analysis; the initial runs selected extracts for close reading, which then suggested lines of analysis and further code runs.

The fieldwork consisted primarily of focus groups, telephone interviews, an online survey and workshops. More ad hoc observation visits enriched the analysis and ensured its firm grounding. Nine focus groups, with local people who had been involved in eight of our cases, plus an additional 'control' non-renewables case, were held at libraries and community facilities.[7] Focus group research is a well-established qualitative research method for studying complex social phenomena, and it is particularly useful for understanding experiences. It can help silent or quieter 'voices' come to the foreground. The purpose here was to get a deeper understanding of public concerns and aspirations regarding decision-making processes. The events included up to twelve local people, including residents, those with business interests and those representing a third sector organisation. In addition, staff and consultants working for some of the applicants as 'public engagement' professionals, who interact directly with local people and manage the statutory pre-application consultation, were interviewed. Interviews were also conducted with national NGOs that did not fit neatly into the roles identified for other actors, and with certain key actors to explore the unique perspectives involved in Navitus Bay. The online survey was a short questionnaire to follow up on the focus group findings with a larger number of people.[8] The survey data were both quantitative and qualitative, providing a snapshot from across the fieldwork, and commentary to unpack the detail. Towards the end of our project, we held workshops with developers and members of ExAs to discuss our emerging findings and recommendations.

The evolution of our collaborative experience is perhaps as important as our use of these formal methodologies. Our interest in the NSIP regime began several years before we applied for funding for this project. We were part of a larger 'climate change technologies' group, convened by Maria. This group explored the ways in which the legal and policy context shaped the implementation of legally guaranteed rights of participation around large wind farms and carbon

---

[7] See 'NSIPs Research', University College London, www.ucl.ac.uk/nsips.

[8] Lucy Natarajan et al., 'Navigating the Participatory Processes of Renewable Energy Infrastructure Regulation: A "Local Participant Perspective" on the NSIPs Regime in England and Wales' (2018) 114 *Energy Policy* 201.

capture and storage.[9] It was supported by the UCL Grand Challenges programme,[10] and whilst this had not been the explicit intention, it turned out to be a 'pilot' project for this bigger piece of work. We were able to pilot our ideas, our ability to work together and also aspects of our methodology, given that earlier work involved both close reading and some focus groups. The smaller group emerged organically, on the basis of shared interests and personal affinity, rather than as an institutional requirement.

UCL is no exception to the pattern of institutional efforts to incentivise cross-disciplinary working, and it has been extremely proactive in stimulating work across faculties. Although UCL seems to have been less directive than we understand might have been the case elsewhere, the encouragement of cross-faculty work has occasionally felt artificial and even burdensome, notwithstanding some undeniably exciting outputs. We benefitted from the less direct, relationship-building benefits of institutional pressure towards collaboration. Relationships build during work on 'a project', creating both personal bonds and familiarity with colleagues' work. With Yvonne as principal investigator, we built on our personal and professional links, as well as our shared sense of the practical and scholarly significance of the NSIPs regime, to apply for ESRC funding for our project.

Disciplines and Their Transgression

Academic disciplines bring with them an organisation, working methods and years of tacit and explicit knowledge that can be enabling and empowering, as well as a more-or-less collectively agreed notion of rigour and quality. Disciplines can also be rigid and restrictive and may fail to flourish in changing contexts.[11] From the initial application to the ESRC, we have described our work as cross-disciplinary. Any discussion of cross-disciplinarity needs to start out by acknowledging the complexity of the ways in which we describe an activity where individuals from

[9] Maria Lee et al., 'Public Participation and Climate Change Infrastructure' (2013) 25 *Journal of Environmental Law* 33; Simon Lock et al., 'Nuclear Energy Sounded Wonderful 40 Years Ago: UK Citizen Views on CCS' (2014) 66 *Energy Policy* 428; Yvonne Rydin et al., 'Public Engagement in Decision-making on Major Wind Energy Projects' (2015) 27 *Journal of Environmental Law* 139.

[10] 'UCL Grand Challenges', University College London, www.ucl.ac.uk/grand-challenges.

[11] See e.g. D. W. Vick, 'Interdisciplinarity and the Discipline of Law' (2004) 31 *Journal of Law and Society* 153.

different academic disciplines work together, or where individuals enrich their own work by calling on insights from other disciplines. Three approaches are commonly identified in the literature.[12] First, 'interdisciplinarity', in which there is 'an attempt to integrate or synthesize perspectives from several discussions'.[13] Second, 'multidisciplinarity', in which there is no effort to transform the disciplines, which remain intact within their own boundaries. And third, 'transdisciplinarity', in which disciplinary boundaries are transcended and broken down. This threefold classification of interdisciplinarity could never capture the variety of work between disciplines, and the boundaries between them must be fluid. In any event, disciplines themselves are constructed and mutable, and their shapes and borders are not inevitable: they are 'constructs borne out of historical processes involving both objects and methods of study; they provide "frames of reference, methodological approaches, topics of study, theoretical canons and technologies"'.[14]

The term 'interdisciplinarity' is often used generically (as well as in the first sense earlier) to capture a spectrum of approaches to working across disciplines;[15] we have worked with the term 'cross-disciplinarity' in the same way. We were never hoping to break down the boundaries of our disciplines on this project, which in any event are not rigid in respect of our individual disciplinary approaches. We are working across at least the three disciplines of law, planning, and science and technology studies (STS). These are all potentially generous disciplines, exploring a very wide range of issues from many perspectives, and using a plurality of methodologies. We each take, broadly speaking, an interdisciplinary approach to our own work. Our project is an example of 'moderate'[16] or 'cognate'[17] interdisciplinarity, rather than radical interdisciplinarity, for example, between the physical sciences and law.

---

[12] E.g. Andrew Barry et al., 'Logics of Interdisciplinarity' (2008) 37 *Economy and Society* 20; Judith Petts et al., 'Crossing Boundaries: Inter-Disciplinarity in the Context of Urban Environments' (2008) 39 *Geoforum* 593.

[13] Barry, 'Logics of Interdisciplinarity', 27.

[14] Petts, 'Crossing Boundaries', 596, citing the Chambers English Dictionary.

[15] Barry, 'Logics of Interdisciplinarity'; Petts, 'Crossing Boundaries'; Pedersen, 'The Limits of Interdisciplinarity'. See also the British Academy on interdisciplinarity as a 'family resemblance concept': 'Crossing Paths: Interdisciplinary Institutions, Careers, Education and Applications', British Academy, July 2016.

[16] Gavin Little, 'Developing Environmental Law Scholarship: Going Beyond the Legal Space' (2016) *Legal Studies* 48.

[17] Petts, 'Crossing Boundaries'.

STS is *itself* described as an interdisciplinary field aiming at the creation of 'an integrative understanding of the origins, dynamics, and consequences of science and technology'; STS has 'through three decades of
interdisciplinary interaction and integration, shifting intellectual
continents and cataclysmic conceptual shocks, perseverance and imagination ... become institutionalised and intellectually influential'.[18] Many
of its ideas and methods have been adopted and employed extensively in
other social science and humanities disciplines, including law and planning studies, but also history, geography and political science. Planning
scholars often come from different disciplinary backgrounds (such as
economics, political science, sociology or geography) as well as from
a variety of multidisciplinary educational routes (such as urban studies
or land economy). Planning scholars embrace many approaches to
research, focusing on particular domains, such as transport or housing;
or practices, such as collaboration, regulation or design; or outcomes,
such as sustainability or inclusion. Planning is theoretically diverse, with
different researchers adopting approaches as distinct as Marxist,
Habermasian or governmentality perspectives, with equally diverse
methodological underpinnings. Legal scholarship is also theoretically
and methodologically diverse.[19] Few academic lawyers consider themselves purely doctrinal scholars, and the call on other disciplines by legal
scholars is diverse in range and depth. Environmental law is especially
permeated by different approaches to interdisciplinarity.[20] Whilst the
pluralism of our disciplines is often generous, it can be conflictual. In law,
crossing some boundaries between legal sub-disciplines can seem much
more transgressive than moving outside law is for environmental
lawyers.

The authors of this chapter were (presumably) invited to participate in
this collection because one of our members (Maria) self-identifies and is
identified as, amongst other things, an *environmental* lawyer. And we
instinctively class this project (in part) as an environmental law project.
But it could equally be described as a planning law project, and it might
matter. Planning law is arguably one of the precursors to our current
environmental law. It was once a hot topic of academic study, forming an

---

[18] Edward J. Hackett et al., 'Introduction' in Edward J. Hackett et al. (eds.), *The Handbook of
      Science and Technology Studies* (Cambridge, MA: MIT Press, 2008), p. 1.
[19] Vick, 'Interdisciplinarity and the Discipline of Law'; David Feldman, 'The Nature of Legal
      Scholarship' (1989) 52 *Modern Law Review* 498.
[20] E.g. Fisher, 'Maturity and Methodology'; Pedersen, 'The Limits of Interdisciplinarity';
      Little, 'Developing Environmental Law Scholarship'.

important core of administrative law scholarship.[21] It went through a period of *relative* academic neglect from the end of the 1980s until very recently. Planning became a practitioner-led area,[22] as fresh issues stimulated administrative law, and the new discipline of environmental law became established, absorbing planning law as a small element within it. Analysing planning as a part of environmental or administrative law must shape its scholarly reception, emphasising the legitimacy of the exercise of state power, or the effectiveness of environmental protection. The construction and role of both publics and expertise may well come into a different sort of focus depending on the perspective taken, and of course the broader contribution of planning law to working out how we want to live (beyond environmental protection) may be neglected. The focus on renewable energy superficially reduces the dilemma, and climate change may partly explain the renewed interest of environmental lawyers in planning. But it reminds us that the boundaries of environmental law, a relatively new discipline, are dynamic and potentially contested. And even in this open-hearted area, what the discipline 'is' cannot be taken for granted.[23] As well as its porous borders, profound but little-addressed disagreements on the value of theory, the value of description and exposition,[24] the role of internal legal analysis, the place for political engagement in scholarship,[25] the necessity and nature of interdisciplinarity and the centrality of method underlie our approaches and our judgements.

Cross-disciplinary work is nothing new, and disciplines necessarily evolve and disappear. The debate about the pressures and directions of interdisciplinarity has intensified over recent years. There seems to be a growing appreciation that certain complex social challenges (climate

[21] See e.g. Patrick McAuslan, 'Administrative Law, Collective Consumption and Judicial Policy' (1983) 46 *Modern Law Review* 1.

[22] Both law and planning have close relationships with practice and the professions, which have not always been happy for scholarly confidence and identity; e.g. William Twining, *Blackstone's Tower: The English Law School* (London: Sweet and Maxwell, 1994).

[23] A focus on reflection and self-criticism within environmental law was started by Fisher et al., 'Maturity and Methodology'. We do not share the pessimistic (although not uniformly pessimistic) perspective on existing environmental law scholarship, primarily because weak and strong scholarship can be found anywhere.

[24] For a continuation of the debate, see Steven Vaughan, 'My Chemical (Regulation) Romance' (2015) 27 *Journal of Environmental Law* 167.

[25] See Jane Holder and Donald McGillivray, 'Bringing Environmental Justice to the Centre of Environmental Law Research: Developing a Collective Case Study Methodology' in Andreas Philippopoulos-Mihalopoulos and Victoria Brooks (eds), *Research Methods in Environmental Law: A Handbook* (Cheltenham: Edward Elgar, 2017).

change, ageing, poverty are frequently cited) demand input from multiple disciplines. This is matched by an assumption, widely but not universally shared, that one of the responsibilities of academics and our institutions is indeed to respond to social challenges. Asking for 'useful' research responds to certain demands that we become more accountable to 'society' for how we spend our time.[26] The social demand goes alongside a sense that academically exciting things can happen when we push at the edges of our disciplines. The perceived importance of interdisciplinarity stimulates an anxiety among some that interdisciplinarity is structurally under-incentivised and under-rewarded in career structures, publishing opportunities and academic funding.[27] This has led to certain institutional changes, which have led in turn to some academics experiencing institutional pressure towards interdisciplinarity, which is thought to attract funding and prestige to universities.

The positive agenda is potentially powerful. But the instrumentality of this approach, addressing particular identified social (and economic and industrial) problems, as well as institutional (university and funding body) needs, brings with it a risk that the 'transient political agenda of the day',[28] or an overly commercial agenda, may dominate. A more recent dilemma is whether work in universities may temporarily mask a loss of capacity and expertise within government.[29] There must also be questions about the ways in which government or other funders identify problems, which as discussed later may involve looking for 'the' answer to small technical questions, isolated from the rich complexity of the discipline. Equally though, 'the' problem is likely to be reframed and re-posed by the researchers during their work.[30]

None of this is either unique to interdisciplinary work or a necessary part of it. Disciplinary work can be instrumental, and work across disciplines need not be. Certain additional questions are raised specifically by interdisciplinarity. Interdisciplinarity is said to have the potential to undermine academic autonomy,[31] empowering the managerial over the intellectual, over 'the relevant collectivity of scholars who are the only people capable of creating and maintaining intellectual value in

[26] E.g. Barry, 'Logics of Interdisciplinarity'.
[27] This is captured by 'Crossing Paths', British Academy, July 2016.
[28] Stefan Collini, *Speaking of Universities* (London: Verso, 2017), p. 198.
[29] See 'Crossing Paths', British Academy, July 2016, on how academic advice to government has allowed government science to absorb funding cuts (expressed without criticism).
[30] Barry, 'Logics of Interdisciplinarity'.
[31] Ibid.

a particular discipline generation to generation'.[32] Further, assessing the quality of interdisciplinary work is a widely acknowledged challenge. It creates difficulties for the scholars and academic development if holding work to the standards of distinct disciplines means that genuinely important interdisciplinary insights are unable to find a home. But equally, the criteria for assessing interdisciplinarity on its own grounds are only beginning to emerge,[33] and developing new scholarly values will take time. Even identifying an appropriate literature may be difficult. One of the delights of cross-disciplinary work is being referred to papers we may not otherwise find, and yet publication can push us back to a particular disciplinary corpus of work.

More specifically, when social problems are packaged in a particular way for academic investigation, we might see an undervaluing of some disciplines relative to others. One discipline might be seen as simply providing a service, 'making up for or filling in for an absence or lack'[34] on behalf of another, rather than entering into a collaboration. A simplistic approach to the division of labour (including seeing the 'social' (sciences) as inevitably and always subsequent and subservient to the 'physical' (sciences)) is likely to reduce understanding of the problem.[35] The danger of instrumentalisation of STS scholarship within large, science-focused interdisciplinary projects is real. It can rest on an unexamined assumption that social scientists 'represent' public views, that 'the social' is simply a barrier to be overcome, or that the 'ethical, legal, social issues' are completely separate from the scientific work.[36] Similarly, other researchers might 'ask lawyers to identify "the law", stripped of complexity and preferably in the form of a rule of obligation that is specific to a limited social setting'.[37] Law though is not 'a datum, a fact, unproblematic and one-dimensional',[38] but as complex and

---

[32] Collini, *Speaking of Universities*, p. 48.

[33] 'Crossing Paths', British Academy, July 2016.

[34] Barry, 'Logics of Interdisciplinarity', pp. 28–29.

[35] Petts, 'Crossing Boundaries', on the perception of the 'social' in energy efficiency as a barrier to be addressed after the science and technology are right.

[36] Andrew Balmer et al., 'Taking Roles in Interdisciplinary Collaborations: Reflections on Working in Post-ELSI Spaces in the UK Synthetic Biology Community' (2015) 28 *Science & Technology Studies* 3; Jane Calvert, 'Collaboration as a Research Method? Navigating Social Scientific Involvement in Synthetic Biology' in N. Doorn et al. (eds), *Early Engagement and New Technologies: Opening up the Laboratory* (Dordrecht: Springer, 2013).

[37] Christopher McCrudden, 'Legal Research and the Social Sciences' (2006) *Law Quarterly Review* 632 at 648.

[38] McCrudden, 'Legal Research and the Social Sciences', 648.

constructed as any other area of social life. Similarly, planning is about more than technocratic development control, including a messy socio-political dimension in its scholarship. It might be satisfying to contribute to this sort of instrumental knowledge in a worthwhile project, even if it does not contribute to our own academic agenda or create genuinely joint knowledge relevant to our own discipline. But it is important to avoid rendering a simplistic account of our own expertise, reinforcing our discipline as either facilitative or a barrier to substance decided elsewhere.[39]

Our Differences

Meaningful work between and across disciplines is difficult.[40] It takes more time than work within a single discipline, it requires patient learning and teaching,[41] there are risks around finding an audience and recognition and there are risks that the whole project will fail to produce anything of interest. Happily, these risks are lessened among a group of collaborators who share the common ground we do, and who are accustomed to working on the edges of their own disciplines. But collaboration even within a single discipline increases the time and risks of academic work, in our output-driven academic culture. Even in our cohesive team, there was potential for disciplinary misunderstandings.

The most obvious issue from the outset was the methodological divide in terms of the core social science methodologies of coding, focus groups and interviews, which Maria had not used directly before, and her focus on reading and analysis, which experience suggests is not always valued as a distinctive contribution to interdisciplinary activities. This did not cause significant problems, essentially through a mutual respect for, and enthusiastic interest in, one anothers' methodology: what we can and cannot learn from 'mere' close reading and analysis, what we can and cannot learn from focus groups. The gap occasionally took more work to bridge with other audiences;[42] a willingness to teach, learn and explore was crucial. Notwithstanding our different starting points, we

---

[39] Liz Fisher, 'The Substantive Role of Law in Framing Energy Transitions: Wind Energy Development in the UK', paper for *Regulating the Energy Transition*, University of Oxford, 30 July 2016.

[40] This is a theme that runs through the literature.

[41] Fisher et al. conceptualise this in terms of the *expertise* needed for environmental law scholarship, Fisher et al., 'Maturity and Methodology'.

[42] Including our advisory group and some of our workshops.

were all involved in the process, reviewing codes and focus group preparation, attending focus groups, discussing findings from the empirical work and from the reading.

A connected, but less obvious and possibly more interesting methodological divide was in the ways we approached the cases. The starting point for Simon and Lucy was the focus group and interview material, emphasising the exploration of participants' experience of the process. Maria undertook a detailed analysis of a single or a small number of particularly appropriate cases for any point, having selected them from an initial reading of all of the cases, and a rereading of some of them. The empirical work was used to enrich the understanding of the documents, and to provide background understanding and context. Maria did not make use of the codes but read and reread the material, placing it in the broader literature (including the other cases), and analysing that case in a way that might tentatively build up to broader conclusions. By contrast, Yvonne used the coding to find a route back into the entire group of cases. However, going back and rereading the text is essential; so although attention to an individual text varies, we both seek to understand the words in context. Yvonne's work focused on generalisations from our group of cases as a whole, and the identification of patterns across cases, using a conceptual framing to identify key features. It can be tricky to find a home for this small-n case study research in the planning literature, notwithstanding its merits, since some reviewers see it as falling between the in-depth case study and aggregate statistical/quantitative analysis.[43]

These different approaches may reflect our disciplinary experiences. The disciplinary divide may be glimpsed in the (un)familiarity of the NSIPs reports, which read like (very long) legal documents. They are structured and argued differently (e.g. a linear argument, 'flatter' language) than material more often analysed in planning, such as media reports and policy and policy-related documentation. The task is not one of trying to 'surface' a storyline or discourse, or looking at metaphors. But our different approaches also reflect individual scholarly practices, preferences and interests. The differences were more productive than they were disruptive, primarily because our approaches were not mutually exclusive. Importantly, there was time in the project for each of us to take the lead in different areas, so that following one approach did not squeeze

---

[43] Joachim Blatter and M. Haverland, *Designing Case Studies Explanatory Approaches in Small-N Research* (Basingstoke, UK: Palgrave MacMillan, 2012).

out another. A productive way of working (not carefully planned) emerged, in which we each wrote to our own discipline, with one person taking the lead in writing for a predominantly legal, STS or planning audience. This also sidestepped the deeper questions about the ontological bases of our different approaches, congruent with but possibly masked by the methodological issues noted earlier. The boundaries between the disciplines were not rigidly maintained, however, even in the 'first drafts'. So for example, the 'legal' papers, led by the lawyer, were not primarily driven by doctrinal legal analysis. They were deeply influenced especially by STS, but also planning scholarship. Importantly, we also had time to learn from one another, without any particular pressure to produce quickly. And this was more carefully planned. Frequent, and reasonably relaxed, discussions of our plans and our drafts were built into our work. We added some material and made suggestions, and each of our publications draws on one anothers' insights. Mutual trust and respect for our different approaches, and a genuine interest in what we might learn from one another were central. The reflective nature of our conversations around the documents and the fieldwork opened up the potential for a more creative approach than we might have achieved on our own. Fieldwork stories, for example about the different tone of the discussions in different focus groups, were helpful in identifying issues for further exploration, and in providing more nuanced ways of thinking about the documentation.

A brief aside about the preparation of this chapter might be illustrative. The four of us had an 'away day' in summer 2017, the main purpose of which was to begin 'brainstorming' our conclusions and recommendations for our practice-oriented closing event (in December 2017). For the first part of that meeting, we had each prepared brief presentations, articulating our 'discipline', our approach to scholarship, what we had learned personally from our collaboration and what we thought of as the most important findings and conclusions from our work thus far. This discussion, including follow-up written contributions, was incorporated into a substantial first draft by Maria, alongside research and reflection on legal scholarship, environmental law scholarship and interdisciplinarity. There was a primarily legal lead for a primarily legal audience, but embedded in the cross-disciplinary collaboration. This draft was circulated twice around the team for amendments, suggestions and additions, plus one final review, and the draft was enriched and improved, and completed in early 2018.

The divisions of a common language are a recurrent theme in discussions of interdisciplinary work. We were not entirely immune from this. Although neither planners nor lawyers ignore cases of protest and unrest, when lawyers talk about 'public participation', we generally turn quickly to legally mandated rights, especially rights to be consulted; planners also focus on institutionalised moments for participation. The NSIPs process fits neatly into this approach. Rather than focusing on a legal or institutional mandate, STS explores, from multiple normative positions,[44] the case for inclusion of publics as a substantive aspect of the construction of good science and technology policy. These different starting points might imply a different focus, in particular a greater emphasis on substantive rather than procedural justice in STS.[45]

But as this example perhaps indicates, terminological confusion is not the main challenge when the collaborators are as inherently concerned by all three disciplines. It is most striking that we developed a common language very quickly, perhaps because we already worked with similar concepts and methodologies and shared a common set of understandings. Our most obvious methodological challenge had nothing to do with cross-disciplinarity or collaboration. Between being told our application for funding had been successful and the formal start date of the project, the government announced that onshore wind in England was to be removed from the NSIPs process.[46] This was admittedly disappointing. However, we had more than enough material to work with, and now a richer perspective on how high-level policy might change, even when one of the purposes of the regime is to avoid having to revisit policy.[47] The rejection of the application for consent in Navitus similarly enriched the material we had to work with, but not in a straightforward way. Our starting point had been that policy framed the way in which publics could be heard in the process, restricting the possibilities for an application to be turned down (and focusing the public participation on mitigation).

[44] See e.g. Jack Stilgoe, Simon Lock and James Wilsden, 'Why Should We Promote Public Engagement with Science?' (2014) 23 *Public Understanding of Science* 4; Jason Chilvers and Matthew Kearnes (eds), *Remaking Participation: Science, Environment and Emergent Publics* (Abingdon: Routledge, 2015).

[45] Andrew Stirling, '"Opening Up" and "Closing Down" Power, Participation, and Pluralism in the Social Appraisal of Technology' (2008) 33 *Science, Technology, & Human Values* 262.

[46] Onshore wind was removed from the NSIP regime in England (SI 2016/306 Infrastructure Planning (Onshore Wind Generating Stations) Order 2016).

[47] For earlier examples, see Susan Owens, 'Siting, Sustainable Development and Social Priorities' (2004) 7 *Journal of Risk Research* 101.

Navitus was clearly an exceptional case, and the construction of evidence in that case provided food for thought.[48]

At a personal level, we have found this project rewarding and worthwhile. Cross-disciplinarity of this type seems to be as much a social as an academic activity,[49] dependent on mutual trust, respect and compatibility, if the work is to be as good as it can be. A little bit of luck can go a long way, but this social and academic good fortune does not just happen. It requires skills of communication, and these can be learned and improved. It also requires confident and modest leadership, not just of the project but also as representatives of our disciplines. In that respect, it is worth saying that the mentoring in different disciplinary approaches came from junior as well as senior members of the team.

Three factors have, we think, been especially important. First, the project was self-motivated and organic. We did not follow an external agenda, but our mutual scholarly interests, although we did reach some conclusions for practice.[50] Second, our project was based on pre-existing relationships. Three of the participants (Yvonne, Simon and Maria) had worked together before, including publishing three papers and holding several events.[51] We began with mutual trust and respect. Lucy had written her PhD under Yvonne's supervision, and they had a strong pre-existing relationship. However, we would not want to dismiss involvement in the more constructed projects. Not only have we all been involved in exciting, if not always straightforward, projects of this sort ourselves. But further, our own project emerged out of the relationship building that has been an element of UCL's institutional encouragement of cross-faculty working.

The first two issues are closely related to the third, which is the importance of time. We began our work together (in the larger group) in 2011; we applied for our funding in 2014 and started the project in July 2015; and it came to a formal end in December 2017. The rewards of collaboration do not always come quickly. We could be relatively confident about our ability to work together before any big risks

---

[48] Lee, 'Landscape and Knowledge'.
[49] See also Gavin Little, 'The Pitfalls and Promises of Interdisciplinary Collaboration', paper for Society of Legal Scholars Conference, 2016.
[50] 'NSIPs Research', University College London, www.ucl.ac.uk/nsips.
[51] Lee et al., 'Public Participation and Climate Change Infrastructure'; Lock et al., 'Nuclear Energy Sounded Wonderful 40 Years Ago'; Rydin et al., 'Public Engagement in Decision-making'; 'UCL Grand Challenges', University College London, www.ucl.ac.uk/grand-challenges.

were taken. Time was also important within the project – time for discussion, a willingness to give time to talking and thinking about work without expecting anything particular in return. And time for outputs to evolve, with all of us working at our own pace and producing work we could be pleased with in our own contexts. Frequent meetings were a vital part of this. The general calmness of the project might largely be attributed to the talent and effectiveness of the research associate working full time on the project, and running the empirical work, as well as to the experience and leadership of the principal investigator.

But we should assess a little more the criteria of success. That is of course a difficult notion to pin down. We might start with the idea that scholarship is about knowledge, with the object 'to discover more about whatever is being considered, and to understand it better'.[52] Our project has certainly allowed each of us to deepen and extend our disciplinary, as well as our cross-disciplinary, knowledge. We have produced work we are proud of, drawing on collective insights from the group. We have also made some proposals for practice. There is always a tension between being truthful to the subtlety of academic findings and being influential. When our recommendations require additional resources for the NSIPs process, they are not likely to be implemented any time soon, although others may have more immediate potential. The quality of our work as a whole is for others to judge, and it is too soon to say what level of contribution we have been able to make even within our own disciplines.

What has been gained by cross-disciplinarity is perhaps not a 'better' or 'more complete' way of knowing,[53] but a completeness that is a different shape from anything we might have produced individually. We did not aim to meet ambitious criteria for interdisciplinarity that require a breaking down of disciplinary borders, or perhaps even a genuine integration between disciplines, and some readers will be disappointed by that.[54] The jeopardy in our collaboration was low, and this certainly did not feel like the 'hazardous disciplinary border zones' described by Judith Petts and her colleagues.[55] There is surely much to be learned in more risky and socially challenging projects.

---

[52] Feldman, 'The Nature of Legal Scholarship'.
[53] Jasanoff, *States of Knowledge*.
[54] See e.g. Catherine Lyall et al., 'The Role of Funding Agencies in Creating Interdisciplinary Knowledge' (2013) 40 *Science and Public Policy* 62.
[55] Petts, 'Crossing Boundaries', 593.

Conclusion

Careful efforts to bring disciplines together have considerable potential benefits, whether as a scholarly extension of our understanding or as a self-conscious effort to respond to social challenges. Our observations in this chapter are personal and reflective and may not be easily applied beyond our own case. Ours has not been the most stretching form of interdisciplinary work, and it developed organically amongst a group of people who knew one another and knew they could work together. Our project was not a narrow instrumental result of institutional pressure, but it did arise out of the incidental relationship-building effects of an institutional effort to incentivise work across faculties. It has been personally and intellectually rewarding. In December 2017, we hosted an 'academic exchange', attended by a mix of academic lawyers and planners, to mark the end of our project. The warmth and intellectual vibrancy of that event suggest much scope for future collaboration between these disciplines, and who knows, perhaps a breaking down of some disciplinary borders.

Bibliography

Barry, Andrew et al., 'Logics of Interdisciplinarity' (2008) 37 *Economy and Society* 20.

Fisher, Elizabeth et al., 'Maturity and Methodology: Starting a Debate about Environmental Law Scholarship' (2009) 21 *Journal of Environmental Law* 213.

Little, Gavin, 'Developing Environmental Law Scholarship: Going Beyond the Legal Space' (2016) *Legal Studies* 48.

Pedersen, Ole, 'The Limits of Interdisciplinarity and the Practice of Environmental Law Scholarship' (2014) 26 *Journal of Environmental Law* 423.

Petts, Judith et al., 'Crossing Boundaries: Inter-Disciplinarity in the Context of Urban environments' (2008) 39 *Geoforum* 593.

Economics and Environmental Law Scholarship

CAROLINE CECOT AND MICHAEL A. LIVERMORE

Introduction

The economic perspective has had an important, if constrained, influence on environmental law scholarship. Despite having a vast influence in other legal areas, economics has penetrated less fully into the field of environmental law. Some scholars, especially those of an economic bent, might bemoan this state of affairs, while others with different ideological or intellectual commitments might celebrate. What is clear is that environmental law scholars have resisted a broader trend within the academic legal community – especially within the United States – toward increasing reliance on the tools and concepts of economics. This resistance has shaped the content of environmental law scholarship as well as, perhaps, its influence among legal scholars and within the broader policy environment.

It is common to draw a line between normative and positive legal scholarship. The normative domain includes scholarship that asks questions about what the law *should* be or how it *ought* to be understood, while the positive domain describes the law, whatever its current state. Within the positive domain, empirical work in particular asks questions about the *causes* and *consequences* of the law.

The field of economics has made contributions to environmental law scholarship on both sides of the normative/positive divide. On the normative side, economics can be understood as embodying a particular set of claims about the appropriate ends of environmental law – typically economically oriented scholars take some form of efficiency and/or welfare as the goal of policy. Much normative scholarship takes up the task of defending or attacking efficiency or welfare as a goal of environmental policy. On the positive side, economics brings a distinctive set of empirical tools – in particular specific methods of data analysis – to the study of the law. A great deal of legal scholarship uses the tools of economics to empirically understand the law, although this trend is relatively less prevalent among environmental law scholars.

In this chapter, we review some of the major normative and empirical contributions of the economic perspective to environmental law scholarship. We argue that, although economics has shaped the normative discourse on environmental law in important ways over the past several decades, the field has largely missed the turn towards economically informed empirical study of the law (with important exceptions). We offer some speculation about why environmental law finds itself outside of the broader empirical trend and discuss some of the potential consequences of this isolation. Our leading conjecture is that it has been the success of normative economics in shaping the conversation on environmental law and policy that has led to a relative lack of enthusiasm for empirical work among environmental law scholars. Finally, we highlight the unique contributions that academic lawyers can make to empirical study of environmental law and policy and call for a new approach that better integrates legal expertise into the quantitative social science research in this field.

Shaping the Normative Conversation

The economic perspective, with its focus on the maximization of social welfare and efficiency, offers normative insights into environmental law and policy. Economic theory can justify government intervention, recommend a socially optimal level of environmental quality, and provide guidance on choosing the method of regulation. Although many of the normative implications of economic theory for environmental law are controversial among environmental law scholars, they have helped define the conversation on environmental policy for several decades.[1]

---

[1] For a more comprehensive treatment of the implications of an economic perspective for environmental law, see Michael Livermore & Richard Revesz, 'Environmental Law and Economics', in Francesco Parisi (ed.), *Oxford Handbook of Law and Economics: Private and Commercial Law* (New York: Oxford University Press, 2017), vol. 2, 509–42; and Richard Revesz & Robert Stavins, 'Environmental Law and Policy', in A. Mitchell Polinsky & Steven Shavell (eds), *Handbook of Law and Economics* (Amsterdam: North-Holland/ Elsevier Science, 2007), pp. 499–589.

Justifying Regulation

The concept of market failure is often cited as a justification for government intervention. Standard economic theory predicts that free markets will generally allocate scarce resources efficiently, without need for government intervention. Important exceptions exist, including unpriced effects on third parties – what are referred to as externalities. Generally speaking, market failure due to the existence of an externality is understood by economic theory to justify government intervention.

Environmental harms such as pollution are a classic example of a negative externality. Unless transaction costs are small and property rights are well defined, private bargaining will not account for third-party effects. Many situations in the environmental context involve high transaction costs and incomplete property rights – air pollution affecting a large downwind population is one obvious example. Economic theory thus supports government intervention that would encourage market participants to internalize the effect of an environmental externality.

Some scholars have argued, however, that this externality-based justification for environmental regulation does not go far enough in defining the appropriate scope of environmental protection.[2] Legal scholars who favour environmental rights, for example, have argued that government intervention can be justified even when externalities are not present.[3] Notwithstanding these critiques, the externality-based justification for environmental protection has been broadly influential among legal scholars and is a mainstay of the environmental law discourse.[4]

---

[2] Mark Sagoff, 'On Preserving the Natural Environment' (1974) 84 *Yale Law Journal* 224–225.

[3] Rena Steinzor, 'Devolution and the Public Health' (2000) 24 *Harvard Environmental Law Review* 366–369. Other legal scholars, relying on insights from behavioural economics, have argued that the existence of systematic irrationality among market participants can also justify government intervention (e.g. John Hanson & Douglas Kysar, 'Taking Behavioralism Seriously: The Problem of Market Manipulation' (1999) 74 *New York University Law Review* 630–745), although it is not clear that the environmental context is one in which such behavioural justifications are unusually common.

[4] We conducted a Westlaw search of 'Secondary Sources' with 'Publication Type' set to 'Law Reviews and Journals' and 'Topic' set to 'Energy and Environment'. There were a total of 69 sources identified. A search of 'externality' or 'externalities' and a date range of 1990 to 2015 returned 1,883 results, roughly one-third of the returns from a similar search of 'Clean Air Act' – arguably the most important statute in all of US environmental law (which returned 5,576 results).

Determining Stringency

The economic perspective also provides a framework for determining the appropriate level of environmental quality – and, consequently, the appropriate goals of government intervention. Applying principles of welfare economics, economic theory identifies the socially desirable level of environmental quality as the level that maximizes satisfaction of individual preferences. Cost-benefit analysis is then used to shed light on social welfare-improving policies by analyzing the difference between the value of the benefits to the beneficiaries and the costs to those who are burdened.

The starting place for contemporary cost-benefit analysis is the Pareto criterion, which favours policies that benefit at least one person while making no other person worse off. Because virtually all policies benefit some individuals while harming others, economists have proposed *potential* Pareto-improving policies (where the winners could theoretically compensate the losers) as an alternative criterion. This Kaldor-Hicks efficient policy maximizes the difference between the value of the gains to the winners and the losses to the losers. Cost-benefit analysis in its contemporary form implements the Kaldor-Hicks criterion by converting gains and losses onto a monetary scale and attempting to maximize net benefits.[5]

Legal scholars have raised a number of critiques of cost-benefit analysis, and there remains no general consensus among them concerning its use in environmental policy.[6] Criticisms include cost-benefit analysis's focus on individual preference satisfaction as the basis for social welfare, its disregard for distributional equity in the analysis, and concerns about incommensurability and commodification, among others.[7] Some legal scholars object to cost-benefit analysis as applied to environmental policymaking in particular, largely due to concerns about undervaluation of environmental benefits.[8] In light of these and other conceptual and

[5] For a welfare-based justification for cost-benefit analysis, see Matthew Adler & Eric Posner, *New Foundations of Cost-Benefit Analysis* (Cambridge, MA: Harvard University Press, 2006).

[6] Frank Ackerman & Lisa Heinzerling, *Priceless: On Knowing the Price of Everything and the Value of Nothing* (New York: The New Press, 2005).

[7] Mark Sagoff, 'On Preserving the Natural Environment' (1974) 84 *Yale Law Journal* 224–225, Matthew Adler, *Well-Being and Fair Distribution: Beyond Cost-Benefit Analysis* (New York: Oxford University Press, 2011); Elizabeth Anderson, *Values in Ethics and Economics* (Cambridge MA: Harvard University Press, 1995), Mary Jane Radin, *Contested Commodities* (Cambridge, MA: Harvard University Press, 2001).

[8] Douglas Kysar, 'It Might Have Been: Risk, Precaution and Opportunity Costs' (2006) 22 *Journal of Land Use & Environmental Law* 1–34.

practical criticisms of cost-benefit analysis, some scholars have argued for alternative approaches to determining the stringency of environmental policy, such as using feasibility analysis to require maximum feasible emission reductions.[9]

Notwithstanding methodological challenges and lingering opposition, cost-benefit analysis has become a staple of US regulatory policymaking since at least 1981, with wide influence on the stringency of environmental policy.[10] In fact, the tool, or at least an informal version of the tool, is increasingly associated by courts with rational agency decision-making.[11] Great strides have been made in valuation methodology that have significantly improved the quality of cost-benefit analyses in the environmental context. In recent years, the tool has been effectively used to justify many stringent environmental regulations, including those aimed at mitigating climate change, leading even some skeptics to at least tentatively accept the technique.[12]

Achieving Environmental Goals

Finally, the economic perspective has something to offer not only in determining the goals of environmental policy but also in choosing the means to achieve policy goals as well as the institutions that are best positioned to deploy those policies. We focus on instrument choice, where the economic perspective has been particularly influential.

A wide range of instruments is available to regulators to achieve a given environmental goal, whether or not that goal was chosen by reference to economic principles. These instruments include command-and-control regulations such as technology-based and performance-based standards, market-based instruments such as pollution taxes and tradeable permits (also referred to as cap-and-trade or emissions trading schemes), labelling and disclosure requirements, and liability rules. In choosing among instruments, the economic perspective focuses on

---

[9] David Driesen, 'Distributing the Costs of Environmental, Health, and Safety Protection: The Feasibility Principle, Cost-Benefit Analysis, and Regulatory Reform' (2005) 32 *Boston College Environmental Affairs Law Review* 1–95.

[10] Richard Revesz & Michael Livermore, *Retaking Rationality: How Cost-Benefit Analysis Can Better Protect the Environment and Our Health* (New York: Oxford University Press, 2008).

[11] Cass Sunstein, 'Cost-Benefit Analysis and Arbitrariness Review' (2017) 41 *Harvard Environmental Law Review* 1–41.

[12] Michael Livermore & Richard Revesz, 'Interest Groups and Environmental Policy: Inconsistent Positions and Missed Opportunities' (2015) 45 *Environmental Law* 1–19.

efficiency or cost-effectiveness and evaluates which instrument is likely to achieve the identified policy goals at least cost to society.

Pigou proposed taxing polluting firms to incentivize pollution reduction, and similar market-based mechanisms remain broadly popular among economists as a way to influence behaviour.[13] Market-based mechanisms are often thought to be superior to command-and-control approaches because they tend to equalize marginal abatement costs across all pollution sources where reductions are possible.[14] Beyond that high-level agreement, however, there is a lively literature within environmental economics concerning the relative merits of various market-based mechanisms such as taxes or cap-and-trade schemes.[15] There is also discussion of how best to extend market mechanisms to nontraditional issues, such as preserving biodiversity.[16]

However, several prominent critiques of market-based mechanisms come from legal scholars as well as economists. One criticism of cap-and-trade schemes that has attracted significant attention is the potential for 'hot spots', or areas of concentrated pollution, to form as a result of emissions trading.[17] As an initial matter, it is not clear that such hot spots would be worse than those that form as a result of command-and-control regulation in highly industrial areas. In any event, ways exist to mitigate these concerns when designing a cap-and-trade scheme, such as limiting trading or including command-and-control backstops.[18] These fixes do, however, chip away at the efficiency advantage of

---

[13] Peter Howard & Derek Sylvan, 'The Economic Climate: Establishing Expert Consensus on the Economics of Climate Change', Institute of Policy Integrity, December 2015.

[14] Gloria Helfand, 'Standards versus Standards: The Effects of Different Pollution Restrictions' (1991) 81 *American Economic Review* 622–634.

[15] Martin Weitzman, 'Prices vs. Quantities' (1974) 41 *Review of Economic Studies* 477–491; Lawrence Goulder & Andrew Schein, 'Carbon Taxes Versus Cap and Trade: A Critical Review' (2013) 4 *Climate Change Economics* 1350010–1350048.

[16] Irene Alvarado-Quesada, Lars Hein, & Hans Peter Weikard, 'Market-Based Mechanisms for Biodiversity Conservation: A Review of Existing Schemes and an Outline for a Global Mechanism' (2014) 23 *Biodiversity & Conservationism* 1–21.

[17] Daniel Farber, 'Pollution Markets and Social Equity: Analyzing the Fairness of Cap and Trade' (2012) 39 *Ecology Law Quarterly* 1–56. This criticism is relevant for controlling global pollutants such as greenhouse gases only to the extent that the emissions of localized pollutants are correlated with the emissions of greenhouse gases. Robert Stavins, 'A Meaningful U.S. Cap-and-Trade System to Address Climate Change' (2008) 32 *Harvard Environmental Law Review* 293–371.

[18] Richard Revesz, 'Markets and Geography: Designing Marketable Permit Schemes to Control Local and Regional Pollutants' (2001) 28 *Ecology Law Quarterly* 569–672.

emissions trading.[19] Scholars have also questioned the morality of allowing emissions trading.[20] Taxes, meanwhile, have been challenged as difficult to calculate, dependent on market structure, and politically infeasible.[21] Some scholars argue that market-based policies are not always superior to well-designed command-and-control policies that are informed by economic principles.[22] Other scholars argue that command-and-control policies are easier to enforce, resulting in lower overall implementation costs in practice.[23]

Empirical Environmental Law Scholarship

In recent years, economically informed empirical work has exploded in influence in legal scholarship. In the United States, there has been a particularly strong growth of quantitatively based empirical scholarship, buoyed in part by the broad availability of accessible statistical software and the increasing availability of data. Now entire conferences and journals, such as the Conference on Empirical Legal Studies (CELS) and the *Journal of Empirical Legal Studies* (JELS), are devoted to empirical legal content, with other journals, including student-edited law reviews, routinely publishing empirical pieces.

While there is no argument that empirical economics plays a large role in contract law, tax law, or criminal law scholarship, to name a few prominent legal fields, the methodology has barely touched environmental law scholarship. At the 2017 CELS, for example, while six out of thirty-five panels were devoted to criminal law issues, no panels discussed environmental law issues. In fact, 'environmental law' is not even a named submission category. In the past five volumes of JELS, volumes ten to fourteen, we identified only one article on an environmental

---

[19] Thomas Tietenberg, 'Tradable Permits for Pollution Control When Emission Location Matters: What Have We Learned?' (1995) 5 *Environmental and Resource Economics* 95–113.

[20] Steven Kelman, *What Price Incentives?: Economists and the Environment* (Toronto: Praeger Publishing, 1981).

[21] Stavins, 'A Meaningful U.S. Cap-and-Trade System'.

[22] Wallace Oates, Paul Portney, & Albert McGartland, 'The Net Benefits of Incentive-Based Regulation: A Case Study of Environmental Standard Setting' (1989) 79 *American Economic Review* 1233–1242.

[23] Daniel Cole & Peter Grossman, 'When Is Command-and-Control Efficient? Institutions, Technology, and the Comparative Efficiency of Alternative Regulatory Regimes for Environmental Protection' (1999) *Wisconsin Law Review* 887–938.

issue.[24] And it seems that empirical work in environmental law appears rarely in law reviews. Out of more than 3,000 environmental law articles published in select law reviews from 2008 to 2015, only ten articles self-identify as empirical in their titles.[25] And environmental law scholarship does not appear to draw from the peer-reviewed environmental economics literature as often as scholarship in other areas draws from relevant economics fields. For example, in the period 2005–2010, the highest-ranked environmental economics journal was cited 179 times in law reviews articles, while the highest-ranked financial economics journal was cited 1,004 times.[26] By contrast, roughly the same number of articles mentioned the Environmental Protection Agency and the Securities and Exchange Commission.[27]

The relative insignificance of empirical work in environmental law scholarship is all the more surprising given that a wealth of empirical questions are relevant to the field. We discuss three particular kinds of relevant empirical work: the valuation of environmental benefits, the effectiveness of environmental policies, and the political and social factors that influence environmental policy choices.

Valuation

One area where empirical scholarship has important implications for environmental law, in part due to the prominent influence of the economic perspective and cost-benefit analysis, is in estimating the economic benefits of environmental protection. Because environmental regulation often affects non-market goods, economic research into hard-to-value benefits can have particular influence over policymaking.

---

[24] Howard Chang & Hilary Sigman, 'An Empirical Analysis of Cost Recovery in Superfund Cases: Implications for Brownfields and Joint and Several Liability' (2014) 11 *Journal of Empirical Legal Studies* 477–504.

[25] This count is based on the list assembled by student editors of the *Environmental Law and Policy Annual Review* at Vanderbilt Law School (e.g. Linda Breggin et al., 'Trends in Environmental Law Scholarship 2008–2015' (2016) 46 *Environmental Law Reporter News & Analysis* 10647). Although the students do not track empirical work, we obtain a rough estimate of the number of empirical articles by taking advantage of the norm of identifying empirical work in the article title. Admittedly, this procedure misses articles that do not identify themselves as empirical in their titles.

[26] We conducted a Westlaw search of 'Secondary Sources' with 'Publication Type' set to 'Law Reviews and Journals' and searched for 'J. Fin. Econ.' and 'J. Envtl. Econ. Mgmt.' with a date range of 2005 to 2010.

[27] A search of 'Securities and Exchange Commission' and 'Environmental Protection Agency' with a date range of 2005 to 2010 returned 5,688 and 5,871 results, respectively.

One benefit underlying many environmental policies is the reduction of mortality risk. The US Environmental Protection Agency (EPA) has adopted a "value of statistical life" to place a monetary value on mortality risk reduction. This value is typically estimated using the hedonic wage method, which takes advantage of real trade-offs individuals make between wages and job-related fatality risks to infer individuals' valuation of risk. The availability of comprehensive wage and fatality data has allowed economists to generate a number of studies on people's willingness to pay to avoid fatality risks, which EPA has used extensively to evaluate its regulations.[28]

Economic tools have been used to value a number of other types of environmental benefits. Economists often prefer estimates based on revealed-preference studies, like the hedonic wage method underlying estimates of VSL. For many years, studies have used hedonic property value methods to estimate the value of local environmental amenities by analyzing how property values change as the environmental attributes of otherwise comparable properties change.[29] In addition, economists have used household production models to infer demand and derive willingness to pay for environmental regulation, such as for ozone control, and travel cost models to value the availability or quality of recreational opportunities.[30]

Where such revealed preference studies cannot be carried out, economists have relied on stated preference surveys that obtain individuals' willingness to pay or accept specific changes in environmental quality based on their answers to hypothetical scenarios.[31] This method can be applied to value a wide range of environmental attributes, including use and non-use values. Because of the potential for biased answers, economists have developed best-practice guidelines, while continuing to study

[28] W. Kip Viscusi, 'The Value of Life: Estimates with Risks by Occupation and Industry' (2004) 42 Economic Inquiry 29–48; US Environmental Protection Agency, 'Guidelines for Preparing Economic Analyses', December 17, 2010.

[29] Sherwin Rosen, 'Hedonic Prices and Implicit Markets: Product Differentiation in Pure Competition' (1974) 82 Journal of Political Economy 34–35.

[30] Mark Dickie & Shelby Gerking, 'Willingness to Pay for Ozone Control: Inferences from the Demand for Medical Care' (1991) 21 Journal of Environmental Economics and Management 1–16; Nancy Bockstael, 'Travel Cost Methods', in Daniel Bromley (ed.), The Handbook of Environmental Economics (Oxford: Blackwell Publishers, 1996); Daniel Phaneuf & V. Kerry Smith, 'Recreation Demand Models', in Karl-Gran Mäler & Jeffrey Vincent (eds), Handbook of Environmental Economics (Amsterdam: North Holland/Elsevier Science, 2005), pp. 671–761.

[31] Robert Mitchell & Richard Carson, Using Surveys to Value Public Goods: The Contingent Valuation Method (Washington, DC: Resources for the Future, 1989).

conditions that support reliable estimates.[32] Recent work has raised the prospect of using neurological imaging to construct less-error-prone studies.[33] However, persistent skepticism of contingent valuation means that the values are sometimes not used in cost-benefit analyses, leaving large categories of benefits unmonetized.[34]

One important recent innovation in environmental valuation concerns the value of reducing greenhouse gas emissions, referred to as the 'social cost of carbon'. Beginning in the 1990s, economists began developing integrated assessment models that link greenhouse gas emissions, temperature changes, and monetary damages.[35] The most established models are the Dynamic Integrated Model of Climate and the Economy (DICE); the Climate Framework for Uncertainty, Negotiation, and Distribution (FUND) model; and the Policy Analysis of the Greenhouse Effect (PAGE) model.[36]

Given the complexity of linked climate-economy-society systems, there is still considerable uncertainty concerning the accuracy of the model estimates, leading some to question their value.[37] In one paper, a legal scholar working with climate modellers helped shed light on

---

[32] Kenneth Arrow et al., 'Report of the NOAA Panel on Contingent Valuation' (1993) 58 Federal Register 4601–14.

[33] Colin Camerer & Dean Mobbs, 'Differences in Behavior and Brain Activity During Hypothetical and Real Choices' (2017) 21 *Trends in Cognitive Sciences* 45–56; Mel Khaw et al., 'The Measurement of Subjective Value and Its Relationship to Contingent Valuation of Environmental Public Goods' (2015) 10 *PLoS ONE* 1–19.

[34] US EPA, 'Final Regulations to Establish Requirements for Cooling Water Intake Structures at Existing Facilities', 79 Federal Register 48300 (Aug. 15, 2014) (Cooling Water Intake Structures rule). The concept of ecosystem services (that natural systems provide valuable goods and services) is another important innovation that has helped inform research on environmental valuation (e.g. T. Brown, J. Bergstrom & B. Loomis, 'Defining, Valuing and Providing Ecosystem Goods and Services' (2007) 47(2) *Natural Resources Journal* 329–76; B. Keeler et al., 'Linking Water Quality and Well-Being for Improved Assessment and Valuation of Ecosystem Services' (2012) 109(45) *Proceedings of the National Academy of Sciences of the United States of America* 18619–24.

[35] Michael Livermore, 'Setting the Social Cost of Carbon', in Daniel A. Farber and Marjan Peeters (eds), *Climate Change Law* (Cheltenham: Edward Elgar Publishing, 2016).

[36] William Nordhaus & Paul Sztorc, *DICE 2013R: Introduction and User's Manual* (New Haven: Cowles Foundation, 2013); David Anthoff & Richard Tol, 'The Uncertainty About the Social Cost of Carbon: A Decomposition Analysis Using FUND' (2013) 117 *Climatic Change* 515–530; Chris Hope, 'Critical issues for the Calculation of the Social Cost of CO_2: Why the Estimates from PAGE09 Are Higher Than Those from PAGE2002' (2013) 117 *Climatic Change* 531–543.

[37] Peter Howard & Michael Livermore, 'Sociopolitical Feedbacks and Climate Change' *Harvard Environmental Law Review* (forthcoming); Robert Pindyck, 'Climate Change Policy: What Do the Models Tell Us?' (2013) 51 *Journal of Economic Literature* 860–872.

a particularly important source of uncertainty in these models, based on their treatment of economic growth.[38] In addition, there are controversial normative questions that include the appropriate discount rate, the treatment of catastrophic risk, and whether global or domestic-only damages should be used.[39] Notwithstanding these controversies, the benefit estimates based on these models are likely the best available.[40] Given the substantial costs imposed by efforts to cut greenhouse gas emissions – or address other environmental concerns – continued work to clarify the important benefits achieved by those efforts remains an important priority for the field.

Policy Effects

Empirical work can also shed light on the effects of the stringency or the design of environmental policies. Such work is critical to serious efforts to identify ways to improve these policies. In this area, knowledge of the legal regimes involved is particularly useful, and legal scholars have done some important work. For example, Chang and Sigman empirically confirmed that the imposition of joint and several liability on parties responsible for contaminated sites substantially increased the government's recovery of cleanup costs.[41] Their finding has implications for the incentives for private parties to sell or lease potentially contaminated property.

But, as in valuation, economists do the bulk of the work. Environmental economists have empirically evaluated the effect of the

---

[38] Elisabeth Moyer et al., 'Climate Impacts on Economic Growth as Drivers of Uncertainty in the Social Cost of Carbon' (2014) 43 *Journal of Legal Studies* 401–425.

[39] Christian Gollier & Martin Weitzman, 'How Should the Distant Future Be Discounted When Discount Rates Are Uncertain?' (2009) 107 *Economics Letters* 350–353; Mark Weitzman, 'Fat-Tailed Uncertainty in the Economics of Catastrophic Climate Change' (2011) 5 *Review of Environmental Economics and Policy* 275–292; Peter Howard & Jason Schwartz, 'Think Global: International Reciprocity as Justification for a Global Social Cost of Carbon' (2017) 42 *Columbia Journal of Environmental Law* 203–295; Ted Gayer & W. Kip Viscusi, 'Determining the Proper Scope of Climate Change Policy Benefits in U.S. Regulatory Analyses: Domestic versus Global Approaches' (2016) 10 *Review of Environmental Economics and Policy* 1–19; Arden Rowell, 'Foreign Impacts and Climate Change (2015) 39 *Harvard Environmental Law Review* 371–421.

[40] Richard Revesz et al., 'Best Cost Estimate of Greenhouse Gases' (2017) 357 *Science* 655.

[41] Howard Chang & Hilary Sigman, 'An Empirical Analysis of Cost Recovery in Superfund Cases: Implications for Brownfields and Joint and Several Liability' (2014) 11 *Journal of Empirical Legal Studies* 477–504.

Clean Air Act's regulation of nonattainment areas,[42] the local effect of hazardous cite designation,[43] the effect of pollution on school absences,[44] and the effect of California's tradeable permit program for nitrogen oxides, to name just a few studies.[45]

Arguably, data on environmental outcomes have been more difficult to obtain than data relevant to other legal fields, where empirical work by legal scholars is more prevalent. But even if this were historically true, such data are increasingly available to scholars. Now even some state and local governments make environmental data publically available and readily accessible on their websites. And in any event, data issues have not stopped environmental economists from producing important work in this area.

Perhaps more concerning, these policy-relevant empirical findings in environmental economics have enjoyed relatively little influence in environmental law scholarship. For example, Fowlie et al. evaluated how emissions changes due to California's tradeable permit program varied by neighbourhood demographic characteristics, finding no statistically significant effects.[46] Previously, the existence of pollution hot spots in minority neighbourhoods due to emissions trading (and California's program, in particular) was essentially assumed.[47] But despite hundreds of articles about emissions trading and environmental justice in environmental law scholarship, only three mention this empirical work.[48]

---

[42] Kenneth Chay, Carlos Dobkin, & Michael Greenstone, 'The Clean Air Act of 1970 and Adult Mortality' (2003) 27 *Journal of Risk and Uncertainty* 279–300.

[43] Michael Greenstone & Justin Gallagher, 'Does Hazardous Waste Matter? Evidence from the Housing Market and the Superfund Program' (2008) 123 *Quarterly Journal of Economics* 951–1003.

[44] Janet Currie et al., 'Does Pollution Increase School Absences?' (2009) 91 *Review of Economics and Statistics* 682–694.

[45] Meredith Fowlie, Stephen Holland, & Erin Mansur, 'What Do Emissions Markets Deliver and to Whom? Evidence from Southern California's NOx Trading Program' (2012) 102 *American Economic Review* 965–993.

[46] Ibid.

[47] Stephen Johnson, 'Economics v. Equity: Do Market-Based Environmental Reforms Exacerbate Environmental Injustice?' (1999) 56 *Washington & Lee Law Review* 111–118.

[48] Alice Kaswan, 'Decentralizing Cap-and-Trade? State Controls Within a Federal Greenhouse Gas Cap-and-Trade Program' (2010) 28 *Virginal Environmental Law Journal* 343–410; Alice Kaswan, 'Climate Change, the Clean Air Act, and Industrial Pollution' (2012) 30 *University of California, Los Angeles Journal of Environmental Law & Policy* 51–119; Daniel Farber, 'Pollution Markets and Social Equity: Analyzing the Fairness of Cap and Trade' (2012) 39 *Ecology Law Quarterly* 1–56.

Determinants of Environmental Policy

As discussed, the economic perspective supports government intervention designed to increase social welfare by addressing market failures
such as externalities. In practice, government intervention might be
influenced by other factors besides the public interest.[49] For example,
the public choice view is that regulation is a response to pressure from
powerful interest groups, perhaps at the expense of social welfare.
In the environmental context, the pressure likely comes from relative
winners and relative losers of different types of government
intervention.[50] And, in fact, descriptive accounts suggest that such
interest group pressure has been a significant factor in the enactment
and design of federal environmental policies, such as the Clean Air Act
and its amendments.[51]

Empirical work in this area can help evaluate the relative strengths of
competing theories in explaining environmental policy. For example,
Pashigian empirically evaluated US House of Representatives' votes on
the Clean Air Act's policy of prevention of significant deterioration to
determine whether tastes for environmental regulation, political philosophy, or self-interest with respect to the relative costs of environmental
regulation likely drives voting behaviour.[52] He found that the self-
interest hypothesis has played a prominent role in enacting environmental regulation. Similar kinds of analyses have been done to explain
differences in environmental policies across countries.[53] Legal scholars
have done some work in this area, too. Notably, experimental work in
'cultural cognition', the idea that cultural worldviews govern individuals'
beliefs about and support for various policies, has helped explain why

[49] For a more detailed discussion of the determinants of environmental policy and its
enforcement, as well as the role of empirical work in evaluating the resulting effect on
the environment, see Cary Coglianese & Catherine Courcy, 'Environmental Regulation',
in *The Oxford Handbook of Empirical Legal Research* (2010).

[50] Nathaniel Keohane, Richard Revesz, & Robert Stavins, 'The Choice of Regulatory
Instruments in Environmental Policy' (1998) 22 *Harvard Environmental Law Review*
313–367.

[51] Clean Air Act of 1970 42 USC §7401 et seq. (1970); Bruce Ackerman & William Hassler,
*Clean Coal/Dirty Air: or How the Clean Air Act Became a Multibillion-Dollar Bail-Out for
High-Sulfur Coal Producers* (New Haven: Yale University Press, 1981).

[52] Peter Pashigian, 'Environmental Regulation: Whose Self-Interests Are Being Protected?'
(1985) 23 *Economic Inquiry* 511–584.

[53] Eric Neumayer, 'Are Left-Wing Party Strength and Corporatism Good for the
Environment? Evidence from Panel Analysis of Air Pollution in OECD Countries'
(2003) 45 *Ecological Economics* 203–220.

groups of people persistently hold certain beliefs about environmental protection, particularly climate change policy.[54]

Overall, there is useful empirical work to be done in the environmental context: it can help determine whether environmental policies will be deemed cost-benefit justified, shed light on whether policies are achieving the desired results, and remind us of the social and economic forces that influence policies, among other things. Of course, there are legal scholars who employ empirical methods or who actively use empirical findings. But in general, environmental law scholarship rarely produces empirical work and has taken inadequate notice of some important empirical insights from economics.

Causes and Consequences

Just as legal phenomena have causes and consequences, so too does legal scholarship. Given the state of affairs described in the preceding two sections, it is worth speculating on why this situation has come about and what it means for the current condition of environmental law scholarship.

The first question is why the normative economic perspective has had greater purchase than economically informed empirical legal studies within environmental law scholarship. One straightforward answer to this question is that it does not take a great deal of economic expertise to grasp the basic normative implications of economics for environmental law and policy. Externalities and the problems of common pool resources are straightforward concepts and their application to the environmental context is often fairly obvious. Pollution and imperfect property rights are classic market failures, and little specific expertise is needed to understand them. The importance of trade-offs to policymaking is readily apparent for any critical observer, and questions concerning how the positive and negative consequences of policy choices should be weighed and evaluated can be discussed – at least at a superficial level – without a strong economic or philosophical background. Similarly, the benefits of more flexible approaches to regulation, such as cap-and-trade programs, are also fairly straightforward and can be understood intuitively without a deep foundation of economic theory. In addition, much of the economically relevant environmental law scholarship amounts to various

[54] Dan Kahan et al., 'Cultural Cognition of Scientific Consensus' (2011) 14 *Journal of Risk Research* 147–174.

critiques levelled against the application of economic thinking to environmental problems. Frequently these critiques take place at a sufficiently high level of abstraction that familiarity with the details of economic theory or models is unnecessary.

Sound empirical work on the law, by contrast, typically requires a technical background. Although widely available statistical packages and collections of data have massively reduced the barriers to engaging in empirical work, some understanding of statistics is a must, and scholars that do not have a strong familiarity with the rules of causal inferences engage in empirical work at their own risk. This is especially true in the context of empirical legal studies, which often rely on observational data rather than controlled experiments. In these cases, statistical controls and sophisticated inferential models are often used, which creates the risk of misinterpretation for the inexperienced.[55] Without a substantial educational investment, this type of research is typically is out of reach.

Nevertheless, as discussed earlier, in other areas of legal scholarship, legal academics have invested the necessary time and resources to develop an empirical skill set, and cross-disciplinary collaborations between law scholars and economists are relatively common. The question is why environmental law has lagged this particular trend. One possible explanation is that environmental law scholars are particularly resistant to or unwilling to engage in quantitative analysis – preferring by virtue of humanistic predisposition to stay on the qualitative side of this great intellectual divide. This explanation is unconvincing, however, because environmental law often involves questions that are riddled with thorny scientific and engineering issues. Environmental law is not an appropriate area for those unwilling to engage in the technical details.

An alternative hypothesis is that environmental law attracts scholars with certain interests and normative commitments that may be at odds with an economic worldview. Perhaps most generally, normative economics is firmly anthropocentric and takes human well-being as the ultimate yardstick to evaluate the desirability of policy choices. The non-human environment is essentially treated as a set of inputs into human well-being, with no independent moral status. Theories within environmental ethics criticize such human-centred approaches by arguing in

---

[55] Joshua Angrist and Jörn-Steffen Pischke, 'The Credibility Revolution in Empirical Economics: How Better Research Design Is Taking the Con out of Econometrics' (2010) 24 *Journal of Economic Perspectives* 3–30.

favour of the innate moral value of non-humans.[56] Animal rights advocates argue that focusing only on human utility amounts to *speciesism* based on morally irrelevant differences.[57] Others argue that collective entities such as species have intrinsic value that ought to be protected.[58] Sentiments like these may motivate both participation in environmental politics and interest in environmental law.

If this is the case, the normative side of economics discourse may have, in a sense, tainted the economics perspective more generally, including research that is more empirical in nature. There are many environmental law scholars who do not look favourably on cost-benefit analysis, who are skeptical of market mechanisms, and who view environmental harms as deontological moral wrongs rather than negative consequences to be balanced against their benefits in a consequentialist calculation. These are all, of course, legitimate positions sincerely held, but they may have the unnecessary side effect of biasing their adherents to the descriptive and empirical side of economic analysis of environmental law. If this conjecture is true, it may be that the success of the normative side of economics in shaping the conversation on environmental law has been a liability for the spread of economically informed empirical study in this area.[59]

Whatever the causes of a relative lack of an environmental law branch of empirical legal studies, it is also worth considering its consequences, both within and outside the legal academy. One immediate consequence is that, by missing one of the most important intellectual movements in the legal academy in the past several decades, environmental law scholars have isolated their field, which has resulted in fewer opportunities for mutually beneficial interactions with other areas of legal scholarship. This is a pity both for environmental law scholars and for the broader scholarly community. Any subfield that is cut off from its intellectual milieu will suffer as it turns inwards to ever more arcane questions that are of interest to a diminishing population of specialists.

[56] D. Ehrenfeld, *The Arrogance of Humanism* (London: Oxford University Press, 1981).

[57] Peter Singer, *Animal Liberation: A New Ethics for Our Treatment of Animals* (New York: HarperCollins, 1975).

[58] Holmes Rolston III, 'Duties to Endangered Species' (1985) 35(11) *BioScience* 718–726.

[59] This conjecture is quite speculative. It's possible, for example, that normative economics, by increasing the relevance of empirical work, actually led to more of such work being done than would have been the case if normative economics had not been so influential. Our instinct is that debates about the legitimacy of normative economics may have tainted the field more generally for environmental law scholars, compared to the counterfactual. But our confidence in that belief is relatively limited.

Furthermore, many areas of law may be denied the benefit of the particular expertise and creative energies of environmental law scholars if the field becomes overly isolated. Environmental law intersects with many broader areas of law, including property law, tort law, administrative law, land use law, local government law, constitutional law, and international law. In many areas, environmental questions pose new and interesting fact patterns that give rise to important precedent. For example, the US Supreme Court decision that establishes the doctrine of deference to agency statutory interpretation is *Chevron* v. *Natural Resources Defense Council*, a case that dealt with a pollution control regulation.[60] Environmental policy often presents interesting issues related to federalism and decentralized government, the role of courts, and policy design and evaluation.[61] Environmental law scholars have important insights to bring to these disparate areas, but they will be less well positioned to do so if they are not engaged in similar intellectual projects. There are also fewer opportunities for collaboration across the university, especially the social sciences, if the empirical tools that have been developed there do not have a home in environmental law scholarship.

A further consequence of the underdevelopment of empirical environmental law scholarship may be a lack of influence within broader policy debates. The election of Donald J. Trump to the US presidency illustrates the degree to which the status of experts in the policymaking process is always tenuous. Scholars of environmental law well know that even physical scientists and public health researchers – who one might think occupy the highest rungs of the expertise hierarchy – can easily be ignored by policymakers when the financial and political stakes are sufficiently high. Nevertheless, it remains the case that expertise on empirical matters is more likely to be heeded than expertise on normative matters: when policymakers are called on to make difficult choices, it is common to consult experts in the relevant scientific disciplines, and relatively uncommon to make calls to professors of moral philosophy. It is fair to bemoan this situation, and a lack of tangible and immediate influence does not imply that normative scholarship is not socially valuable. But, by focusing their energies on normative matters, and allowing the broader trend towards empirical legal study to largely pass them by,

---

[60]   467 US 837 (1984).
[61]   Michael Livermore, 'The Perils of Experimentation' (2017) 126 *Yale Law Journal* 636–708.

environmental law scholars have ceded important territory both to other disciplines (notably the social sciences) and to less scrupulous players (such as consultants on the payroll of affected industry) who are willing to occupy that vacuum.

The Role of Law in Multidisciplinary Environmental Research

Although empirical study of environmental law has not, to date, been a primary interest of scholars in the field, environmental law scholars can make considerable contributions to empirical research on important questions that are relevant to environmental law and policy. The special expertise and abilities of environmental lawyers open the door for several potential roles that they can play as part of interdisciplinary research projects.

As an initial matter, empirical research in the social sciences, public health, and even the life sciences often rely on natural experiments that are provided by legal variation and change. Because policymaking rarely proceeds through a process of randomized controlled trials, information about the effects of policy choices on environmental quality, economic variables, or health can often best be gleaned through observational data. The well-established problem with such observational data is that the lack of randomization raises serious problems of causal inference, as policy choices are themselves endogenous to the systems under study, creating issues of selection bias and unobserved variable bias.

An understanding of legal context, however, can point the way to better identified studies. For example, Greenstone and Gallagher exploit a sharp discontinuity in how hazardous sites are categorized under the US toxic waste cleanup program to study the local consequences of environmental remediation.[62] By limiting their study to sites that are clustered on either side of this discontinuity, Greenstone and Gallagher are able to control for the host of unobserved variables that might be correlated with outcome variables of interest.[63] Essentially, the nature of the legal regime (in which a cutoff exists between sites that are listed and prioritized for cleanup and those that are not) creates a quasi-experiment allowing for more well-founded causal inference. In this and similar studies, understanding a legal regime can provide researchers with the

---

[62] Michael Greenstone & Justin Gallagher, 'Does Hazardous Waste Matter? Evidence from the Housing Market and the Superfund Program' (2008) 123 *Quarterly Journal of Economics* 951–1003.

[63] Ibid.

opportunity to study causation effects that would otherwise be extremely difficult to analyse.

A second major advantage that legal scholars bring to environmental research is a greater familiarity with legal decision-making contexts and the ways that empirical research is – or is not – integrated into environmental policy. This knowledge can help structure research questions and research design so that empirical work can have the maximum possible effects. There are several ways in which knowledge of the policymaking process can help translate research into results. Focusing investments in research on policy areas that may be soon subject to reform efforts can ensure that policymakers can put fresh research findings directly into use. When researchers engage in work that is relevant only to policy areas that are not likely to be subject to revision in the near future, then their findings may be stale by the time decision-makers get around to reforms.

In addition to insights into the timing of reform, legal scholars are also attuned to institutional contexts, such as the jurisdictional level at which policymaking will happen (i.e. between local, provincial/states, or national jurisdictions), or the horizontal allocation of decisional capacity (i.e. between agencies, courts, or legislatures). Understanding the institutional context of decision-making allows researchers to structure research questions and methods to have maximal effects. To take an obvious example, courts deciding questions of liability have very different standards of causation than administrative agencies deciding whether to regulate. Research design that is sufficient for an agency to update its understanding of the toxicity of a chemical is likely to be insufficient for a court operating on a preponderance of the evidence standard. Similarly, local, state, and national regulators are often interested in different social and economic consequences and have different trade-offs between fine-grained analysis and predictive confidence – a municipality may be willing to accept greater uncertainty in exchange for more locally relevant predictions, whereas national regulators may be willing to accept greater aggregation of effects if that reduces the confidence intervals around point estimate predictions. Research that is designed in light of the institutional context in which it will be used is more likely to be influential in practice.

In a related vein, environmental law scholars can also play a vital role in communicating empirical results to the relevant policymaking bodies. This might occur through informal processes, or during the course of formal proceedings such as rule-making or litigation. Of course, a legal scholar can certainly communicate research results without being integrated directly into a research team. Nevertheless, by playing an early role in selecting research questions and methods that are well suited to particular forums, legal scholars will create the conditions that create the best opportunities for successfully relaying research findings to policymakers.

We can think of two additional roles that legal scholars are particularly well suited to play in advancing empirical scholarship on environmental questions. One is in facilitating conversations among disparate academic disciplines in the course of multidisciplinary scholarship. An unusual characteristic of law faculties – especially in the United States – is their interdisciplinary nature. Generally speaking, what brings a law faculty together is not a shared *methodology*, but rather a shared *object of study*. A law faculty may have scholars with backgrounds in economics, history, philosophy, sociology, and anthropology, in addition to scholars with practical experience or expertise in doctrinal analysis. Because they engage colleagues with such diverse backgrounds, legal scholars often become well versed in the skill of interdisciplinary conversation. Part of that skill is grounded in familiarity with the methods, questions, interests, and quirks of many different disciplines. This may be especially true of environmental law scholars, whose work frequently touches on fields as disparate as environmental ethics and climate science. As research tends towards being done by larger and more interdisciplinary teams, environmental law scholars can bring their expertise in framing questions that can be translated into terms that are cognizable within different disciplinary traditions.

The final role is in interpreting environmental law itself as an object that is worthy of study directly as a cultural product, somewhat apart from its role as an instrument of policy or social ordering. There is a budding field within empirical legal studies that is based on the quantitative analysis of legal texts, and which uses tools from network theory, natural language processing, complexity theory, and computer science to understand the law.[64] Environmental law – with its multiple intersections with society and economic and political life, as well as the natural world – is a particularly ripe area for this type of scholarship. Indeed, environmental law scholars were among the first to recognize the resonance between the complexity of natural systems and the law, setting the stage for the application of tools derived from the study of those natural

---

[64] Michael Livermore & Daniel Rockmore, *Law as Data: Computation, Text, and the Future of Legal Analysis* (Santa Fe, AZ: Santa Fe Institute Press, in press).

systems to legal phenomena.[65] As the techniques of computational text analysis become more widespread within the legal academy, environmental law may prove to be an area where they generate particularly important insights. This new wave of empirical legal study, which builds on but is distinct from the more econometrically centred approach that is now widespread, may provide the perfect opportunity for environmental law scholars to join the vanguard of academic lawyers engaged in the empirical study of the law.

Bibliography

Ackerman, Bruce & Hassler, William, *Clean Coal/Dirty Air: or How the Clean Air Act Became a Multibillion-Dollar Bail-Out for High-Sulfur Coal Producers* (New Haven: Yale University Press, 1981).

Ackerman, Frank & Heinzerling, Lisa, *Priceless: On Knowing the Price of Everything and the Value of Nothing* (New York: The New Press, 2005).

Adler, Matthew, *Well-Being and Fair Distribution: Beyond Cost-Benefit Analysis* (New York: Oxford University Press, 2011).

Adler, Matthew & Posner, Eric, *New Foundations of Cost-Benefit Analysis* (Cambridge, MA: Harvard University Press, 2006).

Alvarado-Quesada, Irene, Hein, Lars, & Weikard, Hans Peter, 'Market-Based Mechanisms for Biodiversity Conservation: A Review of Existing Schemes and an Outline for a Global Mechanism' (2014) 23 *Biodiversity & Conservationism* 1–21.

Anderson, Elizabeth, *Values in Ethics and Economics* (Cambridge, MA: Harvard University Press, 1995).

Angrist, Joshua & Pischke, Jörn-Steffen, 'The Credibility Revolution in Empirical Economics: How Better Research Design Is Taking the Con out of Econometrics' (2010) 24 *Journal of Economic Perspectives* 3–30.

Anthoff, David & Tol, Richard, 'The Uncertainty About the Social Cost of Carbon: A Decomposition Analysis Using FUND' (2013) 117 *Climatic Change* 515–530.

Arrow, Kenneth et al., 'Report of the NOAA Panel on Contingent Valuation' (1993) 58 *Federal Register* 4601–4614.

Bockstael, Nancy, 'Travel Cost Methods', in Daniel Bromley (ed.), *The Handbook of Environmental Economics* (Oxford: Blackwell Publishers, 1996).

Breggin, Linda et al., 'Trends in Environmental Law Scholarship 2008-2015' (2016) 46 *Environmental Law Reporter News & Analysis* 10647.

Brown, T., Bergstrom, J., & Loomis, B., 'Defining, Valuing and Providing Ecosystem Goods and Services' (2007) 47(2) *Natural Resources Journal* 329–376.

---

[65] J. B. Ruhl, 'Complexity Theory as a Paradigm for the Dynamical Law-and-Society System: A Wake-Up Call for Legal Reductionism and the Modern Administrative State' (1996) 45 *Duke Law Journal* 849–928.

Camerer, Colin & Mobbs, Dean, 'Differences in Behavior and Brain Activity During Hypothetical and Real Choices' (2017) 21 *Trends in Cognitive Sciences* 45–56.

Chang, Howard & Sigman, Hilary, 'An Empirical Analysis of Cost Recovery in Superfund Cases: Implications for Brownfields and Joint and Several Liability' (2014)11 *Journal of Empirical Legal Studies* 477–504.

Chay, Kenneth, Dobkin, Carlos, & Greenstone, Michael, 'The Clean Air Act of 1970 and Adult Mortality' (2003) 27 *Journal of Risk and Uncertainty* 279–300.

Coglianese, Cary & Courcy, Catherine, 'Environmental Regulation', in *The Oxford Handbook of Empirical Legal Research* (Oxford: Oxford University Press, 2010).

Cole, Daniel & Grossman, Peter, 'When Is Command-and-Control Efficient? Institutions, Technology, and the Comparative Efficiency of Alternative Regulatory Regimes for Environmental Protection' (1999) *Wisconsin Law Review* 887–938.

Currie, Janet et al., 'Does Pollution Increase School Absences?' (2009) 91 *Review of Economics and Statistics* 682–694.

Dickie, Mark & Gerking, Shelby, 'Willingness to Pay for Ozone Control: Inferences from the Demand for Medical Care' (1991) 21 *Journal of Environmental Economics and Management* 1–16.

Driesen, David, 'Distributing the Costs of Environmental, Health, and Safety Protection: The Feasibility Principle, Cost-Benefit Analysis, and Regulatory Reform' (2005) 32 *Boston College Environmental Affairs Law Review* 1–95.

Ehrenfeld, D., *The Arrogance of Humanism* (London: Oxford University Press, 1981).

Farber, Daniel, 'Pollution Markets and Social Equity: Analyzing the Fairness of Cap and Trade' (2012) 39 *Ecology Law Quarterly* 1–56.

Fowlie, Meredith, Holland, Stephen, & Mansur Erin, 'What Do Emissions Markets Deliver and to Whom? Evidence from Southern California's NOx Trading Program' (2012) 102 *American Economic Review* 965–993.

Gayer, Ted & Viscusi, W. Kip, 'Determining the Proper Scope of Climate Change Policy Benefits in U.S. Regulatory Analyses: Domestic versus Global Approaches' (2016) 10 *Review of Environmental Economics and Policy* 1–19.

Gollier, Christian & Weitzman, Martin, 'How Should the Distant Future Be Discounted When Discount Rates Are Uncertain?' (2009) 107 *Economics Letters* 350–353.

Goulder, Lawrence & Schein, Andrew, 'Carbon Taxes Versus Cap and Trade: A Critical Review' (2013) 4 *Climate Change Economics* 1350010–1350048.

Greenstone, Michael & Gallagher, Justin, 'Does Hazardous Waste Matter? Evidence from the Housing Market and the Superfund Program' (2008) 123 *Quarterly Journal of Economics* 951–1003.

Hanson, John & Kysar, Douglas, 'Taking Behavioralism Seriously: The Problem of Market Manipulation' (1999) 74 *New York University Law Review* 630–745.

Helfand, Gloria, 'Standards versus Standards: The Effects of Different Pollution Restrictions' (1991) 81 *American Economic Review* 622–634.

Hope, Chris, 'Critical issues for the Calculation of the Social Cost of CO_2: Why the Estimates from PAGE09 Are Higher Than Those from PAGE2002' (2013) 117 *Climatic Change* 531–543.

Howard, Peter & Livermore, Michael, 'Sociopolitical Feedbacks and Climate Change' *Harvard Environmental Law Review* (forthcoming).

Howard, Peter & Schwartz, Jason, 'Think Global: International Reciprocity as Justification for a Global Social Cost of Carbon' (2017) 42 *Columbia Journal of Environmental Law* 203–295.

Howard, Peter & Sylvan, Derek, 'The Economic Climate: Establishing Expert Consensus on the Economics of Climate Change', Institute of Policy Integrity, December 2015.

Johnson, Stephen, 'Economics v. Equity: Do Market-Based Environmental Reforms Exacerbate Environmental Injustice?' (1999) 56 *Washington & Lee Law Review* 111–118.

Kahan, Dan et al., 'Cultural Cognition of Scientific Consensus' (2011) 14 *Journal of Risk Research* 147–174.

Kaswan, Alice, 'Decentralizing Cap-and-Trade? State Controls Within a Federal Greenhouse Gas Cap-and-Trade Program' (2010) 28 *Virginal Environmental Law Journal* 343–410.

Kaswan, Alice, 'Climate Change, the Clean Air Act, and Industrial Pollution' (2012) 30 *University of California, Los Angeles Journal of Environmental Law & Policy* 51–119.

Keeler, B. et al., 'Linking Water Quality and Well-Being for Improved Assessment and Valuation of Ecosystem Services' (2012) 109(45) *Proceedings of the National Academy of Sciences of the United States of America* 18619–18624.

Kelman, Steven, *What Price Incentives?: Economists and the Environment* (Toronto: Praeger Publishing, 1981).

Keohane, Nathaniel, Revesz, Richard, & Stavins, Robert, 'The Choice of Regulatory Instruments in Environmental Policy' (1998) 22 *Harvard Environmental Law Review* 313–367.

Khaw, Mel et al., 'The Measurement of Subjective Value and Its Relationship to Contingent Valuation of Environmental Public Goods' (2015)10 *PLoS ONE* 1–19.

Kysar, Douglas, 'It Might Have Been: Risk, Precaution and Opportunity Costs' (2006) 22 *Journal of Land Use & Environmental Law* 1–34.

Livermore, Michael, '*Setting the Social Cost of Carbon*', in Daniel A. Farber and Marjan Peeters (eds), *Climate Change Law* (Cheltenham: Edward Elgar Publishing, 2016).

Livermore, Michael, 'The Perils of Experimentation' (2017) 126 *Yale Law Journal* 636–708.

Livermore, Michael & Revesz, Richard, 'Interest Groups and Environmental Policy: Inconsistent Positions and Missed Opportunities' (2015) 45 *Environmental Law* 1–19.

Livermore, Michael & Revesz, Richard, Environmental Law and Economics', in Francesco Parisi (ed.), *Oxford Handbook of Law and Economics: Private and Commercial Law* (New York: Oxford University Press, 2017), vol. 2, p. 509.

Livermore, Michael & Rockmore, Daniel, *'Law as Data: Computation, Text, and the Future of Legal Analysis* (Santa Fe, AZ: Santa Fe Institute Press, in press).

Mitchell, Robert & Carson, Richard, *Using Surveys to Value Public Goods: The Contingent Valuation Method* (Washington, DC: Resources for the Future, 1989).

Moyer, Elisabeth et al., 'Climate Impacts on Economic Growth as Drivers of Uncertainty in the Social Cost of Carbon' (2014) 43 *Journal of Legal Studies* 401–425.

Neumayer, Eric, 'Are Left-Wing Party Strength and Corporatism Good for the Environment? Evidence from Panel Analysis of Air Pollution in OECD Countries' (2003) 45 *Ecological Economics* 203–220.

Nordhaus, William & Sztorc, Paul, *DICE 2013 R: Introduction and User's Manual* (New Haven: Cowles Foundation, 2013).

Oates, Wallace, Portney, Paul, & McGartland, Albert, 'The Net Benefits of Incentive-Based Regulation: A Case Study of Environmental Standard Setting' (1989) 79 *American Economic Review* 1233–1242.

Pashigian, Peter, 'Environmental Regulation: Whose Self-Interests Are Being Protected?' (1985) 23 *Economic Inquiry* 511–584.

Phaneuf, Daniel & Smith, V. Kerry, 'Recreation Demand Models', in Karl-Gran Mäler & Jeffrey Vincent (eds), *Handbook of Environmental Economics* (Amsterdam: North Holland/Elsevier Science, 2005), pp. 671–761.

Pindyck, Robert, 'Climate Change Policy: What Do the Models Tell Us?' (2013) 51 *Journal of Economic Literature* 860–872.

Radin, Mary Jane, *Contested Commodities* (Cambridge, MA: Harvard University Press, 2001).

Revesz, Richard, 'Markets and Geography: Designing Marketable Permit Schemes to Control Local and Regional Pollutants' (2001) 28 *Ecology Law Quarterly* 569–672.

Revesz, Richard et al., 'Best Cost Estimate of Greenhouse Gases' (2017) 357 *Science* 655.

Revesz, Richard & Livermore, Michael, *Retaking Rationality: How Cost-Benefit Analysis Can Better Protect the Environment and Our Health* (New York: Oxford University Press, 2008).

Revesz, Richard & Stavins, Robert, 'Environmental Law and Policy', in A. Mitchell Polinsky & Steven Shavell (eds), *Handbook of Law and Economics* (Amsterdam: North-Holland/Elsevier Science, 2007), pp. 499–589.

Rolston, Holmes, III., 'Duties to Endangered Species' (1985) 35(11) *BioScience* 718–726.

Rosen, Sherwin, 'Hedonic Prices and Implicit Markets: Product Differentiation in Pure Competition' (1974) 82 *Journal of Political Economy* 34–35.

Ruhl, J. B., 'Complexity Theory as a Paradigm for the Dynamical Law-and-Society System: A Wake-Up Call for Legal Reductionism and the Modern Administrative State' (1996) 45 *Duke Law Journal* 849–928.

Sagoff, Mark, 'On Preserving the Natural Environment' (1974) 84 *Yale Law Journal* 224–225.

Singer, Peter, *Animal Liberation: A New Ethics for Our Treatment of Animals* (New York: HarperCollins, 1975).

Steinzor, Rena, 'Devolution and the Public Health' (2000) 24 *Harvard Environmental Law Review* 366–369.

Sunstein, Cass, 'Cost-Benefit Analysis and Arbitrariness Review' (2017) 41 *Harvard Environmental Law Review* 1–41.

Tietenberg, Thomas, 'Tradable Permits for Pollution Control When Emission Location Matters: What Have We Learned?' (1995) 5 *Environmental and Resource Economics* 95–113.

US Environmental Protection Agency, 'Guidelines for Preparing Economic Analyses', December 17, 2010.

Viscusi, W. Kip, 'The Value of Life: Estimates with Risks by Occupation and Industry' (2004) 42 *Economic Inquiry* 29–48.

Weitzman, Mark, 'Fat-Tailed Uncertainty in the Economics of Catastrophic Climate Change' (2011) 5 *Review of Environmental Economics and Policy* 275–292.

Weitzman, Martin, 'Prices vs. Quantities' (1974) 41 *Review of Economic Studies* 477–491.

8

What Is the Point of International Environmental Law Scholarship in the Anthropocene?

TIM STEPHENS

Abstract

This chapter considers the implications of the Anthropocene for the study of international environmental law. This new 'human era' in Earth's history upends many traditional assumptions about the purpose and function of environmental law. It has decisively erased the (already untenable) distinction between the human and natural worlds such that many of the historic concerns of environmental law (such as wilderness protection) now appear as vainglorious acts in the face of global environmental transformation. As the Anthropocene challenges our understanding of international environmental law, so it must necessarily challenge our understanding of research in the field. The chapter argues that if international environmental law research is to maintain its meaning and relevance, it will need to draw on the insights provided by Earth systems science and Earth systems governance literature and embrace clear objectives to maintain a habitable planet.

Introduction

The chapter considers the challenges that the advent of the Anthropocene poses for the study of international environmental law. The Anthropocene concept is increasingly used by the scientific community to describe the current geological period in which humanity has become the dominant force of global environmental change. The term appears likely to acquire formal approval as a unit of the geological time

This chapter draws upon some of the author's previous work, including Tim Stephens, 'Reimagining International Environmental Law in the Anthropocene' in Louis Kotzé (ed.), *Environmental Law and Governance for the Anthropocene* (Oxford: Hart Publishing, 2017), p. 31.

scale by the International Commission on Stratigraphy.[1] However, it is the more general meaning of the term as a description of human-induced change to the global biosphere (the sum of all biota) and geosphere (atmosphere, hydrosphere, cryosphere, and upper lithosphere)[2] which is most relevant for our purposes. As Steffen et al. put it, '[t]he Anthropocene provides an independent measure of the scale and tempo of human-caused change – biodiversity loss, changes to the chemistry of atmosphere and ocean, urbanization, globalization – and places them in the deep time context of Earth history.'[3] It is this meaning which captures the extent of human impacts on the Earth system and describes activities which can be managed through the rules and institutions of international environmental law.

The Anthropocene upends many traditional assumptions about the purposes and functions of environmental law at national, regional, and global levels. Most obviously, the pace and scale of Earth system change undermines many of the traditional, place-based, concerns of environmental law which are becoming increasingly futile gestures in the face of global environmental transformation. It is argued in this chapter that this new era represents a critical turning point for the study of international environmental law as it raises the question as to what purpose(s) this area of international law should now serve. In seeking to address this question, the chapter commences with an overview of the history of international environmental law and leading accounts of its goals. The chapter then assesses the implications of Earth system science and Earth system governance literature for international environmental law research, and it concludes with a suggested agenda for international environmental law scholarship in the Anthropocene.

The Anthropocene and the History of International Environmental Law

The Anthropocene concept was first popularised by Paul Crutzen and Eugene Stoermer more than fifteen years ago.[4] But it is only recently that

[1] Jan Zalasiewicz, Colin Waters, & Martin J. Head, 'Anthropocene: Its Stratigraphic Basis' (2017) 541 *Nature* 289.

[2] Owen Gaffney & Will Steffen, 'The Anthropocene Equation' (2017) 4(1) *The Anthropocene Review* 53.

[3] Will Steffen et al., 'The Anthropocene: From Global Change to Planetary Stewardship' (2011) 40(7) *Ambio* 739, 757.

[4] Paul J. Crutzen, 'Geology of Mankind' (2002) 415 *Nature* 23.

the term has become widely used in scientific circles and has had a broader influence in the social sciences.[5] The Anthropocene Working Group of the International Commission on Stratigraphy has been tasked with determining whether the Anthropocene is truly a new geological time unit and, if so, when it began.[6] The dawn of the nuclear age in the middle of the twentieth century has been identified as the likely starting point of this new era, as it was at this time that the expansion in industrial activities and energy use left a geological footprint.[7]

The concept is elegantly captured in Gaffney and Steffen's 'Anthropocene Equation, $\frac{dE}{dt} = \frac{f(H)}{A,G,I \to 0}$, in which the variable 'H', representing humanity, has become the primary force of change to the Earth ('E') system over time ('t'), with astrophysical ('A') forcings, geophysical ('G') forcings and internal ('I') dynamics tending to zero.[8] Conceived in this way, the Anthropocene has obvious relevance for international environmental policy and law because the disturbance to Earth's biogeophysical systems is seriously impairing the health of the planet's environmental systems and the socio-economic systems that they support. But the Anthropocene is more than simply a new term to describe global environmental decline, something with which international environmental law has been concerned for some time. Instead, the Anthropocene foregrounds the reality of the deeply connected human-nature relationship.

For most of human history, spatially and temporally limited human impacts on the environment have served to obscure the interdependence of human and natural systems. However, planetary changes such as climate change mean this symbiosis can no longer be ignored. Hamilton notes that global environmental transformation in the Anthropocene 'is now telling us that the modern division of the world into a box marked "Nature" and one marked "Human" is no longer tenable'.[9] We are in a post-natural epoch, a 'New Earth' in which human and natural forces are intermixed

[5] Jeremy Davies, *The Birth of the Anthropocene* (Berkeley: University of California Press, 2016).

[6] Jan Zalasiewicz et al., 'When Did the Anthropocene Begin? A Mid-Twentieth Century Boundary Level Is Stratigraphically Optimal' (2015) 383 *Quaternary International* 196.

[7] Zalasiewicz et al., 'Anthropocene: Its Stratigraphic Basis'.

[8] Gaffney & Steffen, 'The Anthropocene Equation', 53.

[9] Clive Hamilton, 'Human Destiny in the Anthropocene' in Clive Hamilton, Christophe Bonneuil, & François Gemenne (eds), *The Anthropocene and the Global Environmental Crisis* (Abingdon: Routledge, 2015), p. 32.

and inseparable.[10] As Biermann puts it, the Earth is now 'an inter-
dependent integrated social-ecological system'.[11]

There are many lessons from the Anthropocene for international
environmental law. First among these is that the Earth must be
viewed as a single dynamic system with multiple intersecting environmental subsystems. This is a genuinely novel perspective. Despite
the attachment of 'international' to environmental law to connote its
global reach, much of the focus of this area of international law has
been on environmental issues within defined spatial boundaries (e.g.
the protection of heritage areas) or relating to specific environmental
subjects (e.g. types of pollution). A related realisation now confronting international environmental law is that in the post-natural world
we now inhabit, law cannot seek to protect nature as an external
object separate from human influences. There is no 'pure' nature or
wilderness, not even in the remotest places on Earth such as
Antarctica.[12] As Purdy argues, in the Anthropocene, '[t]he world
we inhabit will henceforth be the world we have made.'[13]

If many of international environmental law's traditional goals (e.g.
habitat preservation in a pristine and natural condition) now seem out
of reach, and the tools used to achieve them (e.g. protected areas) are
less effective, what should international environmental law now strive
to do? A fatalistic response is that international environmental law is
pointless because many of Earth's environmental systems have passed
a point of no return. A more appropriate answer is that global
environmental change significantly conditions the purposes that international environmental law can now serve and demands a fresh
appraisal of the content and effectiveness of multilateral environmental treaty regimes.

In developing this latter response, it is helpful to consider the goals that
international environmental law have traditionally served. History in

---

[10] Simon Nicholson & Sikina Jinnah, 'Introduction: Living on a New Earth' in
Simon Nicholson and Sikina Jinnah (eds), *New Earth Politics: Essays from the
Anthropocene* (Cambridge, MA: MIT Press, 2016), p. 7.

[11] Frank Biermann, *Earth System Governance: World Politics in the Anthropocene*
(Cambridge, MA: MIT Press, 2014), p. 16.

[12] Tim Stephens, 'The Antarctic Treaty System and the Anthropocene' (2018) 8 *The Polar
Journal* 29.

[13] Jedediah Purdy, 'Surviving the Anthropocene: What's Next for Humanity?' ABC Religion
and Ethics, available at www.abc.net.au/religion/articles/2016/03/01/4416386.htm.

international law casts a long shadow,[14] and international environmental law is no exception. In reflecting on the past, present, and future of international environmental law, we can separate its development into three main periods: the modern era which extended for most of the twentieth century and concluded in the early 1970s, a postmodern era from the 1970s onwards in which there was a rapid growth in a disparate range of environmental regimes, and a post-nature era in which international environmental law is beginning to confront the implications of the Anthropocene (Table 8.1). Scholarship in international environmental law has also tended to follow in the footsteps of these periodic developments in the law rather than itself generating significant normative change.

Modern International Environmental Law and Scholarship

The modern period of international environmental law comprised most of the twentieth century, until the last three decades when awareness of global environmental challenges led to the adoption of the 1972 Stockholm Declaration and other instruments which guided the consolidation and evolution of global environmental policy and law.

Applying 'international environmental law' to this period is something of a conceit given that the term only began to be used after it ended. Bodansky describes this period as one in which international law relating to the environment might best be termed 'international conservation law'.[15] This body of law was composed of treaties addressing natural resources such as fisheries, seals, whales, and some topics of wildlife conservation. An example is the 1902 Convention to Protect Birds Useful to Agriculture[16] adopted by a collection of European governments. A strong emphasis of environmental norms throughout this period was on instrumentalist and utilitarian values: the natural environment as a source of living and nonliving materials for human consumption and as a place of recreation.[17]

---

[14] Anne Orford, 'International Law and the Limits of History' in W. Werner, A. Galán, & M. de Hoon (eds), *The Law of International Lawyers: Reading Martti Koskenniemi* (Cambridge: Cambridge University Press, 2015).

[15] Daniel Bodansky, *The Art and Craft of International Environmental Law* (Cambridge, MA: Harvard University Press, 2011), p. 10.

[16] Convention to Protect Birds Useful to Agriculture, Paris, 19 March 1902, in force 6 December 1905, BFSP (1902) 102.

[17] See Ed Couzens, *Whales and Elephants in International Conservation Law and Politics: A Comparative Study* (Abingdon: Routledge, 2014), chap. 2.

Table 8.1 *Periods in international environmental law and international environmental law scholarship.*

	Modern	Postmodern	Anthropocene
Period	Modern	Postmodern	Post-nature
Values	Instrumental values predominate (utilisation, dominion)	Instrumental and inherent values (utilisation, management, conservation)	Instrumental values predominate (utilisation, conservation, geoengineering)
Human/Nature Connection	Humanity and environment separate	Humanity and environment connected	Humanity and environment inseparable
Conception of Nature	Nature as threat	Nature as object	Nature as threat (crisis model of lawmaking?)
Conception of Ecosystems	Limited conception of ecosystems	Maintenance of ecosystem services	Global ecosystem 'management' (negative emissions, SRM etc.)
Conception of Earth	No concept of Earth system	Some conception of Earth systems	Concept of total Earth system
Environment and Development	Environment as inexhaustible resource for development	Sustainable development (weak form – linear economy)	Sustainable development (strong form – safe and just space – circular economy)
Objectives	No clear goals	Disparate goals (fragmentation, proliferation)	Overarching goal?

In this era, the environment appears in treaty texts and legal treatises as a (mostly) inexhaustible resource for development. The goal of many treaty regimes was therefore to facilitate greater exploitation, subject to few limits, with the primary goal of maintaining peaceful relations between the states in competition for resources. The *Bering Fur Seals* case and the treaty it helped generate for the management of Alaskan fur seals by Britain, Russia, and the United States is an example of this.[18] There was very little appreciation of interconnected human/nature relations. Humanity and nature were viewed as radically separate, with nature either a threat to be confronted and overcome or a resource to be exploited. Moreover, this era featured a compartmentalised view of nature itself, with the emerging concept of ecosystem in the scientific literature[19] having very limited influence on environmental policy and law.

Postmodern International Environmental Law and Scholarship

The postmodern period in international environmental law and environmental law scholarship commenced in the early 1970s. It was a phase in which scientific research on environmental issues acquired substantial influence within governments, environmental movements in developed countries organised and asserted political influence, comprehensive national environmental laws and policies were adopted, and global environmental texts were concluded in response to global environmental challenges.

These developments took place against the backdrop of debates between north and south on global developmental pathways. International environmental law and research in the field therefore became subsumed within broader debates concerning economic development. This epitomised the postmodern character of the period, with established certainties giving way to a variety of competing perspectives. This is seen in the emergence of the discourse of sustainable development, a highly pliable concept with a meaning shifting according to the perspective of the user of the term.[20] For governments in the north the emphasis was on environmental protection, while for those in the south the primary concern remained development to alleviate poverty. Sustainable development served as a shared vision. While there were disagreements about what it required, there was consensus that economic expansion could be reconciled with environmental protection. This was a linear perspective of development, subscribing to neo-liberal economic

---

[18] *Bering Sea Fur Seals (Great Britain v. United States)* (1898) 1 Moore 755

[19] See e.g. A. G. Tansley, 'The Use and Abuse of Vegetational Concepts and Terms' (1935) 16 *Ecology* 284, 299.

[20] See generally Bill Adams, *Sustainable Development: Environment and Sustainability in a Developing World*, 3rd edn (Abingdon: Routledge, 2009).

theory which maintains that continuous economic growth is possible despite the finite limits of the Earth system.[21]

Ecological science began to gain recognition in international environmental law during this era, as seen in the 1992 Convention on Biological Diversity which sought to safeguard ecosystems and biodiversity.[22] We also see the arrival of clearly utilitarian notions of ecosystem services, which emphasised the need to sustain environmental systems to provide food, fibre, and other resources for human societies. Treating ecosystems as a provider of services, and as a type of natural 'capital', involved the commodification of the natural world and allowed environmental problems to appear in mainstream economic analysis.[23]

Unlike the modern period, therefore, there was a mixture of disparate approaches in this postmodern period, with international environmental law serving both instrumental purposes and, to a lesser extent, higher goals in protecting inherent environmental values.[24] The variety of perspectives and the sheer number of environmental treaties at this time began to give rise to concerns around normative proliferation and fragmentation. Despite this diversity, most of these treaties and other texts viewed nature as an object of regulation largely separate from humanity.

There remained therefore limited understanding of the embeddedness of human societies within natural systems, despite the wealth of scholarship in environmental theory making just this point.[25] Moreover, there was very little reflection in international environmental law texts of the character of the Earth as a dynamic system. As early as the 1970s, there was some understanding of Earth as a single complex system composed of the interaction of biological and geophysical forces, as captured in Lovelock's Gaia hypothesis.[26] But this was not expressed to any

---

[21] For a comprehensive critique, see Kate Raworth, *Donut Economics: Seven Ways to Think Like a 21st Century Economist* (White River Junction, VT: Chelsea Green Publishing, 2017), p. 23.

[22] Convention on Biological Diversity, Rio de Janeiro, 5 June 1992, in force 29 December 1993, 1760 UNTS 143. Art. 2 contains a definition of an ecosystem as 'a dynamic complex of plant, animal and micro-organism communities and their non-living environment interacting as a functional unit.'

[23] See generally Partha Dasgupta, *Human Well-Being and the Natural Environment* (Oxford: Oxford University Press, 2002).

[24] Alexander Gillespie, *International Environmental Law, Policy, and Ethics*, 2nd edn (Oxford: Oxford University Press, 2014).

[25] See generally Robyn Eckersley, *Environmentalism and Political Theory* (London: University College London Press, 1992).

[26] James E. Lovelock, *The Age of Gaia* (Oxford: Oxford University Press, 1995).

significant extent in positive international environmental law or in international environmental law scholarship. There were isolated exceptions, such as the recognition by the International Court of Justice in the *Nuclear Weapons Advisory Opinion* that 'the environment is not an abstraction but represents the living space, the quality of life and the very health of human beings, including generations unborn.'[27]

A telling example of a pre-Anthropocene environmental treaty is the 1991 Alpine Convention that seeks to protect the European Alps.[28] This treaty regime demonstrates limited engagement with the radical systemic change underway as the Alps lose their permanent and seasonal snow and ice cover.[29] Subsequent additions to the treaty have shown some awareness of global pressures on the Alps (e.g. the 2007 Alpine Climate Declaration[30]), but the regime is otherwise mostly inward looking. It also fails to acknowledge the functional importance of the Alps beyond the immediate Alpine environment itself (such as its capacity to reflect solar radiation, the Albedo effect[31]).

This and many other environmental treaties are typical of 'Romantic environmentalism'[32] in designating areas as places to be protected because of their natural and/or cultural significance. The language of the Alpine regime is steeped in this approach, describing the Alps 'as an archive of natural history and the history of civilisation'[33] leaving the impression that the region is a kind of museum, gallery, or library rather than a dynamic environment deeply connected to global environmental systems. This is an 'old-world' environmental ethic, which subscribes to a pastoral environmentalism in which the aesthetic value of wilderness is thought to be protected and maintained in perpetuity by the mere act of legal designation.

---

[27] *Legality of the Threat or Use of Nuclear Weapons* [1996] ICJ Rep 226, [29].

[28] Alpine Convention, 7 November 1991, in force 6 March 1995 (1991) 31 ILM 767, available at www.alpconv.org.

[29] Daniel Farinotti, Alberto Pistocchi, & Matthias Huss, 'From Dwindling Ice to Headwater Lakes; Could Dams Replace Glaciers in the European Alps?' (2016) 11 *Environmental Research Letters* 1.

[30] Alpine Declaration on Climate Change, adopted November 2006, Declaration made under the Alpine Convention, available at www.alpconv.org/en/convention/protocols/Documents/AC_IX_declarationclimatechange_en_fin.pdf.

[31] See generally A. Gobiet, '21st Century Climate Change in the European Alps – A Review' (2014) 493 *Science of the Total Environment* 1138.

[32] Jedediah Purdy, *After Nature: A Politics for the Anthropocene* (Cambridge, MA, Harvard University Press, 2015), p. 231.

[33] Protocol on the Implementation of the Alpine Convention of 1991 in the Field of Soil Conservation, 16 October 1998, in force 16 November 1998, OJ L 337/29, Art. 1(2).

Post-Nature International Environmental Law and Scholarship

The Anthropocene marks the transition from humanity being a passive inheritor of global environmental conditions set by forces beyond its control to being the trustee of planetary environmental stability.[34] The Anthropocene has arisen only very recently in human history and practically instantaneously in Earth's geological history. The characteristics of the Anthropocene are therefore mostly new to international environmental law and research, and they challenge the conventional regulatory approach which 'presupposes a separation between humans and the natural world'.[35]

Bodansky observes that today it is evident that the 'boundaries of what constitutes an "environmental" issue have already become blurred. Problems such as global warming and loss of biological diversity result from a wide variety of factors, including population growth, energy use, consumption patterns, and trade.'[36] Indeed, he argues, if 'everything is interconnected, then everything becomes an environmental problem',[37] in which case international law is effectively synonymous with international environmental law. However, this is not how international law operates in practice, with the human/nature separation still clearly manifest in the way in which governments and other international legal actors approach environmental issues. There have been some promising developments, such as the International Court of Justice's embracing of a whole ecosystem approach in valuing environmental damage in its decision in *Certain Activities Carried Out by Nicaragua in the Border Area (Costa Rica v. Nicaragua)*.[38] In assessing the compensation owed by Nicaragua in respect of dredging and other activities in an area found to be within Costa Rican territory, the Court noted that 'it is appropriate to approach the valuation of environmental damage from the perspective of the ecosystem as a whole, by adopting an overall assessment of the impairment or loss of environmental goods and services prior to recovery, rather than attributing values to specific categories of environmental goods and services and estimating recovery periods for each of them.'[39]

---

[34] Steffen et al., 'The Anthropocene: From Global Change to Planetary Stewardship', 249.
[35] Bodansky, *Art and Craft*, p. 10.
[36] Ibid. 10–11.
[37] Ibid. 12.
[38] *Certain Activities Carried Out by Nicaragua in the Border Area (Costa Rica v. Nicaragua)* [2018] ICJ Rep
[39] Ibid. [78].

Despite the seriousness of the global ecological crisis, there have been very limited new responses by governments. While some commentators see promise, with environmental stewardship moving to the centre of global concerns,[40] Dryzek observes that the twenty years following the 1992 Rio Declaration have seen 'retreat in global ambitions' and while global economic governance has become increasingly sophisticated 'global environmental governance is under-developed and weak.'[41] For international environmental law, it has mostly been 'business as usual' with limited innovations in normative and conceptual content, processes, and institutions to confront the reality of the new era.

Searching for a Teleology of International Environmental Law

What then should the purpose of international environmental law now be if previous certainties no longer hold? Is this even a meaningful question given that international environmental law is now such a large body of law with distinctive regimes with individualised objects and goals?

There has been relatively little engagement with the question of international environmental law's purpose in the literature. In opening their treatise, Birnie, Boyle, and Redgwell describe the term 'international environmental law' as one that is 'used simply as a convenient way to encompass the entire corpus of international law, public and private, relevant to environmental problems'.[42] Viewed in this way, international environmental law is not a discrete subfield of international law having its own internal logic and purpose. While elements of international environmental law might be said to have certain aims and objectives, Birnie et al. avoid the suggestion that international environmental law possesses an overarching goal.

Others have been more willing to consider international environmental law in purposive terms, although there is considerable variation in accounts of what its purposes are. Sands, Peel, Fabra, and MacKenzie are

---

[40] Robert Falkner & Barry Buzan, 'The Emergence of Environmental Stewardship as a Primary Institute of Global International Society' *European Journal of International Relations*, published online 1 December 2017 https://doi-org.ezproxy1.library.usyd.edu .au/10.1177/1354066117741948.

[41] John Dryzek, 'Global Environmental Governance' in Teena Gabrielson, Cheryl Hall, John M. Meyer, & David Schlosberg (eds), *The Oxford Handbook of Environmental Political Theory* (Oxford: Oxford University Press, 2016), pp. 533–534.

[42] Patricia Birnie, Alan Boyle, & Catherine Redgwell, *International Law and the Environment*, 3rd edn (Oxford: Oxford University Press), p. 2.

open to the suggestion that international environmental law as a whole has a teleology supplied by environmental principles, with sustainable development sitting atop a loose hierarchy of organising norms.[43] Dupuy and Viñuales see international environmental law in a similar way, with the 'two main ideas underlying international environmental law [being] the need to prevent environmental harm while striking a satisfactory balance among the different considerations at play'.[44] These 'different considerations' include the body of principles and concepts of international environmental law, including sustainable development. Louka is more economical in her summary of international environmental law's purpose, noting that as a branch of public international law, it shares its same fundamental purpose, which is 'the maintenance of peace among states with regard to the management of global commons'.[45]

Accepting that it is possible to describe international environmental law as having a purpose or a collection of purposes, the question that naturally follows is a normative one. What purpose *should* international environmental law serve? What goal or goals can be justified on ethical and practical grounds? In introducing the *Oxford Handbook of International Environmental Law*, Bodansky, Brunnee, and Hey observe that international environmental law is 'a distinct field – distinct not simply in the sense of addressing a discrete set of problems ... but also in the stronger sense of having its own characteristic structure and process, and its own set of conceptual tools and methodologies'.[46] They specifically address the purposes of international environmental law, noting its historic 'anthropocentric bias' in being concerned not with protecting the environment per se 'but because of its value to humans – its importance for human health, economics, recreation and so on'.[47] They also acknowledge that international environmental law has undergone some 'evolution from

---

[43] Philippe Sands, Jacqueline Peel (with Adriana Fabra and Ruth Mackenzie), *Principles of International Environmental Law* 3rd edn (Cambridge: Cambridge University Press, 2012), p. 9.

[44] Pierre-Marie Dupuy & Jorge E Viñuales, *International Environmental Law* (Cambridge: Cambridge University Press, 2015), p. 54.

[45] Elli Louka, *International Environmental Law: Fairness, Effectiveness, and World Order* (Cambridge: Cambridge University Press, 2006), p. 67.

[46] Daniel Bodansky, Jutta Brunnee, & Ellen Hey, 'International Law: Mapping the Field' in Daniel Bodansky, Jutta Brunnee, & Ellen Hey (eds), *The Oxford Handbook of International Environmental Law* (Oxford: Oxford University Press, 2008), p. 5.

[47] Ibid. 15.

a utilitarian to a more environmentally oriented ethic' and has increasingly 'displayed a more ecocentric approach'.[48]

This framing is the classic division in much scholarship on international environmental law that categorises global norms of environmental governance according to whether they are designed to serve human objectives or whether instead they are focused on protecting the natural world for its own sake.[49] The divide remains between 'shallow ecology' and 'deep ecology' (and between 'light green' and 'deep green' environmentalism), with 'shallow ecology' and 'light green' environmentalism describing the need to protect the environment for the primary purpose of avoiding threats to human health, comfort, and survival, and 'deep ecology' and 'deep green' environmentalism according all living things and all natural systems a moral considerability that means they are inherently deserving of protection.

Most accounts seldom engage with environmental ethics and philosophy in any comprehensive way.[50] They have in any event become increasingly redundant in the Anthropocene, as this era clearly erases the already untenable distinction between natural and human systems. There is no 'pure' nature that can be protected in its own right in a period in which the entire natural world has experienced to greater or lesser extent the influence of human activities. Therefore, it makes little sense to speak of a utilitarian, anthropocentric environmental law on the one hand and an inherent-value, ecocentric environmental law on the other. For this reason, Lorimer has argued that 'the Anthropocene offers a shock to thought, a catalyst for new modes of conservation' which avoids the binary choice between 'greater mastery' of the environment and 'forms of naturalism' that imagine a 'return to Nature'.[51]

The Anthropocene brings to the fore the reality of the coupled human-natural system. It is impossible to escape the physical reality of this new Earth in which human and natural forces are intertwined. The extent of human interference has been so large that it is impossible to turn back the clock to the old Earth. Many changes are irreversible over tens of thousands, hundreds of thousands, or even millions of years. It is likely,

---

[48] Ibid. 16.

[49] Gillespie, *International Environmental Law, Policy and Ethics*, p. 13.

[50] With some notable exceptions, such as Christopher D. Stone, *Should Trees Have Standing? Law, Morality and the Environment*, 3rd edn (Oxford: Oxford University Press, 2010).

[51] Jamie Lorimer, *Wildlife in the Anthropocene: Conservation After Nature* (Minneapolis: University of Minnesota Press, 2015), p. 179.

for instance, that glacier mass loss is irreversible even if the Paris Agreement 1.5°C/2.0°C temperature goal is reached,[52] and looking farther over the horizon, climate change has probably delayed the onset of the next ice age by hundreds of thousands of years.[53]

The purpose of international environmental law in the Anthropocene therefore cannot be to protect or restore Eden. But beyond this what should international environmental law seek to do? As suggested later, it may be possible to offer an ethically principled response to this question. However, in practical terms, the answer that the international community settles upon may be determined by the unpredictable trajectory that the Anthropocene takes, because the other major dimensions to the Anthropocene beyond scale and irreversibility are the pace of change and the likelihood of severe impacts on human societies.[54] In this context, it is conceivable that in response to crisis, instrumentalist and utilitarian values will reassume central importance in international environmental law in an attempt to protect communities from environmental change. Indeed this is already beginning to occur in the context of geoengineering technologies which are being presented by advocates as a techno-fix to address global environmental problems.[55]

'Eco-modernists'[56] celebrate the Anthropocene as the epitome of human control of the global environment and advance grand geoengineering proposals in service of a Panglossian belief that humanity can enjoy a 'good Anthropocene'.[57] But it is a logical fallacy that because humanity has assumed a position of 'domination' over the environment that it must therefore have within its grasp the capacity to superintend the Earth's biophysical systems now and in the future. The mastery is only imagined, given that the disruption being wrought upon Earth's systems is likely to be beyond that which can be truly controlled. As Hansen et al. put it, '[t]here is a possibility, a real danger, that we

[52] Ben Marzeion et al., 'Limited Influence of Climate Change Mitigation on Short-Term Glacier Mass Loss' (2018) *Nature Climate Change*, doi:10.1038/s41558-018-0093-1.
[53] A. Ganopolski, R. Winkelmann, & H. J. Schellnhuber, 'Critical Insolation – CO_2 Relation for Diagnosing Past and Future Glacial Inception' (2016) 529 *Nature* 200 at 201.
[54] Gaffney & Steffen, 'The Anthropocene Equation', 58.
[55] For general discussion of the international legal response, see Karen Scott, 'International Law in the Anthropocene: Responding to the Geoengineering Challenge' (2013) 34 *Michigan Journal of International Law* 309.
[56] Clive Hamilton, 'The Theodicy of the 'Good Anthropocene' (2015) 7 *Environmental Humanities* 233.
[57] See 'The Ecomodernist Manifesto', available at www.ecomodernism.org/manifesto.

will hand young people and future generations a climate system that is practically out of their control.'[58]

Earth System Science, Planetary Boundaries, and Earth System Governance

A re-imagination of international environmental law that takes seriously the challenges of the Anthropocene needs to engage more closely with natural and social science research in relation to global environmental change and global environmental governance. When it comes to grappling with planetary change, international environmental law scholarship is substantially underdeveloped in comparison with Earth system science and Earth system governance literature. Earth systems scientists have tracked global environmental changes, and they have also sought to map out policy-relevant 'planetary boundaries' that define the 'safe operating space for global societal development'.[59] The planetary boundaries framework identifies the main global environmental systems essential for maintaining the integrity of the planet as a self-regulating system.[60] The approach also 'identifies levels of anthropogenic perturbations below which the risk of destabilization of the Earth system is likely to remain low'.[61] There are nine processes highlighted as critical to the Earth system but which are being substantially modified by human activities. These are climate change, novel entities, upper-atmosphere ozone depletion, atmospheric aerosols, ocean acidification, biogeochemical flows, freshwater use, land-system change, and biosphere integrity. For humanity to live within planetary boundaries entails that 'provisioning systems must be fundamentally structured to enable basic needs to be met at a much lower level of resource use.'[62]

International relations literature is increasingly considering the implications of this for global environmental governance. Prominent in this

---

[58] James Hansen et al., 'Ice Melt, Sea Level Rise and Superstorms' (2016) 16 *Atmospheric Chemistry and Physics* 3761.

[59] W. Steffen et al., 'Planetary Boundaries: Guiding Human Development on a Changing Planet' (2015) 347(6223) *Science* 736.

[60] Ibid.

[61] Ibid.

[62] Daniel W. O'Neill et al., 'A Good Life for All Within Planetary Boundaries' (2018) 1 *Nature Sustainability* 88 at 92.

research is the work of Oran Young,[63] Frank Biermann,[64] Stevenson and Dryzek,[65] and other scholars associated with the Earth Systems Governance Project.[66] In contrast, with some exceptions, most accounts of international environmental law have yet to come to terms with the immense consequences that the Anthropocene poses for global environmental governance. Even relatively recent texts and monographs on international environmental law make no mention of the idea and continue to treat global environmental issues in the manner characteristic of the postmodern period described earlier.[67]

A sustained attempt to introduce the insights of Earth system science and political theory to international environmental law research is provided by Kim and Bosselmann who argue that respect for planetary boundaries should be the central objective of international environmental law in the Anthropocene.[68] Drawing on natural law reasoning, they contend that 'respecting planetary boundaries is a dictate of reason' and that this should be the *grundnorm* of international environmental law.[69] Kim and Bosselmann make the point that while international environmental law does have some normative coherence thanks to its suite of principles,[70] these norms are too general in nature to provide clear guidance to stay within planetary boundaries. This is not only a failure of international environmental law as a whole but is also a weakness of many individual environmental regimes that have overly broad objects and purposes when clear, science-based benchmarks and targets are needed.

International environmental law must achieve a very difficult balance in the Anthropocene. It will need to become more pragmatic and focused on protecting environmental systems to sustain human civilisation. While large-scale technologies such as carbon dioxide removal will

[63] Oran Young, *Governing Complex Systems: Social Capital for the Anthropocene* (Cambridge, MA: MIT Press, 2017).
[64] See especially Biermann, 'Earth System Governance'.
[65] Hayley Stevenson & John S. Dryzek, *Democratizing Global Climate Governance* (Cambridge: Cambridge University Press, 2014), p. 210.
[66] Earth System Governance, www.earthsystemgovernance.org/about.
[67] See e.g. (the very fine) Dupuy & Viñuales, *International Environmental Law*.
[68] Rak E. Kim & Klaus Bosselmann, 'International Environmental Law in the Anthropocene: Towards a Purposive System of Multilateral Environmental Agreements' (2013) 2 *Transnational Environmental Law* 285.
[69] Ibid. 290.
[70] Eloise Scotford, *Environmental Principles and the Evolution of Environmental Law* (Oxford: Hart Publishing, 2017).

almost certainly be implemented to stay within planetary boundaries, at the same time governments must not succumb to a technocratic temptation towards 'quick fixes' in substitution for preventative measures.[71] In this context, a central conundrum will be how to maintain international environmental law's ethical and principled core that serves principles of ecological integrity, fairness and justice,[72] and not to embrace a 'survivalist' ethic which discards fundamental values in service to wholly instrumentalist and utilitarian objectives. It may appear paradoxical, but the conditions for an effective environmental law in the Anthropocene are ultimately to be found in a less anthropocentric environmental law, as 'anthropocentrism [is] at the core of the ecological crisis.'[73]

Conclusion

Researchers in international environmental law are not often afforded an opportunity to reflect critically on the enterprise with which we are engaged. Instead we have generally taken the role of observers and technicians, describing the law as it has developed and offering views as to how the normative framework and the institutions that support it could be refined.

As with other areas of international law research, there is a capacity for international environmental law scholarship to have an impact on the development of the law. This can occur in a number of ways, from influencing governments directly in their negotiating positions in international fora, through to academic writings being recognised as a subsidiary means for the determination of rules of law.[74] However, where an influence has been felt it has often been incremental rather than radical, with international courts reluctant to grasp the full significance of concepts and principles such as sustainable development.[75] This in turn may have encouraged international environmental law scholarship to be

---

[71] Kevin Anderson & Glen Peters, 'The Trouble with Negative Emissions' (2016) 354 *Science* 182.

[72] See generally Peter Lawrence, *Justice for Future Generations: Climate Change and International Law* (Cheltenham: Edward Elgar, 2014).

[73] Klaus Bosselmann, *Earth Governance: Trusteeship of the Global Commons* (Cheltenham: Edward Elgar, 2015), p. 34.

[74] Statute of the ICJ, Art. 38(1)(d).

[75] Tim Stephens, *International Courts and Environmental Protection* (Cambridge: Cambridge University Press, 2009).

less ambitious than it could be in assessing the legal implications of global environmental change.

It has been argued in this chapter that the Anthropocene demands much more than an account of the law as it is, or for progressive change over time. Instead it requires a wholesale re-examination and re-imagination of international environmental law's objectives. An immediate priority for international environmental law research is to identify the conditions for a just and effective international environmental law in this new era. From the discussion in this chapter, four such conditions appear as fruitful starting points for a new international environmental law research agenda that takes seriously the challenges of the Anthropocene.

First, the core organising principles of international environmental law require affirmation and further development to recognise the central goal of protecting and restoring Earth's life support system.[76] To discard international environmental law's foundational concepts, such as the prevention and precautionary principles and common but differentiated responsibility which reflect international agreement on ethical principles for organising responsibility for and responses to environmental crisis, would be unrealistic and unproductive. Second, environmental treaty regimes need rapid transformation to incorporate clear, science-based, global goals based on the insights of Earth system science and the planetary boundaries framework. A third priority is the achievement of a fair allocation of benefits and burdens to create a safe and just space for humanity within planetary boundaries. This is an enormous challenge, as distributive justice has proven extremely difficult to implement in environmental treaty regimes, as the climate example clearly shows. Fourth, and related, the achievement of global environmental goals is likely to be achieved only if the process for setting global targets and allocating national responsibilities takes place in a deliberative and ecologically reflexive process that is perceived as fair.[77]

Bibliography

Biermann, Frank, *Earth System Governance: World Politics in the Anthropocene* (Cambridge, MA: MIT Press, 2014).
Bodansky, Daniel, *The Art and Craft of International Environmental Law* (Cambridge, MA: Harvard University Press, 2011), p. 10.

---

[76] Kim & Bosselmann, 'International Environmental Law in the Anthropocene'.
[77] Stevenson & Dryzek, *Democratising Global Climate Governance*.

Bodansky, Daniel, Jutta Brunnee, & Ellen Hey, 'International Law: Mapping the Field' in Daniel Bodansky, Jutta Brunnee, & Ellen Hey (eds), *The Oxford Handbook of International Environmental Law* (Oxford: Oxford University Press, 2008), p. 5.

Bosselmann, Klaus, *Earth Governance: Trusteeship of the Global Commons* (Cheltenham: Edward Elgar, 2015), p. 34.

Crutzen, Paul J., 'Geology of Mankind' (2002) 415 *Nature* 23.

Davies, Jeremy, *The Birth of the Anthropocene* (Berkeley: University of California Press, 2016).

Gaffney, Owen & Will Steffen, 'The Anthropocene Equation' (2017) 4 *The Anthropocene Review* 53.

Gillespie, Alexander, *International Environmental Law, Policy, and Ethics*, 2nd edn (Oxford: Oxford University Press, 2014).

Hamilton, Clive, 'The Theodicy of the "Good Anthropocene"' (2015) 7 *Environmental Humanities* 233.

Kim, Rak E. & Klaus Bosselmann, 'International Environmental Law in the Anthropocene: Towards a Purposive System of Multilateral Environmental Agreements' (2013) 2 *Transnational Environmental Law* 285.

Purdy, Jedediah, *After Nature: A Politics for the Anthropocene* (Cambridge, MA: Harvard University Press, 2015), p. 231.

Steffen, Will et al., 'Planetary Boundaries: Guiding Human Development on a Changing Planet' (2015) 347(6223) *Science* 736.

Stevenson, Hayley, & John S. Dryzek, *Democratizing Global Climate Governance* (Cambridge: Cambridge University Press, 2014).

Young, Oran, *Governing Complex Systems: Social Capital for the Anthropocene* (Cambridge, MA: MIT Press, 2017).

Zalasiewicz, Jan, Colin Waters, & Martin J. Head, 'Anthropocene: Its Stratigraphic Basis' (2017) 541 *Nature* 289.

Reflections on the Future of Environmental Law Scholarship and Methodology in the Anthropocene

LOUIS J. KOTZÉ

1 Introduction

Scientists believe we are entering a new geological epoch called the Anthropocene, in which humans have become a force of nature, essentially dislodging the harmony of the Earth's intertwined system that has hitherto prevailed in the relatively stable Holocene epoch. While its existence has yet to be formally confirmed, the Anthropocene as a trope undoubtedly already confronts environmental law scholars with unique challenges concerning the need to critically question, and ultimately to re-imagine, those methodological and scholarly foundations, perspectives and approaches related to the discipline of environmental law.

It is my hypothesis that for environmental law scholars, the socio-ecological crisis signified by the Anthropocene epoch (marked as this crisis is by rapidly intensifying levels of change, complexity and uneven-ness) presents unique regulatory, normative and more importantly for present purposes methodological and scholarly challenges that will have to be addressed if environmental law scholars were to make any mean-ingful contribution to confronting head on this epoch's innumerable complex regulatory challenges. As I hope to show, because of the Anthropocene, there is a convincing case to be made out in support of critically re-interrogating the current state and future of environmental law scholarship, including many of the trite epistemological, ontological, ethical and methodological impulses, assumptions and approaches that accompany this decades-old characterization of the juridified regulatory interventions associated with environmental protection.

In Section 2, I provide brief introductory perspectives with the view to situating the debate on environmental law scholarship in the

Anthropocene. Section 3 sets out what the Anthropocene means in general terms, including its relevance for social sciences, humanities and environmental law. Section 4 identifies in broad terms some of the possible implications of the Anthropocene for environmental law scholarship. It specifically highlights and elaborates three considerations that I believe we should consider if we are to produce scholarship alongside appropriate methodologies that could more usefully respond to Anthropocene exigencies. These are the need for transdisciplinarity, integration and transnationality; the need to confront head on the pervasive anthropocentrism of environmental law and its scholarship; and the need for environmental law and its scholarship to become more inclusive and representative.

Three caveats apply to the discussion that follows: (i) While there will certainly be other considerations that could be fleshed out in a more comprehensive inquiry (including a taxonomical study that could also make a more convincing case for re-ordering and reclassifying the rules governing the Earth system in the Anthropocene), I believe the considerations outlined later represent in broad terms the most immediate concerns potentially bedevilling the future legitimacy and usefulness of environmental law as a juridical discipline for the Anthropocene around which scholars will convene. (ii) Without an objective standard of measurement or criteria which I have not developed, I will refrain from judging the quality of Anthropocene environmental law scholarship that has emerged to date. Passing judgement on the quality of scholarship could easily become a subjective exercise that falls victim to generalizations, while running the risk of being characterized as an elitist pursuit. (iii) The analysis does not focus on the entire spectrum of environmental law since its development in the 1970s; it only concerns itself with the scholarship that has been emerging since the early 2000s when the idea of the Anthropocene was first introduced.

2   Situating the Debate

Environmental law as a discipline has been around approximately fifty years now, but reflections on the state of environmental law scholarship have only been emerging in the past decade. Apart from the sustained work of a few commentators,[1] such reflections have not yet been fully

---

[1]   See, for example, E. Fisher et al., 'Maturity and Methodology: Starting a Debate about Environmental Law Scholarship' (2009) 21(2) *Journal of Environmental Law* 213–250;

taken up in mainstream academic debates. Moreover, to date, little attention has been given to the potential impact of the Anthropocene trope on environmental law scholarship, despite this trope being increasingly utilized by environmental law scholars. I believe it is timely and apt to commence with such a conversation here, even though it would only be a tentative tipping of the toe in the water.

An important precursor to such an interrogation would be to distinguish between the (not unrelated as I will show) state of environmental law as a *regulatory intervention* and the *scholarship* that engages with this regulatory intervention. With the overarching goal of achieving anthropocentric sustainable development, environmental law has developed since its birth around the 1970s as a regulatory response to localized, silo-based problems of environmental pollution and nature conservation, which it has treated in a fragmented manner. It has failed, alongside other socially constructed normative interventions that aim to regulate human behaviour, to keep humanity from crossing critical planetary boundaries that exemplify the Anthropocene's socioecological crisis in concrete terms:[2]

> [E]ffective environmental legislation must at a minimum act as legal boundaries that prevent human activities from reaching and breaching planetary boundaries, defined as the safe space for mankind to operate within ... In other words, legal boundaries must translate the physical reality of a finite world into law and thereby delimit acceptable levels of human activity.[3]

Because we have already crossed three of the nine planetary boundaries, and as we are fast approaching the other six,[4] it is evident that environmental law has failed to meaningfully contribute to regulatory efforts that aim to keep humanity from reaching and breaching these boundaries. To this end, several of the failures and deficiencies of environmental law

Ole Pedersen 'The Limits of Interdisciplinarity and the Practice of Environmental Law Scholarship' (2014) 26 *Journal of Environmental Law* 423–441; Ole Pedersen, 'Modest Pragmatic Lessons for a Diverse and Incoherent Environment Law' (2013) 33(1) *Oxford Journal of Legal Studies* 103–131.

[2] J. Rockström et al., 'A Safe Operating Space for Humanity' (2009) 461 *Nature* 472–475.

[3] G. Chapron, Y. Epstein, A. Trouwborst & J. López-Bao, 'Bolster Legal Boundaries to Stay within Planetary Boundaries' (2017) 1 *Nature Ecology and Evolution* 1–5 at 1.

[4] The nine boundaries are biodiversity, climate change, biogeochemical flows (all three crossed), stratospheric ozone depletion, atmospheric aerosol loading, ocean acidification global freshwater use, land system change, and chemical pollution (all six fast approaching).

are explicated by the Anthropocene's human-induced signatures which loosely characterize environmental law as being

- Incompatible with Earth system complexities and unresponsive to Earth system changes;
- Too supportive of anthropocentric neo-liberal economic development through, among others, its prioritization of the politically powerful, but ethically weak, concept of sustainable development; and
- Discriminatory to the extent that it often excludes minorities and other vulnerable categories of people, thus shutting out alternative modes of inclusive socioecological care.[5]

These factors are all apparent in environmental law, and they legitimize and reinforce the type of human behaviour that is causing the Anthropocene,[6] while allowing and actively perpetuating environmental destruction, growing inter- and intra-species hierarchies, human rights abuses and socioeconomic and ecological injustices.[7] These concerns are increasingly (although not nearly sufficiently) being considered by legislators, courts, politicians and states in their efforts to reform the regulatory aspects of environmental law.

More importantly for present purposes, however, is the state of the scholarship that critiques environmental law as a regulatory intervention, including scholarship dealing with its successes and failures and proposals for reform and future development. Scholars have obviously been engaging intellectually with environmental law for many years now, but we have been neglecting *why* and *how* we as scholars engage with the normative and regulatory *problematique* of environmental law, and *what* we are doing and what we should be doing as scholars to interrogate this *problematique*; including considerations such as methodology, the quality of scholarship, the role of ethics in scholarship, the question of transdisciplinarity and issues of representivity. While questions arising from the state of environmental law as a regulatory intervention and the scholarship that engages with this regulatory intervention are two separate issues, as

---

[5] L. Kotzé, 'Rethinking Global Environmental Law and Governance in the Anthropocene' (2014) 32(2) *Journal of Energy and Natural Resources Law* 121–156.

[6] R. Kim & K. Bosselmann, 'International Environmental Law in the Anthropocene: Towards a Purposive System of Multilateral Environmental Agreements' (2013) 2 *Transnational Environmental Law* 285–309.

[7] A. Grear, 'Deconstructing Anthropos: A Critical Legal Reflection on "Anthropocentric" Law and Anthropocene "Humanity"' (2015) 26 *Law and Critique* 225–249.

Fisher et al. argue,[8] I believe the Anthropocene's human-induced signatures described earlier usefully characterize some of the short-comings of environmental law scholarship as well, especially when viewed through the epistemological lens of the Anthropocene. More particularly, as I will argue, environmental law scholarship could be described as being

- Insufficiently aligned with Earth system complexities and unresponsive to Earth system phenomena, which will require a systems approach and methodologies that actively embrace transdisciplinarity and transnationalism;
- Too accommodative of, and uncritical towards, neo-liberal anthropocentrism and the achievement of economic prosperity for some privileged humans at all cost, which will require a fundamentally different ecologically centred ontological reorientation and ethical approach underlying scholarship and methodologies; and
- Under-representative of the diverse and often neglected voices and concerns of marginalized sectors in society, including especially nature, the poor, women, children and members of indigenous communities who are the most severely affected by Anthropocene exigencies, which will require more inclusive and representative scholarship and methodologies aimed at achieving inter- and intra-species socioecological justice.

These considerations, as I will argue, have to be addressed by environmental law scholars as they start engaging with and developing the nascent body of 'Anthropocene environmental law scholarship' (for lack of an alternative phrase).

3　The Anthropocene and Its Relation to Law

The Anthropocene epoch is a period in Earth's geological history signalling an unprecedented global socioecological crisis where humans act as geological agents capable of dominating and changing the Earth system.[9] As a consequence, virtually all global environmental indicators have been rising exponentially, showing that 'the Earth system has clearly moved outside the envelope of Holocene variability.'[10] To this end, the

---

[8] Fisher et al., 'Maturity and Methodology'.
[9] Simon Lewis & Mark Maslin, 'Defining the Anthropocene' (2015) 519 *Nature* 171–180.
[10] Will Steffen, Jacques Grinevald, Paul Crutzen & John McNeill, 'The Anthropocene: Conceptual and Historical Perspectives' (2011) 369 *Philosophical Transactions of the Royal Society* 842–867 at 850–851.

(distinctly multidisciplinary) Anthropocene Working Group recently concluded that there is probably convincing evidence to formalize the Anthropocene in the near future as the new geological epoch.[11] Yet, whether or not it is formalized, what is already clear from the burgeoning and ever-expanding academic and popular literature is that the Anthropocene concept 'has captured an ever-widening audience and emerged as a powerful trope'.[12] As a discursive category, the Anthropocene now occupies a central position in the human-environment relations discourse.

To this end, the Anthropocene has many scholarly manifestations or utilities: it could signify a complex time of accelerated anthropogenic change; it could be a narrative framing of contemporary life and futures; it could act as a lens through which to view multispecies worlds in formation; and/or it could be a spatial and material manifestation of specific economic, scientific, and political practices.[13] Baskin therefore correctly points out that '[t]he Anthropocene does not need to be an object of scientific inquiry by geologists and stratigraphers, or even a formally-recognised geological epoch, in order to have an impact.'[14] As it stands, the Anthropocene is 'paradigm dressed as epoch'[15] and has entered the *Zeitgeist* in spectacular fashion. In addition, the Anthropocene radically unsettles the philosophical, epistemological and ontological grounds on which both the natural sciences and the social sciences/humanities have traditionally stood. To this end, the Anthropocene

> is not simply a neutral characterisation of a new geological epoch, but it is also a particular way of understanding the world and a *normative guide to action*. It is ... more usefully understood as an ideology – in that it provides the ideational underpinning for a particular view of the world, which it, in turn, helps to legitimate.[16]

Because such a new world view or ideology 'heralds an opening of sorts, a clarion call for change',[17] as Baker argues, this change must also be

---

[11] J. Zalasiewicz et al., 'The Working Group on the Anthropocene: Summary of Evidence and Interim Recommendations' (2017) 19 *Anthropocene* 55–60 at 59.

[12] Grear, 'Deconstructing Anthropos', 226.

[13] Amelia Moore, 'The Anthropocene: A Critical Exploration' (2015) 6 *Environment and Society: Advances in Research* 1–3 at 1.

[14] Jeremy Baskin, 'Paradigm Dressed as Epoch: The Ideology of the Anthropocene' (2015) 24 *Environmental Values* 9–29 at 12.

[15] Ibid. 10.

[16] Ibid. 10–11 (emphasis added).

[17] Shalanda Baker, 'Adaptive Law in the Anthropocene' (2015) 90(2) *Chicago-Kent Law Review* 563–584 at 567.

reflected in, and carried through, our regulatory institutions, especially if one agrees with the view that the Anthropocene offers some sort of 'normative guide to action', which very particularly highlights the connection between the Anthropocene trope and law. Law has the potential not to change the Earth system but to influence human impacts on the Earth system, while enabling humans to adapt to an increasingly erratic Earth system and to become more resilient. To this end, law as a regulatory social institution is a crucial ingredient in any response strategy to the Anthropocene, notably to the extent that it could work to increase resilience; enable society to sustain and absorb socioecological stresses and impacts, external interference and complex and unpredictable changes; and to confront the many complex uncertainties of the Earth system, while striving to protect and even enhance ecological integrity.[18] If law must play a central role in regulatory efforts responding to the Anthropocene, it could reasonably be expected that legal scholars will increasingly be required to grapple with the implications of the Anthropocene for environmental law, as well as with the practice of scholarship around the Anthropocene's juridical domain.

4 The Implications of the Anthropocene for Environmental Law Scholarship

Generally speaking, scholarship focusing on the Anthropocene has been steadily emerging and expanding at an exponential rate since the early 2000s, following the term's first formal introduction.[19] These initial inquiries, while far too extensive to map here, were mostly based in the natural sciences (notably geography, stratigraphy, geology, archeology and ecology), which to date still remain the dominant domains of scholarly activity and focus in this regard. Anthropocene research has been published over the years in a range of journals dealing specifically with the foregoing scientific areas. Perhaps also reflecting on the increased maturity of Anthropocene scholarship is the creation of issue-specific scientific journals directly related to the Anthropocene, through which such scholarship is gradually gaining importance, legitimacy and recognition (if perhaps not yet full maturity) in a remarkably short space of time. Some journals include *Anthropocene Review, Anthropocene,*

---

[18] Jonas Ebbesson, 'The Rule of Law in Governance of Complex Socio-ecological Changes' 2010(20) *Global Environmental Change* 414–422 at 414.
[19] P. Crutzen and E. Stoermer, 'The "Anthropocene"' (2000) 41 *International Geosphere-Biosphere Programme Global Change Newsletter* 17–18.

Elementa: Science of the Anthropocene and *Anthropocene Coasts.* The majority of publications in these journals hail from the natural sciences, although the journals are all branded as 'multidisciplinary' and often include social science and humanities contributions.

One of the most notable first forays into the humanities and social sciences domains occurred through the work of political scientists (see especially the work of Biermann),[20] that sought to connect and interrogate aspects of global environmental governance through the Anthropocene lens, and more specifically, to connect it with the Anthropocene's imagery of an integrated Earth system that requires integrated modes of polycentric, reflexive and multi-scalar global governance alongside a systems approach. In growing attempts to more critically engage with questions centring on 'meaning, value, responsibility and purpose in a time of rapid and escalating change',[21] humanities and social science scholars from a diverse range of specialties from ethics and economics to religion and anthropology have increasingly been engaging with the Anthropocene. In fact, the social sciences and humanities are now considered an integral part of the Anthropocene research agenda. As Lövbrand et al. encouragingly note:

> We believe the social sciences are well equipped to push the idea of the Anthropocene in new and more productive directions. Interpretation, differentiation and re-politicization represent central traits of this next generation of Anthropocene scholarship, in which a plurality of actors are welcomed to deconstruct established frames of the planet and its inhabitants and to experiment with new ones. It is promising to note that conversations of this kind now are unfolding in diverse academic settings. Across the humanities and social sciences, scholars are adopting the Anthropocene concept to raise critical questions on environmental politics, culture, identity and ethics.[22]

Law seems to have warmed to the idea of the Anthropocene only much later, but it is a steady and promising enterprise that has, for the most part, been using the Anthropocene as an epistemological lens through which to reassess and to critique, in both a backwards and forwards-looking view, the many and varied aspects of (environmental) law in this

---

[20] F. Biermann, *Earth System Governance: World Politics in the Anthropocene* (Cambridge, MA: MIT Press, 2014).

[21] E. Lövbrand et al., 'Who Speaks for the Future of Earth? How Critical Social Science Can Extend the Conversation on the Anthropocene' (2015) 32 *Global Environmental Change* 211–218 at 212.

[22] Ibid., 217.

proposed new epoch. While it is difficult to pinpoint the first juridical enquiry that dealt with the Anthropocene, I believe it is probably correct to say that Kim and Bosselmann's 2013 interrogation of international environmental law through the Anthropocene lens was one of the first and most influential.[23] Other international law–focused enquiries such as by Vidas, Robinson, Stephens, and Scott soon followed,[24] while yet other accounts have reflected on the constitutional and ethical aspects of (environmental) law in the Anthropocene.[25] More recently in 2017, the first comprehensive and systemized collection of work focusing specifically on a diverse set of sub-disciplinary areas of juridical and governance areas appeared.[26] It broadly reflects upon the Anthropocene and the implications of its discursive formation in an attempt to trace some initial, radical, future-facing and imaginative implications for environmental law and governance.

What this (perhaps crude and rather brief) summary of the developmental trajectory of Anthropocene environmental law scholarship suggests is that the idea of the Anthropocene and its accompanying imagery has not yet been taken up with overwhelming enthusiasm by general legal and environmental law scholars. Some legal scholars are to some extent recognizing the Anthropocene's value as a new paradigmatic trope, and they are applying this trope in areas of international (environmental) law, constitutional law, climate and disaster management, global environmental governance and ethics, among others. But this has only occurred since 2013 and in a rather haphazard manner which does not suggest the deliberate and widespread emergence of any coherent and systemized scholarly body of work critically reflecting on Anthropocene environmental law. That being said, there is considerable potential for legal

---

[23] R. Kim & K. Bosselmann, 'International Environmental Law in the Anthropocene: Towards a Purposive System of Multilateral Environmental Agreements' (2013) 2(2) *Transnational Environmental Law* 285–309.

[24] Nicholas Robinson, 'Fundamental Principles of Law for the Anthropocene?' (2014) 44 *Environmental Policy and Law* 13–27; Karen Scott, 'International Law in the Anthropocene: Responding to the Geoengineering Challenge' (2013) 34(2) *Michigan Journal of International Law* 309–358; D. Vidas et al., 'International Law for the Anthropocene? Shifting Perspectives in Regulation of the Oceans, Environment and Genetic Resources' (2015) 9 *Anthropocene* 1–13; Tim Stephens, 'Disasters, International Law and the Anthropocene' in S. Breau and K. L. H. Samuel (eds), *Research Handbook on Disasters and International Law* (Cheltenham: Edward Elgar, 2016).

[25] Grear, 'Deconstructing Anthropos'; L. Kotzé, *Global Environmental Constitutionalism in the Anthropocene* (Oxford: Hart Publishing, 2016).

[26] L. Kotzé (ed.), *Environmental Law and Governance for the Anthropocene* (Oxford: Hart Publishing, 2017).

scholarship to more fully respond to the Anthropocene – not least because the arrival of the Anthropocene mind-set has various implications for environmental law as a social regulatory institution, as well as various and varied implications for scholars engaging intellectually with environmental law.

First, the Anthropocene provides a fresh analytical perspective to environmental law scholars, which could potentially facilitate deeper epistemological and ontological enquiries into regulatory interventions that dictate human behaviour on Earth. Law, after all, is deeply implicated in the systems that have caused the Anthropocene (also in the sense that law might be an autopoietic system that defines, maintains and reproduces itself).[27] Such a realization allows an opening up, as it were, of hitherto prohibitive closures in the law, of the legal and regulatory discourse more generally, and of the world order that the law operatively maintains, towards other understandings of global environmental change and ways to mediate this change through a specific type of law that is more attuned to the challenges of the Anthropocene. Through the new epistemological lens of the Anthropocene, environmental law scholars will increasingly be required to question and critically revisit the epistemic assumptions and normative and regulatory limits and deficiencies of environmental law and its regulatory domain, possibly even progressing towards the formulation of second-generation environmental law (something along the lines of what Rose calls the 'new wave' of environmental law)[28] that is tailor made for the Anthropocene. The potential of a *Lex Anthropocena* or body of Earth System Law emerging in the process is an exciting prospect with such a taxonomical process predominantly being driven by scholars. In fact, the Earth System Governance Task Force on Earth System Law was established in 2107, and it will formulate proposals related to the ethical, ontological, practical and structural aspects of Earth System Law which involves a fundamental re-ordering and reclassification of the rules governing the Earth system in the Anthropocene.[29] Such an endeavour

[27] See, generally, Gunther Teubner, *Law as an Autopoietic System* (Oxford: Blackwell Publishers, 1993); and in the environmental law context specifically, Andreas Philippopoulos-Mihalopouos, 'Critical Autopoiesis: the Environment of the Law' in Bald de Vries & Lyana Francot (eds.), *Law's Environment: Critical Legal Perspectives* (The Hauge: Eleven International Publishing, 2011) 45–62.

[28] Carol Rose, 'Environmental Law Grows Up (More or Less), and What Science Can Do to Help' (2015) 9(2) *Lewis and Clarke Law Review* 273–294.

[29] 'Task Force on Earth System Law', Earth System Governance, www.earthsystemgovernance.org/research/taskforce-on-earth-system-law/.

may very well signal the first scholarly attempts to shape next-generation environmental law.

Second, while some focused categories such as climate change (which are part of the Anthropocene's planetary boundaries imagery) are already said to be providing such a unifying theme,[30] environmental law scholars now have an integrated and all-encompassing framework or reference to more systematically study the role of law in mediating the human-environment interface in a very broad sense – one that in fact demands an integrated consideration of all nine planetary boundaries. The Anthropocene and its planetary imagery relate to the entire Earth system, which is far more holistic than the silo-based problem objectification frameworks or categories such as ocean acidification, air pollution and water pollution that environmental law scholars have been employing to date. This might potentially overcome criticism related to fragmentation often levelled against environmental law and its scholarship. Moreover, the idea of an integrated Earth system usefully points to the problem of fragmenting, for the sake of law and governance purposes, the Earth into separate jurisdictional areas, instead of allowing for more fluid, transnational, polycentric and reflexive forms of law and governance that resonate with an integrated and causally linked Earth system. The steady emergence of the field of transnational environmental law, exemplified in this instance by its specialized journal among others,[31] is perhaps already an indication of a broader recognition by environmental law scholars of the need to invite a systems approach into the domain of environmental law scholarship which could contribute to overcoming the barriers of siloism, fragmentation and compartmentalization.[32]

Third, the Anthropocene revolves around the centrality of *Anthropos* (the human), which forces recognition and acceptance of human centrality in dislodging the Earth system, as well as law's complicity in deliberately creating and maintaining privileging hierarchies that are being sustained by and through law:

---

[30] See Daniel Farber, Chapter 10, this volume.
[31] *Transnational Environmental Law.*
[32] Although, admittedly, the debate on the scope and advantages of a transnational approach to environmental law should not be overdrawn, as it arguably is not unconditionally beneficial to a clear and focused future taxonomical development of environmental law. After all, the proponents of transnational environmental law often paint it as including all public and private norms at all geographical levels directly and indirectly related to the environment: if everything is transnational environmental law, then nothing is.

> [S]uch hierarchies implicate a systemically privileged juridical 'human' subject whose persistence subtends – to a significant and continuing extent – the neoliberal global juridical order as a whole, and that these hierarchical commitments also significantly undermine the ability of the international legal order to respond to climate crisis, environmental degradation and the intensifying imposition of structural disempowerment on vast and growing numbers of human beings.[33]

Through the lens of the Anthropocene, the prevalence and persistence of anthropocentrism and associated patterns of neo-liberal socioeconomic development that must meet the present and future needs of (some privileged) humans at all (ecological) cost, including the myriad resulting inter- and intra-species injustices occurring as a result of the foregoing, are brought to the fore. Confronting the persevering and overpowering *Anthropos* and the many hierarchies that are promoted through law, including the many failures and deficiencies of law to counter such impulses, will be a main challenge to environmental law scholars in future.

Fourth, related to all the foregoing, the Anthropocene is useful to environmental law scholars because it brings with it a set of scientifically more robust assumptions to the table, which require less proof (or which have already been proven in other scientific fields) and which could be utilized to contextualize and/or justify legal analysis. These include, among others, the fact of human domination, the extent and consequences of human domination and the integrated nature of the Earth system.

One way to start thinking about the possible ways in which environmental law scholarship could embrace the foregoing epistemological, ontological, regulatory, scholarly and methodological challenges and opportunities presented by the Anthropocene is to focus on the three main areas of concern suggested earlier that I believe currently bedevil environmental law scholarship.

4.1   Transdisciplinarity, Integration and Transnationality

The Anthropocene will require environmental law scholars to discard the prevailing understanding of environmental law and its fragmented, mono-disciplinary and nation-state–focused methodologies and epistemological assumptions. It will instead require a conscious effort to

---

[33] Grear, 'Deconstructing Anthropos', 227.

imagine and to resituate our scholarship within a newly conceptualized notion of Earth system law. The view that environmental law scholarship has been a decidedly mono-disciplinary, nation state–focused and silo-based exercise that operates within neatly confined political, legal and geographical boundaries is now generally accepted. As Chapron et al. say:

> [T]he use of 'non-legal' sources in legal scholarship has historically been considered inappropriate in many legal cultures. Further, because co-authored publications are unusual in the legal academy and are often discounted by law faculties, legal academics may be discouraged from participating in interdisciplinary scholarship. We believe stubborn walls between disciplines must now be torn down as an increased collaboration between legal scholars and conservation academics is urgently needed.[34]

The Anthropocene arguably does not only require lawyers to collaborate with political scientists and ecologists in an ad hoc fashion. The move towards transdisciplinarity should be far more profound. What might instead be critical would be the creation of an entirely new legal discipline which 'transcends traditional disciplinary boundaries, which are barriers to effectively addressing environmental problems'.[35] This would represent a convergence of transdiciplinarity around the *problematique* of the Anthropocene. It is one 'in which there is the development of a "transcendent language, a meta-language, in which the terms of all the participants' languages are, or can be, expressed"'; it concerns 'the development of a new ambitious intellectual paradigm of environmental studies'.[36] Such a new legal discipline could be Earth System Law.

A systems approach to the re-imagination and reconceptualization of environmental law and its accompanying scholarship is in part driven by the realization that the Anthropocene invites a holistic perspective on a globally interconnected and reciprocally related Earth system; Earth system changes; and the connection between the Earth system, its changes and the increasingly globalized human social system and the impact of humans on the Earth system. The expanding human social system is a result of globalization, and it has become a central feature of the Anthropocene.[37] More particularly, the 'planetary-scale social-ecological-geophysical system' interrelationship underlying the

---

[34] Chapron et al., 'Bolster Legal Boundaries to Stay within Planetary Boundaries' 4.

[35] Fisher et al., 'Maturity and Methodology'.

[36] Ibid. 234.

[37] Frank Oldfield et al., 'The Anthropocene Review: Its Significance, Implications and the Rationale for a New Transdisciplinary Journal' (2014) 1(1) *The Anthropocene Review* 1–7 at 4.

Anthropocene and its human-inclusive view of the Earth system suggest that human-driven socioeconomic processes are becoming an integral part of natural Earth system process[38] and are able to change the Earth system in profound ways. While the 'global' imagery of the Anthropocene should not be generalized by implying that the same socioecological conditions occur and are experienced by everyone everywhere in exactly the same way, the arrival of the Anthropocene arguably requires of us to start thinking about law, politics and social ordering in planetary terms: 'discussions of the Anthropocene necessarily require thinking at the scale of the biosphere and over the long term. This is a planetary issue, matters at the large scale require some consideration of ethical connection and, perhaps, the implicit invocation of a single polity, however inchoate.'[39]

One way to think about law revolving around a single global polity in planetary terms is through the lens of Earth system science, and more specifically through the lens of Earth system governance. Recognizing the connectivity, nonlinearity, and complexity of socioecological processes, Earth system science is concerned with the 'study of the Earth's environment as an integrated system in order to understand how and why it is changing, and to explore the implications of these changes for global and regional sustainability'.[40] Fundamentally rooted in Earth system science, Earth systems governance has been developed as a reactive counter-narrative to localized, state-based and narrowly focused regulatory approaches to environmental issues through the trite application of an issue-specific environmental law regime that focuses on pollution control, nature conservation and wildlife, among others, and that predominantly employs formal, state-based law and state institutions.

With reference to a more open, holistic, flexible, multi-scalar, and multi-actor regulatory approach that is better able to capture and address the many complex global developments that transform the bio-geophysical cycles and processes of the Earth system, the complex relations between global transformations of social and natural systems and

---

[38] Will Steffen et al., 'The Anthropocene: From Global Change to Planetary Stewardship' 2011(40) *Ambio* 739–761 at 740.

[39] Simon Dalby, 'Anthropocene Ethics: Rethinking "The Political" after Environment'. Paper presented at International Studies Annual Convention, Montreal, Canada, 2004. Available at www.yumpu.com/en/document/view/42485216/anthropocene-ethics-rethinking-the-political-after-environment/3.

[40] Ada Ignaciuk et al., 'Responding to Complex Societal Challenges: A Decade of Earth System Science Partnership (ESSP) Interdisciplinary Research' (2012) 4 *Current Opinion in Environmental Sustainability* 147-158 at 147.

the multi-scale consequences of ecological transformation, Biermann et al. define Earth system governance as follows:

> [T]he interrelated and increasingly integrated system of formal and informal rules, rule-making systems and actor networks at all levels of human society (from local to global) that are set up to steer societies towards preventing, mitigating and adapting to global and local environmental change and, in particular, earth system transformation.[41]

Earth system governance clearly is not only concerned with ways to influence and direct the Earth system (the governance of aspects of technological innovations that are able to change the Earth system might resort under its ambit): '[E]arth System governance is [also] about the human impact on planetary systems. It is about the societal steering of human activities with regard to the longterm stability of geobiophysical systems.'[42] Because law is particularly adept at steering human behaviour, it is a crucial aspect of Earth system governance. Any Earth system governance–based regulatory response, including its juridical elements, must respond to persistent Earth system uncertainty; nurture new responsibilities and modes of cooperation as a result of inter- and intra-generational, spatial and socioecological interdependence between people, countries, species and generations; respond to the functional interdependence of different aspects of the Earth system and Earth system transformations; respond to the needs of an increasingly integrated globalized society; and respond to extraordinary degrees of socioecological harm.[43]

What does the foregoing mean for environmental law and its attending scholarship? In line with the global imagery of the Anthropocene, the epistemological shift caused by Earth system governance seeks to avoid the state-bound, localized and issue-specific territorial trap to which environmental law is often falling victim. Such a shift also challenges this regulatory territorial trap by suggesting alternative mappings of

---

[41] Frank Biermann et al., 'Navigating the Anthropocene: The Earth Systems Governance Project Strategy Paper' (2010) 2 *Current Opinion in Environmental Sustainability* 202–208 at 203. See also for a more detailed conceptual analysis, Frank Biermann, '"Earth System Governance" as a Cross-cutting Theme of Global Change Research' (2007) 17 *Global Environmental Change* 326–337; and more recently, Frank Biermann, *Earth System Governance: World Politics in the Anthropocene* (Cambridge, MA: MIT, 2014).

[42] Frank Biermann, 'The Anthropocene: A Governance Perspective' (2014) 1(1) *The Anthropocene Review* 57–61 at 59.

[43] Biermann, 'Earth System Governance', 329–330.

social and political phenomena on a planetary scale that might contribute
to better understanding and responding to contemporary regulatory
transformations in the Anthropocene.[44] In so doing, the Anthropocene
challenges the 'cartographic imagination of the social sciences'[45] and
more specifically of environmental law, by inviting a global regulatory
perspective that acknowledges the interconnectedness and reciprocity of
Earth system processes and phenomena – a perspective that moves away
from an issue-specific governance approach to a more holistic one.[46] It is
also a perspective that discards the prevailing primacy of localized and
territorially bound administrative categories of the (local) nation-state
that are used to govern global environmental problems (such as climate
change),[47] and a perspective that sees the regulatory space not only as one
defined by sovereign territories but increasingly as one that is also being
shaped transnationally by global environmental phenomena, change and
regulatory institutions of which laws is a critical part.[48] An intrinsically
rooted regulatory advantage of thinking about environmental issues in
these interconnected global Earth system terms is that we are able to
'build a unified political project, based upon the common ecological fate
we all share'.[49]

Through the Anthropocene's lens and in tandem with the Earth
system governance metaphor, it becomes possible to envision an inter-
meshed global regulatory space for law that must address a whole range
of multilevel, reciprocal and interconnected regulatory socioecological
problems. This space also includes various governance levels, normative
arrangements and multiple state and non-state actors, which manifest in
a multilevel spatial (geographic), temporal (applicable to present and

---

[44] Simon Dalby, 'Geographies of the International System: Globalization, Empire and the
Anthropocene' in Pami Aalto, Vilho Harle & Sami Moisio (eds), *International Studies:
Interdisciplinary Approaches* (London: Palgrave Macmillan, 2011), 126.

[45] Ibid. 143.

[46] Hill notes that 'there is an increasing focus from the global change community on the
need for human society and the governance systems that moderate our actions and
decisions to operate within multiple inter-connected earth systems.' Margot Hill,
Climate Change and Water Governance: Adaptive Capacity in Chile and Switzerland
(New York: Springer, 2013), 5.

[47] Dalby, 'Geographies of the International System', 144.

[48] Hans Günter Brauch, Simon Dalby & Úrsula Oswald Spring, 'Political Geoecology for the
Anthropocene' in Hans Günter Brauch et al. (eds), *Coping with Global Environmental
Change, Disasters and Security Threats, Challenges, Vulnerabilities and Risks* (New York:
Springer, 2011), 1453.

[49] Mark Whitehead, *Environmental Transformations: A Geography of the Anthropocene*,
Kindle edition (Abingdon: Routledge, 2014), 481.

future generations) and causal setting (interacting Earth system processes). Ideal characteristics of this global regulatory space could include global hybrid law (including adaptive and interacting legal and quasi-legal structures); multi-scalarity where a range of state and non-state actors in a variety of interactions contributes to internalize norms transnationally through a process of interpretation, internalization and enforcement; multidisciplinarity and ultimately, greater regulatory responsiveness to better address the type of socioecological transformations that characterize the Anthropocene.[50]

4.2 Confronting Anthropos

Acting as a collective term encapsulating the apocalyptical exigencies of many single issues through its expression of urgency, the Anthropocene 'is a concept which is perhaps big enough to urge transformation on the level of values and ontology in a way that could never have happened in response to one singular societal or environmental challenge, from globalization to climate change.'[51] To this end, the Anthropocene's ontological turn usefully emphasizes the critical need to discard notions of neo-liberal anthropocentrism, both as the underlying foundation of our regulatory responses (including that of environmental law) and as an assumed given that cannot and should not be criticized by scholars. In short, the Anthropocene urges environmental law scholars to speak up and to speak out against pervasive neo-liberal anthropocentrism and to more fully embrace notions of ecocentric Earth system care and integrity that would at once serve to foster greater inter- and intra-species socioecological justice.

To the extent that we need to change human behaviour as a matter of moral inter- and intra-generational and inter-species responsibility, we will also have to revisit our socio-juridical institutions that mediate the human-environment interface, including the ethical and moral foundations of these institutions. As the Amsterdam Declaration on Global Change suggests: '[A]n ethical framework for global stewardship and

[50] Hari Osofsky, 'Scales of Law: Rethinking Climate Change Governance', PhD thesis, Oregon University (2013), 45–49, available at https://scholarsbank.uoregon.edu/xmlui/bitstream/handle/1794/13297/Osofsky_oregon_0171A_10730.pdf?sequence=1.
[51] Helen Pallett, 'The Anthropocene: Reflections on a Concept-Part 1', Topograph: Contested Landscapes of Knowing: Blogspot, available at http://thetopograph.blogspot.de/search?updated-min=2013-01-01T00:00:00-08:00&updated-max=2014-01-01T00:00:00-08:00&max-results=14.

strategies for Earth System management are urgently needed. The accelerating human transformation of the Earth's environment is not sustainable.'[52] In fact, if we accept that '[T]he collapse of any credible distinction between humans and nature forces humanity to modify ethical codes or political aspirations',[53] as is currently the case in the Anthropocene, then an Anthropocene ethic of care that is instead cast in limits-on-growth terms is probably long overdue. One of the clearest ways to give expression to such an ethic is through law and the type of scholarship we practice.

Law is an expression of society's shared ethics. Law is crafted as a result of being based on a specific ethic; law has a distinct ethical orientation that is broadly reflective of a certain attitude that members of society have towards each other as well as of the attitude towards other non-human, but living, and nonliving constituents of the Earth system. Environmental law likewise derives its legitimacy in part from ethics, where a specific ethical orientation steers environmental law and associated institutions and processes to achieve a specific outcome; ethics justify the existence of an environmental law system; ethics determine the relationship between environmental law and other socio-institutional regulatory institutions such as religion; and ethics help to determine the rules that structure environmental law.

To date, there is neither any systemized and generally accepted ethical framework that has gained universal acceptance for the purpose of the Anthropocene (although some, like Kim and Bosselmann, have made tentative proposals in this regard)[54] nor is any Anthropocene-specific ethic currently expressed through environmental law. Questions pertaining to what is right and wrong, just and unjust, and the multiple potential duties and responsibilities vis-à-vis the Earth system that are suitable for the Anthropocene are increasingly being asked. The formulation of an ethical framework has accordingly just begun, and it will likely continue along an undulating path of which neither the direction nor the final destination is yet clear.

---

[52] 'Amsterdam Declaration on Global Change', available at www.colorado.edu/AmStudies/lewis/ecology/gaiadeclar.pdf.

[53] Simon Dalby, 'Ecology, Security, and Change in the Anthropocene' (2007) 8(2) *Brown Journal of World Affairs* 155–164 at 161.

[54] They convincingly propose that ecological integrity should become the *Grundnorm* of the international environmental law order in the Anthropocene. See Rakhyun Kim & Klaus Bosselmann, 'International Environmental Law in the Anthropocene: Towards a Purposive System of Multilateral Environmental Agreements' (2013) 2(2) *Transnational Environmental Law* 285–309.

While the precise content of an Anthropocene ethic is (still) unclear, it is possible at this stage to speculate about this ethic's general orientation. The central tenet of much of the work that is concerned with formulating an Anthropocene ethic revolves around key themes such as ecological resilience, ecological integrity, greater human responsibility, ecocentrism, and inter- and intra-species justice.[55] These broader themes collectively suggest that an Anthropocene ethic should be turning its back on the orthodox preservationist ethos that is cast in traditional environmentalism, and often in neo-liberalist terms, where wealth creation is solely dependent on the transformation of the Earth and its resources from their natural forms and on the conservation of these resources for human benefit. If one accepts that the Anthropocene is the clearest expression yet of anthropocentric behaviour and its effects, and that anthropocentrism is the main cause of the current socioecological crisis as some believe it is,[56] an Anthropocene ethic should be discarding palliatives such as weak sustainable development and the pervasive constructions of anthropocentrism that are permeating law and other regulatory institutions, thus working to reinforce claims for a universal morality and some responsibility to care for the biosphere. This responsibility of care could usefully be considered by scholars through the lens of the Anthropocene which shows us a new living reality of human domination of the biosphere where humans are no longer external observers and beneficiaries of a vulnerable Earth and its system from which they are somehow removed. Humans have become an integral part of a vulnerable biosphere and in the process we are becoming vulnerable ourselves as a result of our own activities and the power we exert over the vulnerable biosphere and its many and varied components.

4.3   Inclusivity and Representivity

Related to the foregoing is the need for environmental law and its scholarship to more fully embrace the concerns and interests of the marginalized and the oppressed including, for example, nature, non-white people, LGBTQ people, women, children, indigenous people, the poor and more generally people from the Global South – broadly referred

---

[55] See, for example, Louis Kotzé, 'Human Rights and the Environment in the Anthropocene' (2014) *Anthropocene Review* 1–24.

[56] Already in 1992, Bosselmann succinctly declared that '[D]er Anthropozentrismus ist die tiefste Ursache der ökologischen Krise.' Klaus Bosselmann, *Im Namen der Natur: Der Weg zum ökologischen Rechsstaat* (Bern: Scherz, 1992), 14.

to as the 'others'. The 'othering' tendencies of law are evident from, among others, 'the late arrival of equality and anti-discrimination laws (inadequately) addressing the oppression of "outsider" subjectivities based on gender, race, age, sexuality – and so forth.'[57] Grear says:

> Indeed, the very existence of equality and anti-discrimination provisions are, in a sense, law's own legislative acknowledgement of law's failures of inclusion – a formal (and revealingly flawed) addressal of law's 'otherings'. Moreover, law's othering patterns are profoundly persistent. The arrival of intersectional analysis – an important attempt to expose the mutually reinforcing vectors of oppression implicated in the sheer patterned multiplicity of 'the others of law' reveals an important clue to the crux of the problem: the existence of a particularistic 'human subject' as the 'centre' around which its 'others' struggle for full legal recognition.[58]

Law (including environmental law) is seen to elevate the interests of certain humans (or 'particularistic human subjects') above everything and anyone else, thereby creating profound inter- and intra-species hierarchies and resulting injustices. In so doing, (environmental) law privileges a group of certain privileged humans for which it provides freedom from want and suffering, while allowing them (although I should say 'us' as I am included in this privileged category) to live in pristine environments safely enclosed and protected against the onslaughts of an erratic nature and from the perceived plundering by the poor. This 'identifiable elite' as Grear says,[59] is broadly characterizable as the property-owning, white masculinist legal subject of Northern descent. The fact of environmental law scholarship's own (late) admission to its failures to engender greater inter- and intra-species environmental justice, as well as the steadily emerging body of scholarship focusing on precisely this issue, is testimony to the othering, hierarchical and exclusionary tendencies of environmental law and its scholarship.

Yet, in the same way that the Anthropocene dissolves the human-nature divide, it might very well also dissolve the many privileging hierarches, or at least perceptions of such hierarchies, that are being created by law. As Chakrabarty says: 'there are no lifeboats here for the rich and the privileged.'[60] What would instead be crucial for any future

---

[57] Grear, 'Deconstructing Anthropos', 231.
[58] Ibid.
[59] Ibid., 230.
[60] D. Chakrabarty, 'The Climate of History: Four Theses' (2009) *Critical Inquiry* 197–222 at 221.

vision of Anthropocene law and its attendant scholarship is to be far more critical towards the actual and potential tendencies of law to promote subversive forms of (neo-)colonialism, imperialism, neo-liberal capitalism and exploitation aimed at natural resource extraction for the benefit of the world's privileged. Conscious efforts will also have to be made to dissolve the North-South divide and its related hierarchies,[61] while embracing alternative ways of understanding and confronting the myriad injustices as a result of this divide.

5   Conclusion

If environmental law were to remain relevant as an area of scholarship that focuses on and informs the design of regulatory interventions to mediate the human-environment interface, the way in which scholars engage with environmental law will arguably have to become better attuned and more sensitive to the new regulatory realities that are collectively being symbolized by the Anthropocene. The term 'Anthropocene' has the potential, irrespective of its precise formal status as a term of art, to serve as a powerful discursive tool in the production of a new and groundbreaking juridical imaginary and to capture important ground in debates concerning the response of environmental law and its scholarship to human behaviour in a possibly new geological epoch.

Bibliography

Biermann, F., *Earth System Governance: World Politics in the Anthropocene* (Cambridge, MA: MIT Press, 2014).

Fisher, E. et al., 'Maturity and Methodology: Starting a Debate about Environmental Law Scholarship' (2009) 21(2) *Journal of Environmental Law* 213–250.

Grear, A., 'Deconstructing Anthropos: A Critical Legal Reflection on 'Anthropocentric' Law and Anthropocene 'Humanity'' (2015) 26 *Law and Critique* 225–249.

Kim, R. & Bosselmann, K., 'International Environmental Law in the Anthropocene: Towards a Purposive System of Multilateral Environmental Agreements' (2013) 2 *Transnational Environmental Law* 285–309.

---

[61] See, among others, C. Gonzalez, 'Bridging the North-South Divide: International Environmental Law in the Anthropocene' (2015) 32 *Pace Environmental Law Review* 407–434.

Kotzé, L., 'Rethinking Global Environmental Law and Governance in the Anthropocene' (2014) 32(2) *Journal of Energy and Natural Resources Law* 121–156.

Kotzé, L. (ed.), *Environmental Law and Governance for the Anthropocene* (Oxford: Hart Publishing, 2017).

Pedersen, O., 'The Limits of Interdisciplinarity and the Practice of Environmental Law Scholarship' (2014) 26 *Journal of Environmental Law* 423–441.

The Unifying Force of Climate Change Scholarship

DANIEL A. FARBER

Environmental law scholarship has always suffered from something of an identity crisis. Scholars have periodically felt the need to defend the idea that there is a distinctive field of law in play, as opposed to a conglomerate of different statutes dealing with problems of pollution or preservation of nature. It has not always been easy to identify how to draw a boundary around "environmental" issues and the body (or bodies) of law bearing on them.[1] In addition, legal scholarship on environmental issues has had a tendency to bleed into questions of science or policy. In some respects, climate change intensifies these conundrums, making a broader range of statutes and doctrines relevant to environmental law, such as energy regulation. It also involves deep engagement with issues of economics, science, and technology.

This chapter argues that climate change provides a unifying thread, fostering a deeper unity in environmental law and a more coherent identity for environmental law scholarship. The chapter begins with a review of the development of environmental law in one country, the United States, and the coevolution of legal scholarship, including the recent expansion of interest in climate change. It then considers the coherence issue in environmental law and the way that climate change may provide a connecting thread. Finally, it discusses how the climate change issue amplifies some existing characteristics of legal scholarship such as interdisciplinarity.

---

[1] The question of whether environmental law has any inner coherence goes back many years. As one of the first generation of American legal scholars in the field commented in 2004, "[o]ver the years, many have observed that the impressive formal superstructure of environmental law masks persistent doubts about the existence of a "there" in environmental law." A. D. Tarlock, "Is There a There There in Environmental Law" (2004) 19 *Journal of Land Use* 213 at 217.

1   A Changing Legal Landscape: The Case of the United States

Environmental law is still a relatively youthful field. As we know it today, it hardly predates the 1970s, although precursors can no doubt be found dealing with forests or game preservation going back many centuries. Legal scholarship has evolved as the legal landscape itself has evolved over the past four decades.

1.1   The Initial Stage

The United States was initially a leader in the development of environmental law. Environmentalism took hold most strongly in urban areas and in certain coastal regions.[2] During the 1960s, environmental groups such as the Sierra Club had expanded dramatically, and there was a spate of new federal legislation, such as the Wilderness Act of 1964 and smaller initiatives dealing with air and water pollution.[3]

As this ferment grew, scholars began to advocate conceptualizing environmental law as a distinct field of interest. At a 1969 meeting in Washington, DC, pioneering scholars from across the country met to discuss the contours of this emerging field. However, they agreed that it would be premature to try to define the field. Instead, they agreed, it was best understood in reference to "the 'hideous fact' of 'environmental decay,'" and legal responses to that problem would define the field.[4]

By 1970, the year of the first Earth Day, public support for the environment reached a high pitch.[5] The result was a wave of new environmental legislation that lasted until Ronald Regan took office in 1980. Much of this wave of legislation took place under Richard Nixon, an unlikely candidate for environmental champion. Nixon took forceful positions[6] on behalf of the environment in his earlier

---

[2] See S. P. Hays, *Beauty, Health, and Permanence: Environmental Politics in the United States, 1955–1985* (Cambridge: Cambridge University Press, 1987), 41–45. For more on the emergence of the environmental movement, see J. A. Layzer, *Open for Business: Conservatives' Opposition to Environmental Regulation* (Cambridge, MA: MIT Press, 2012), 11.

[3] Hays, *Beauty, Health, and Permanence*, 53.

[4] R. J. Lazarus, *The Making of Environmental Law* (Chicago: University of Chicago Press, 2004), 48.

[5] James Turner, *The Promise of Wilderness: American Environmental Politics Since 1964* (Seattle: University of Washington Press, 2012), 95–97.

[6] For instance, in his 1970 State of the Union address, Nixon called for urgent action and warned that material wealth is not identical with true well-being. Layzer, "Open for Business," 33.

years as president.[7] Nixon was concerned about Senator Ed Muskie as a potential Democratic opponent and wanted to meet this potential challenge, while also limiting the ability of Democrats to exploit the issue in the off-year congressional elections.[8] As a biographer puts it, "Nixon loved to confound the enemy"; "[s]tealing the Democrats' clothes was Nixon's old Tom Sawyer trick – he had pulled it on Senator Ed Muskie by pushing for environmental laws."[9] In a major message to Congress, President Nixon took an emphatically pro-environmental position and followed up by creating the Environmental Protection Agency (EPA) and the National Oceanic and Atmosphere Administration (NOAA).[10] In 1970, he signed the National Environmental Policy Act (NEPA), the first of a wave of legislation such as the Clean Air Act over the next few years.[11] He also called for an emissions tax on sulfur dioxide and for a national land use law.[12]

Nixon soon began to rethink his environmental policies; by 1972, he had decided to side more with industry.[13] Indeed, on his last day in office after his impeachment, he vetoed EPA's budget.[14] In the meantime, environmentally protective regulation of public lands had begun to spark a backlash in the West and in Alaska.[15] Yet, despite Nixon's inconsistent attitudes, he presided over some of the most significant environment initiatives in history.

This period saw a sharp rise in the amount of legal scholarship on the environment. A Westlaw search produced striking results.[16] In 1965, a total of 21 articles in US law reviews used the terms "environmental" or "pollution." By 1970, the number had doubled to 52. In 1975, the count had doubled again to 107, roughly where it remained in 1980. Environmental law courses were just beginning to emerge at law schools

---

[7] Hays, *Beauty, Health, and Permanence*, 58.
[8] Lazarus, *Making of Environmental Law*, 75–76.
[9] Turner, *Promise of Wilderness*, 348.
[10] Lazarus, *Making of Environmental Law*, 76.
[11] Turner, *Promise of Wilderness*, 104. For a listing of significant environmental legislation (mostly from 1970 to 1981), see C. M. Klyza & D. J. Sousa, *American Environmental Policy: Beyond Gridlock*, rev. edn. (Cambridge, MA: MIT Press, 2013), 33.
[12] Layzer, "Open for Business," 38.
[13] Lazarus, *Making of Environmental Law*, 77.
[14] Ibid. 78.
[15] Ibid. 94.
[16] The search was conducted on the Secondary Sources – Law Reviews & Journals database on January 8, 2018.

across the country, so the first group of environmental scholars had not had time to train students at this point.

1.2 Backlash and Legal Maturity

The election of Ronald Reagan marked the end of the period of creative legislative activity of the 1960s and 1970s. Reagan used his First Inaugural Address to reiterate his opposition to regulation, announcing that "government is not the solution to our problems; government *is* the problem."[17] Yet, he was able to accomplish little in terms of regulatory reform in Congress.[18] During the Reagan years, "Congress did not roll back a single substantive statutory protection, and in 1984 and 1986 it expanded the protections afforded by two hazardous waste control and cleanup statutes."[19]

The Reagan administration marked very nearly the last phase of legislative creativity in US environmental law. The last truly significant legislation was passed in 1990. In that year, the George H. W. Bush administration "pressed Congress to enact much-needed amendments" to the Clean Air Act.[20] Congress also enacted the Oil Pollution Act of 1990.[21]

Since that time, Congress has played only a secondary role in the evolution of US environmental policy.[22] Although it has occasionally managed to block actions by federal agencies and even more rarely to issue new mandates, the focus of environmental policy making has shifted to administrative agencies such as the EPA. This has resulted in increasingly complex legal doctrines as agencies have attempted to use existing statutes to address new priorities, sometimes with support from the courts and sometimes checked by judicial disapproval.[23]

---

[17] Ronald Reagan, *Inaugural Address* (January 20, 1981), transcript available at www .reaganfoundation.org/pdf/SQP012081.pdf.

[18] Lazarus notes that "Congress enacted none of the Reagan administration's proposals to reduce the various federal environmental and natural resource laws." Lazarus, *Making of Environmental Law*, 103.

[19] Thomas O. McGarity, *Freedom to Harm: The Lasting Legacy of the Laissez Faire Revival* (New Haven, CT: Yale University Press, 2013), 73.

[20] Ibid. 101.

[21] Ibid. 104.

[22] R. J. Lazarus, "Environmental Law at the Crossroads: Looking Back 25, Looking Forward 25" (2013) 2 *Michigan Journal of Environmental and Administrative Law* 267–271.

[23] Ibid. 272.

As major new federal legislation came to a halt, US legal scholars focused more intently on how to interpret the existing statutes and on the potential for action by agencies such as EPA. This tended to bring environmental law closer to administrative law. As the Supreme Court became more conservative, environmental scholars also became drawn into constitutional issues about the extent of standing and on protection of private property rights. Justice Antonin Scalia was a leader on the Supreme Court in these fields, writing important opinions protecting landowners from "excessive" regulation[24] and restricting the scope of standing at the expense of environmental plaintiffs.[25]

The most important administrative single innovation may be a 1980 executive order, that is, an order issued by the president to direct the action of federal administrative agencies. In his first week in office, President Reagan signed Executive Order 12,291.[26] Building on initial efforts during the Carter administration,[27] the executive order required systematic use of cost-benefit analysis in designing new regulations.[28] Section 2 directed that "major" regulations be promulgated only if, "taking into account the condition of the particular industries affected [and] the condition of the national economy," the potential benefits to society outweigh the potential costs and net benefits are maximized.[29] In 1993, President Bill Clinton issued an executive order continuing the use of the Office of Information and Regulatory Affairs (OIRA) to review regulatory cost-benefit analyses but attempting to streamline the process of review.[30] With some additional minor changes, the Clinton order remains in effect today. The result of these executive orders has been to

---

[24] *Lucas* v. *South Carolina Coastal Council*, 505 US 1003 (1992) (unconstitutional to prohibit construction on vulnerable coastal land).

[25] *Lujan* v. *Defenders of Wildlife*, 504 US 555 (1992) (no standing to litigate application of Endangered Species Act outside the United States).

[26] Executive Order No. 12,291, 3 Code of Federal Regulations 127 (1982) (signed by Reagan on February 17, 1981). Notably, a year earlier, the Supreme Court's decision in *Industrial Union Department* v. *American Petroleum Institute* (The Benzene Case), 448 US 607 (1980), gave a major boost to fledging efforts to implement quantitative risk assessment as a regulatory tool. See W. Boyd, "Genealogies of Risk: Searching for Safety, 1930s–1970s" (2012) 39 *Ecology Law Quarterly* 895–987, 978–79 (discussing how quantitative risk assessment, a prerequisite for the use of cost-benefit analysis, became the dominant regulatory approach).

[27] McGarity, *Freedom to Harm*, 70 (discussing how Carter signed an executive order requiring agencies for the first time to repeal regulations that were not cost-beneficial).

[28] Ibid. at 72–73.

[29] Executive Order No. 12,291, 3 Code of Federal Regulations 127 (1982).

[30] Executive Order No. 12,866, 3 Code of Federal Regulations 638 (1994), reprinted as amended in 5 USC. § 601 (2012).

permeate US environmental law with economic analysis, making it impossible to understand the field without taking this interdisciplinary perspective into account.

This economic turn in the regulatory sphere also had its effects on environmental scholarship. To see the impact of these developments on legal scholarship, another Westlaw search is illuminating.[31] In 1980, there were 22 articles using the terms "cost-benefit analysis," "emissions trading," "cap and trade," or "emissions tax." By 1990, there were 256. In 2000, there were 613, and in 2010, there were 1,308. The counts for 2016 was slightly lower (1,090) but still very significant. These articles are sometimes doctrinal, debating whether use of these techniques is consistent with statutes or judicial doctrines. Others are theoretical, either making normative arguments for or against these economic tools or using economic analysis to debate how these methods should be applied. Empirical research is not unknown but seems less common than in some other areas of law such as securities regulation or in other fields such as environmental economics.

Environmental law scholars vigorously debated the legitimacy of cost-benefit analysis. Among the ethical issues were (and still are) placing a monetary value on human life; placing a monetary value on endangered species or unique ecosystems; and using economic techniques that tend to reduce the significant of long-term harms, especially those involving future generations. Beyond these ethical issues, legal scholars found themselves drawn into debates about whether agencies were correctly applying tools such as techniques for valuation of ecosystem services or methods of calculating the value of human life or ecosystems. Outside of cost-benefit analysis, economics has also influenced legal scholars to consider the use of market-based instruments such as emissions trading and emissions taxes that were advocated by economists.

Another particularly striking area for agency innovation is climate change. In the 1970s, when the key environmental law statutes were passed, climate change was at most a peripheral concern if it was considered at all. By the time climate change had emerged after 1990 as a major regulatory issue, the window for new environmental legislation had closed. So the initiative in US law has come from elsewhere: administrative agencies, with a push from the Supreme Court. At this writing, the future of these efforts is hotly contested.

---

[31] The search was conducted on the Secondary Sources – Law Reviews & Journals database on January 8, 2018.

Climate change has naturally become an increasing interest of legal scholars. An online search through Westlaw reveals the following:[32] in 1990, there were 69 US law review articles referring to "climate change" or "global warming." In 2000, there were 183. In 2010, there were 1,557. In 2016, the number was 1,404, showing that growth had leveled off.[33] There were 4,773 articles that year using the terms "environmental" or "pollution." Thus, articles mentioning climate change were (very roughly) a third of all environmental scholarship.

2 Environmental Law and the "Law of the Horse"

Given the diverse set of statutes, environmental issues, and legal doctrines involved in environmental law, it may seem susceptible to Frank Easterbrook's "law of the horse" critique.[34] For those unfamiliar with this allusion, it stems from a debate over whether cyberlaw should be recognized as a distinct field of legal scholarship. Judge Easterbrook criticized the concept of "cyberlaw" as a separate field, saying rather that it is akin to a course on the "law of the horse," which would simply involve compiling cases from diverse fields of law that happened to involve horses.[35] He viewed this as a foolish endeavor:

> Lots of cases deal with sales of horses; others deal with people kicked by horses; still more deal with the licensing and racing of horses, or with the care veterinarians give horses, or with prizes at horse shows. Any effort to collect these strands into a course on "The Law of the Horse" is doomed to be shallow and to miss unifying principles. Teaching 100 percent of the cases on people kicked by horses will not convey the law of torts very well.[36]

Easterbrook was not successful in killing "Law and Cyberspace" courses. As a critic of Easterbrook's said, "the intervention, though brilliant, produced an awkward silence, some polite applause, and then quick

[32] The search, too, was conducted on the Secondary Sources – Law Reviews & Journals database on January 8, 2018.
[33] The reason for using 2016 rather than 2017 as the final year is that many law reviews with 2017 cover dates will not actually be published until 2018, so the 2017 count as of January 2018 would be incomplete.
[34] F. H. Easterbrook, "Cyberspace and the Law of the Horse" (1996) *University of Chicago Law Forum* 207–216.
[35] Ibid. 208.
[36] Ibid. 208–209.

passage to the next speaker."[37] Although no one was quite persuaded, Easterbrook's intervention reshaped the discussion: "Talk shifted in the balance of the day, and in the balance of the contributions, to the idea that either the law of the horse was significant after all, or the law of cyberspace was something more."[38]

Nevertheless, Easterbrook's essay has left a permanent mark. The invariable response in the American legal academy to anyone proposing the recognition of a new area of law is that the supposed new area is simply another example of the law of the horse. In the case of environmental law, the argument against the coherence of the field would take two forms. First, much of environmental law can be seen as applying more general principles of law to specific settings. Second, both the factual settings and the statutory schemes involved in environmental law are quite diverse and their interrelations are not obvious.

As to the first criticism, the argument would be that much of environmental law involves legal processes that involve other bodies of law. Agency actions are the subject of administrative law, while treaties are part of international law. Liability for environmental damages can be seen as part of tort law. Application of environmental laws often involves principles of legislation or statutory interpretation. Some parts of environmental law may involve constitutional issues about the rights of private property owners, federalism, or limits on judicial authority. From this perspective, environmental law can be seen as just the application of more general legal principles.

This critique seems to assume that one field of law cannot intersect with another, but there are numerous examples of intersection fields. For instance, intellectual property law is enforced through litigation, but it clearly is not merely a subfield of civil procedure. Similarly, financial regulation, like much of environmental law, is conducted by agencies, but that does not make it a branch of administrative of law because it has its own special rules and policies. Bankruptcy law involves debts that are contractual in nature and security interests that are a type of property, but it is not merely a branch of contract or property law.

The question is whether different aspects of environmental law have at least as much in common with each other as with other relevant fields. This certainly seems to be true, at least to a certain extent. For instance,

---

[37] Lawrence Lessig, "The Law of the Horse: What Cyberlaw Might Teach" (1999) 113 *Harvard Law Review* 501–549.
[38] Ibid.

someone who understood California's climate change regime would find it easier to understand the EU's climate change regime than a general expert in EU law, though the surrounding legal contexts are quite different.

In any event, the second critique is in some sense more serious. The first critique merely demotes environmental law to a subfield of some other legal field. The second critique suggests that environmental law does not really exist at all as a field, because it is merely a collection of unrelated bodies of law that happen to deal with somewhat analogous subjects. In other words, unlike the critique that environmental law is not really a field, this critique insists that it is many different fields with little in common. The laws governing air pollution may be quite distinct from those governing water pollution, while toxic chemicals may be subject to yet another legal regime, such as the REACH Directive in the EU. Laws governing endangered species, preservation of forests, overfishing, public lands, offshore oil drilling, and so forth may seem even more scattered and unrelated. Similarly, at the international level, separate treaties deal with subjects as diverse as ocean protection, the ozone layer, and trade in toxic chemicals.

Clearly, these subjects have some basics in common.[39] They all involve human interaction with nonhuman physical or biological systems. The fact that these areas became subject to specialized legal regulation indicates a dissatisfaction with private law ordering or with completely discretionary government control of resources. It also indicates that society places some value on these nonhuman systems, either instrumental or intrinsic. Still, in concrete terms, a subject such as air pollution is quite different from preservation of wildlife, and the legal regimes are correspondingly different, at least apart from issues of process.[40] This raises the question of whether these subfields have more than a family resemblance. Section 3 argues that climate change has become the nexus between environmental problems, making them part of a connected network of issues rather than merely similar but isolated islands in an archipelago.

[39] These characteristics of environmental systems are discussed in an earlier effort to identify defining features of environmental law. T. S. Aagaard, "Environmental Law as a Legal Field: An Inquiry in Legal Taxonomy" (2010) 95 *Cornell Law Review* 223–282, 263.
[40] Tarlock views these process issues as the only real unifying principles in environmental law. Tarlock, "Is There a There There?" 220.

3   Climate Change as a Unifying Theme

Climate change may provide connective tissue for environmental law because its causes and its consequences encompass nearly all the major aspects of the field. Climate change is caused by the emission of greenhouse gases. These come from manufacturing and the energy sector, two major causes of air and water pollution. Methods of addressing climate change are almost guaranteed to address air pollution issues in particular by reducing reliance on combustion processes and the use of oil refineries, prime sources of pollution. Moreover, extraction, processing, and transportation of fossil fuels are implicated in a host of environmental problems from land disturbance to water pollution. Other carbon emissions result from land use change, particularly deforestation, and implicate that branch of environmental law.

In terms of its effects, climate change again is deeply connected with other areas of environmental concern. In understanding the link between biodiversity and climate change, we need to begin with a grasp of the current and future trajectories of the climate. Perhaps the simplest way to grasp these effects is to consider the effects of the type of warming we would expect to see if there were no effective program to reduce global emissions. A report by the World Bank provides a succinct view of the impacts of 4°C average warming (or about 7°F). The report provides a dire list of consequences: "the inundation of coastal cities; increasing risks for food production potentially leading to higher malnutrition rates; many dry regions becoming drier, wet regions wetter; unprecedented heat waves in many regions, especially in the tropics; substantially exacerbated water scarcity in many regions; increased frequency of high-intensity tropical cyclones; and irreversible loss of biodiversity, including coral reef systems."[41]

In this high climate change scenario, according to the World Bank, biodiversity will also be threatened. This cannot be considered terribly surprising, since plants and animals are generally no more immune from heat waves, droughts, cyclones, and flooding than are humans, crops, and domesticated animals. Because of the rapid pace of climate change, "[m]any species will be unable to disperse rapidly enough to track the

---

[41] "Turn Down the Heat: Why a 4°C Warmer World Must be Avoided," World Bank (2012), v, available at www.worldbank.org/en/topic/climatechange/publication/turn-down-the-heat-climate-extremes-regional-impacts-resilience.

changing climate and remain within their 'climate envelope' of temperature and precipitation."[42]

Climate change will also have severe effects on oceans. Several lines of
evidence converge to suggest that "the combination of changes in ocean
surface temperatures, increasing ocean acidity, and a host of other
stresses could bring coral reef ecosystems to critical ecological tipping
points within decades rather than centuries, and that some regions of the
ocean are already near that point from a biogeochemical perspective."[43]
Human activities are key stressors that will combine with climate change
to impact marine ecosystems. As the Intergovernmental Panel on
Climate Change (IPCC) puts it, "[s]trong interactions with other
human impacts like eutrophication, fishing, and other forms of harvest-
ing accelerate and amplify climate-induced changes."[44]

The world now seems to have clearly entered the Anthropocene,
a geological period dominated by humans[45] in much the same way as
the Jurassic was dominated by dinosaurs. Humans have already begun to
change the climate; unless we take serious steps to limit emissions, the
changes may become severe. We have also had a massive impact on
ecosystems everywhere on the planet, while accelerating the pace of
extinction far beyond the prior rate.

The rise of the sea level and the destruction of some rare butterflies
may seem unrelated, and sometimes they may be. But we saw that at
a larger scale, biodiversity and climate are closely related, given the
impact of climate change on biodiversity and the feedback loop from
deforestation back to climate change. Because neither our activities nor

[42] R. Primack, *Essentials of Conservation Biology*, 5th edn (Sunderland, MA: Sinauer
Associates, Inc., 2010), 208. For further discussion of effects on biodiversity, see
A. E. Camacho, "Managing Ecosystem Effects in an Era of Rapid Climate Change" in
D. A. Farber & M. Peeters (eds.), *Elgar Encyclopedia of Environmental Law* (Cheltenham,
UK: Edward Elgar, 2016), 355.

[43] A. C. Janeros et al., "Biodiversity" in Peter Backlund, Anthony Janetos, & David Schimel,
*The Effects of Climate Change on Agriculture, Land Resources, Water Resources, and
Biodiversity in the United States* (Washington DC: US Climate Change Science
Program and the Subcommittee on Global Change Research, 2008), 162.

[44] H. Pörtner et al., "Ocean Systems" in IPCC, *Climate Change 2014: Impacts, Adaptation,
and Vulnerability. Part A: Global and Sectoral Aspects. Contribution of Working Group II
to the Fifth Assessment Report of the Intergovernmental Panel on Climate Change*
(Cambridge: Cambridge University Press, 2014), 465.

[45] Whether to make this designation official is still under consideration, but it seems clear
that humans have had a massive impact on the planet already. See Hillary Young,
"The Hitchhiker's Guide to the Anthropocene" (2015) 347 *Science* 955. For further
thoughts on the implications of this new era for the legal system, see E. Biber, "Law in
the Anthropocene Epoch" (2017) 106 *Georgetown Law Journal* 1.

our impacts on the planet are localized, it is increasingly easy for events in one location, such as a biofuel mandate, to impact biodiversity in a far-removed portion of the world. An early ecological slogan was that "everything is connected to everything else."[46] That slogan has, if anything, even greater relevance today.

Runaway carbon emissions pose perhaps the greatest risk of playing havoc with the planet, including its ecological systems. Biodiversity and climate mitigation are now closely linked. As we attempt to create an international regime to control carbon, control of deforestation is a necessary component, with a co-benefit of preserving biodiversity. This effort is emblematic of the functional connection between mitigation and forest preservation. Moreover, efforts to preserve biodiversity must now take climate change into account, whether in relatively mature domestic biodiversity laws or in the still-developing international biodiversity regime. One of the challenges in adapting to climate change is finding ways to preserve biodiversity.

At a deeper level, climate change focuses our attention on interlinked global systems, each of which is composed of smaller, localized subsystems: the Earth's physical systems (primarily represented by the atmosphere but also oceans), global economic activities (particularly the energy system), and the biosphere (especially carbon and biodiversity stores such as rainforests). Climate change teaches us that all three systems are intricately connected, locally and globally. Thus, to a large extent, environmental law can be seen as the study of the legal regime (also local to global) governing the interactions of these systems.

4   Climate Change and Trends in Environmental Law Scholarship

In addition to bringing seemingly unrelated aspects of environmental law into closer relationship, climate change may also accentuate some existing aspects of environmental while adding new ones.

4.1   Transnational Legal Scholarship

Given that climate change involves global systems with local linkages, it is not surprising that the governance regime mixes the local and the global. Traditionally, there has been a stark contrast between international law and domestic law, with international law being reserved for actions of

---

[46] B. Commoner, *The Closing Circle* (New York: Random House, 1971), 33.

nation-states. This dichotomy has begun to break down in the climate change arena, as other actors have begun to take independent actions across national borders to address the issue. Some theorists have spoken of the emergence of polycentric governance systems to address climate change.[47]

In a number of countries, prominently including the United States, subnational governments have begun to address climate change and to link with one another.[48] This trend most prominently includes the state of California, whose programs have achieved international prominence. California has also entered into cooperation agreements with other countries and subnational governments.[49] But the trend is not limited to the United States.

Although this climate change scholarship is in the forefront of this shift in legal scholarship, similar changes are taking place in other fields. The trend is prominent enough to lead to the publication of a successful new journal, *Transnational Environmental Law*.

4.2 Linkages with Other Fields

Given that the primary source of greenhouse gases is the energy system, it is not surprising that energy law and climate change law are now closely linked. In particular, energy law has become increasingly concerned with efforts to decarbonize the energy system through expanded use of renewable energy and energy conservation.[50] The energy system is globally linked through trade, but many drivers and impacts are local, as with climate change.

One area of linkage from global climate to local governance is land use planning. In cities, poor planning contributes to sprawl, increasing the use of automobiles and trucks that spew greenhouse gases.[51] Moreover, urban planning needs to take into the account how climate change will impact cities, particularly those that may be subject to

[47] H. M. Osofsky, "Polycentrism and Climate Change" in Daniel Farber & Marjan Peeters (eds.), *Climate Change Law* (Cheltenham, UK: Edward Elgar, 2016), 325.
[48] K. H. Engel, "Climate Change Federalism" in Farber & Peeters, *Climate Change Law*, 337.
[49] D. A. Farber & C. P. Carlarne, *Climate Change Law* (St. Paul, MN: Foundation Press, 2018), 186–187.
[50] A. B. Klass, "Climate Change and the Convergence of Environmental and Energy Law" (2013) 4 *Fordham Environmental Law Review* 180–204.
[51] W. W. Buzbee, "Transportation as a Climate Wedge and Challenge Under United States Law" in Farber & Peeters, *Climate Change Law*, 438.

flood risks.[52] Outside of cities, control of land use in coastal areas looms large as a climate change adaptation issue.[53] Indeed, the adaptation to climate change is an issue that will impact many fields of law.[54]

This expansion of environmental law beyond its traditional boundary reinforces a trend outside of the climate change area in which environmental considerations are increasingly factored into statutes dealing primarily with non-environmental matters.[55] Moreover, it is also possible for non-environmental areas such as insurance law to be used as tools to address climate change and other environmental issues. Given the way that climate change and its causes affect so many different aspects of human life, we can only expect to see a further expansion of environmental law beyond its heartland.[56]

4.3   Interdisciplinarity

Climate change epitomizes the interdisciplinarity that is often found in environmental law. The scientific foundation of climate change law, climate science, includes both research into the atmosphere and oceans along with studies of how ecosystems store or release carbon.[57] But economics is also basic to climate change law.[58] Emissions trading and carbon taxes have figured heavily in greenhouse gas reduction strategies. Moreover, regulatory policy cannot be assessed fully without consideration of another economic concept, the social cost of carbon.

Most importantly, climate change science mandates consideration of an important new concept in environmental law: "non-stationarity."[59] Environmental law, and even non-environmental fields such as property law, assume that background conditions will remain relatively stable

[52] L. G. Sun & B. Curtis, "Urban Planning and Climate Change" in Farber & Peeter, "Climate Change Law," 649.

[53] M.R. Caldwell and M.L. Melius, "Coastal Issues," in Farber and Peeters, *Climate Change Law*, 579.

[54] J. B. Ruhl & J. Salzman, "Climate Change Meets the Law of the Horse" (2013) 62 *Duke Law Journal* 975, 1010.

[55] T. S. Asgaard, "Environmental Law Outside the Canon" (2014) 89 *Indiana Law Journal* 1240.

[56] T. S. Asgaard, "Environmental Law's Heartland and Frontiers" (2015) 32 *Pace Environmental Law Review* 511.

[57] Farber & Carlarne, *Climate Change Law*, 29–38.

[58] Ibid., 38–55.

[59] Ruhl & Salzman, "Law of the Horse," 93–94.

despite occasional fluctuations and slow long-term shifts.[60] But climate science tells us that we are in the midst of many years, if not centuries, of change that will impact how to think about a diverse range of environmental issues and programs, including wildlife refuges, fisheries, water quality, and forestry. Rather than seeking permanent solutions to issues in these areas, we are beginning to see a greater appreciation for adaptive management and other flexibility mechanisms.

5 Conclusion

Environmental law has always had a loose coherence given the common focus of its subfields on aspects of nature and associated preservation-oriented values. As climate change becomes an increasingly important focus of environmental law, it provides a linkage between these subfields. As we learn from climate science, the global climate system interacts intensively with ecosystems around the world, driven by large-scale human activities such as forestry and energy production, and in turn impacting human society profoundly.

We thus begin to glimpse the larger shape of the human/natural systems that bridge scales from local to global. This chapter has argued that this emerging understanding will help shape our view of the associated legal institutions that mediate between humans and the surrounding world. An early product of this understanding is an increasing coherence within environmental law scholarship.

Bibliography

Aagaard, Todd S., "Environmental Law as a Legal Field: An Inquiry in Legal Taxonomy" (2010) 95 *Cornell Law Review* 223.

Biber, Eric, "Law in the Anthropocene Epoch" (2017) 106 *Georgetown Law Journal* 1.

Easterbrook, Frank H., "Cyberspace and the Law of the Horse" (1996) *University of Chicago Law Forum* 207–213.

Farber, Daniel A. & Carlarne, Cinnamon P., *Climate Change Law* (St. Paul, MN: Foundation Press, 2018).

Hays, Samuel P., *Beauty, Health, and Permanence: Environmental Politics in the United States, 1955–1985* (Cambridge: Cambridge University Press, 1987).

---

[60] Farber & Carlarne, *Climate Change Law*, 238–240.

Layzer, Judith A., *Open for Business: Conservatives' Opposition to Environmental Regulation* (Cambridge, MA: MIT Press, 2012).

Lazarus, Richard J., *The Making of Environmental Law* (Chicago: University of Chicago Press, 2004)

McGarity, Thomas O., *Freedom to Harm: The Lasting Legacy of the Laissez Faire Revival* (New Haven, CT: Yale University Press, 2013).

Tarlock, A. Dan, "Is There a There There in Environmental Law" (2004) 19 *Journal of Land Use* 213.

Environmental Law Scholarship in a Developing Country – An Alternative Discourse

CAMENA GUNERATNE

Introduction

Legal scholars have been engaged in a critical examination as to the nature, role and objectives of environmental law scholarship, questioning its relevance as an academic discipline. Much of this discourse is located in common law jurisdictions of developed countries that share common perspectives about the nature of environmental law and its role in environmental regulation and management.

In this chapter, I use a developing country's experience of environment and development to argue for an alternative discourse in both environmental law and the scholarship that informs it. I contend that there cannot be a uniform definition of what constitutes environmental law scholarship, and it must inevitably adapt to differing jurisdictions, needs and social realities, wherever they are located. In this chapter, I consider the ambit of this sub-discipline of law, and its relevance and impacts in a developing country that is confronting issues of environmental degradation, poverty and development. In doing so, I will offer suggestions as to how scholarship in this field can positively contribute to this process in terms of wider impact, research methodologies and responding to current challenges.

1 The Discourse on Legal Scholarship and Environmental Law

Legal scholarship has been the subject of much debate within the field and legal scholars themselves have questioned its role, purpose and objective. They have asked what legal scholars contribute to the academic pursuit of knowledge and to the pursuit of justice. It has been alleged that legal scholarship is normative and its aim is not to create new knowledge but merely to analyse the current status of the law to consider what it should be. At its best, it seeks to develop a more just world rather than a more knowledgeable one. For that reason, legal scholarship is not true scholarship, the defining goal of which is to uncover subtle and interesting truths in the pursuit of knowledge within the discipline of a recognized academic field. The comment has been made that '[i]t is too professional or too normative to be true "scholarship" for some critics and too academic for others. It is too disorganized, undisciplined, or disperse: no one can articulate widely shared standards of quality, or even a widely shared method that defines the discipline.'[1]

The questions raised as to the purpose of legal scholarship have been asked with even greater intensity and self-doubt in regard to environmental law. Environmental law scholarship has been defined as scholarship predicated on ideals common to all legal scholarship but which addresses 'the special kind of problems that are discovered in the study of laws and legal systems that relate to the environment'.[2] Writers from the United Kingdom are pessimistic about the nature and state of environmental law as a legal discipline and perceive it as one that has yet to come of age, and which is immature, incoherent and marginal to mainstream legal scholarship.[3] US scholars take a more positive view and contend that since the birth of modern environmental law forty years ago the subject has matured considerably and reached a level of stability.[4] However, they too agree that the area is highly fragmented and unduly complicated and needs an overall vision or descriptive framework to make it coherent.[5] Interestingly, the literature does not appear to indicate that a similar debate has arisen among scholars in developing countries. This is possibly because environmental law scholarship in many of these countries has a strong element of

---

[1] Robin West, 'The Contested Value of Normative Legal Scholarship' (2016) 66 *Journal of Legal Education* 6; Robin West & Danielle Citron, 'On Legal Scholarship' available at www .aals.org/wp-content/uploads/2014/08/OnLegalScholarship-West-Citron.pdf; Gavin Little, 'Developing Environmental Law Scholarship: Going Beyond the Legal Space' (2016) 36(1) *Legal Studies* 48.

[2] Elizabeth Fisher, Bettina Lange, Eloise Scotford & Cinnamon Carlarne, 'Maturity and Methodology: Starting a Debate about Environmental Law Scholarship' (2009) 21(2) *Journal of Environmental Law* 213.

[3] Ibid., 213; Ole W. Pedersen, 'Modest Pragmatic Lessons for a Diverse and Incoherent Environmental Law (2013) 33(1) *Oxford Journal of Legal Studies* 103 at 105.

[4] Todd S. Aagaard, 'Environmental Law as a Legal Field: An Inquiry in Legal Taxonomy' (2010) 95(2) *Cornell Law Review* 221 at 223.

[5] Aagaard, 'Environmental Law as a Legal Field'.

activism with academics contributing to the development of the law within and outside a legal setting.

The uncertainty as to the nature and status of environmental law as an academic discipline has largely to do with the uncertainty as to what the speciality encompasses. Macrory notes that one of the challenges of environmental law is to define its boundaries.[6] Several writers have attempted to define these boundaries, the scope of which ranges from all laws that affect or have to do with the natural environment,[7] to those whose primary purpose is to protect the natural environment, to the most restrictive – that is, those laws which are based on an environmental ethic.[8] A narrow definition encompassing such issues as pollution and nature conservation law may bring some certainty to the field but does not address all environmental challenges. Conversely, as Aagaard argues, an over-inclusive definition that encompasses all laws which impact on the environment but which were enacted without any consideration of environmental interests would lead to confusion. Aagaard appears to take the middle ground – environmental law encompasses laws that deal with human impacts on the natural environment, and he notes that such a definition 'will allow us to study the various approaches that law making institutions take to environmental management'.[9]

The attempts to define the boundaries of environmental law reflect the perhaps unresolvable debate as to the nature of the discipline – is it simply a collection of any laws relating to the environment which may be used to resolve environmental problems, or is it based on a fundamental set of principles that give it credence as an identifiable legal discipline?[10] The first question also gives rise to another that would precede it – namely, how does one define 'environment' and identify 'environmental' problems?

---

[6] Richard Macrory, 'Maturity and Methodology': A Personal Reflection' (2009) 21(2) *Journal of Environmental Law* 251.

[7] Pedersen, 'Modest Pragmatic Lessons', 105.

[8] Aagaard, 'Environmental Law as a Legal Field', 261.

[9] Ibid., 263. Dernbach carries the role of environmental law a step further, citing its role in ensuring sustainability. He defines sustainable development as environmentally sustainable human development and notes that environmental law and natural resources law are essential foundations to achieve this objective and are reasonably well developed in the United States and many other countries. See John C. Dernbach, 'The Essential and Growing Role of Legal Education in Achieving Sustainability' (2011) 60(3) *Journal of Legal Education* 489 at 490.

[10] Macrory, 'Maturity and Methodology', 252; Pedersen, 'Modest Pragmatic Lessons'.

In this chapter, I argue that the accepted width and breath of environmental law as a legal field and as an academic discipline and its acceptance as such has diverged between scholars of developed and developing countries. Environmental law in developed common law jurisdictions has a relatively narrow definition as a response to the global ecological crisis, generally covering remedies for environmental harms under areas such as tort law, public nuisance, planning law and others.[11] While it expanded to address issues such as pollution, waste, and species protection and then transitioned to those such as transport, resource use, climate change and biodiversity, it remains focused on the role of law in regulating the human impacts on the natural environment.[12]

In this chapter I reflect on the experience of a developing country, Sri Lanka, and argue that environmental law, though a much more recent academic discipline, has evolved in response to the very different environmental challenges faced by such a country in grappling with issues of poverty, development and good governance. I will examine how environmental law scholarship has been both informed and driven by these factors; in the context of the Sri Lankan experience, I will argue that a new discourse in environmental law is needed to make a meaningful contribution to issues of environment and development.

2   A Developing Country Perspective on Sustainable Development and the Environment

To deconstruct the nature, scope and objectives of environmental law in countries such as Sri Lanka, it is necessary to consider the principle of sustainable development as it evolved in the international sphere and was defined within these countries. By the late 1960s, understandings of development, economic growth and progress started pointing towards sustainable development. The many reasons for this include the realization of the impacts of human population growth, unchecked industrialization together with pollution and resource depletion on the global

---

[11] An expansive definition of environmental law research has been defined as research which analyses any legal issues focused on pollution, species or habitat conservation, land use, natural resource management, or climate change. Robert L. Fishman & Lydia Barbash-Riley, 'Empirical Environmental Law Scholarship', 44 *Ecology Law Quarterly* (2018) 101 at 106.

[12] Macrory, 'Maturity and Methodology', 254.

environment and the Earth's carrying capacity.[13] While the theory and practice of sustainability and concerns about the impacts of human activity on the planet have historical roots going back centuries,[14] the succinct conceptualization contained in the Brundtland Commission report of 1986, 'Our Common Future,' gave it a renewed impetus in the latter half of the twentieth century. The earlier conceptualization of sustainability as protecting ecosystems and natural resources evolved into an acknowledgement that development must maintain an equilibrium between environmental protection, economic growth and social justice.

The convergence of issues of environment and development progressed relatively slowly, and the process reflected the divergent viewpoints of developed and developing countries. Affluent developed countries conceptualized environmental issues primarily as conservation and pollution control and on questions as to how economic growth, particularly in the Global South, would impact the natural environment. This standpoint was often at odds with the position of developing countries whose over-riding priorities of human development and poverty alleviation took precedence over environmental protection.

Concurrently with the Brundtland Commission report, a parallel development agenda emerged with the Declaration on the Right to Development. The declaration sought to infuse a human rights–based approach to development with particular emphasis on social and economic rights.[15] Developing countries were grappling with issues that were generally omitted from the sustainable development discourse, including problems of extreme poverty, vertical and horizontal inequity, conflict over the possession and use of natural resources and a disadvantageous international economic order. The emphasis on human development enunciated in the declaration coalesced with the agenda of developing countries, which sought to ensure distributive justice, equity and inclusiveness in development, including in resource allocation and use. The two conceptualizations of development advanced

[13] Jacobus A. Du Pisani, Sustainable Development – Historical Roots of the Concept (2006) 3(2) *Environmental Sciences* 83, 89.
[14] Ibid.; Ulrich Grober, 'Deep Roots – A Conceptual History of "Sustainable Development"' (Nachhaltigkeit) available at https://bibliothek.wzb.eu/pdf/2007/p07-002.pdf.
[15] 'Development is a Human Right', United Nations Human Rights Office of the High Commissioner, www.ohchr.org/EN/Issues/Development/Pages/Backgroundrtd.aspx; 'The Right to Development at a Glance', United Nations Human Rights Office of the High Commissioner, www.un.org/en/events/righttodevelopment/pdf/rtd_at_a_glance.pdf.

by the Brundtland Commisson and the Declaration on the Right to Development in effect forced a meeting point of environment and development.

Since the Rio Conference, the confluence of sustainable development and human development has evolved in the international sphere. The process was facilitated by a series of world conferences addressing issues of environment, social development, population, gender and human rights, which shifted the focus from the human environment to environment and development, to sustainable development and to the human right to development.[16] The human right to development was rooted in the human rights discourse rather than in the environment-based sustainable development discourse. The right to development introduced what are now called the third generation of human rights merging the first two generations of civil and political with economic, social and cultural rights. The third generation of human rights includes both the right to development and the right to environment.[17] It also reflected the universality and indivisibility of human rights expressed in the Preamble to the two International Covenants on Human Rights which both stressed that one category could not be fulfilled without the other.[18] This meeting of the two agendas paved the way for a greater parity among the three pillars of sustainability – environmental, economic and social.

In developing countries, there was an initial resistance to environmental protection, which was perceived as an obstruction to development and poverty alleviation. However, policy shifts and attitudinal change eased the tensions between issues of environment and development as these countries acknowledged that economic growth and development without environmental protection and conservation was essentially self-destructive. The shift to a new paradigm of sustainable development in states' laws and policies also marked the development of a new environmental law in these countries.[19] The consistent articulation

---

[16] 'Sustainable Development Timeline', International Institute for Sustainable Development, www.iisd.org/pdf/2012/sd_timeline_2012.pdf.

[17] Alexandre Kiss, 'An Introductory Note on a Human Right to Environment' in Edith Brown Weiss (ed.), *Environmental Change and International Law* (New York: United Nations University Press, 1992), 199.

[18] See the Preambles to the International Covenant on Civil and Political Rights, 999 UNTS. 171: 6 *ILM* 368 (1967) and International Covenant on Economic, Social and Cultural Rights 993 UNTS 3: 6 *ILM* 368 (1967).

[19] Kilaparti Ramakrishna, 'The Emergence of Environmental Law in the Developing Countries: A Case Study of India' (1985) 12(4) *Ecology Law Quarterly* 907.

of the countries of the Global South of their development agenda has now found expression in the 2030 Sustainable Development Goals (SDGs).[20]

The Millennium Development Goals (MDGs), which had preceded the SDGs, had focused almost entirely on eradicating extreme poverty and on the provision of basic human needs for the peoples of the Global South. They included only one goal addressing environmental sustainability[21] and did not make an explicit link between environmental protection and human development. The SDGs on the other hand offer a renewed paradigm of development, integrating the three pillars of sustainable development into an overarching objective rather than conceptualizing them as competing priorities. Human development, progress and welfare are addressed in all their dimensions predicated on the efficient use of a declining natural resource base. While the MDGs were designed as targets to be achieved by developing countries with the assistance of the developed nations, the SDGs require equal commitment and action from all nations. Most importantly, the SDGs are 'universally anchored in human rights' and grounded in a human rights agenda, directly tackling inequalities within peaceful, just and inclusive societies and ensuring human rights and dignity.[22]

In this context of the renewed paradigm of sustainable development, I will explore the nature and scope of environmental law in Sri Lanka and the way in which it has evolved to meet the challenges of development and sustainability. I will examine environmental law scholarship and the role of scholars and researchers in informing, responding to and guiding the legal process on human rights, development and environmental protection.

3   Environmental Law Scholarship – The Sri Lankan Experience

In the context of the current developmental paradigm, I argue that the role of the environmental law scholar in Sri Lanka must necessarily be to

---

[20] 'Sustainable Development', United Nations, https://sustainabledevelopment.un.org/?menu=1300.

[21] 'Millennium Development Goals', United Nations, Goal 7 – Ensure Environmental Sustainability.

[22] Yesudas Choondassery, 'Rights-based Approach: The Hub of Sustainable Development' (2017) 8(2) *Discourse and Communication for Sustainable Education* 17; 'Transforming Our World: Human Rights in the 2030 Agenda for Sustainable Development', United Nations Human Rights Office of the High Commissioner, www.ohchr.org/Documents/Issues/MDGs/Post2015/TransformingOurWorld.pdf; John H. Knox, 'Human Rights, Environmental Protection, and the Sustainable Development Goals' (2015) 24(3) *Washington International Law Journal* 517.

impact on, and contribute to, the development process. Environment law in Sri Lanka, both as an academic discipline and as the practice of law and policy, has moved beyond conservation and management of the natural environment and into the realm of human rights and development founded on the sustainable use of natural resources. Although it has not been redesignated in these terms, the conceptualization of environmental law scholarship has moved in parallel into the field of sustainable development law.

The redefining of environmental law as sustainable development law was driven initially by legal practitioners rather than by scholars. The 1980s and 1990s could be described as the formative years of environmental law in Sri Lanka in terms of both legislation and case law. The introduction of environmental law teaching into Sri Lankan universities in the mid-1990s was preceded by a body of statutory law, which formed a regulatory and management framework on protection of natural resources from the impacts of human development. This body of law was consistent with the narrower definition of environmental law discussed earlier and followed the direction of sustainability in the international sphere.

Concurrent with the statutory process, public interest lawyers often working for environmental non-governmental organizations began initiating litigation in courts challenging the state on matters of environment and development. A considerable number of these cases were filed questioning state action, including on development projects that adversely impacted the natural environment and, increasingly, communities. Litigation sought enforcement of statutory duties by state agencies through writs[23] and on several occasions petitioned for judicial review of legislation impacting environment and development.[24] Others filed on behalf of peoples and communities drew heavily on constitutional provisions on fundamental rights.[25] The lawyers initiating this case law had not received training in environmental law as a specific discipline but

---

[23] For example, *Center for Eco-Cultural Studies and Others* v. *Director General Department of Wildlife Conservation and Others* (2016) CA/WRIT/370/2015 (unreported); *Fernando and Others* v. *Urban Council Kesbewa and Others* (2014) CA/177/2010 (Writ) (unreported).

[24] For example, *Supreme Court Special Determination No 24/2003 and 25/2003 on the Water Services Reform Bill* (unreported) (2003); *Supreme Court Special Determination 26/2003 on the Land Ownership Bill* (2003)(unreported).

[25] Camena Guneratne, 'Using Constitutional Provisions to Advance Environmental Justice – Some Reflections on Sri Lanka' (2015) 11(2) *Law, Environment and Development Journal* available at www.lead-journal.org.

were well versed in constitutional rights, and therefore resorted to constitutional remedies to achieve justice for their clients, and for environmental regulation. Much of this case law was founded on inequality in benefits from the development process and from the adverse impacts of environmental degradation. Consequently, environmental law transitioned, almost inadvertently, into the area of human rights and social justice.[26]

As mentioned earlier, environmental law scholars initially played a subsidiary role to the practitioners in this process. Their function was limited to doctrinal scholarship, documenting, commenting on and analysing the law that was being produced in the courts, as well as critically reviewing the legislation enacted by Parliament. However, over time this role evolved into a more proactive one, and as teaching and research developed in the law schools, scholars began to redefine the field. Environmental law scholarship soon encompassed comparative jurisprudence, particularly in the South Asian region, which drew heavily on human rights standards. The deconstruction of the rights to life and environment by South Asian judges, particularly in India, opened up new areas of social and economic rights and issues of social justice in sustainable development. Exploring the case law that had drawn heavily on human rights, academics also began explicating the area of environment and human rights, the right to development and social and economic rights.

Both curricula and research in environmental law began to expand to encompass any field that might impact the development process or natural resources. Areas of law that were distinctive in the law school curricula, such as international trade, intellectual property rights and human rights, were embraced within environmental law to the extent that they impacted development or the environment, and these subjects too were often redefined. This trend reflected the ethos that fine distinctions could not be made between economic development, social justice and environmental conservation which were all intrinsically intertwined, and issues of environment, trade and commerce and foreign investment, among others, were conceptualized as issues of development.

[26] Ibid.

4 Future Directions

4.1 Linking Environment and Human Rights

The 2030 SDGs have given renewed impetus to the study of a human rights–based approach to sustainable development. The notion that development is a complex process that must be founded on human rights and environmental sustainability is now widely accepted and validated by the SDGs which offer new opportunities for Southern perspectives on development.[27] While some goals more directly confront environmental protection and sustainability,[28] all the goals and their targets link human rights and environment.

In the light of the SDGs, it is pertinent to assess future directions of environmental law scholarship in Sri Lanka. A writer has noted that 'Rather than reducing itself to a reactive, ponderous and disciplinary-confined position, environmental law is ethically obliged to assume a much more active role in what is currently happening on the planet.'[29] This exhortation carries even greater force in developing countries where the launch of the SDGs has made it necessary for environmental law scholars to reassess their role and functions in implementing them, and to consider whether in order to make a positive impact on development, it has become necessary to once again re-conceptualize the field, questioning its purpose, methodology and beneficiaries. Universities globally have a unique role in accelerating implementation of the goals, and higher education institutions particularly in developing countries have a crucial role to play in national development.[30] The role of the environmental law scholar in this scenario will be discussed below.

---

[27] Oluf Langhelle, 'Sustainable Development and Social Justice: Expanding the Rawlsian Framework of Global Justice' (2000) 9 *Environmental Values* 295; Karin Arts, 'Inclusive Sustainable Development: A Human Rights Perspective' (2017) 24 *Current Opinion in Environmental Sustainability* 24.

[28] 'Sustainable Development Goals', United Nations, Goals 6, 7, 11, 13, 14 and 15.

[29] Andreas Philippopoulos-Mihalopoulos, 'Critical Environmental Law as Method in the Anthropocene' in Andreas Philippopoulos-Mihalopoulos (ed.) *Research Methods in Environmental Law: A Handbook* (Cheltenham, UK: Edward Elgar, 2017), chap. 6.

[30] It has also been noted that the goals cover a range of specific areas in which higher-education institutions can make a positive contribution in teaching, research, community engagement and advisory services; Goolam Mohamedbhai, 'SDGs – A Unique Opportunity for Universities', University World News, Issue 392, 27 November 2015, - www.universityworldnews.com/article.php?story=2015112512342677.

4.2 *The Contribution and Impact of Environmental Law Scholarship*

To assess the impact of environmental law scholarship, at the outset we must determine for whom the environmental law scholar writes or should write. The answer in short must be for everyone. Assuming that the primary objective of environmental law scholarship is action-oriented research, it follows that to have the widest possible impact, such scholarship should not be confined to academia alone. Therefore, the targets of environmental law scholarship, both research and teaching, must include students (both law and non-law), lawyers, judges, policy-makers, developmental specialists and the community, among others. Since the primary function of an academic is teaching, scholarship in environmental law must inform this process. Teaching is not confined to students alone and must include the wider legal community of both judges and lawyers as well as those outside it.

A related question to the previous one, which has been often posed, is whether environmental law scholarship can and does have an impact beyond the community of legal scholars. The answer to this question is that this is a necessity if the objective of scholars is to contribute to development. As discussed earlier, while lawyers and judges initiated the practice of environmental law, it has been supplemented by the scholarship of academics who have engaged in legal and judicial training. Similarly, scholars have contributed to law and policy, interacting with technocrats and policymakers, thus ensuring the links between research and application of the law to respond to social and political realities. Extending environmental law scholarship into the public space will extend its reach to those outside the academy and will have a greater impact and influence on policymaking. Importantly, it will also help to ensure the accountability of the state for good governance, environmental regulation and protection of human rights.

A challenge that must be overcome in writing and teaching for those beyond the academy is that research must necessarily be comprehensible to those without a legal background. For many legal scholars, this poses particular challenges which are, however, not insurmountable. Writing for those within the legal field including judges and lawyers will not pose much difficulty, but writing for non-lawyers will be a more arduous task. Writers from the UK take the view that teaching and writing for non-lawyers further marginalizes the field,[31] but it is argued that

---

[31] Fisher et al., 'Maturity and Methodology', 221.

environmental law should not be perceived as an esoteric discipline, and in fact doing so would test the skills of the scholars.

4.3   Interdisciplinary Approaches and Legal Scholarship

In making this wider impact, environmental law scholarship must necessarily move beyond the traditional methodologies of legal scholarship. Environmental laws scholars cannot and should not operate in a vacuum or in silos. In practice, lawyers have crossed the boundaries from a narrow perception of environmental law as regulating and managing natural resources into areas of constitutional law, administrative law and human rights. Scholars, teaching and researching environmental law, have found themselves functioning in areas of intellectual property, consumer protection, international trade and investment, and corporate law to name a few. The pressing need for climate change mitigation and adaptation has also carried researchers into fields such as agriculture, energy and construction law.

Taking environmental law scholarship forward in the context of the human rights–based approach to development as explicated in the SDGs will require a radical rethinking of the field. To impact development and inform litigation, policy and legal reform, environmental law scholarship must take an instrumental approach, described as a conception of 'law as a tool for sustaining changing aspects of social life'.[32] Research on human rights and sustainable development must be carried out, not as a purely academic exercise, but for achieving the targets of the SDGs and harmonizing with human rights commitments. A question that needs to be addressed is whether the predominantly doctrinal research which legal scholars engage in will be sufficient for this purpose.

As noted, environmental law scholars have crossed the boundaries between the various subsets of law. This will not pose much difficulty, and legal research within these subsets can be conducted within the familiar methodology of doctrinal studies. However, to produce action-oriented research that responds to social realities and development, and which proactively impacts both litigation and policy, I argue that to make a practical contribution outside the legal community, environmental law scholars must be receptive to the contribution of other disciplines. This

---

[32] Austin Sarat & Thomas R Kearny (eds), *Law in Everyday Life* (Ann Arbor: University of Michigan Press, 1995), 23.

inevitably poses greater challenges including venturing into alternative methodologies.

Macrory cites three methodologies that should guide environmental law scholarship. These are 'black letter law', requiring intense and critical analysis of legislation and case law, and an activity whose importance should not be underestimated; sociolegal studies, designed to illuminate how law actually works in practice; and what one might describe as policy-orientated scholarship, which explores the contribution that law and legal techniques might make to the resolution of challenging policy issues.'[33]

While doctrinal research or black letter law forms the foundation of legal scholarship, engaging in the other two forms of research advocated by Macrory would require an interdisciplinary approach. The call for interdisciplinarity in the study of law is a long-standing one and[34] although the question is still heavily debated, there seems to be some agreement that legal research would be enhanced by drawing upon the social sciences. It is argued that environmental law scholarship is a subject where interdisciplinarity, and adopting a range of alternative research methodologies, is not only desirable but also necessary to further the instrumentality of the field. Writers engaged in critiquing environmental law scholarship acknowledge that '[t]he most important development in legal scholarship over the past quarter century has been the rise of empirical research', while also noting that '[e]nvironmental law, while not immune from the trend of increasing contributions from empirical research, nonetheless seldom incorporates insights from empirical investigations. An empirical agenda could facilitate reforms to improve environmental law's effectiveness.'[35] Owen and Noblet point out that environmental law in practice is highly interdisciplinary, noting that environmental lawyers work closely with environmental scientists, and environmental law is a response to the findings of scientific research.[36] They argue that a similar level of interdisciplinary engagement in academia would be useful. Given that these comments have been

---

[33] Macrory, 'Maturity and Methodology', 252.

[34] Dave Owen & Caroline Noblet, 'Interdisciplinary Research and Environmental Law' (2015) 41 *Ecology Law Quarterly* 887; William Boyd, Douglas A. Kysar & Jeffrey J. Rachlinski 'Law, Environment, and the "Nondismal" Social Sciences' (2012) 8 *Annual Review Law and Social Sciences* 183.

[35] Fishman & Barbash-Riley, 'Empirical Environmental Law Scholarship'; see also Fisher et al., 'Maturity and Methodology'.

[36] Owen & Noblet, 'Interdisciplinary Research', 887.

made with reference to a relatively narrow view of what environmental law encompasses, it would be even more applicable to a redefined field that includes all aspects of sustainable development founded on human rights. Further, development is a field that is in itself interdisciplinary and requires the input of social sciences, natural sciences and the hard sciences, and law must be included in the discourse.

There is general agreement that legal research on human rights and sustainable development would be greatly enriched by the contribution of social sciences disciplines. De Feyter points out that the process of legalization of human rights established law as the dominant discipline in the field. Lawyers perceived legalization as the final phase in the development of human rights and took the view that only legal rights could qualify as human rights, thus diminishing the relevance of other disciplines to the topic. However, there are limitations to the legal enforcement of human rights, including problems of compliance, the limited impacts of litigation on society and legalization as the ultimate definition of human rights, and such issues could be explained by other disciplines.[37] Social sciences disciplines could also assist the legal scholar in interpretation of texts (which is a primary function of a lawyer) and help to determine whether the protection afforded to individuals operates in reality.[38]

Integrating law with social sciences in human rights research will not be an easy endeavour. Since lawyers by and large have little or no grounding in social sciences research methodologies, collaboration with scholars who do would become necessary, and this carries its own challenges. Further questions include what exactly the collaboration would entail and how it would benefit instrumental legal research on development and rights.

One of the objectives of sociolegal studies, as observed by Macrory, is to illuminate how law works in practice. In a specific context, the SDGs include targets and indicators, which have to be met within the given time frame. Human rights researchers have pointed to the need for statistical data to measure developmental outcomes and determine whether the indicators have been met.[39] Since law is a discipline that is

---

[37] Koen De Feyter, 'Law Meets Sociology in Human Rights' (2011) 40(1) *Development and Society* 45 at 49.

[38] De Feyter, 'Law Meets Sociology', 63.

[39] 'A Human Rights Based Approach to Data: Leaving No One Behind in the 2030 Agenda for Sustainable Development', United Nations Human Rights Office of the High Commissioner, 2015, available at www.ohchr.org/Documents/Issues/HRIndicators/

essentially data deficient, social scientists who work on evidence-based research are better able to develop tools for such data collection. However, writers have noted that there is a tension between law and the social sciences particularly in regards to conceptualization.[40] While lawyers do not generally examine the impacts of laws and legal systems in reality, social scientists who do so may overlook or misinterpret the applicable legal standards, thus affecting both data collection and analysis.[41] The literature also points to the omissions in human rights research, among both legal and social science scholars, and these potential pitfalls will have to be given consideration.[42]

The meeting point of legal scholars and social scientists is obviously not confined to data collection alone. Macrory's third objective of legal research is policy-oriented scholarship. This is another endeavour in which collaboration between lawyers and social scientists would be beneficial, as the law must respond to the social context within which it is located. Here too the potential obstacles to such collaboration would be the diverse ways in which different disciplines understand and prioritize development and rights, and barriers of conceptualization, norms and methodologies would need to be overcome.

Examples of interdisciplinary efforts in law and policymaking in non-environmental fields in Sri Lanka include criminal law and children's rights, where multidisciplinary teams of legal and medical personnel and sociologists brainstormed to reach agreement on the law relating to the age of consent and statutory rape, and the minimum age of marriage. It is clear that the policy on such issues required the contribution of all three areas of expertise, since the ages of consent and marriage have social and health implications which form the rationale for the law. Similarly, in the fields of environment and development and in the context of the SDGs, the input of a range of disciplines becomes necessary to guide law and

GuidanceNoteonApproachtoData.pdf; 'Human Rights and Data, Tools and Resources for Sustainable Development', The Danish Institute for Human Rights, 2017, available at www.humanrights.dk/sites/humanrights.dk/files/media/dokumenter/udgivelser/sdg/data_report_2016.pdf.

[40] Paola Cesarini & Shareen Hertel, 'Interdisciplinary Approaches to Human Rights Scholarship in Latin America' (2005) 37 *Journal of Latin American Studies* 793 at 795.

[41] Fons Coomans, Fred Grünfeld & Menno T. Kamminga, 'Methods of Human Rights Research: A Primer' (2010) 32(1) *Human Rights Quarterly* 179 at 181.

[42] Ibid. 181; Russel Lawrence Barsh, 'Measuring Human Rights: Problems of Methodology and Purpose' (1993) 15(1) *Human Rights Quarterly* 87.

policy in context. Those needed include historians and anthropologists who can decipher concepts of sustainability which are intrinsic in countries such as Sri Lanka so that they can be adapted and applied to present-day scenarios. Justice C. G. Weeramantry drew upon 'some wisdom from the past relating to sustainable development' and 'principles of traditional legal systems' in elucidating the principle of sustainable development in the present day, citing the works of novelists, historians and engineers to support his thesis.[43] Legal scholars and practitioners conversant with disciplines beyond their own can potentially contribute a diversity of 'worldviews, biases and heuristics'[44] to the development of current paradigms of development and equity.

5 Conclusion

Environmental law in Sri Lanka has moved beyond regulation and management of the environment and into the realm of sustainable development and human rights. This direction has been underscored by the international framework on development founded on human rights, as explicated in the SDGs. This chapter has argued that to maintain its relevance, environmental law scholarship in Sri Lanka must keep pace with these developments and must positively influence law and policy reform for national development and social change. In doing so, such scholarship should not be confined by a narrow definition of what environmental law entails but should proactively contribute to the continuous redefining of the subject to meet current realities of environmental sustainability, human development and rights. To ensure that environmental law scholarship has the widest possible impact, both within and outside the legal community, scholars must also move beyond the familiar methodologies of legal research and engage not only with other relevant areas of law but also with non-law disciplines including the social sciences. It is by doing so that environmental law scholarship, far from being marginal, will acquire a distinctive relevance.

---

[43] Gabcikovo-Nagymaros Project (Hungary/Slovakia) (Separate Opinion of Vice President Weeramantry) [1997] ICJ Rep 7, at 94. This trend was also followed in a seminal case in Sri Lanka where the court laid down guidelines for the state in managing natural resources; *Bulankulame* v. *The Secretary, Ministry of Industrial Development and Others* [2000] 3 *Sri Lanka Law Reports* 243.

[44] Note the comments of Pedersen, 'Modest Pragmatic Lessons', 119.

Bibliography

Aagaard, Todd S., 'Environmental Law as a Legal Field: An Inquiry in Legal Taxonomy' (2010) 95(2) *Cornell Law Review* 221.

Çeşarini, Paola & Hertel, Shareen, 'Interdisciplinary Approaches to Human Rights Scholarship in Latin America' (2005) 37 *Journal of Latin American Studies* 793.

De Feyter, Koen, 'Law Meets Sociology in Human Rights' (2011) 40(1) *Development and Society* 45.

Dernbach, John C., 'The Essential and Growing Role of Legal Education in Achieving Sustainability' (2011) 60 (3) *Journal of Legal Education* 489.

Du Pisani, Jacobus A., 'Sustainable Development – Historical Roots of the Concept' (2006) 3(2) *Environmental Sciences* 83.

Fisher, Elizabeth, Lange, Bettina, Scotford, Eloise & Carlarne, Cinnamon, 'Maturity and Methodology: Starting a Debate about Environmental Law Scholarship' (2009) 21(2) *Journal of Environmental Law* 213.

Fishman, Robert L. & Barbash-Riley, Lydia, 'Empirical Environmental Law Scholarship' (2018) 44 *Ecology Law Quarterly* 101.

Guneratne, Camena, 'Using Constitutional Provisions to Advance Environmental Justice – Some Reflections on Sri Lanka' (2015) 11(2) *Law, Environment and Development Journal*, available at www.lead-journal.org.

Knox, John H., 'Human Rights, Environmental Protection, and the Sustainable Development Goals' (2015) 24(3) *Washington International Law Journal* 517.

Macrory, Richard, 'Maturity and Methodology': A Personal Reflection' (2009) 21 (2) *Journal of Environmental Law* 251.

Owen, Dave & Noblet, Caroline, Interdisciplinary Research and Environmental Law, (2015) 41 *Ecology Law Quarterly* 887, available at http://scholarship.law.berkeley.edu/elq/vol41/iss4/2.

Pedersen, Ole W., 'Modest Pragmatic Lessons for a Diverse and Incoherent Environmental Law (2013) 33 (1) *Oxford Journal of Legal Studies* 103.

Sarat, Austin & Kearny, Thomas R. (eds) *Law in Everyday Life* (Ann Arbor: University of Michigan Press, 1995).

President Trump, the New Chicago School and the Future of Environmental Law and Scholarship

JASON J. CZARNEZKI AND SARAH SCHINDLER[†]

I want to say thank you to each and every one of you, because the EPA touches on the lives of every single American every single day. You help make sure that the air we breathe, the water we drink, the foods we eat are safe. You protect the environment not just for our children but their children. President Barack Obama, remarks to US Environmental Protection Agency (EPA) staff.[1]

Environmental Protection, what they do is a disgrace. Donald Trump, speaking about EPA.[2]

We're going local. Have to go local. Environmental protection – we waste all of this money. We're going to bring that back to the states . . . We are going to cut many of the agencies. Donald Trump, speaking about EPA.[3]

1 Introduction

NEPA, RCRA, ESA, CWA, CAA, FIFRA, TSCA.[4] What do all of these acronyms have in common? They are federal environmental statutes that

---

[†] We wish to thank Audrey Friedrichsen, Katherine Fiedler, Bridget Crawford, the Pace Law Faculty's Summer 10/10 Series, and the Colloquium for Environmental Scholarship participants for their insights on this project.

[1] Barack Obama, "Remarks by the President to EPA staff," The White House, January 10, 2012, available at www.whitehouse.gov/the-press-office/2012/01/10/remarks-president-epa-staff.

[2] Diane Regas, "A Warning for Donald Trump: Gutting EPA Would Be Harder – And More Perilous – Than You Think," Forbes, November 17, 2016, available at www.forbes.com /sites/edfenergyexchange/2016/11/17/a-warning-for-donald-rump-gutting-epa-would-be -harder-and-more-perilous-than-you-think/#1910edb32d92.

[3] Tom Shoop, "Donald Trump's Plan for Cutting Government," Government Executive, February 26, 2016, available at www.govexec.com/federal-news/fedblog/2016/02/donald-trumps-plan-cutting-government/126242/.

[4] National Environmental Policy Act of 1969 (NEPA), 42 USC §§ 4321–47 (1969); Resource Conservation and Recovery Act of 1976 (RCRA), 42 USC §§ 6901-92k (1976); Endangered Species Act of 1973 (ESA), 16 USC §§ 1531–44 (1973); Federal Water Pollution Control

were originally passed by Congress in the 1960s and 1970s. (Yes, to the surprise of many, President Nixon was the "Environmental President.") This influential group of federal environmental statutes has traditionally defined the substantive boundaries of the field of environmental law. They are the statutes that have historically made up the bulk of the standard environmental law curriculum, and many environmental law attorneys have focused on these statutes for their entire careers.[5] However, given the lack of new federal environmental legislation over the past forty years (at least in the traditional sense)[6] and the establishment of new research techniques, scholars, practitioners, and politicians have begun to redefine the field of environmental law: they have expanded the substantive areas that it includes, and the tools used to achieve its desired goals.

Recent presidents including Bill Clinton, G. W. Bush, and Barack Obama have refined how environmental law has been enacted and carried out. For example, due to Congress's decades-long inaction on environmental issues and in the interest of abating the climate crisis,[7] President Obama employed both administrative law techniques and his executive authority to shape the implementation and enforcement of our existing environmental laws: the Clean Power Plan was created under the Clean Air Act (CAA); the Waters of the US Rule was created under the Clean Water Act; and the Paris Agreement was entered into under the president's plenary powers to manage foreign affairs and make executive agreements, the CAA, and existing treaties such as the 1992 Framework Convention on Climate Change. These actions represent expansive readings of the underlying statutes and are being challenged by those who want these statutes and powers to be read narrowly.

Indeed, under President Trump, the scope of public environmental law will most certainly narrow. Trump called Obama's remark, that

---

Act (Clean Water Act, CWA), 33 USC §§ 1251–1388 (1972); Clean Air Act (CAA), 42 USC §§ 7401-7671q (1970); Federal Insecticide, Fungicide, and Rodenticide Act (FIFRA), 7 USC §§ 136-36y (1910); Toxic Substances Control Act (TSCA), 15 USC §§ 2601–97 (1976).

[5] When one of the authors of this chapter worked at a large national law firm in the Environmental Law practice group, she interacted primarily with these federal statutes.

[6] See David W. Case, "The Lost Generation: Environmental Regulatory Reform in the Era of Congressional Abdication" (2014) 25 *Duke Environmental Law & Policy Forum* 49.

[7] We note exceptions, among others, of the Clean Air Amendments of 1990, the reforms of the Toxic Substances Control Act, 15 USC§§ 2601–97 (1976), in The Frank R. Lautenberg Chemical Safety for the 21st Century Act, Pub. L. No. 114-182, 130 Stat. 448 (2016), and the Microbead-Free Waters Act of 2015, Pub. L. No. 114-114, 129 Stat. 3129 (2015).

global climate change is one of the greatest threats facing the United States and the world, "one of the dumbest statements that [he's] ever heard,"[8] and he has expressed a desire to diminish the role of the EPA and withdraw many of Obama's environmental regulations, with the help of EPA Administrator Scott Pruitt. Thus, it seems likely that the future of environmental law will depend not upon traditional federal command-and-control legislation or executive branch maneuvering, but instead upon activating environmentalism through expanded substantive areas and innovative regulatory techniques that fall outside the existing, traditional norms of environmental law and legal scholarship.

This chapter is an attempt to acknowledge this monumental change, recognizing that these barriers to traditional environmental regulation have and will continue to force an expansion in the boundaries of environmental law and legal scholarship, and in our approaches to environmental regulation. Specifically, the chapter suggests the following in response to the lack of new "traditional" environmental law: (1) environmental law will continue to expand as a discipline and scholarly area of inquiry to include new subfields outside the traditional fields of air quality, water quality, and pollution control to attack environmental problems;[9] and (2) environmental law will continue to focus on alternative methods of environmental regulation by expanding regulatory techniques, expanding the notion of what can be considered a regulated entity beyond that of large institutional stationary sources, and – in light of the new presidential administration – moving away from public environmental regulation and toward private environmental governance.

Section 2 of this chapter considers the expanding notion of what constitutes environmental law. It explores the ways in which environmental lawyers and scholars have expanded substantive boundaries to include subfields outside of the traditional areas of air and water pollution, toxics, and natural resources law to include energy law, local land use law, food and agriculture law, global environmental law, and animal law.

---

[8] Tal Kopn & Heather Goldin, "Donald Trump: Obama Climate Change Remarks One of 'Dumbest Things' Uttered in History," CNN, November 30, 2015, available at www.cnn .com/2015/11/30/politics/donald-trump-obama-climate-change-dumbest-thing/.

[9] Ours is not an attempt to create a restatement of existing environmental law or a taxonomy of environmental law. See Tracy Hester et al., "Restating Environmental Law" (2015) 39 *Columbia Journal of Environmental Law* 1; Todd Aagaard, "Environmental Law as a Legal Field: An Inquiry in Legal Taxonomy" (2010) 95 *Cornell Law Review* 221.

Section 3 considers the ways in which environmental law scholars, lawyers, and policy makers (both politicians and some industry players) are pursuing alternative methods by which to regulate environmental harms. While this change has been building for a number of years, it seems to have taken on new urgency in light of the Trump administration's views regarding the role of the federal government in protecting the environment. A new wave of scholars has been seeking to broaden the environmental law field beyond the methods employed by the aforementioned traditional federal statutes. These new regulatory techniques are part of what Lawrence Lessig describes as the "New Chicago School."[10] The idea is that federal, state, and local governments are not limited to traditional lawmaking to achieve regulatory goals; rather, they can be more creative in their environmental regulatory approaches by considering the way that law interacts with other behavioral controls such as markets, social norms, and architecture.

Section 4 considers more specifically the role that the Trump administration will have in changing the way that policymakers and advocates approach environmental regulation. Here, we suggest that we might see a return to the "Old Chicago School" methods. While the New School has urged law to operate indirectly and in conjunction with other forms of regulation, the Old School looked to alternatives to law; it sought ways to regulate in the absence of law. Here, we see an important role for private individuals and private industry to do more through the use of these alternative regulatory approaches (and for legal scholars to write about them) even if law and lawmakers turn their backs on the project of environmental protection.

This chapter asserts that the environmental field is changing and expanding – with respect to the substance that is being taught and written about in the legal academy, the regulatory devices that governments are using, and the role of private actors and lower levels of government – as a response to a lack of federal congressional initiative on environmental issues. These approaches will likely continue, given the Trump administration's apparent view that environmental regulation should not be the purview of the federal government. This change in environmental law is real and increasingly necessary. And by acknowledging that there are now more answers to the question "what is environmental law and what tools do we use to impose it," we can more confidently navigate the new

---

[10] Lawrence Lessig, "The New Chicago School" (1998) 27 *Journal of Legal Studies* 661.

administration and its potential lack of interest in environmental protection.

2 Expanding the Substantive Boundaries of a Discipline

The traditional canon of environmental law has included the subjects of air pollution, water, toxics, and endangered species under a series of federal statutes primarily passed and amended more than four decades ago, such as the Clean Air Act, Clean Water Act and the Comprehensive Environmental Response, Compensation, and Liability Act (CERCLA). Even today, we are dealing with modern-day environmental problems like climate change and wetlands protection through relatively old statutes like the Clean Air Act (via the Clean Power Plan) or Clean Water Act (given the Water of the US Rule), as attempts to expand or substantially revise federal environmental law have not come to pass (e.g., failure of the Clean Water Restoration Act bill to gain sufficient congressional support).

The substantive evolution of the canon in adding new subfields is a result of the lack of new environmental statutes in the traditional fields (e.g., air and water), as well as the realization that the traditional subfields, without revision, cannot handle modern environmental problems. To end this stagnation, scholars and policy makers now see a need to be creative in expanding the field and, as discussed in Section 3, the lens through which one views how the government, private entities, and individuals can and should create environmental reform. This section lays out the substantive subfields that have grown beyond the Eastern US focus of air, water, and other forms of pollution law, and the Western US public lands and natural resources law tradition.

Perhaps the first subfield to become firmly planted in the environmental and natural resources law tradition was energy law. In light of global climate change, interests in greenhouse gases, renewable energy, fracking, and energy distribution grids have expanded the field's scope beyond oil, gas, and electricity rates. And in 2013, the Association of American Law Schools retitled its Natural Resources Law section to include Energy Law. In other words, energy law was an early expansion to the discipline of environmental law that we now have more recently seen in the areas that follow.

The current wave of the expansion of environmental law first includes the incorporation of land use law, which has itself grown to include urban planning and sustainability. For example, a number of land use scholars have written about sustainability devices like green building, the redevelopment of shrinking cities, development and redevelopment in disaster zones, and tools for adaptation and mitigation that local governments can use in the face of climate change.[11] There has also been a rise in scholarship about smart growth, and the recognition that dense development is sustainable development. All of these land use and planning tools can create more environmentally friendly places and are a key part of this new, expanded field of environmental law.

Second, with the rise of "locavores" and books like Michael Pollan's *Omnivore's Dilemma*, food and agriculture law and policy have risen to national prominence and interest among law students and law scholars. Two new casebooks on food and agriculture law have been published,[12] with at least one more on the way, and (Master of Laws (LLM)/certificate programs and food law centers and clinics have proliferated in American law schools.[13] There has also been a rise in food law scholarship and conferences, and there is now a food law professor listserv.

Third, there has been a transition from traditional international environmental law, focusing on international agreements like the Montreal Protocol, to "global environmental law."[14] Environmental law must now contend with the globalization of environmental harm and the democratization of

---

[11] See, e.g., Keith Hirokawa, "Local Planning for Wind Power: Using Programmatic Environmental Impact Review to Facilitate Development" (2010) 33 *Zoning and Planning Law Report* 1; Keith Hirokawa & Ira Gonzalez, "Regulating Vacant Property" (2010) 42 *Urban Lawyer* 627; Sarah Schindler, "The Future of Abandoned Big Box Stores: Legal Solutions to the Legacies of Poor Planning Decisions" (2012) 83 *University of Colorado Law Review* 471 (2012); Sarah Schindler, "Following Industry's LEED: Municipal Adoption of Private Green Building Standards" (2010) 62 *Florida Law Review* 285; Lisa Grow Sun, "Smart Growth in Dumb Places: Sustainability, Disaster, and the Future of the American City" (2011) *Brigham Young University Law Review* 2157.

[12] Susan Schneider, *Food, Farming, and Sustainability: Readings in Agricultural Law* (Durham, NC: Carolina Academic Press, 2011); Mary Jane Angelo, Jason J. Czarnezki, & William S. Eubanks II, *Food, Agriculture and Environmental Law* (Washington, DC: Environmental Law Institute, 2013).

[13] Richard Lazarus, "Food Law Is the Next Great Area for Environmental Litigation" (2016) 33(1) *The Environmental Forum* ("For example, Vermont boasts of a degree in food law; Pace has a joint food law initiative with NRDC; UCLA has an exciting program for Food Law and Policy Studies; and even my own Harvard Law School has an active food law program, including a food law clinic").

[14] "[G]rowing international linkages are blurring the traditional divisions between private and public law and domestic and international law, promoting integration and harmonization," and leading to the creation of "global environmental law." Tseming Yang & Robert V. Percival, "The Emergence of Global Environmental Law" (2009) 36 *Ecology Law Quarterly* 615 at 616 and 664 (noting further that "Global environmental law is an evolving set of substantive principles, tools and concepts derived from elements of

pollution sources,[15] and "environmental legal norms have become increasingly internationalized."[16] This blurring has occurred not only in sectors of law but also in substantive environmental issues and processes to ameliorate environmental degradation. However, the globalization of environmental law and policy is not without irony. Pollution sources remain domestic and increasingly localized despite international impacts. Local cultures of consumption have spread throughout the globe. These factors have necessitated international cooperation on environmental and public health issues, even in traditionally domestic fields like food safety, and have forced policy makers and scholars alike to renew their focus on the developing world.

Fifth, animal law, with the help of the emergence of food and agriculture law, has developed as a subfield within the discipline. Animal law courses are now taught at most law schools, and dedicated animal law journals are filled with articles addressing the way that animals are currently treated under the law (mostly as property) and the protections (or, more often, lack thereof) that they are afforded. While much of animal law focuses on the animals themselves, there is also a tie to environmental law and sustainability, especially with respect to the Concentrated Animal Feeding Operations (CAFOs) in which most animals that are raised for food in the United States are kept.[17] These CAFOs result in runoff, contribute to global warming, and result in land use conflicts as development intrudes into formerly agricultural land. Some similar issues are raised by Right-to-Farm laws.[18]

Finally, we suspect, and perhaps predict, that other related fields will be accepted as subfields into the environmental law nexus and incorporated into the mainstream curriculum and legal scholarship. These fields might include sustainable business/corporate social responsibility, community and economic development, public health law, and international trade and the environment.

---

national and international environmental law. Yet, it also represents a significant shift in the evolution of environmental law field").

[15] Jason J. Czarnezki, *Everyday Environmentalism: Law, Nature, and Individual Behavior* (Washington, DC: Environmental Law Institute, 2011), 141 (citing Timothy P. Duane, "Environmental Planning and Policy in a Post-Rio World" (1992) 7 *Berkeley Planning Journal* 27 at 31).

[16] Yang & Percival, "The Emergence of Global Environmental Law," 615.

[17] See, e.g., David N. Cassuto, "The CAFO Hothouse: Climate Change, Industrial Agriculture and the Law," Animals & Society Institute Policy Paper, 2010.

[18] Right-to-Farm laws intersect with nuisance and zoning law and are typically invoked when there are use conflicts in a given area.

While some traditionalists might cling to a vision of environmental law as defined by the aforementioned group of federal statutes, many emerging scholars and lawyers agree that the field has grown bigger in the way described in this section. Further, not only have we witnessed an expansion in the substantive nature of that which constitutes the field of environmental law, but we have also experienced growth in the nature of the tools that we use to protect the environment. The next section will address that change.

3   The New Chicago School and Regulatory Expansion

A new wave of environmental law scholars has taken a page from the New Chicago School. These scholars look, from a theoretical standpoint, to alternative forms of regulation such as shifting social norms and using the law to modify the architecture of the built environment to change behavior.[19] Lessig describes the New Chicago School as follows:

> Both the old school and new share an approach to regulation that focuses on regulators other than the law. Both, that is, aim to understand structures of regulation outside law's direct effect. Where they differ is in the lessons that they draw from such alternative structures. From the fact that forces outside law regulate, and regulate better than law, the old school concludes that law should step aside. This is not the conclusion of the new school. The old school identifies alternative regulators as reasons for less activism. The new school identifies alternatives as additional tools for a more effective activism. The moral of the old school is that the state should do less. The hope of the new is that the state can do more.[20]

The alternative regulatory approaches that Lessig cites – markets, norms, and architecture – do not fall completely outside the scope of law but instead may be embraced by and used in conjunction with law.[21] For example, the law can be used to regulate markets, and markets then create

---

[19]   See, e.g., Sarah Schindler, "Architectural Exclusion" (2015) 124 *Yale Law Journal* 1934; Katrina Fischer Kuh, "When Government Intrudes: Regulating Individual Behaviors That Harm the Environment" (2012) 61 *Duke Law Journal* 1111.

[20]   Lessig, "The New Chicago School," 661.

[21]   Ibid., 672 ("These techniques of direct and indirect regulation are the tools of any modern regulatory regime. The aim of the New Chicago School is to speak comprehensively about these tools – about how they function together, about how they interact, and about how law might affect their influence. These alternative constraints beyond law do not exist independent of the law; they are in part the product of the law. Thus the question is never "law or something else." The question instead is always to what extent is a particular constraint a function of the law, and more importantly, to what extent can the law effectively change that constraint.").

change; the law can require educational programs that influence societal and industry norms; zoning laws can require certain features of the built environment that result in control over individual behavior.

Complementing the substantive boundaries discussed in Section 2, procedurally the new environmental law paradigm considers how law is (and should be) shaped, how behavior is altered, and it sometimes seeks to measure impacts empirically.[22] In other words, government action can and should influence norms (perhaps in a much stronger "push" rather than a Sunstein nudge as discussed in the Conclusion), take advantage of the rise of incentives and markets, and think differently about regulation. Thus, in addition to substantive boundary pushing, environmental law is now embracing alternative forms of regulations and expanding the scope of traditional government regulation. This section discusses the Old School and describes the New Chicago School and its application to environmental law.

3.1 The Old School and the New School

As it is traditionally understood, the Chicago School of legal thought asserts that economic efficiency should be the goal of law and policy. This well-known school of law and economics grew to prominence when many of its foremost proponents were professors or affiliated faculty at the University of Chicago School of Law.[23] Law and economics came to dominate discussions of legal theory and became a key framework through which many scholars began to analyze law and policy. This view also had a dramatic impact on Supreme Court opinions. When most legal academics hear the "Chicago School," this is the history that comes to mind.

---

[22] Lisa Bernstein et al., "The New Chicago School: Myth or Reality?" (1998) 5 *University of Chicago Law School Roundtable* 1 at 11 ("Meares: Now, a final word on all this. One thing I can say about the New Chicago School, if there is one, is that when you are working with norms, you have to be very much concerned about empirical questions. It is very difficult to make predictions about what is going to happen. It is very labor-intensive. A very important part of this work is not just theorizing about the ways in which the standard conception of economics might be wrong, but also a willingness to go out there and do the legwork in the eleventh district in the city of Chicago, in the highest crime district in the city, and see what's actually really going on.").

[23] Robin I. Mordfin & Marsha Ferziger Nagorsky, "Chicago and Law and Economics: A History" (2011) Fall Edition, *University of Chicago Alumni Magazine*, available at www .law.uchicago.edu/alumni/magazine/fall11/lawandecon-history.

Lawrence Lessig coined the term "New Chicago School" in a talk given at a 1998 conference on "Social Norms, Social Meaning, and the Economic Analysis of Law." According to Lessig's description, the Old Chicago School is more than mere law and economics. As he envisions it, the Old School focused broadly on seeking out alternative regulatory tools that could serve as substitutes for law. Of course, law and economics were an important piece of this, but the Old School more broadly sought to supplant law with these other forms of regulation, including markets, norms, and architecture.

As Lessig describes it, the New School examines these same tools but recognizes that they are inherently intertwined with law. We can, and should, use law not just to pass statutes or to ban certain activities but to create laws that will have the effect of altering norms, markets, and architecture. In this way, Lessig recognizes that governments can do more than merely "regulate" in the traditional sense. They can look to other forms of regulation to alter the behavior of the governed. Environmental law and environmental policy makers have been doing this for many years.

3.2   The New Chicago School and the Role of Law

The New Chicago School could be viewed as a new version of law and economics.[24] It does not seek to displace law with alternative forms of regulation; rather, it views each of those alternative forms of regulation as *subject* to law.[25] As Lessig noted, "Law can select among these various techniques in selecting the end it wants to achieve. Which it selects depends on the return from each."[26] The key is matching the appropriate regulatory tool to the behavior or harm that should be abated.[27]

One question that this chapter seeks to answer is, does the New Chicago School exist? Well-known scholars like Eric Posner, Richard

---

[24] See Bernstein et al., "The New Chicago School," 1 (wherein moderator Richard Epstein included himself as part of the "old law and economics" and referred to the New Chicago School as the "new law and economics").

[25] Lessig, "The New Chicago School," 666. See also Lawrence Lessig, *Code: Version 2.0* (New York: Basic Books, 2006), 123 (noting the regulatory constraints of the law, social norms, the market, and architecture).

[26] Lessig, "The New Chicago School," 672.

[27] Czarnezki, *Everyday Environmentalism*; James Salzman, "Teaching Policy Instrument Choice in Environmental Law: The Five P's" (2013) 3 *Duke Environmental Law and Policy Forum* 363.

Epstein, and Randy Picker were initially extremely skeptical of its existence,[28] blaming its label on a Jeffrey Rosen article in *The New Yorker*.[29] Indeed, the perception in 1998 was that this New School lacked coherent methodology.[30] To this point, Posner stated the following at a roundtable at the University of Chicago Law School:

> Now, I'm going to tell a "New Chicago School" story about the New Chicago School. This is my prediction, which will occur, I would say, with twenty percent probability. Rosen chose to write about a handful of scholars [including Ellickson, Kahan, and Lessig, who are still leaders in this area of social norms literature] when a hundred could have been included in his article. This, of course, immediately engaged all the insecurities and jealousies that academics are famous for. What might happen now is that some scholars will write articles charging that there is nothing coherent, interesting, or new about the New Chicago School. But in order to make this argument, they are going to have to describe what the New Chicago School is. And as they describe it, gradually the School will take on meaning. Some will be embarrassed to be identified with such ideas and disassociate themselves. Other people will join the School and defend it. Gradually, over time, the New Chicago School will develop into

---

[28] Bernstein et al., "The New Chicago School," 30–31 ("Audience Member 9: Did any of you tell Jeffrey Rosen that there was no New Chicago School, or did he miss it? Epstein: He did not ask. Not only that, you've got to understand he did not quite understand the old Harvard school. His description of Langdell was, to put it mildly, wrong. One of the reasons you misconstrue novelty is you don't understand the past. If you haven't read the classical authors, you can describe them in two sentences and get them wrong. It's not necessarily perverse, but it is inaccurate. Picker: The story here is no school, no story. He's a journalist building up a story, and if the existence of a Chicago school is a useful fiction for doing that, I'm all in favor of it.").

[29] Jeffrey Rosen, "The Social Police: Following the Law, Because You'd Be Too Embarrassed Not To," *The New Yorker*, October 20 and 27, 1997.

[30] Bernstein et al., "The New Chicago School," 12–13 ("Posner: Now, what's the New Chicago School? Many of you know that the term was coined by Larry Lessig at a symposium last spring. My view is that there is very little to this school. There was very little at that time, and there is very little now. First of all, there is no coherence in methodology. As you can see, I like to use game theory, Tracey likes to use sociology, Randy uses computer-generated models, Dan uses a variety of sources. Second, there is no unity in normative implications. We all have different ideas about what one should do. It's not like the old Chicago School, or other schools, in which there was an ideological and normative label that was easily attached to it. The only thing that unifies us is subject matter. We all talk about social norms, although we use the term in different ways. We talk about how the government can affect people's beliefs. But people have been talking about these things for ten, twenty, thirty, forty, a hundred, a thousand years. So at the time that Lessig wrote this comment, my view was that his claim would die a deserved death almost immediately. And I think it would have except for the intervention of the all-powerful media.").

a coherent body of thought. So when that happens, there will be a New Chicago School.[31]

We suggest that Posner was right. This coherent body of thought is developing in the field of environmental law and has been embraced by new scholars, yet it remains in need of further definition. This chapter seeks to ensure that the "Posner Prophecy" comes true.

3.3   Application to Environmental Law

At least two components of the New Chicago School are gaining traction as it relates to environmental regulation and scholarship: (1) the expansion of the notion of regulated entities to include individuals and (2) the activation and changing of social norms through regulation. Another component progresses beyond these two and will be necessary due to the failure of public national action in the environmental arena: (3) the expansion of avenues for regulation such as local activism and private governance through public action, private initiatives, and public-private partnerships.

First, the individual can and should be viewed as a regulated entity in the context of environmental protection. In recent years, legal scholars and local governments have expressed interest in examining individual behavior and its impacts on the environment, and some have gone so far as to begin treating the individual as a polluter.[32] This is new because traditional environmental law has thought of large-scale industries and institutions as the polluters that should be regulated as opposed to individuals. The law is still struggling with whether and how to regulate individual actors and other small sources of pollution. For example, lawn mowers, leaf blowers, and watering hoses all seem puny when examined individually. However, individual environmentally harmful actions in the aggregate have significant environmental impacts; some states and localities have recognized this and have decided that more must be done to target regulation on these behaviors.[33] For example, anti-idling

---

[31] Bernstein et al., "The New Chicago School," 13.

[32] Michael Vandenbergh, "Order without Social Norms: How Personal Norm Activation Can Protect the Environment" (2005) 99 *Northwestern University Law Review* 1101; Michael Vandenbergh, "Individual as Polluter" (2005) *Environmental Law Reporter*, available at http://papers.ssrn.com/sol3/papers.cfm?abstract_id=847804.

[33] See Czarnezki, *Everyday Environmentalism*; Katrina Fischer Kuh, "Personal Environmental Information: The Promise and Perils of the Emerging Capacity to Identify Individual Environmental Harms" (2012) 65 *Vanderbilt Law Review* 1565.

regulation has been proposed by some legal scholars as a method to dramatically reduce carbon emissions.[34]

An advantage of direct regulation of individual action is that it makes the costs of regulation more transparent, though this may invite public or political resistance.[35] This resistance, however, should not be presumed to present an insurmountable obstacle to the use of direct mandates to regulate environmentally significant individual behaviors,[36] especially since such behaviors have significant environmental costs.

Second, environmental law can influence social norms. Jeffrey Rosen's 1997 article in *The New Yorker*, "The Social Police: Following the Law, Because You'd Be Too Embarrassed Not To," notes that social-norms theorists favor enlisting the government in ambitious programs of creating new norms, noting Ellickson's conclusion from *Order Without Law*: "People frequently resolve their disputes in a cooperative fashion without paying any attention to the laws."[37]

While Rosen described the movement as "still defining itself," he noted that it might "change the way we think about law and regulation in the twenty-first century."[38] Policy makers are already using both small-scale and large-scale regulation to shift norms leading to behavior change. Examples include requiring calorie-menu labeling, the installation of bike lanes, and allowing chickens in residential backyards. Often, major government initiatives are needed to change social norms. For example, recycling norms did not emerge from primarily bottom-up, informal, causal processes; governments passed laws in this area.[39] That said, norm change is often insufficient without the development of adequate and convenient infrastructure (what Lessig has called architecture). "In fact, increasing convenience is so effective that individual commitment toward the desired behavior bears little relationship to whether someone

---

[34] Michael P. Vandenbergh, Jack Barkenbus, & Jonathan Gilligan, "Individual Carbon Emissions: The Low-Hanging Fruit" (2008) 55 *University of California Los Angeles Law Review* 1701 at 1723–30 (calculating the environmental benefits of changes in idling behavior and describing the use of anti-idling laws in conjunction with public information campaigns to reduce vehicle idling).

[35] Katrina Fischer Kuh, "When Government Intrudes: Regulating Individual Behaviors That Harm the Environment" (2012) 61 *Duke Law Journal* 1111 at 1125–26.

[36] Ibid.

[37] Rosen, "The Social Police," 172–73.

[38] Ibid. 172.

[39] Steven Hetcher, "Norms as Limited Resources" (2005) 35 *Environmental Law Reporter* 10770.

will engage in it."[40] That said, norm change is difficult and still not totally understood.[41] This empirical quandary forces us to question what role public law should directly play in norm change, and at what level and to what extent public law should simply influence and promote private and local innovation.

Third, due to the challenges of regulating large-scale individual action and the limits of norm change, two alternative avenues of regulation must be pursued: (1) encouraging actions by local governments that are in a better position to understand and change individuals in their communities and (2) promoting and supporting private environmental governance (e.g., sustainable business, corporate social responsibility, green and sustainable public procurement) through both public law, private initiatives, and public-private partnerships. The advantage of these options is that, while they help progressive values of environmental protection, they promote traditionally conservative values of supporting local control and promoting business innovation.

Local communities are key to norm change, especially in a large and diverse country like the United States:

> In a heterogeneous liberal democracy, there's often too much disagreement about social norms at the national level for the federal government to try to manipulate values without taking sides in the culture wars. This means that norms cascades of the future may come from partnerships between local governments and the traditional sources of moral values: local community groups, schools, and churches. And they may involve activities that bear little resemblance to traditional law enforcement.[42]

In particular, Katrina Fischer Kuh suggests that local governments are the key players in capturing individual harms, often through changes in physical architecture and through the use of traditional regulation to change social norms.[43]

---

[40] "The manner in which the expressive function of law works to transform norms is not clearly understood." Ann Carlson, "Recycling Norms" (2001) 89 *California Law Review* 1231 at 1236.

[41] Andrew Green, "You Can't Pay Them Enough: Subsidies, Environmental Law, and Social Norms" (2006) 30 *Harvard Environmental Law Review* 407 at 431.

[42] Rosen, "The Social Police," 180–81.

[43] Katrina Fischer Kuh, "Capturing Individual Harms" (2011) 35 *Harvard Environmental Law Review* 155 at 166 ("The capacity of local governments to change the physical architecture of communities is an important way that local governments influence individual lifestyles and behaviors and the environmental harms they occasion. This also supports local involvement in climate mitigation efforts. However, while this Article incorporates local control over the built environment into its analysis, the

While individuals should be regulated entities as discussed earlier, private environmental governance in the corporate sector (what might be thought of as social norms for industry) will also need to gain traction, especially given the large carbon footprint of industrial activities.[44] Michael Vandenbergh defines private environmental governance as "actions taken by non-governmental entities that are designed to achieve traditionally governmental ends such as managing the exploitation of common pool resources, increasing the provision of public goods, reducing environmental externalities, or more justly distributing environmental amenities."[45] Importantly, he includes private standard-setting activities such as global private and labeling certification systems for consumer products and "bilateral standard-setting in the definition of private environmental governance, such as when private supply chain contracts include provisions that are designed to reduce the environmental harms arising from the suppliers' operations."[46] The inadequacy of public environmental law has led to a rise of certification systems like those established by the Marine Stewardship Council and Forest Stewardship Council, as well as private labeling schemes like dolphin safe tuna.[47]

Companies are additionally moving now toward true cost accounting of their supply chain and developing life-cycle costing methodologies, at least at some points in the supply chain to measure their carbon and environmental footprints, as well as to meet consumer demand for more environmentally friendly products. Also, public law can promote more eco-friendly supply chains and innovation in product development as, for example, recently done in the new European Union Public Sector Directive that encourages the purchasing of sustainable goods and services by public institutions:

> It is no longer sufficient to assume that government is the only or even the best actor for many environmental problems. The available environmental instruments are not limited to those that governments have the legal

Article focuses on two different types of regulation of behavior: norm management and direct mandates."). Ibid. 170 ("Significantly local governments possess community information important for ascertaining which concrete norms are feasible to activate and translate into behavior change in a community.").

[44] Michael P. Vandenberg, "Reconceptualizing the Future of Environmental Law: The Role of Private Climate Governance" (2015) 31 *Pace Environmental Law Review* 382.

[45] Michael P. Vandenbergh, "Private Environmental Governance" (2013) 99 *Cornell Law Review* 129 at 146–48.

[46] Ibid.

[47] Ibid. 161–62

authority, expertise, and political will to implement. Positive law and government action are still very important, but private environmental governance is surprisingly important for many of the most pressing environmental problems. The key conceptual step offered by private governance is that public action is not the only way to achieve public ends. This is a deceptively simple proposition, but it is remarkable how often the question asked in public debates is "what can government do?" The existence of private governance suggests that the question should be whether a public or a private actor can be mobilized and whether a public or private governance option, or some mix of the two, will produce the desired outcome.[48]

Private environmental governance has the ability to influence corporate norms, and thus could be useful given the large environmental impacts of corporations. Going forward, due to the Trump administration's hostility to public environmental law and its unwillingness to deal with the climate crisis, it seems that we must rely on private environmental governance.

4   Conclusion – Donald Trump and a Return to the Old School?

The election of Donald Trump raises a number of questions. One of the most important for legal scholars is, what of the role of law? Given the cabinet nominations and appointments that President Trump has made, it is quite possible that both the executive and legislative branches of government will turn away from the use of law to regulate, at least in the traditional sense. Indeed, Trump's former advisor Steve Bannon stated publicly that they were seeking a "deconstruction of the administrative state."[49] Thus, the New School model – which seeks ways to use the law to alter norms, markets, and architecture – might no longer hold much force.

Thus, we believe that we might see a return to the Old School, where we must find ways to use norms, markets, and architecture directly, in lieu of law, to change behavior. This means reliance on local and community initiatives (the public itself rather than public law) and private behavior (changing personal choices and placing both external and internal pressure on industry action). And by focusing their scholarship

---

[48] Ibid. 198–99.
[49] Philip Rucker & Robert Costa, "Bannon Vows a Daily Fight for 'Deconstruction of the Administrative State,'" *Washington Post*, February 23, 2017.

on these alternatives to traditional law, legal scholars can help to encourage these actions and increase public awareness of their benefits.

Rosen asserted that the "libertarian camp ... is skeptical whether government can do very much to transform people's taste, no matter how hard it tries."[50] In contrast, "the more leftist liberal norm scholars ... believe that an activist government can transform social norms on a national scale."[51] The question now is whether liberal activism (from lawmakers, scholars, and citizens) combined with libertarian individualism can sufficiently influence environmental norms, markets, and the built environment to avoid a total environmental crisis in the face of climate change and a president who appears hostile to environmental interests.

Bibliography of Selected Works

Bernstein, Lisa et al., "The New Chicago School: Myth or Reality?" (1998) 5 *University of Chicago Law School Roundtable* 1.

Czarnezki, Jason J., *Everyday Environmentalism: Law, Nature, and Individual Behavior* (Washington, DC: Environmental Law Institute, 2011).

Fischer Kuh, Katrina, "When Government Intrudes: Regulating Individual Behaviors That Harm the Environment" (2012) 61 *Duke Law Journal* 1111 (2012).

Lessig, Lawrence, "The New Chicago School" (1998) 27 *Journal of Legal Studies* 661.

Vandenbergh, Michael, "Order without Social Norms: How Personal Norm Activation Can Protect the Environment" (2005) 99 *Northwestern University Law Review* 1101.

Vandenbergh, Michael, "Reconceptualizing the Future of Environmental Law: The Role of Private Climate Governance" (2015) 31 *Pace Environmental Law Review* 382.

---

[50] Rosen, "The Social Police," 176.
[51] Ibid. 179.

13

EU Environmental Law and European Environmental Law Scholarship

LUDWIG KRÄMER

The impact of languages

The European Union (EU)[1] is not a State, but consists of twenty-eight sovereign States with different legal cultures which often enough demonstrate their sovereignty by vetoing common initiatives; by voting in the UN Security Council; and by promoting or slowing down measures in foreign policy, fiscal matters, trade or environmental policy issues,[2]. In this EU, twenty-four official languages are used, and the number of non-official languages is considerably higher. Any discussion of European scholarship must begin with this fundamental issue of languages. Indeed, the English language which was, until 1973, not even a recognized language in the EU, has developed since then into the dominant language in the EU and remains today, for the vast majority of environmental law scholars, the second language, though it never developed into the lingua franca of environmental law and policy.[3] And while English has become the leading language of the EU and the majority of environmental law publications in the EU are published in English and, thereby, implicitly transport Anglo-Saxon ideas, principles and objectives, there remains a wealth of legal research and publications in French, German, Italian, Spanish, Dutch, Polish and all the other EU

---

[1] The term 'EU' is used throughout this contribution, though between 1958 and 1993, the EU figured as EEC (European Economic Community), and from 1993 till 2009 as EC (European Community).

[2] Matters in the environmental policy area which were, until now, not accepted to be tackled at EU level include legislation on the protection of soils, on access to justice, on environmental inspectors and effective enforcement tools, on corporate environmental responsibility, the corporate veil problem in environmental matters, the protection of European oceans or on general measures to protect biodiversity.

[3] The working language of the European Court of Justice (CJEU) is French.

languages.[4] The wealth of the different legal cultures within the EU is not fully exploited by environmental law scholars.

Indeed, environmental law scholars within the EU mainly work in their mother languages. This may find some confirmation in the rough survey which this author made: the Italian *Trattato di Diritto Ambientale*[5] refers in Volume I to 1,285 publications in Italian, 187 in English, 28 in French, 14 in Spanish and 5 in Portuguese. A Spanish *Tratado de Derecho Ambiental*[6] refers to 633 publications in Spanish, 18 in English, 12 in French, 4 in German and 4 in Italian. In Kloepfers German book *Umweltrecht*[7] the author indicates in the first five chapters (424 pages), 1,329 publications in German and 15 publications in English; no title in another language is quoted. Books on EU environmental law do not fare much better: in Maria Lee's book on *EU Environmental Law*,[8] I counted 648 quotations of authors in English and one in German. Joan Scott's *Environmental Protection. European Law and Governance* has 308 quotations in English, 2 in French and 1 in Italian.[9] Astrid Epiney quotes 220 German, 43 English and 12 French authors.[10] Simon Charbonneau does not quote any literature.[11] Patrick Thieffry mentions in his bibliography 195 French and 8 English sources.[12] Eve Truilhé-Marengo quotes 406 French, 32 English sources and 1 Italian author;[13] Angel Moreno Molina quotes 51 English, 28 Spanish, 5 French and 1 German author.[14]

These few figures show at the same time, how important the national language is for information, education and research on the environment and how much know-how and input from other legal cultures gets lost,

---

[4] It will be seen if and to what extent the Brexit will progressively change the role of the English language and anglo-saxon thinking in the EU environmental law and policy thinking.

[5] P. dell'Anno & E. Picozza (eds.), *Trattato di Diritto Ambientale*, (Padua: CEDAM, 2012).

[6] L. Ortega Álvarez & C. Alonso García (eds), *Tratado de Derecho Ambiental* (Valencia: Tirant Lo Blanch, 2013).

[7] M. Kloepfer, *Umweltrecht*, 3rd.edn (Beck: München, 2004).

[8] M. Lee, *EU Environmental Law* (Oxford and Portland: Oxford University Press, 2005).

[9] J. Scott (ed.), *Environmental Protection. European Law and Governance* (Oxford: Oxford University Press, 2009).

[10] A. Epiney, *Umweltrecht der Europäischen Union*, 3rd edn (Nomos: Baden-Baden, 2013).

[11] S. Charbonneau, *'Droit Communautaire de l'Environnement* (Paris: L'Harmattan, 2006).

[12] P. Thieffry, *Droit de l'Environnement de l'Union Européenne*, 2nd edn (Brussels: Bruylant, 2011).

[13] E. Truilhé-Marengo, *Droit de l'Environnement de l'Union Européenne* (Brussels: Larcier, 2015).

[14] A. Moreno Molina, *Derecho Comunitario del Medio Ambiente* (Madrid: Marcial Pons, 2006).

when environmental law discussions are so strongly dominated by the English language as at present. It is true that scholars who work in the area of international environmental law,[15] where English is even more dominant, are more frequently working and publishing in English. However, international environmental law plays a rather limited role in the elaboration and application of EU environmental law. Also, its relevance appears to be limited in continental EU Member States, where statute law prevails, common law plays little role and where international environmental law is mainly imported through the measures taken by the European Union. And as EU environmental law was and is systematically drafted and adopted in all official languages of the EU, there is no particular reason for scholars to work on the basis of an English version of the EU legislative acts.

Two main consequences of this linguistic point of departure spring to mind: on the one hand, environmental law scholars within the EU, hampered by the language barrier which makes them all too often express in English only what they are able to express, saw and see no or a very limited possibility to form associations or other groupings at the EU level, to discuss, influence, shape or criticize EU environmental law. There are well-established national environmental law associations in most, if not all, EU Member States which regularly meet to discuss topics of common interest, publish books or articles, cooperate in research projects, advise public authorities and so on. Some of these national associations are more oriented towards academic scholars; others are more open to lawyers from public authorities and private companies. In contrast to these national associations, European associations of environmental law scholars or of environmental lawyers generally hardly exist. The European Association of Environmental Law (Association européenne de droit de l'environnement, AEDE) was set up in1992 but is barely active at present.[16] The European Environmental Law Forum (EELF) limits itself largely to organizing an annual environmental law conference and publishing the conference papers.[17] The Avosetta Group consists of some 30 environmental law academics but also meets only once a year and limits itself to exchange concepts.[18] Overall, no

[15] It goes beyond the scope of this chapter to look at the question of to what extent international environmental law, until now, neglected other streams of legal thinking (indigenous law, law from Asia and Africa, Russian and Chinese law etc.).
[16] https://uia.org/s/or/on/1100061072.
[17] European Environmental Law Forum, www.eelf.info/about-eelf.html.
[18] Avosetta Group, www.avosetta.jura.uni-bremen.de.

continuous, integrating EU structure for environmental law scholars exists. This situation is made more serious by the fact that most of the environmental non-governmental organizations which are active at EU level worked, at least until very recently, without having a lawyer on their staff.

On the other hand, the reaction of environmental law scholars to legal proposals, policy initiatives, incidents or other events with an EU dimension is heavily influenced by the linguistic problem, sketched out earlier: the legal writings commented on the impact of the EU law on events or incidents at the *national* law and policy level. Very little, if any, consideration is given to the geographical area 'EU' and the positive or negative impact that the initiative might have on the *European* environment. The academic scholars re-act – mainly in 'their' language – to initiatives from the EU institutions. At best, they advise their national government how this or that environmental problem could be responded to within the EU. However, the EU Member States do not have the right to take environmental legislative initiatives at the EU level, not even via the European Parliament; that right is exclusively vested in the European Commission.[19] As a consequence of this legislative construct, national initiatives for new EU-wide legislation have to pass the Commission's assessment to determine whether or not they are really in the EU environmental, social, economic and political interests.

Environmental law scholarship within the EU is therefore compartmentalized; the scholars frequently sit and research in their legal corner, without knowing that in some other Member State an environmental scholar is brooding over the same problem. Environmental scholars have struggled to overcome these hurdles, for example, by joining forces and formulating environmental provisions, such as a restatement of law, a model law or detailed provisions on solving a specific problem.[20] Environmental law scholars have very rarely proposed joint initiatives to suggest measures, laws or structures to improve the environmental

---

[19] Consolidated Version of the Treaty on the Functioning of the European Union, articles 192 and 294, OJ 2008 No C115/47 at 133–134 and 173–175.

[20] This is different from EU consumer law, where the EU Consumer Law Group, a loose grouping of scholars and NGO representatives, made proposals, for example, on package holidays (now Directive 2015/2302/EU on package travel and linked travel arrangements, OJ 2015 No. L326, p. 1) or on unfair contract terms (now Directive 93/13/EEC on unfair terms in consumer contracts, OJ 1993 No. L95, p. 29). Of course, this kind of drafting of EU provisions was and is frequently practiced by professional organizations in numerous areas such as insurance law, cosmetic and pharmaceutical law, industrial standards, motor vehicle legislation etc.

situation in the EU as a whole. There were, of course, often enough intense cooperation activities on specific research projects, which were mainly mandated by public authorities. However, such cooperation did not lead to regular, more general cooperation, and certainly not to scholars concentrating on EU environmental law.

The linguistic problem is the most obvious and persistent problem for pooling environmental law capacities within the EU and addressing common environmental problems. But it is far from being the only one. Some other obstacles to EU-wide continuous cooperation among environmental law scholars are enumerated hereafter but cannot be elaborated in detail. The first obstacle was and is the objective of European integration as such: historically, the European integration concept might have been a consequence of the Second World War, security considerations and economic pressure ('the economy needs the bigger market'). Quality-of-life considerations did not play a significant role in the beginning of the integration process. And environmental law scholars, who might be, in all prudence, considered to be rather skeptical to security considerations and were more inclined to see in economic growth a challenge to the environment, saw a limited usefulness for the environment in the European integration process. This led to the statement, often heard in the 1970s and 1980s, that environmental law scholars were not interested in the European integration, and general EU scholars – quite numerous in continental Europe – were not interested in the environment.

Furthermore, environmental law scholars in Europe depend to a large extent on public funding for their research.[21] However, domestic public authorities tend to engage with the question of the impact of EU measures on the national economy and ecology rather than promoting altruistically research for improving the European environment as a whole. The idea that when trade and industry organize themselves at an EU (or global) level, the environment which organizes itself at national level would be phased out[22] did not gain any significant interest with either researchers or public/private funders. At the same time, a position which is too critical of national environmental legislation and the implementation and enforcement of EU provisions might lead

---

[21] Funding by charities is rare in the EU and private funding was and is not particularly interested in financing environmental research.

[22] The similarity to the Marxist slogan of the nineteenth century: 'Workers of all countries, unite' is obvious.

to a greater hesitation in public authorities when it comes to making research funds available.

Perhaps, it should also be mentioned that European environmental law scholars in their majority appear to be non-political. They work to preserve, protect and improve the quality of the environment but are not too much interested in political debates and controversies, for example, on the pros and cons of European integration. As EU integration is an eminently political undertaking and remains largely a process in the interest of economic interests, environmental law scholars approached it more with mistrust than with positive expectations. Integration was not considered 'sexy'.

All these elements may have influenced environmental law scholars' approach to EU environmental law policy and its achievements. Nuances might exist from one person and one country to the other. The overall result, though, is clear: environmental law scholars within the EU remained largely in their national contexts, integrating themselves little, showing some reservation to the EU integration process as a whole and reacting more to environmental law initiatives coming from the EU than seriously acting to contribute to a EU-wide environmental standard setting.

The EU Institutions and Environmental Law Scholars

When the EU, in the legal form of the European Economic Community (EEC) was established in1958, 'environment', 'environmental policy' and 'environmental protection' were not mentioned in the EEC Treaties, and practically no environmental policy existed in the EEC Member States. It were two members of the European Commission, Altiero Spinelli (Italy) and Sicco Mansholt (Netherlands), who favoured, in the late 1960s, the idea that the EEC should also look into environmental issues. Having received the green light from the first-ever meeting of the EEC Heads of State and Governments (Paris, 1972), the European Commission set up an administrative department for the environment,[23] and the EEC adopted an environmental action pro-gramme in 1973, where it announced a series of measures, in particular to combat environmental pollution and harmonize national environ-mental legislation. However, very little environmental legislation existed

---

[23] Environment and Consumer Protection Service (SEPC) was set up on 1 January 1973. This service later became the Directorate General for the Environment.

in the nine Member States at that time,[24] and the Commission, which had the task of initiating environmental legislation, was often enough literally sitting before a blank sheet of paper. No legal research existed on priority necessities, methods to tackle pollution and good or bad legislative practices. Environmental organizations which were just forming them selves at EU level, were ready to denounce bad agricultural practices or industrial accidents but were not able to indicate what a European approach to environmental problems should look like. And existing Commission departments on agriculture, industry, transport or competition successfully prevented the Commission's SEPC from elaborating environmental rules that would impact 'their' territory.

In view of this situation and without any political or legal support from the outside, the Commission administration decided to propose legislation in areas where other administrations were not active. In pursuance thereof, directives were proposed and adopted in the areas of waste[25] and water,[26] and later, with active political support from nature conservation organizations, on birds and some endangered species,[27] as well as, due to policy concerns of the European public on the 'Waldsterben' (dying forests), on air pollution.[28] Product-related legislation was more driven by pressure from producers but aptly used to introduce some environmental aspects.[29]

Two examples might illustrate the experiences gained in the first decades of EU environmental policy. In 1976, a major industrial accident took place in Seveso (Italy), where toxic chemicals were released into the environment. The Commission wanted to reduce the risk of such accidents by preventive measures, but there was no legal research available to orient it nor was there any corresponding national legislation; the only 'model' was US legislation which tried to stop accidents through fixing

---

[24] For this reason, the question of a comparative law analysis was not posed.

[25] Directive75/439/EEC on waste oils, OJ 1975 No. L 194, p. 23; Directive 75/442/EEC on waste, OJ 1975 No. L194, p. 39; Directive 76/403/EEC on PCB/PCT waste, OJ 1976 No. L108, p. 41; Directive 78/319/EEC on dangerous waste, OJ 1978 No. L84, p. 43.

[26] Directive 75/440/EEC on surface water, OJ 1975 No. L194, p. 26; Directive 76/160 on bathing water, OJ 1976 No. L31, p. 1; Directive 76/464/EEC on the discharge of pollutants into water, OJ 1976 No. L129, p. 23.

[27] Directive 79/409/EEC on birds, OJ 1979 No. L103, p. 1; Regulation 348/81 on whales, OJ 1981 No. L39, p. 1; Reg.3626/82 on trade in endangered species, OJ 1982 No. L384, p. 1; Directive 83/129/EEC on seal pups, OJ 1083 No, L91, p. 30.

[28] Directive 84/360/EEC on air pollution, OJ 1984 No. L188, p. 20; Directive 86/609/EEC on combustion plants, OJ 1986 No, L358, p. 1.

[29] Directive 79/117/EEC on banning some pesticides, OJ 1979 No. L33, p. 36; Directive 79/831/EEC on permitting new chemicals, OJ 1979 No. L259, p. 10.

severe financial sanctions when an accident had happened. The way ultimately chosen by the EU, to act through preventive measures,[30] was pure administrative innovation: the industrial installations concerned had to elaborate emergency plans for the site, store chemicals safely and keep the surrounding population informed of their activities; after an accident they had to report to the authorities on the causes, the effects and the measures to avoid repetition. Also in the area of environmental impact assessment for projects,[31] no academic research led the way; US legislation existed and France had just adopted national legislation. The EU officials thus had to draft legislation according to their own common sense[32] and look for Member States unanimous approval for it.

Generally, in the 1970s and in the early 1980s, environmental law scholars – as well as scholars from adjacent faculties such as economics, biology or political science – did not appear, in writing or in person, at the European level to provide input into the legislation, which remained largely in the hands of EU and national administrations. This explains some specificities in EU environmental acts which appear at odds with the general environmental policy line. For example, the directive on the prevention of major accidents of industrial installations[33] excluded nuclear installations from its field of application, because in particular France insisted on such an exclusion.[34] The directive on the environmental impact assessment of some projects[35] excluded projects which had been adopted by legislative acts; Denmark had insisted on this exclusion, as it wanted to build a bridge to link with Sweden and did not wish the project to be interfered with.[36] That same directive provided that the right of the concerned public to participate in the assessment procedure for projects with potential transboundary effects be taken over by intergovernmental consultation.[37] This provision was again due to France wanting to avoid giving citizens of other Member States a right to participate in the assessment procedure of its nuclear plants, some of

[30] Directive 82/501/EEC on the prevention of industrial accidents, OJ 1985 No. L230, p. 1.
[31] Directive 85/337/EEC on environmental impact assessment, OJ 1985 No L175, p. 40.
[32] This common sense had limits: for example, the exclusion of golf courses or the limitation to pipelines of more than 40 km of length in Annex I was due more to the influence of lobbying.
[33] Directive 82/501.
[34] Until 1993, decisions on environmental matters had to be unanimous.
[35] Directive 85/337.
[36] Directive 85/337, Article 1(5). In the meantime, the CJEU considerably restricted the field of application of this provision.
[37] See Directive 85/337, Article 7.

which had been constructed close to the borders with other Member States, gave citizens of other Member States a right to participate in the assessment procedure. During the adoption of both directives which took several years, no critical comment from environmental law scholars was heard.

The first significant legal contribution to the discussion on EU environmental policy and law was made not by an environmental law scholar, but by an environmental law practitioner: in 1984, Nigel Haigh published a book, in which he scrupulously examined each EU environmental act and the legislative discussion in the UK.[38] He concluded that the impact of EU environmental law on Member States environmental law was considerable.[39]

At almost the same time (1985), the EEC Treaty was amended to include, among other issues, a chapter on environmental policy. Again the drafting of the different provisions of what is now Articles 191 to 193 of the Treaty on the Functioning of the European Union (TFEU), was the exclusive work of Commission and later also Council officials, with no direct or indirect contribution from environmental law scholars.[40] Following the EU Treaty amendment, literature on EU environmental legislation sprang up, also encouraged by the emergence of an increasing number of environmental judgments of the EU Court of Justice.[41]

As mentioned earlier, however, this environmental literature was mainly re-active, commenting and elaborating on the existing EU environmental legislation and its impact on the EU Member States, mainly on the respective author's State. Proposals on how to amend or improve the existing EU legislation were rare. For this reason, it was tempting and at the same time easy for the EU administration – the Commission, the European Parliament and the Council – to largely ignore this literature

---

[38] N. Haigh, *EEC Environmental Policy and Britain: An Essay and a Handbook* (London: Environmental Data Services, 1984).

[39] This was about the time when a controversy between the EU Commission and the UK government broke out as to the legal meaning of an EU environmental directive. This controversy was brought to some end by Case C337/89, *Commission* v. *UK* [1992] ECLI 456 and C56/90, *Commission* v. *UK* [1993] ECI 307. The recent diverging discussions on air pollution in the UK show, though, that it might not altogether be over.

[40] This explains the limited number of environmental law principles in the present Article 191(2) of the TFEU; in the mid-eighties, many more environmental principles were discussed at the international level which later were assembled in the Rio principles of 1992.

[41] At the CJEU, an environmental law scholar, Professor Manfred Zuleeg, acted as a judge between 1988 and 1994, leaving his handwriting in a number of remarkable judgments on environmental law.

and to continue to work with EU environmental action programmes and their implementation.[42]

Part of this self-restraint of law scholars may also have to do with the legislative decision-making process at the EU level which is not always transparent: Commission proposals for legislation were, for a long time elaborated without the possibility of the general public knowing about them,[43] though transparency improved over the years. However, the Commission continues to publish its assessment of alternative legislative options only after it has officially made its proposals.[44] And when the procedure in the Council enters into the so-called trilogue stage[45] – a procedure more and more frequently used – discussions remain almost entirely confidential, until the final outcome. The same confidentiality reigns for decisions in the so-called comitology, where a committee of Member States' representatives and the Commission decide on executive or implementing acts. This lack of transparency might partly explain the reservation of environmental law scholars to engage in discussions on the shaping of EU environmental law.

However, the result is that the large majority of EU environmental legislation is prepared and passed through the legislative or regulatory decision-making process without input from legal scholars. Some examples – out of many more – are EU legislation on the right of access to environmental information or participation in environmental decision-making,[46] the framework directives on fresh and marine

---

[42] The environmental sector is, next to the sector on research, the only policy sector where the EU worked, since 1973, with four- or five-year action programmes which fixed objectives and priorities for EU measures. At present, the environmental action programme is running, OJ 2013 No. L354, p. 171.

[43] This led E. Rehbinder in 1985 to the comment that access to Commission documents was easier for vested interest groups than for the general public; E. Rehbinder & R. Stewart, *Environmental Protection Policy* (Berlin-New York: Walter de Gruyter, 1985), 334. This issue is of particular relevance in environmental law matters, as the protection of the environment is of *general* interest.

[44] See on this Court, joined cases T-424/14 and T-425/14 *ClientEarth v. Commission* [2015] ECLI 848.

[45] The trilogue procedure is nowhere fixed in writing. It consists of meetings behind closed doors of a limited number of members of the European Parliament, the Commission and the Council to discuss a Commission proposal for legislation. When a compromise is reached, the European Parliament and the Council formally adopt it; thus it may happen – and this is not exceptional – that a Commission proposal for legislation is not discussed by the Parliament's plenary at all.

[46] Directive 2003/4 on access to environmental information, OJ 2003 No. L41, p. 26; Directive 2003/35 on public participation in decision-making, OJ 2003 No. L56, p. 17.

waters,[47] on drinking water[48] or urban waste water,[49] on air pollution,[50] habitat protection[51] and invasive alien species;[52] the legislation on waste management,[53] ship recycling,[54] offshore- oil and gas extraction,[55] greenhouse gas emission trading[56] or renewable energies.[57] The majority of this legislation was conceived, drafted and shaped almost entirely by the EU and the national environmental administrations.

The situation with regard to international environmental law which becomes applicable within the EU is not significantly different. A considerable number of legal scholars from different Member States of the EU actively participate in the discussions of international environmental law, contribute to the drafting of environmental agreements and try to spread concepts and principles of international environmental law at home.[58] However, as a result of the rather restrictive application of international agreements, concepts or principles by the Court of Justice of the European Union (CJEU), international environmental agreements only play some role in EU environmental law, when the EU itself adopted an international legislative act to apply its objectives, principles and structures within the EU. As far as can be seen, environmental law scholars made limited efforts to engage a discussion to gradually improve this situation.

Environmental Law Scholars and the Environment in Europe

This overview gives the impression of being rather critical of the approach taken by environmental law scholars towards the EU. However, the position of these scholars only reflects the general situation

[47] Directive 2000/60 on freshwater, OJ 2000 No. L327, p. 1; Directive 2008/56 on marine waters, OJ 2008 No. L164, p. 19.
[48] Directive 98/83, OJ 1998 No. L330, p. 32.
[49] Directive 91/271, OJ 1991 No. L135, p. 40.
[50] Directive 2008/50, OJ 2008 No. L152, p. 1.
[51] Directive 92/43, OJ 1992 No. L206, p. 7.
[52] Regulation 1143/2014, OJ 2014 No. L317, p. 35.
[53] Directive 2008/98, OJ 2008 No. L312, p. 3.
[54] Regulation 1257/2013, OJ 2013 No. L330, p. 1.
[55] Directive 2013/30, OJ 2013 No. L178, p. 66.
[56] Directive 2003/87, OJ 2003 No. L275, p. 32.
[57] Directive 2009/28, OJ 2009 No. L140, p. 16.
[58] As an example, the *Draft International Covenant on Environment and Development*, 5th edn (Gland: IUCN 2015), may be quoted which lists 120 contributors (1st to 5th eds), out of which 39 are Europeans. The work was conducted exclusively in English.

of the EU: the EU is not a State and there is no European public opinion, certainly not on environmental matters. When lawyers wish to illuminate,[59] they have limited space in the EU building to shine, but they need space where they can be effective – and that is at present to a large extent the Member State's space. That scholars do not see the necessity to continuously work beyond national borders and try to counterbalance the efforts of globalization – or the European globalization organized by the EU – is regrettable but cannot be enforced against the will of scholars.

I see as the first task of an environmental scholar not to illuminate, but to protect the environment with the means of law. A scholar has the skills and the know-how to improve the quality of life of humans, animals and plants, to protect the natural and human-made environment and to call for measures to prevent environmental human-made disasters such as climate change, the loss of biodiversity, the omnipresence of chemicals, the wasteful management of resources, the pollution of oceans or the unsustainability of our cities. It is quaint to believe that the main environmental problems can be solved at the level of the nation-state, at a time when demographic and economic growth puts the whole planet at risk. Whether one likes it or not, the EU constitutes the attempt to bring the European continent together to jointly confront global problems of the twenty-first century; global integration, a world government, is not feasible and the United Nations is not even able to set up a World Environment Organization as it did for trade in the form of the World Trade Organization or for agriculture in the form of the Food and Agricultural Organization. In this sense, the EU is arguably the second-best attempt to reconcile environmental needs and globalization.

With all their skills and all their know-how, environmental law scholars in Europe should try to discuss issues which are more or less similar for the whole European continent and concentrate less on their own country, all the more as this would allow a sort of transfer of know-how that would also benefit countries that are less advanced in environmental matters, illuminate more this entire continent and less their own country, all the more, as there are also environmentally more and less progressive countries on this continent.[60] There is enough work to do which concerns the whole of Europe and would need the joint input of scholars.

---

[59] See Fisher, Chapter 3, this volume.

[60] An analysis of the national environmental legislation will find that in Central and Eastern Europe, but also in Greece, Cyprus and Malta, Italy, Spain, Portugal, Ireland and Luxemburg almost 100 per cent of the national environmental provisions have their

What Farber discusses with regard to the US[61] is also correct for the EU: climate change requires integrated European actions and might have a unifying effect. Such joint scholarly initiatives are not limited to the reduction of greenhouse gas emissions, but might extend to the end of coal and lignite production and consumption, the promotion of renewable energies, the over-consumption of fossil fuels in private transport, the energy efficiency in European buildings and other issues.

Environment and human rights are other topics which are severely neglected by EU environmental scholars. This topic has, through the European Convention on Human Rights and Fundamental Freedoms, a clear transnational dimension and it would be useful if lawyers from different legal cultures could jointly bring this issue to the forefront of public discussions. Why is it, for example, only possible for a judge in the United States to declare that the individual right to life 'includes the right to a climate system capable of sustaining human life',[62] or for a court in India to state that the right to life 'includes the right to enjoyment of pollution-free water and air for full enjoyment of life'?[63] There are rudiments of such a human right in the discussions on clean air[64] and clean water,[65] but little effort is made to elaborate on this or to extend this discussions to other areas such as the noise or the waste sector, the right to see effective measures taken against climate change and the right to enjoy biodiversity.[66]

Furthermore, it is surprising, how little attention environmental law scholars pay to the implementation and enforcement of existing national and EU environmental provisions – a topic which appears to be the most relevant of environmental law[67] and which could well be reconciled with

---

roots in EU legislation. Even the United Kingdom estimates this figure to be about 80 per cent, Germany estimates the figure to be around 75 per cent.

[61] See Farber, Chapter 10, this volume.

[62] *Kelsey Cascadia, Rose Juliana et al. v. United States et al.*, Case No.6:15-cv01517 – TC, US District Court of the District of Oregon, Order of 10 November 2016.

[63] *Subash Kumar v. State of Bihar*, [1991] AIR SC 420, Supreme Court of India, Decision of 9 January 1991.

[64] See Case C361/88, *Commission v. Germany* [1991] ECLI 224; Case C237/07 *Janecek* [2008] ECLI 447.

[65] See Case C237/07; C664/15 *Protect* [2017] ECLI 987.

[66] The discussion on animal rights will sooner or later also have to be taken up by environmental lawyers.

[67] It is submitted that there are a huge number of environmental provisions in existence at local, regional, national, EU and in particular at international levels which are not applied. The environment would be considerably better off if these provisions were actually complied with.

their preference for discussions of the national state of the environment. What help is there for the threatened environment in Europe by having provisions which are not complied with? The figure of 400,000 premature deaths per year due to air pollution in the EU[68] should cause an outcry by lawyers in all countries but rather appears to be taken as the toll to pay for the quality of modern life.

Environmental lawyers in Europe have, until now, not really taken up the discussion about environmental justice which occurred some years ago in the United States and which had pointed to the problems of industrial pollution, dangerous or polluting installations or infrastructures with all their side effects that are more often experienced in areas where underprivileged persons – in the broad sense – live. Europe also has areas of ethnic and other minorities, immigrant quarters, low-income areas and regions and agglomerations where less influential parts of the population dwell. They also should enjoy protection of their environment, but little legal research exists so far.

Lenin once declared that academics were trying to explain the world, but that he and his comrades were going to change it. An environmental law scholar should not limit himself/herself to explanations, illuminations or justifications. Rather he/she should see what can be done to change the state of affairs by preserving, protecting and improving the environment with the means of law, at national, European and global levels.

Bibliography

Bergkamp, L. & Goldsmith, B. (eds), *The EU Environmental Liability Directive - A Commentary* (Oxford: Oxford University Press, 2013).

Bohne, E., 'The Implementation of the IPPC Directive from a Comparative Perspective and Lessons for its Recast. Journal for European Environmental & Planning Law' (2008), 1, 319.

Born, H., Cliquet, A., Schoukens, H., Misonne, D. & VanHoorick, G. (eds), *The Habitats Directive in Its EU Environmental Law Context - Europe Nature's Best Hope?* (Oxon: Rutledge, 2015).

---

[68] See European Environment Agency, Air Quality in Europe (Copenhagen: European Environment Agency, 2017), 55. The figure is carefully broken down for each EU Member State. The EU Commission also quotes similar figures, see Commission COM (2005) 447 p. 2; COM (2013) 918 p. 5.

García Ureta, A. (ed.). *Nuevas perspectivas del Derecho ambiental en el siglo XXI -New perspectives on environmental law in the 21th century* (Madrid: Marcial Pons, 2018).

Jans, J. & Vedder, H., *European Environmental Law after Lisbon*. 4th edn (Groningen: Europa Law Publishing, 2012).

Josefsson, H. & Baaner, L., 'The Water Framework Directive – A Directive for the Twenty-first Century?' *Journal of Environmental Law* (2011) 463.

Kingston, S., *Greening EU Competition Law and Policy* (Cambridge: Cambridge University Press, 2011).

Krämer, L., *EU Environmental Law*. 8th ed. (London: Sweet and Maxwell, 2015).

Lange, B., 'EU Directive on Industrial Emissions: Squaring the Circle of Integrated, Harmonised and Ambitious Technology Standards?' *Environmental Law Review* (2011) 199.

Macrory, R. (ed.), *Reflections on 30 Years of EU Environmental Law: A High Level of Protection?* (Groningen: Europa Law Publishing, 2006).

Misonne, D., 'The Importance of Setting a Target: The EU Ambition of a High Level of Protection'. *Transnational Environmental Law* (2015) 11.

Peeters, M. & Uylenurg, R. (eds), *EU Environmental Law – Legal Perspectives on Regulatory Strategies* (Cheltenham and Northampton, MA: Edward Elgar, 2014).

Petersen, M., 'European Soil Protection Law after the Setback of December 2007 - Existing Law and Outlook'. *European Energy and Environmental Law Review* (2008) 146.

Scott, J. (ed.), *Environmental Protection. European Law and Governance* (Oxford: Oxford University Press, 2009).

Van Calster, G. & Reins, L., *EU Environmental Law* (Cheltenham and Northampton, MA: Edward Elgar, 2017).

Vogelezang-Stoute, E., 'Regulating Uncertain Risks of New Technologies: Nanomaterials as a Challenge for the Regulator' in M. Peeters & R. Uylenurg (eds), *EU Environmental Legislation- Legal Perspectives on Regulatory Strategies* (Cheltenham and Northampton, MA: Edward Elgar, 2014), 211.

14

The Culture of Environmental Law and the Practices of Environmental Law Scholarship

OLE W. PEDERSEN

The first and most striking feature to emerge from this collection of essays is that environmental law scholarship is perceived by environmental law scholars themselves as encompassing a wide range of methodologies, topics, disciplines and considerations. Environmental law scholarship caters to a wide range of approaches to scholarship, and the scholars considering the discipline their home represent a diverse range of backgrounds. Not only do they come from different jurisdictions, carrying with them understandings of scholarship anchored in their unique legal cultures, but these scholars also come to rely on and make use of a diverse set of methodologies and understandings of what scholarship is. Whilst methodological rigour is seen as important, there is not an exclusive commitment to a specific methodology.[1] This 'internal diversity', to use Maldonado's phrase, might even be seen as calling into question whether we are at all talking about one coherent discipline.[2] In the least, it becomes clear that environmental law scholarship is highly contingent, in the sense that a given body of scholarship – and indeed each piece of scholarship – reflects a unique set of circumstances. These circumstances include, for example, the legal framework of environmental law and regulation of the jurisdiction at hand and the institutional drivers and pressures as well as lived scholarly experiences of each individual scholar.[3] In other words, the very understanding of what

---

[1] See also Cecot & Livermore, Chapter 7, this volume.

[2] E.g. Maldonado, Chapter 4, this volume; Lee et al., Chapter 6, this volume; and Farber, Chapter 10, this volume.

[3] E.g. Fisher, Chapter 3, this volume; Guneratne, Chapter 11, this volume. On personal experiences see e.g. Angela Mae Kupenda, 'Personal Essay – On the Receiving End of Influence: Helping Craft the Scholarship of My Students and How Their Work Influences Me' on https://jotwell.com/wp-content/uploads/2014/07/Kupenda-Personal-essay-on-influence.pdf.

falls within the confines of environmental law will vary from jurisdiction to jurisdiction.

An added feature which underscores the permeable nature of the boundaries of environmental law scholarship as a discipline is the wide-spread understanding that environmental law scholarship is by its very nature interdisciplinary.[4] Whether this is asserted as a descriptive observation by reference to the strong links between environmental law and other disciplines in the social or natural sciences or whether it is put forward as a prescriptive claim, arguing that environmental law scholarship ought to learn from other disciplines, the interdisciplinary nature of environmental law scholarship is uncontroversial. That of course is not to say that engaging in interdisciplinary work is easy – the account put forward by Lee et al. shows that interdisciplinary scholarship poses challenges for those scholars brave enough to expressly pursue scholarship through an interdisciplinary project.[5] But it also highlights the centrality and importance of the environmental law scholar's ability to rely on considerations and frameworks ordinarily thought to be external to legal scholarship.

One important implication, however, emerges from this. If interdisciplinarity is so important to environmental law and environmental law scholarship, if it becomes a central or defining characteristic of the discipline, it arguably ceases to be interdisciplinarity as ordinarily understood.[6] That is, interdisciplinary scholarship becomes a disciplinary feature of environmental law scholarship – it is what environmental law scholars do (or at least what a large share of us do) – so much so that environmental law scholarship becomes synonymous with scholarly engagement with other disciplines. If this is the case, the strong reliance on external disciplines ultimately results in these disciplines being internalised into the discipline of environmental law.[7] Interdisciplinarity consequently becomes the disciplinary characteristics of environmental law scholarship.

[4] E.g. Chris Hilson, 'Editor's Foreword' (2008) 20 *JEL* 1; Pieraccini, Chapter 5, this volume. In making this argument, I take interdisciplinarity to include what is by some termed multidisciplinary and transdisciplinary scholarship. See Jerry A. Jacobs, *In Defense of Disciplines* (Chicago: University of Chicago Press, 2013).
[5] Lee et al., Chapter 6, this volume.
[6] Ole W. Pedersen, 'The Limits of Interdisciplinarity and the Practice of Environmental Law Scholarship' (2014) *JEL* 423–441.
[7] Louis Menand, *The Marketplace of Ideas* (New York: Norton & Company, 2010), 119.

On this reading, the broad focus of environmental law scholarship and its interdisciplinary nature result in environmental law scholarship reflecting its object of study – environmental law. Environmental law itself is often seen as defying traditional legal boundaries between the public and the private as well as between the international, the federal and the local.[8] Though this poses challenges for environmental law scholars when it comes to the ability to engage with and criss-cross jurisdictional boundaries which remain firmer in other disciplines of law and legal scholarship, purely as a matter of observation, a central characteristic of environmental law scholarship is that those engaging in it must maintain a level of scholarly flexibility. Again, given that scholars from time to time have called into question whether environmental law itself constitutes an orderly discipline, scholars would be forgiven for pondering whether it is at all possible to conceptualise environmental law scholarship as a coherent whole.[9]

In response to the broad disciplinary confines and the contingency of its scholarship, the most constructive way to conceptualise environmental law scholarship is as a practice embedded within a broader legal culture: the practice being environmental law scholarship and the culture being environmental law as a body of law. In defining environmental law scholarship and its antecedent object of study as a practice and a culture respectively, the point is not so much to prescribe a particular form of methodology for the discipline.[10] The point is simply – in a descriptive sense – to try and capture what environmental law is and what environmental law scholars do. The concept of legal culture is ordinarily used as a term to explain the differences between legal systems. Such differences are evidently important from the perspective of a comparative scholar who needs to be alert to the finer cultural differences between superficially similar rules and concepts found in different jurisdictions.[11] Conversely, the term legal culture is applied here on the level of a specific legal subject and discipline – that of environmental law. On this reading, a legal culture captures the values, ideas, habits and

---

[8] E.g. Elisabeth Fisher, *Environmental Law: A Very Short Introduction* (Oxford: Oxford University Press, 2017).

[9] E.g. Zygmunt Plater, 'Environmental Law and Three Economies: Navigating a Sprawling Field of Study, Practice, and Societal Governance in Which Everything Is Connected to Everything Else' (1999) 23 *Harv. Envtl. L. Rev.* 359.

[10] See for this e.g. Paul W. Kahn, *The Cultural Study of Law* (Chicago: University of Chicago Press, 2009).

[11] Eloise Scotford, *Environmental Principles and the Evolution of Environmental Law* (Oxford: Bloomsbury, 2017).

practices embodied in a given subject.[12] Environmental law defined as
a culture is thus a domain 'with a distinctive history, terminology and
personnel'[13] which is different from the history and terminology of, say,
corporate law, constitutional law and contract law (though there might
be overlaps).[14] Each legal culture (or subculture) thus contains and
exhibits 'a repertoire of actions, practices and beliefs that are relatively
flexible and open to change',[15] giving force to 'ideas, values, attitudes, and
opinions'.[16]

Conceptualising legal domains as cultures in this way explains the
differences between legal subject areas when it comes to issues such as
what constitutes sources of law and doctrines in each field of law and
when it comes to the question of what constitutes valid reasons in the
debates taking place within a subject area. For example, the answer to the
question of what constitutes a valid source of law will vary from, say,
contract law to environmental law though there are likely to be some
similarity. Environmental lawyers will likely hesitate little in invoking so-
called environmental principles when discussing points of law (on the
assumption that these principles are legally relevant) whereas lawyers in
other areas of law might well hesitate invoking what they see as policy
considerations.[17] The point is that each subculture of law stands apart
from other subcultures by reference to its constituent parts.

Though the attempt to conceptualise law as a culture with several
subcultures is not necessarily new or entirely problem free, the main
advantage from our perspective is that it provides a platform on which to
explore the role of scholarship. Again, the point is that each legal culture
will be host to not only different sources of law, values and doctrines but
that these differences will give rise to and find expression in different

[12] David Nelken, 'Thinking about Legal Culture' (2014) Asian Journal of Law and Society 255–274.
[13] Sally Engle Merry, 'What Is Legal Culture? An Anthropological Perspective' (2010) 5 J. Comp. L. 40, 47.
[14] Similarly, defining environmental law as a culture and its scholarly community as a practice by way of reliance on ideas and concepts derived from scholars engaged in cultural studies of law does not necessarily mean that the attempt to do so is interdisciplinary. It simply means that, as a matter of description, this is what environmental law and environmental law scholarship looks like.
[15] Merry, 'What Is Legal Culture?' 42.
[16] Lawrence M. Friedman, 'Is There a Modern Legal Culture?' (1994) 7 Ratio Juris 117, 118.
[17] In saying this, the point alluded to earlier about the need to appreciate the finer differences in legal cultures between different jurisdiction remains highly relevant, considering that the legal nature and thereby relevance of so-called environmental principles will vary from jurisdiction to jurisdiction, e.g. Scotford, Environmental Principles.

practices, including a scholarly practice. Each practice (including a scholarly practice) will thus operate within and be shaped by the contours, histories and values of each culture. In addition to scholarly practices, wider legal practices within the culture of environmental law may include practices of adjudication (in which the main participants are judges and legal practitioners) and practices of legislative drafting and amendment (in which the main participants are legislators and administrative agencies). In each culture of law, the constituent parts of each practice will vary slightly from culture to subculture. The practice of environmental law before the courts will consequently vary from the practice of, say, human rights litigation not only in terms of the participants (e.g. differences in the types of adjudicators as well as adjudicatory institutions) but also when it comes to the ways in which the practice is practically conducted in terms of what arguments can be advanced and methods of litigation used.[18] Similarly, the practice of legislative drafting of environmental law rules will vary from the drafting of commercial codes and legal rules as a result of the nature of the values, habits and beliefs within each practice. But what does it mean specifically to define environmental law scholarship as a practice?

A practice is necessarily an inherently social enterprise.[19] That is, the defining feature and genesis of a practice is the community of participants which sets out the 'agreed criteria of what are reasonable or unreasonable readings'.[20] Thus, a practice facilitates what Fish calls a 'bounded-argument space' in which 'the arguments that can be made and the arguments that just won't fly are formally identified and known to everyone working in the field.'[21] Environmental law scholarship is thus 'an institutionalised social practice', and scholarship is validated by reference to its contribution to the practice and the value which the participants put on a given work of scholarship.[22] On this reading,

---

[18] See Aagaard, Chapter 2, this volume.

[19] Hans-George Gadamer, *Reason in the Age of Science* (Cambridge, MA: MIT Press, 1996). See also Ian Ward, 'Literature and the Legal Imagination' (1998) 49 N. Ir. Legal Q. 167 and Fisher, Chapter 3, this volume.

[20] Christopher McCrudden, 'Legal Research and the Social Sciences' (2006) LQR 632, 634. Naturally, this boundary setting by a practice's participants is not formalised through the creation of formal criteria but through scholarly activities such as peer review, mentoring, citations and the organising of conferences.

[21] Stanley Fish, *Winning Arguments: What Works and Doesn't Work in Politics, The Bedroom, The Courtroom and the Classroom* (New York: HarperCollins, 2016) 72.

[22] Pierre Schlag, 'Spam Jurisprudence, Air Law, and the Rank Anxiety of Nothing Happening (A Report on the State of the Art)' (2009) 97 *Geo. L. J.* 803, 805. See also

disciplines defined as a practice stand apart from those disciplines (such as e.g. the natural and medical sciences) which are primarily defined by reference to their adherence to *a priori* established methodology. As seen in this collection of essays, a central feature of environmental law scholarship is its refusal to commit to a particular methodology. A practice is consequently a deliberative practice in so far as a central feature of it is, very basically, the writing, publishing and communication of scholarly outputs seeking to engage considerations of what the law is, what it ought to be and how it ought to work.[23] This self-regulating and self-referential nature of a scholarly practice means that the practice itself defines 'whatever it is one has to know or believe in order to operate in a manner acceptable to its members'.[24]

A scholarly practice, moreover, serves the important purposes of providing a minimum level of stability in a given field of study.[25] In securing a level of stability, a practice is also an inherently practical endeavour[26] – practical in the sense that the scholars participating in the practice will constantly make decisions and choices shaping the confines of the practice.[27] Such decision-making includes, for example, decisions made in the context of a scholar's independent research as to what questions to engage with and how to answer these (i.e. questions of methodology) as well as decisions made in the context of other scholars' work in the process of commenting on and reviewing this scholarship. When making such decisions, scholars consequently execute individual plans and choices, though this is done from within the confines of the communal practice simultaneously co-determining the collective concerns and priorities of the practice. To Gadamer, practice is consequently 'conducting oneself and acting in solidarity'.[28]

Central to the practice of scholarship is thus the commitment of those taking part in a practice to a common and mutually agreed-upon set of understandings and ground rules (though often these rules remain

Edward L. Rubin, 'The Evaluation of Prescriptive Scholarship' (1990) 10 *Tel Aviv U. Stud. L.* 101.

[23] Pierre Schlag, *Laying Down the Law* (New York: New York University Press, 1996).

[24] Clifford Geertz, *The Interpretation of Cultures* (Fontana Press, 1973), 11. See also Menand, *The Marketplace of Ideas.*

[25] Gadamer, *Reason in the Age of Science*, 76; Geertz *The Interpretation of Cultures*, 18.

[26] This is of course not to imply that a practice cannot engage with questions of theory.

[27] See also Thomas Kuhn, *The Structure of Scientific Revolutions*, 2nd edn (Chicago: University of Chicago Press, 1970).

[28] Gadamer *Reason in the Age of Science*, 87. See also Richard J Bernstein, *Beyond Objectivism and Relativism* (Philadelphia: University of Pennsylvania Press, 1983).

unspoken). The practice is consequently a reflection of a perspective embedded within the practice. Importantly, however, the argument that scholarship is conducted from an internal perspective of a practice is not to be taken to mean that the practice only engages in traditional doctrinal scholarship, excluding perspectives on the law and materials which are traditionally seen as external to the law.[29] As noted earlier, central to the practice of environmental law scholarship is the commitment to methods and considerations which may well be thought external in other practices and areas of legal scholarship. On this account, the practice of environmental law scholarship is very likely to be markedly different from practices in other areas of legal scholarship because the practice of environmental law scholarship maintains a commitment to external perspectives.[30]

If indeed the practice of scholarship is a social practice, it necessarily follows that the practice is not static. Instead it develops over time with the scholarly focus and inclinations of its participants. As Czarnezki and Schindler note, the boundaries of the discipline and its scholarship will continue to expand.[31] Though commentators debate whether the ability of a scholarly practice to change and realign itself over time is desirable, the point made here is not so much a prescriptive assessment as it is a reflection of what has actually taken place in environmental law scholarship over the years. Freyfogle, for example, argues that 'when it began in earnest, environmental law scholarship was a value-drive enterprise ... [this] characteristic has become less evident, with an increasing number of scholars in the field displaying little passion about environmental law ills.'[32] Though Freyfogle's observation is no doubt right, the question of whether the change in focus is something to begrudge is open to debate. To some, the idea that environmental law scholarship is necessarily wedded to pursuing a specific outcome goes against the very definition of scholarship.[33] Similarly, in response to those decrying the lack of conformity within the practice, it might even be argued that a 'function of scholarship is to afflict the intellectually

---

[29] McCrudden 'Legal Research and the Social Sciences', 633–634.

[30] McCrudden does, however, suggest that this feature is one which is found in legal research more generally, ibid. 642.

[31] Czarnezki and Schindler, Chapter 12, this volume.

[32] Eric T. Freyfogle, 'Five Paths of Environmental Scholarship' (2000) U. Ill. L. Rev. 115, 128.

[33] Elizabeth Fisher et al., 'Maturity and Methodology: Starting a Debate about Environmental Law Scholarship' (2009) 21 JEL 213; David Feldman, 'The Nature of Legal Scholarship' (1989) 52 MLR 498.

comfortable', disturbing the scholarly tranquillity of those who desire a common outlook from within a practice.[34] This point is particularly important considering that one of the risks which emerge from the self-referential nature of conceptualising environmental law scholarship as a social practice is that it might result in conformist scholarship.[35] In response to this risk, any social enterprise, including practices of scholarship, might 'learn to value both having opinions and keeping an open mind, to mix the delights of winning an argument with the pleasures of being good listeners'.[36] Again, this highlights the argument that central to a practice of scholarship is the collegial commitment of its participants to a common goal: the preservation and evolution of the practice.

More generally, the potential for the focus of a practice to diverge suggests two things.[37] First, either the practice of environmental law scholarship is so broad that it can accommodate divergent perspectives relating to its core purposes within itself or, second, several sub-practices emerge and form within the wider practice. The reality is likely to be a combination of both of these points. Notwithstanding the accommodating nature and diversity found in environmental law scholarship, the sheer depth and size of the practice suggest that within the broad confines of the practice, several smaller practices are found. Some of the sub-practices could for instance include scholarship engaging primarily with climate change law, environmental law and economics, environmental rights and environmental taxation (to mention just a few). Each of these sub-practices emerges as its own institutionalised social order with its own agreed-upon criteria and understandings of what constitutes reasonable readings and vocabularies in the execution of the scholarship. This diversification does, however, take place within the confines of the broader practice that is environmental law scholarship. The 'environmental' in environmental taxation and the 'environmental' in environmental rights are what sets these subjects and practices apart from tax scholarship and human rights scholarship more generally.

From this it may well be argued that the practice of environmental law scholarship is more porous and less firm than other practices of legal

---

[34] McCrudden 'Legal Research and the Social Sciences', 640.

[35] E.g. David Bryden, 'Scholarship about Scholarship' (1992) 63 *U. Colo. L. Rev.* 641.

[36] Albert O. Hirschman, 'Having Opinions – One of the Elements of Well-Being?' (1989) 79 *The American Economic Review* 75, 78.

[37] Andreas Philppopoulos-Mihalopoulos & Victoria Brooks (eds), *Research Methods in Environmental Law* (Cheltenham: Edward Elgar, 2017).

scholarship.[38] The permeable nature of the practice may indeed explain why environmental law scholarship is perceived as immature by some commentators.[39] On this reading, immaturity is not the diagnosis but the symptom of the youth of the subject (relatively speaking) as well as the open-ended and multilayered nature of the culture of environmental law and the practice of environmental law scholarship itself. To the extent it is at all desirable, the ability to firm up and solidify the confines of the practice is likely to only emerge with time. Charges of immaturity may therefore not be as unsettling as they are likely to be perceived by some participants in the practice of environmental law scholarship. In fact, imposing and contemplating anxiety over one's practice is one way to advance the practice and ultimately to pursue excellence.[40] Ironically, the willingness to reflect on and engage with concerns of immaturity, as attempted in this collection, in itself shows a presence of maturity.

To the extent an 'ideal environmental law scholar' (to use Austin's phrase) emerges from this, it seems that this scholar ought at least to maintain a commitment to the social practice that she is part of.[41] This commitment ought to, at a minimum, entail the reciprocal willingness to engage in a reflective manner with the scholarship being conducted within the practice with the view to maintaining the practice itself.[42] This means not only that the environmental law scholar ought to be prepared to engage meaningfully and rigorously with the work of other scholars in the practice but also that the scholar necessarily must tolerate a certain degree of scrutiny of her own work. Bruising as this can be, it is the price of admission to the practice of environmental law scholarship. This commitment to continuous engagement and reflection also means that the scholar is forced to constantly evaluate her own work against a benchmark which ideally does not stand still. If the participants in the scholarly practice continue to produce new scholarship and thereby reconfigure the boundaries and agreements holding the practice

---

[38] See also Fish, *Winning Arguments*, 170, arguing, 'not all bounded spaces are the same; in some the boundaries are not as rigorously policed as they are in others.'

[39] Fisher et al., 'Maturity and Methodology'.

[40] Edward L. Rubin, 'The Evaluation of Prescriptive Scholarship' (1990) 10 *Tel Aviv U. Stud. L.* 101, 111–112.

[41] Arthur Austin, 'The Postmodern Infiltration of Legal Scholarship' (2000) 98 *Mich. Law. Rev.* 1504.

[42] See also Paul W. Kahn, 'Freedom and Method' in Geert van Gestel et al. (eds), *Rethinking Legal Scholarship: A Transatlantic Dialogue* (New York: Cambridge University Press, 2016), 499–524.

together, the practice will as a result be a vibrant community. This vibrancy will in turn secure a less stale scholarly debate.

But the commitment to the practice also entails an obligation to the principle of contingency: a commitment to contingency of the scholarly endeavour and the law itself in the sense that the very nature of scholarship – as well as environmental law – will vary from scholar to scholar, from jurisdiction to jurisdiction and from one political environment to another.[43] Whilst this variation contributes to vibrancy, it also makes it difficult for scholars to identify and develop universal foundations for the discipline of environmental law which will be applicable across jurisdictional boundaries.[44] Consequently, when trying to do so, the environmental law scholar must keep in mind the principle of contingency and accept the inherently local nature of her endeavour.[45] With the commitment to contingency also comes an acceptance of the likelihood that the scholarly endeavour is likely to be 'messy' (much like environmental law itself).[46] The culture of environmental law thus exemplifies and embodies what Rubin has called 'the transformation of the law' – a transformation which Czarnezki and Schindler are alert to.[47] This transformation has taken place over decades in response to the changing role and function of the state and its regulatory character in modern societies. As noted earlier, environmental law, in most jurisdictions, consists not just of traditional primary law provisions enacted by legislative assemblies and enforced by impartial judiciaries but of policies, principles, rules, decrees and regulations, interpreted and enforced by administrative agencies and applied to a wide range of legal subjects. In this legislative diversity of law and rules, ideals of legal coherence and methodological unity are unproductive if not unsuitable if we as scholars aim to understand the

[43] E.g. Guneratne, Chapter 11, this volume; Czarnezki and Schindler, Chapter 12, this volume; Krämer, Chapter 13, this volume.
[44] Scotford, *Environmental Principles*; Ole W. Pedersen, 'The Contingent Foundations of Environmental Law' (2018) *JEL* forthcoming.
[45] On this reading, environmental law scholarship does not necessarily constitute a *lingua franca* as suggested by Neil Duxbury, 'A Century of Legal Scholarship' in Peter Cane & Mark Tushnet (eds), *The Oxford Handbook of Legal Studies* (Oxford: Oxford University Press, 2003), 950–974.
[46] Carol M. Rose, 'Environmental Law Grows Up (More or Less), and What Science Can Do to Help' (2005) 9 *Lewis & Clark L. Rev.* 273.
[47] See Czarnezki & Schindler, Chapter 12, this volume; Edward L. Rubin, 'From Coherence to Effectiveness' in Geert van Gestel et al. (eds), *Rethinking Legal Scholarship*, 310–350.

law.[48] This 'messiness' need not, however, be perceived as something negative as long as the scholarship is conducted with rigour, diligence and commitment to the social practice of environmental law scholarship.

An additional theme to emerge from this collection is that there is a real potential (as well as desire) for environmental law scholars to shape societal debates and to impact on decisions made beyond the academy.[49] Indeed, as discussed by Pieraccini,[50] in the UK, the ability to influence matters beyond the academy is increasingly required by higher education institutions. Against this, it is worth making the point that neither the quality nor the scholarly relevance of scholarship ought to be conflated with its ability to reach out to policymakers, lawmakers or judiciaries. As Flexner reminds us: '[the] great discoveries which had ultimately proved to be beneficial to mankind had been made by men and women who were driven not by the desire to be useful but merely by the desire to satisfy their curiosity.'[51] Of course Flexner's point is made not in the context of legal scholarship (he does in fact concede that the motive of usefulness is dominant in legal research by virtue of its historical link to the legal profession) but in the context of scientific work more generally. Nevertheless, the argument that the rigorous dedication to a given piece of scholarship – 'obsessive dedication' to use Fisher's phrase – implies the value of that scholarship irrespective of whether or not it has any wider utility.

As exemplified by this collection, the practice of environmental law scholarship is home to a wide variety of scholarly ways of doing scholarship. This is inevitable. As recently observed by Fisher: 'understanding the legal substance of environmental law requires understanding of the place of law and the environment in the world.'[52] Similarly, understanding environmental law scholarship requires an understanding of the place of scholarship and the role it plays in environmental law more widely. Whether scholarship is seen as being a purpose-driven exercise aimed at reforming the law or whether it is seen as something entirely self-contained, this chapter has argued that the most fruitful way to

---

[48] Rubin notes that it might well be worthwhile 'simply to acknowledge that law means something different in the administrative state than it did before.' Ibid., 328.
[49] E.g. Cecot & Livermore, Chapter 7, this volume; Guneratne, Chapter 11, this volume; Krämer, Chapter 13, this volume.
[50] See Pieraccini, Chapter 5, this volume.
[51] Abraham Flexner, 'The Usefulness of Useless Knowledge' (1939) 179 Harpers 544, 545.
[52] Fisher, A Very Short Introduction, 3.

conceptualise environmental law scholarship is as a social practice con-ducted by the scholars who self-identify with that practice.

Bibliography

Fisher Elizabeth et al. 'Maturity and Methodology: Starting a Debate about Environmental Law Scholarship' (2009) 21 *JEL* 213.

Kahn, Paul W., *The Cultural Study of Law* (Chicago: University of Chicago Press, 2009).

McCrudden, Christopher, 'Legal Research and the Social Sciences' (2006) *LQR* 632.

Pedersen, Ole W., 'The Limits of Interdisciplinarity and the Practice of Environmental Law Scholarship' (2014) *JEL* 423–441.

Rubin, Edward L., 'From Coherence to Effectiveness' in Geert van Gestel et al. (eds), *Rethinking Legal Scholarship: A Transatlantic Dialogue* (Cambridge: Cambridge University Press, 2016), 310–350.

Schlag, Pierre, 'Spam Jurisprudence, Air Law, and the Rank Anxiety of Nothing Happening (A Report on the State of the Art)' (2009) 97 *Geo. L. J.* 803.

Scotford, Eloise, *Environmental Principles and the Evolution of Environmental Law* (Oxford: Hart Publishing, 2017).

INDEX

Aagaard, Todd S. 3, 180
abundance of scholarship 1–2
academic context *see* environmental
    law as discipline; legal scholarship
academic lawyers *see* lawyers, academic
administrative permits 21
agriculture law scholarship 200
Alpine Convention 129
animal law 201
Anthropocene as geological era 123–29,
    172–73
Anthropocene concept in scholarship
    Earth system science 135–37
    ethics 157–58
    history of environmental law 122–31
    implications for scholarship 140–41,
        146–60
    international environmental law 6–7,
        121–22, 137–38
    relation to law 144–46
    situating the debate 141–44
    teleology 131–35
Anthropocene Working Group 144–46
Anthropos 150–51
    see also human-centred approaches
attorneys
    comparison to academic lawyers
        16–18
    meaning of laws 13
    policymaking 15–16
audit culture, institutional constraints
    64–70

behaviors, environmental law 206–7
Biber, Eric 21
Biermann, Frank 135–36
black letter law 190–93
Bosselmann, Klaus 136

boundaries in environment *see*
    planetary boundaries
boundaries of environmental law
    199–202, 228–31
    see also environmental law as
        discipline; interdisciplinarity
boundaries of science 73–74
Brundtland Commission 182–83

Camacho, Alejandro 21–22
cap-and-trade schemes 101–2
Carlson, Ann 21
Cecot, C. 5–6
certification schemes 207–8
Clean Air Act 108–9, 196, 199
Clean Water Act 13–14, 196, 199
climate change
    Anthropocene era 123–29, 172–73
    discipline of environmental law 6–8
    Earth system science 135–37
    iterative federalism 21
    post-nature 130–31
    valuation methods 103–6
    see also Anthropocene concept in
        scholarship
climate change scholarship 162
    'law of the horse' 168–70
    and trends in environmental law
        173–76
    as a unifying theme 171–73
    United States legal landscape 163–68
Clinton presidency, environmentalism
    movement 166–67
command-and-control policies 101–2
community *see* institutions; social
    context
comparative advantage 10–11, 18
Comte, Auguste 71

239

Conference on Empirical Legal Studies
  (CELS) 102–9
conservation law 21–22, 125, 183–84
constitutional law 54–56
constitutive STS scholarship 72–73
contemporary context of
  environmental law 1–9
contingency, environmental law
  scholarship 236–37
contractualism 53–54
cost-benefit analysis 99–100,
  103–6, 167
craft expertise, environmental law
  26–32, 40
  materials of the craft 35–38
  using obsessive energy 38–40
cross-disciplines see interdisciplinarity;
  multidisciplinarity;
  transdisciplinarity
Crutzen, Paul 122–23
culture, understanding model of
  environmental law scholarship
  52–57
culture of environmental law 227–38
Czarnezki, Jason J. 8–9

de Sousa Santos, B. 62
deep ecology 133
de-extinction 21–22
developing country scholarship 8, 178
  discourse on legal scholarship and
    environmental law 178–81
  environmental law in Sri Lanka
    184–86, 193
  future directions 187–93
  sustainable development and
    environment 181–84
development
  academic lawyers 188–89
  developing country scholarship
    181–84
  Sustainable Development Goals
    183–84, 187–88, 189
  see also sustainable development
disciplinary context see environmental
  law as discipline
Dryzek, John S. 131, 135–36
Durkheim, Émile 71

Earth system science 135–37, 152–56
Easterbrook, Frank 168–70
ecocentric approaches 132–35
ecological injury 20–21
ecological science 128
eco modernists, Anthropocene concept
  134–35
economic development see
  development
economic perspective 96–97
  causes and consequences 109–13
  empirical environmental law
    scholarship 96–97, 102–9, 110–13
  multidisciplinary environmental
    research 113–16
  and New Chicago School 202–4
  normative legal scholarship 97–102,
    109–13
ecosystem services 128, 130
emission trading 101–2
empirical environmental law
  scholarship 5–6, 96–97, 102–9,
  110–13
energy law 22–23, 199
enforcement
  craft expertise 37–38
  European Union 224–25
English language, European Union
  212–17
environmental harms 98
environmental justice 225
environmental law as discipline
  Anthropocene concept implications
    140–41, 146–60
  climate change scholarship trends
    173–76
  contemporary context 1–9
  craft expertise 26–32,
    40
  culture and practice 227–38
  developing country scholarship
    184–86, 188–93
  discourse on legal scholarship and
    environmental law 178–81
  empirical economics 102–9
  environmental protection 199–202
  European Union 217–25
  institutions 32–35

legal scholarship's contribution to
  10–25
materials of the craft 35–38
New Chicago School 206–10
normative legal scholarship 96–102
using obsessive energy 38–40
see also interdisciplinarity;
  international environmental law;
  models of environmental law
  scholarship
environmental law treatises 43–46
environmental protection
  developing country scholarship
    181–84
  European Union 217–22
  justifying environmental protection 98
  New Chicago School 206–10
  Trump presidency 195–99
  valuation methods 103–6
Environmental Protection Agency
  195–99
environmentalism
  Romantic 129
  shallow vs. deep ecology 133
  United States 163–65
epistemological challenges, scholarship
  4, 70–74
equality
  environmental justice 225
  environmental law 158–60
ethics
  academic and non-academic lawyers
    16–17
  Anthropocene concept 157–58
  human-centred approaches 110–11
  and lawmaking 157
  teleology of international
    environmental law 131–35
European Association of Environmental
  Law (AEDE) 214–15
European Environmental Law Forum
  (EELF) 214–15
European Union
  discipline of environmental law 9
  impact of languages 212–17
  institutions and scholars 217–22
  scholars and the environment in
    Europe 222–25

expertise
  craft expertise 26–32, 40
  discipline of environmental
    law 3
  empirical environmental law
    scholarship 112–13
  materials of the craft 35–38
  using obsessive energy 38–40
explanation model 48–52
externalities 98, 109–10

Farber, Dan 19–20
federalism, climate change 21
Feldman, David 30–31, 34
Fisher, Elizabeth 3, 60, 237–38
food law scholarship 200
Freeman, Jody 22–23
Freyfogle, Eric T. 233–34
funding
  European Union 216–17
  interdisciplinary context 68–70, 83

geological era of Anthropocene 123–29,
  172–73
  see also Anthropocene concept in
    scholarship
global context *see* international
    environmental law;
    transnationality
Global Research Council 68–69
global warming *see* climate change
globalization, international
    environmental law 200–1
goals of environmental policy 100–2
goals of international environmental
    law 131–35
government intervention
  Anthropocene concept 142
  determining stringency 99–100
  goals of environmental policy 100–2
  law vs. policy 12–15
  market failure 98
Griffith, J. 62
Guneratne, Camena 8

Hawkins, Keith 37–38
hazardous waste sites categorization
  113–14

history of environmental law
  Anthropocene concept 122–31
  distinctive role of legal academics
    20–21
  European Union 217–22
human rights
  developing country scholarship 183,
    187–88, 189
  and EU scholarship 224
  interdisciplinary context 191–93
human-centred approaches
  Anthropos 150–51
  normative economics 110–11
  teleology of international
    environmental law 131–35
  see also Anthropocene concept in
    scholarship

idiographic knowledge 70–74
inclusivity, environmental law 158–60
individual action, environmental law
    206–7, 208–10
institutional challenges 4
institutions
  discipline of environmental law
    32–35
  epistemological challenges 74
  European Union 217–22
  interdisciplinary context 33, 64–70
  multidisciplinary research 114
  practices of environmental law
    scholarship 237–38
instruments, government intervention
    100–2
interactional STS scholarship 72–73
interdisciplinarity 4–9
  climate change scholarship 175–76
  developing country scholarship
    189–93
  environmental law boundaries
    199–202, 228–31
  epistemological challenges 70–74
  explanation model of environmental
    law 50–51
  human rights 191–93
  institutions 33, 35, 64–70
  legal academics' understanding of
    law 14–15

scientific community 60–64, 74–76
sustainable development 191–93
see also multidisciplinarity;
  renewable energy case study;
  transdisciplinarity
Interdisciplinary Research Advisory
  Panel (IDAP) 66–67
international environmental law
  Anthropocene concept implications
    6–7, 121–22, 137–38
  Anthropocene concept in modern
    scholarship 124–27
  Anthropocene concept in post-
    modern scholarship 126, 127–29
  Anthropocene concept in post-
    nature scholarship 130–31
  globalization 200–1
  transdisciplinarity 84, 151–56,
    174–75
iterative federalism, climate
  change 21

Jasonoff, S. 72–73, 74
Journal of Empirical Legal Studies
  (JELS) 102–9
journals, environmental law 102–9,
  146–56
judicial practice
  reform model of environmental law
    46–48
  ways of doing scholarship
    231–38
justice, reform model of environmental
  law 46–48

Kaldor-Hicks criterion 99
Kim, Rak E. 136
knowledge, epistemological challenges
  70–74
Kotzé, Louis 6–8
Krämer, Ludwig 9

labeling schemes 207–8
land use law 199–200
language use
  European Union 212–17
  interdisciplinary renewable energy
    case study 92–93

Latour, B. 72–73
law
    Anthropocene concept 144–46
    environmental protection in US
        195–99
    environmental protection subjects
        199–202
    legal academics' understanding of
        12–15
    multidisciplinary research 113–16
    New Chicago School 202–10
    Trump presidency 210–11
    United States legal landscape 163–68
    see also environmental law as
        discipline; government
        intervention; legal scholarship;
        policy
law faculties, multidisciplinary
    research 115
'law of the horse' 168–70
lawmaking
    distinctive role of legal academics
        20–21
    and ethics 157
    non-academic lawyers 15–16
    reform model of environmental law
        46–48
    Sri Lanka 184–86
    see also policymaking
lawyers, academic
    comparative advantage 10–11
    comparison to non-academic
        lawyers 16–18
    development 188–89
    distinctive role of 18–24
    vested interests 24–25
lawyers, non-academic, contribution to
    environmental law 15–18
Lazarus, Richard 20–21
Lee, M. 4–5
legal academics see lawyers, academic
legal consciousness 61–63
legal cultures 227–38
legal pluralism 61–63
legal practice
    reform model of environmental law
        46–48
    ways of doing scholarship 231–38

legal scholarship
    comparative advantage 10–11
    contribution to environmental law
        10–25
    developing country perspective
        178–81
    distinctive role of legal academics
        18–24
    interdisciplinary renewable energy
        case study 84–86, 89–94
    multidisciplinarity 113–16
    non-academic lawyers 15–18
    non-legal scholarship 11–15
    see also environmental law as
        discipline
less developed countries see developing
    country scholarship
Lessig, Lawrence 202–4
life-cycle costing 209–10
Livermore, M. A. 5–6
local communities, environmental law
    208–10
Lock, S. 4–5

Macrory, Richard 190–93
Maldonado, David Bonilla 3–4,
    227–28
market failure 98
market-based mechanisms 101–2,
    202–4
    see also economic perspective
materials of environmental law
    craft expertise 35–38
    systematization model of
        environmental law 43–46
methodologies
    craft expertise 27–32
    developing country scholarship
        190–93
    diversity of 227–28
    explanation model of environmental
        law 50–51
    interdisciplinary renewable energy
        case study 81–83, 89–94
    materials of the craft 36,
        37–38
Millennium Development Goals
    (MDGs) 184

Mode 1/Mode 2-knowledge
    production 75
models of environmental law
    scholarship 41–42, 57–58
    explanation model 48–52
    reform model 46–48
    systematization model 42–46
    understanding model 52–57
modern era, Anthropocene concept
    124–27
multidisciplinarity
    Anthropocene concept 146–56
    case for 75–76
    meaning of 84
    role of law 113–16
    see also interdisciplinarity;
        transdisciplinarity

Natarajan, L. 4–5
nation states, and EU scholarship
    215–17
    see also government intervention
navigable waters 13–14
negative externalities 98,
    109–10
New Chicago School 202–10
Nixon presidency 163–65,
    195–96
nomothetic knowledge 70–74
non-academic lawyers, contribution to
    environmental law 15–18
non-legal scholarship 11–15
normative legal scholarship 96–102,
    109–13

Obama presidency, environmental law
    196–97
obsessive energy, discipline of
    environmental law 38–40
oversupply of scholarship 1–2

Pareto criterion 99
permitting 21
Pieraccini, M. 4, 237
Pigouvian tax 101–2
planetary boundaries
    Anthropocene concept 124–27,
    142–43

Earth system science 135–37
post-nature 130–31
planning, interdisciplinary renewable
    energy case study 80–83, 84–86,
    89–94
policy
    empirical economics 106–9
    vs. law 12–15
    see also government
        intervention; law
policymaking
    discipline of environmental law 3
    empirical economics 109–13
    European Union 217–22
    multidisciplinary research 114–15
    non-academic lawyers 15–16
    see also lawmaking
policy-orientated scholarship 190–93
political positions, scholarship 41, 217
pollution
    climate change 171–73
    European Union 222–25
    as externality 98, 109–10
    hazardous waste sites categorization
    113–14
    law as craft expertise 37–38
    scope of environmental law 168–70,
    199–202
    see also environmental protection
pollution reduction instrument 101–2
Popper, Karl 71
population, developing country
    scholarship 181–84
positive legal scholarship, economic
    perspective 96–97, 102–9
positivism 71–72, 74
Posner, Eric 204–6
post-modern, Anthropocene concept
    126, 127–29
post-nature, Anthropocene concept
    130–31
Power, Michael 65
practices of environmental law
    scholarship 1–9, 227–38
    see also attorneys; craft expertise;
        lawyers, academic; lawyers, non-
        academic
private governance 208–10

quantitative empirical scholarship 5–6, 102–9

Reagan presidency, environmentalism movement 163, 165, 166–67
reform model 46–48
regulation *see* government intervention; law; policy
renewable energy case study
   differences between disciplines 89–94
   disciplines and their transgression 83–89
   personal reflections on interdisciplinarity 79–80, 95
   the project 80–83
representivity, environmental law 158–60
Research Excellence Framework (REF) 63–70
responsibility in scholarship 1–2
revealed-preferences 103–6
Rio Declaration 128, 131
Romantic environmentalism 129
Rosen, Jeffrey 204–6, 207–8, 211
Ruhl, J. B. 21
Rydin, Y. 4–5

Schindler, Sarah 8–9
scholarship *see* Anthropocene concept in scholarship; climate change scholarship; environmental law as discipline; models of environmental law scholarship
Science and Technology Studies (STS)
   epistemological challenges 71–74
   interdisciplinary renewable energy case study 84–85, 89–94
   scientific community 64
scientific community
   explanation model of environmental law 48–52
   interdisciplinary overlap with environmental law 60–64, 74–76
Sennett, Richard 31, 38–39
shallow ecology 133
slippage 19–20
social context

craft expertise 29–31
environmental law scholarship 3–5
institutions 32–33, 34–35
practices of environmental law scholarship 231–38
social norms, and environmental law 207–10
social sciences
   Anthropocene concept 146–56
   explanation model of environmental law 48–52
socio-legal research 61, 62–63, 190–93
speciesism 110–11
Sri Lanka
   environmental law scholarship 184–86, 193
   interdisciplinarity 192–93
stated-preferences 104–5
Stephens, Tim 6–8
Stern Review 66
Stevenson, Hayley 135–36
Stoermer, Eugene 122–23
Stone, Christopher 18–19
Strathern, M. 64–65
subject matter *see* materials of environmental law
supply chain 209–10
sustainable development
   Anthropocene concept 127–28
   developing country scholarship 181–84
   interdisciplinarity 191–93
   Sri Lanka 184–86
Sustainable Development Goals (SDGs) 183–84, 187–88, 189
systematization model 42–46
systems approach 135–37, 152–56

taxation, pollution 101–2
teaching, systematization model of environmental law 42–46
teleology, Anthropocene concept 131–35
terminology
   interdisciplinary renewable energy case study 92–93
   language in the European Union 212–17

transdisciplinarity
  Anthropocene concept 151–56
  climate change scholarship 174–75
  meaning of 84
  see also interdisciplinarity;
    multidisciplinarity
transnationality
  Anthropocene concept 151–56
  climate change scholarship 173–74
treatises 43–46
Trump presidency
  discipline of environmental law 8–9
  environmental protection in US
    195–99
  role of law 210–11
  status of experts 112–13

understanding model 52–57
United Kingdom Research Excellence
  Framework (REF) 63–70

United States
  climate change scholarship
    163–68
  environmental protection under
    Trump 195–99, 210–11
  quantitative empirical scholarship
    102–9
  transnational scholarship 173–74

validation of science 73
valuation methods 103–6
vested interests 24–25

Weberian models 42
  see also models of environmental law
    scholarship
willingness to pay/accept 103–6
Windelband, Wilhelm 70–71

Young, Oran 135–36